A Handbook of Practical Wisdom

The Practical Wisdom in Leadership and Organization Series

Series Editors
Wendelin M. Küpers, Massey University, New Zealand
David J. Pauleen, Massey University, New Zealand

Gower's Practical Wisdom in Leadership and Organization Series provides a platform for authors to articulate wiser ways of managing and leading and of reassessing both practice within organisational settings and organisational research.

Books in this series focus on the art and practice of inquiry and reflexivity and explicitly connect with challenges and issues of 'praxis' in the field of organization and management, be that academic research or in situ management practice. Rather than offering closure and final answers, contributions to this series invite further critical inquiry, interdisciplinary conversations and exploration. The aim is to engage authors and readers – students, academics, and practitioners alike – in reflexive and critical dialogue.

By thus engaging readers, these books play an important role in teaching, learning and informing in university classrooms, management boardrooms, and public policy forums.

The Series Editors – Dr Wendelin Küpers is an Associate Professor in the School of Management and Dr David Pauleen is an Associate Professor of Business Information Systems in the same School at Massey University, New Zealand. Dr Küpers teaches in the areas of management, organisation studies and research methodology and Dr Pauleen teaches knowledge management and other topics and is Chair of the Massey School of Management's PhD Committee. Both are published authors and are the co-editors of *A Handbook of Practical Wisdom* (Gower, 2013).

A Handbook of Practical Wisdom

Leadership, Organization and Integral Business Practice

Edited By

**WENDELIN KÜPERS AND
DAVID J. PAULEEN**

School of Management, Massey University, Albany, New Zealand

Routledge
Taylor & Francis Group

LONDON AND NEW YORK

First published 2013 by Gower Publishing

2 Park Square, Milton Park, Abingdon, Oxfordshire OX14 4RN
52 Vanderbilt Avenue, New York, NY 10017

Routledge is an imprint of the Taylor & Francis Group, an informa business

First issued in paperback 2019

Gower Applied Business Research
Our programme provides leaders, practitioners, scholars and researchers with thought provoking, cutting edge books that combine conceptual insights, interdisciplinary rigour and practical relevance in key areas of business and management.

British Library Cataloguing in Publication Data
A handbook of practical wisdom : leadership, organization
  and integral business practice.
  1. Intellectual capital. 2. Knowledge management.
  3. Wisdom.
  I. Kupers, Wendelin. II. Pauleen, David J., 1957-
  658.4'038-dc23

The Library of Congress has cataloged the printed edition as follows:
Küpers, Wendelin.
  A handbook of practical wisdom : leadership, organization and integral business practice / by Wendelin Küpers and David J. Pauleen.
    pages cm. -- (The practical wisdom in leadership and organization series)
  Includes bibliographical references and index.
  ISBN 978-1-4094-3993-6 (hardback) -- ISBN 978-1-4094-3994-3 (ebook) -- ISBN 978-1-4094-7469-2 (epub) 1. Leadership. 2. Management. I. Pauleen, David J., 1957- II. Title.
  HD57.7K8667 2013
  658.4'092--dc23

                                                                    2013012955

ISBN 13 : 978-1-4094-3993-6 (hbk)
ISBN 13 : 978-0-367-60621-3 (pbk)

Contents

List of Figures

List of Tables

Notes on Contributors

Roberto Biloslavo is a Full Professor in Management at the University of Primorska, Slovenia, Faculty of Management Koper. His research work is focused on management and leadership, knowledge management, strategic management and sustainable development. In the last four years, he was a Vice-Rector for Academic Affairs at the University of Primorska. Beside teaching and researching, he consults for different domestic and international companies about vision and mission statement development, knowledge management and leadership development. This experience led him to consider wisdom as the foundation of good practice.

Maree Boyle is a Senior Lecturer within the Griffith Business School at Griffith University, Australia. Her research interests include gender, work and organizations, emotions in the workplace, sociology of work and organizations and qualitative research approaches. Her work has been published in *Organization*, *Journal of Business Research* and *European Management Journal* and the *Handbook of Organizational Research Methods*.

Peter Case is a Professor of Management and Organization Studies, James Cook University, Townsville, Australia. He also holds a part-time chair at the University of West of England and visiting professorship at the University of Leicester. His research interests encompass corporate social and environmental responsibility, leadership ethics and organization theory. Peter's early fascination with oriental philosophy eventually matured into a fully fledged engagement with Buddhist philosophy and meditation. He has practiced *vipassan* (insight) meditation for 25 years, including time spent in monastic training. This chapter represents a synthesis of his personal interest in Buddhism with his professional interest in organization and leadership studies. Peter served as general editor of *Culture & Organization* (2007–10) and is currently a member of the editorial boards of *Leadership*, *Leadership & Organizational Development Journal*, *Business & Society Review* and the *Journal of Management, Spirituality and Religion*. Publications include *The Speed of Organization* (2006: CBS & Liber), *John Adair: the Fundamentals of Leadership* (2007: Palgrave), *Worldly Leadership* (2012: Palgrave) and *Belief and Organization* (2012: Palgrave).

Mark Edwards is an Assistant Professor at the Business School, University of Western Australia, where he teaches in the areas of business ethics, sustainability and organizational transformation. Mark's PhD thesis was awarded a distinction and was published in 2010 in the *Routledge Studies in Business Ethics* series. The book focuses on the integration of theories of organization and applies this to the fields of organizational transformation and sustainability. He is currently working on several research projects and publications including a general approach to the topic of transformational change (with SUNY Press) and marketing strategies and sustainability (Cambridge University Press) and case studies in ethics and marketing (Cambridge University Press). Mark has published on a diverse range of topics including sustainability, organizational transformation, management education, futures studies and business ethics. Current research and teaching interests include the study of global business ethics, climate change and worldviews, organizational sustainability and the development of metatheoretical research. Mark is on the editorial board for two journals that focus on integrative approaches to research and practice.

Jay Martin Hays has been at Swinburne University of Technology, Melbourne, Australia, since 2010, developing the university's Industry Engaged Learning curriculum and community engagement frameworks, including new Service Learning, internship and workplace learning units. Jay previously taught management and leadership courses at the Australian National University (ANU) in Canberra, Australia. It was at ANU where Jay realized that the management curriculum lacked depth, nuance, meaningfulness and twenty-first-century relevance. He began to redress this lacuna by introducing experiential components and aspects of wisdom into his seminars and courses. Jay tried to get learners to expand their thinking about leadership and better prepare them for leadership roles; for example, by exploring with them how leading wisely would differ from traditional leadership models and considering the implications and consequences of a wise course over more typical approaches. His efforts to improve his own teaching and to enrich and make higher education more relevant have been recognized by nominations for numerous international honours including the American Order of Merit, International Educator of the Year and Gold Medal for Australia. Jay has been researching and writing on wisdom since 2006.

Ali Intezari is a Doctoral Researcher in the Department of Management, Massey University, Auckland, New Zealand. His current research interests include knowledge management, organizational knowledge culture, wisdom, decision-making and emergence in the business world. He holds a Master's degree in Management Information Systems from the Institute of Higher Education & Research for Management & Planning, Tehran, with an emphasis on Knowledge Management, and he holds a Bachelor's degree in Public Administration. He has had some journal articles published in this field. Mr Intezari is currently studying wisdom and its possible implications for management as part of his PhD dissertation.

Claire Jankelson is currently an honorary Associate at Macquarie Graduate School of Management in Sydney, Australia, where she also runs a hermeneutic circle for Phd's. Through teaching Management and Research courses for decades, the core value of her teaching is the action of facilitating learning. She enjoys a particular interest in research that makes a difference: to practice, for the participants and to our planet. Further to a consulting practice on effective leadership, she is the editor of the *Journal of Spirituality, Leadership and Management*, a journal that nurtures the connection between the three named phenomena.

Bernd Kleimann (born 1966) studied philosophy and German literature at the Universities of Marburg and Tübingen. He was a member of the Aesthetical Education Graduate School at the University of Hamburg and earned his doctoral degree in philosophy from the University of Gießen (2002). After holding lecturer positions at different German universities, he has worked since 2001 as a scientific employee with the Higher Education Information System in Hannover, a publicly run institution supporting German higher education through research, consultancy and software development. Currently, he is conducting a research project (in cooperation with Leibniz University, Hannover) on German university presidents that is funded by the German Research Foundation.

Wendelin Küpers is an Associate Professor at the School of Management, Massey University, Auckland, where he teaches in the areas of management/leadership, organization studies and research methodology. Previously he worked for several years in the business world and has been affiliated with different universities in Europe. In his phenomenological and interdisciplinary research he explores an integral and processual understanding of managing and organizing especially focusing on embodied, emotional and aesthetic dimensions involved. Besides editing and publishing books and journal articles, Wendelin is engaged in various editorial and review activities and serves as conference co-convenor.

Bernard McKenna is an Associate Professor in the University of Queensland Business School in Australia where he teaches mostly at graduate level. He has published extensively in such journals as *Applied Linguistics*, *Social Epistemology*, *Public Administration Review*, *Management Communication Quarterly*, *Critical Discourse Studies* and *Leadership Quarterly* and is on the editorial board of five journals. He recently co-authored *Managing Wisdom in the Knowledge Economy* (Routledge, 2010). As a critical scholar in a business school, Bernard came to understand that wisdom was the fundamental virtue that was absent in outcomes such as the GFC and unsustainable lifestyles.

David J. Pauleen (PhD) is an Associate Professor in the School of Management, Massey University, Albany, New Zealand. His interest in wisdom and wise practice stems from a combination of his academic research and classroom experience in knowledge management and his personal experience as a long-time meditator. Other research interests include personal knowledge management, emerging work practices, cross-cultural information and knowledge management and virtual team leadership, dynamics, communication and technology. His work has appeared in such journals as the *Journal of Management Information Systems*, *Sloan Management Review*, *Business Insight (Wall Street Journal & Sloan Management Review)*. He is also editor of the books, *Virtual Teams: Projects, Protocols and Processes* (2004), *Cross-Cultural Perspectives on Knowledge Management* (2007), and *Personal Knowledge Management: Individual, Organizational and Social Perspectives* (2011).

Amanda Roan is a Senior Lecturer in Human Resource Management, Employment Relations and Organizational Behaviour at the UQ Business School, University of Queensland, Australia. Her research is broadly focused around workforce participation with a special interest in gender diversity and why women remain under-represented in higher levels of management. Her interest in wisdom arises out of the way women leaders are represented in business and an interest in feminist theory. She has published in national and international journals including the *Journal of Industrial Relations*, *Management Learning* and *Philosophy of Management*.

David Rooney is an Associate Professor at UQ Business School, the University of Queensland, Australia. He has researched, taught and published in the areas of the knowledge economy, knowledge management, wisdom, leadership and organizational change. His books include *Public Policy in the Knowledge-Based Economy*, the *Handbook on the Knowledge Economy*, *Knowledge Policy* and *Wisdom and Management in the Knowledge Economy*. Rooney has also published in many leading academic journals including *The Leadership Quarterly*, *Public Administration Review*, *Human Relations* and *Management Communication Quarterly*.

Foreword

Practical wisdom (*phronesis*) is an ancient, enigmatic, and intractable notion yet the manner of its workings and its influence on public life, professional practice and civil society remains little understood. Despite its profound effect on virtually every aspect of modern life, full understanding and comprehension of practical wisdom continue to elude us at every turn. In the light of recent upheavals in the financial and corporate worlds, and more broadly the increasingly contested nature of expert knowledge and the professionalized systems of control associated with them, it is timely to inquire into the limits of such forms of knowledge and to consider if the ancient notion of practical wisdom can add something valuable to our comprehension of the human condition. Such consideration is age-old, beginning in the West with Socrates, who recognized that we are only wise in so far as we are able to recognize and accept our limitations. Wisdom, thus, is the antidote to human overconfidence and the managerial *hubris* that often follows. At an individual level such wisdom entails the ability to fold one's knowledge, interests and capabilities into a coherent set of predispositions and to act without the expectation of a settled pre-eminence; a capability for enduring and coping with uncertainty that the poet John Keats called the 'negative capability'. To be wise is not to be 'clever', to have full or accurate knowledge of a condition, or to be known for excellence in a specific area or activity, but to be constantly aware of the limits and limitations of knowledge.

Despite the pre-eminence of wisdom in ancient thought, it has slipped from the scholarly map. More recently, however, a number of management and organizational scholars have begun to re-engage with the concept. These studies have identified wisdom as a capacity for what Aristotle (NE 1142a27, 1143b8, 2002) called *phronesis*, the kind of prudential judgement by which equivocal circumstances are negotiated and acted upon with a view for the common good. In Aristotle's framework, practical wisdom or *phronesis* is regarded as an excellence of character perfected through relentless practice and eventual habituation (Dunne, 1993: 266–268; Flyvbjerg, 2001). Wise people transmit their insights through exemplary behaviour and thoughts so that the judgments they make reveal an exemplary internalized disposition that is communicated to others around them. In the *Nichomachean Ethics* Aristotle distinguishes between five forms of knowledge; art, scientific knowledge, practical wisdom (*phronesis*), philosophic wisdom and intuitive reason. For him philosophic wisdom (*Sophia*) is unquestionably the highest form of knowledge arrived at through the integration of scientific knowledge (*episteme*) with intuitive reason (*logos*). Yet *Sophia* is 'remarkable, admirable, difficult and divine, *but useless* (NE, 1141b6-7, emphasis added) because it is only attained with the benefit of leisure. Practical wisdom or *phronesis* on the other hand can only be known by 'considering who are the persons we credit with it' (NE 6.5.1140a25) thereby implying that it is more a characteristic of a person than a form of knowledge. *Phronesis* is associated with what a *phronimos* does. Thus, 'we think Pericles and men like him have practical wisdom…because they can see what is good for themselves and what is good for men in general' (NE 6.5.1140b5-10). Furthermore, 'practical wisdom is a virtue and not an art' (NE6.5.1140b-24). Whilst in the intervening period of some 2000 years since Aristotle many have written about the notion of prudence and practical wisdom, their true practical import to our everyday lives and especially to the world of business remains inadequately examined.

These preliminary insights on the nature of practical wisdom and its relevance to the world of practical affairs help us to delineate the focus and preoccupation of the papers in this timely collection. Wendelin Küpers and David Pauleen are to be highly complimented for their substantial effort to bring the basics of good business practice back into focus amidst the global chaos and turmoil of the last few years. Amidst the relentless emphasis on instrumentalized and rational-calculative actions in the conduct of business, this volume offers a welcome respite; an opportunity to step back and ask more fundamental questions about the future and viability of our current business models.

Without doubt, there is an urgent need to reset managerial priorities and corporate agendas to take into account the need for acting not just in the immediate self-interests of individual corporations but for the greater common good. The papers in this important collection address such urgent issues and I am heartened that there are those amongst us who are prepared to take the risk to forge a new and more prudent approach to the conduct of business that takes into consideration the wider social and ecological ramifications of local business actions.

Robert C H Chia

References

Aristotle, 2002. *Nichomachean Ethics* (translated by Sarah Broadie and Christopher Rowe). Oxford University Press, New York.

Dunne, J. 1993. *Back to the Rough Ground*. Notre Dame: University of Notre Dame Press.

Flyvbjerg, B. 2001. *Making Social Sciences Matter: Why Social Inquiry Fails and How it Can Succeed Again*. Cambridge: Cambridge University Press.

Acknowledgement

We, the editors, acknowledge with particular gratitude the support of the School of Management and the College of Business at Massey University for the Practical Wisdom Symposium held at the university in December 2011. We also want to express our appreciation of the generosity of spirit of all our contributors in working on their chapters presented here and for their responsiveness to our editorial and reviewers' requests. We would especially like to thank the chapter reviewers, our excellent copy editor, Jackie Bell as well as the very engaged Production Editor Kevin Selmes and Martin West at Gower Publishing for their helpful support and assistance in making this book possible.

Introducing a Handbook of Practical Wisdom for Our Times

At a time when the threat of total annihilation no longer seems to be an abstract possibility but the most imminent and real potentiality, it becomes all the more imperative to try again and again to foster and nurture those forms of communal life in which dialogue, conversation, phronesis, practical discourse and judgment are in need for being concretely embodied in our everyday practices. (Bernstein 1983: 229)

The world we are living in is poised in a fragile state of precariousness. Bernstein's warning has not lost its urgency. On the contrary, the decades since this declaration have confirmed the peril of not bringing wisdom to bear in our 'everyday practices'. Our contemporary realities are characterized by various forms of insanity and folly, marked by various interdependent economic, social and environmental calamities and ecological crisis, which while being unpredictable in their reach and implications are calling for wise counsel to develop more responsible and sustainable ways of living.

The need for practical wisdom is evidenced by the current financial and economic crisis. Caused by a combination of individual, socio-cultural, legal, political and institutional failures and irresponsible non-sustainable business practices, it is reinforced by a short-termism to environmental and development issues. As we observe in the daily news, the impacts of this are generating worldwide contagions, far-reaching effects and erratic consequences on local and global levels, affecting human and non-human realities in a sinking world (Stiglitz 2010). This crisis manifests not only flawed economic and other theories or unbalanced dysfunctional practices and policies, but also in a lack of wisdom in contemporary business and society. Contrary to the spirit of Socratic wisdom, in which we are wise insofar as we recognize and accept our limitations, we are experiencing the opposite in organizational, managerial and political hubris.

We are replete with smart people and agencies working in unwise ways and directions (Sternberg 2004). Their foolishness is often caused by lack of humility, a complacent attitude and narcissism or systemic self-referentiality that conspire against both creativity and wisdom. What we find in organizations is what Alvesson and Spicer (2012) recently described as a ambigious 'functional stupidity' defined as inability and/or unwillingness to use reflective capacities in anything other than narrow and circumspect ways functioning as doubt-control and uncertainty-coping mechanism (Alvesson and Spicer 2012).

Some of the best-educated and most eloquent professionals and sophisticated institutions have observed or mediated processes leading to the recent disastrous events in the financial markets. Basic insights and practices of practical wisdom have been violated not only in the financial and economic sector but in the business world, society and the environment at large. If the current financial and ongoing ecological crisis that is unprecedented in kind and scale have taught us one thing, it is that without practical wisdom, business cannot be sustainable, no matter how sophisticated the financial or managerial formula. On the contrary, according to Dennis Meadows along with the authors of the book *Money and Sustainability* (Arnsperger, Goerner and Brunnhuber 2012), the prevailing financial system is incompatible with long-term sustainability due to currency monopoly, monetary policy-induced compulsory growth and resultant cycles of boom–bubble–bust, hyper-inequities in wealth distribution and the devaluation of social capital.

The predicament of our unwise situation manifests also in the world of business, where we observe not only a series of corporate scandals and spectacular organizational failures, but also various forms of unethical behavior at workplaces, often on behalf of the organization (Umphress and Bingham, 2011). Likewise the lack of wisdom is apparent in the amoral, toxic or ugly practices of leader- and followership (Lipman-Blumen 2005), described by Kellerman (2004) as incompetent, operationally rigid, intemperate, callous, corrupt, insular, and evil. All of these problematic issues and ethical failures to execute moral agency, on the micro-, meso- and macro-levels, indicate personal, socio-cultural and systemic pathologies and dysfunctionalities of unwise practices and realities.

These and many other problematic issues require and call for alternative and transformational responses. Perhaps this multifaceted crisis is an essential phase in a larger process in the transformation and revision of underlying world-views. As such it may serve as an opportunity for regeneration towards and instituting wiser forms of organization and leadership as well as the wholesome renegotiation and integration of businesses and economics into a greater and more caring and sustainable society and planetary culture.

As Dickens expressed 150 years ago in his famous tale of two cities (1859), ours is still an age of wisdom and an age of foolishness. Like for him, our epoch is one of belief and of incredulity, a season of light and of darkness, a spring of hope and a winter of despair, in which we are having still and again everything and nothing before us. What we are experiencing today seems to be both a world of con-fusion and a longing for a new 'fusing' orientation, both an 'Age of Unreason' or imploding endarkenment (Ventura 1993) and an age of potential enlightenment as well as various shades and ambiguities in between. Perhaps it is not an accident that wisdom has been symbolized as an owl, as this animal can see in darkness and takes flight in the twilights of closing dusk or opening dawn.

Looking Back and Moving Forward

When entering the worlds of practice and research on wisdom or the lack of it, it becomes evident that these are situated in a historical continuum even as new understandings, forms and interpretations emerge. Debates about a supposed perennial or universal wisdom versus various forms of socially constructed and culturally mediated conceptualizations of wisdom manifest the complexities involved in conceiving its ever-elusive nature. Often being part of spiritual and religious traditions, those questions and suggestions of how to live in a wise and meaningful way have been with us since humans appeared on Earth. Practices of sapience and incarnations of so called sages have been and are present in all cultures throughout time from ancient paganism to today's postmodernism .

However as studies in history, philosophy, theology, political science as well as natural science, including recent findings in neuro-science indicate, wisdom has been defined, revived and contested over time in varied ways and disciplines.

Therefore, we strongly argue for the need for a historically informed and critical contextualization and cross-disciplinary exploration of the multidimensional phenomena of practical wisdom. Such historically and critically reflexive approach can help to work out a more comprehensive understandings, and develop more adequate pragmatic, political and institutional and other implications and consequences. In this way, practical wisdom yields a contemporarily relevant meaning not only in organization and management research and practices. Rather, it reveals its significance also for the wider social, societal and political and ecological spheres in which today's business and economics are playing such enormous, far-reaching and often problematic roles.

A timely and critical reinterpreting of wisdom requires considering the historico-socio-ethico and political conditions of its own operation (Long 2002) in order not only to comprehend what we are inheriting, and where we find ourselves situated, but also who and what are we going to become in relation to wisdom.

This orientation towards looking backwards for moving forward implies also reconsidering the origin of what economics means as this can help us remember and reinterpret functions and connections of practical wisdom.

Historically, economics as *oikonomiké* (Crespo 2008) was understood as a kind of habitual and prudent 'household management', which in the Aristotelian conception mainly reinforces the immanent proficiency of the human being (NE VI, 8). Economics entailed a moral orientation and action, and incorporated virtues to facilitate prudent performance. Trade and market were seen in a serving role. In contrast, today we live in an era of market triumphalism, where money takes the place of moral values and virtues (Sandel 2012). Through an eroding marketization of everything, including health, education, public safety, security, criminal justice, environmental protection, recreation and other social goods, civic values, virtues and practices of sociability are crowded out.

Though the situation described above is hugely problematic, using 'wisdom' to address it is not without its own danger. Critically, elegiac jeremiads to lost virtues can be part of an anti-liberalism-oriented communitarian, traditionalism and civic moralism, which end in empty declamation or are in danger of being misused for an enforced virtuous politics and neo-authoritarian practices or regimes. Equally, there exists the real danger that traditional virtues, including practical wisdom, will be commoditized and co-opted as part of the market-society in which social relations are embedded in economic relations, rather than economy being embedded in social relations (Polanyi 1944).

Connecting wisdom to modern organizations has also had its historical forerunners. For example, it was 37 years ago that a group of organizational scholars (Hedberg, Nystrom and Starbuck 1976) thought deeply about 'organizing' wisdom. In the context of advocating the concept of a self-organization, they suggested that tents could replace ossified palaces and invited organizations and scholars investigating them to 'ride' on organizational seesaws. In this way, balanced with a kind of nomadic wisdom, for these authors indecision could then promote exploration, unlearning and re-learning, and an ambiguity of roles could produce flexibility. Instead of relying on formal metrics or benchmarks, organizational members would design their own sensors and experiments with new ideas, deriving satisfaction from creatively designing interactions that build new processes, and thereby create and recreate the organization. These researchers identified six seesaws, which intertwine in organizational settings: consensus and dissension, contentment and dissatisfaction, resource abundance and scarcity, faith in goals and doubt, consistency and instability and finally wisdom, rationality and imperfection. Accordingly they acknowledged that: 'Cooperation requires minimal consensus'; 'Satisfaction rests upon minimal contentment'; 'Wealth arises from minimal affluence'; 'Goals merit minimal faith'; 'Improvement depends on minimal consistency' and finally *'Wisdom demands minimal rationality'*.

In summary they stated: 'A self-designing organization can reach a dynamic equilibrium through the non-rational proliferation, the redundancy and improvisation of processes; and these proliferating processes, as they collide, contradict and interact, *produce organizational wisdom'* (Hedberg, Nystrom and Starbuck 1976: 63).

Many lessons and questions for the study and practice of organization and leadership can be drawn from this historical thought experiment, including the still relevant, critical and in many ways encompassing role of wisdom in self-organizing systems.

The Limits of Practical Wisdom and the Status of Embodied *Prâxis*

As much as the revived interest in wisdom has been triggered by current difficulties, a possible danger would be to see in it a simple solution or remedy for the same. In recognizing the limits of our technical-rational capacities to diagnose and treat current problems, while dealing with uncertainty, an instrumentalized or principle-based governing *phrónêsis* would not be the way to go. According to Kemmis (2012) a *phrónêsis* that serves to re-enchant a disenchanted world of demoralized, desecrated and devalued professionalism is in danger of becoming another version of *tékhnê* or a set of moral principles. Thus it cannot guarantee that the good will be done, for anyone, let alone for everyone. The hope of recovering *phrónêsis* from the deformity of practical reasoning caused by scientism, technocratic rationality and means–ends instrumentalism is problematic and may itself be unwise.

Challengingly we therefore ask: can practical wisdom provide resources for conceptualizing and leading practice under modern and postmodern conditions without itself becoming a victim of its problematic conditionalitiess? Can *phrónêsis* be seen as a placeholder for the 'something more' that we are looking for in our thinking about the practice of professionals: a longing for a newly understood and enacted praxis (Kemmis 2012) that is a morally committed action while being oriented and informed by traditions (Kemmis and Smith 2008)?

For Kemmis (2012: 150), 'Praxis is the action itself, in all its materiality and with all its effects on and consequences for the cultural-discursive, material-economic, and social-political dimensions of our world in its being and becoming. Praxis emerges in "sayings", "doings", and "relatings"'. Importantly, these modes of praxis are part of the living embodiment of human beings. Accordingly, the practice in the *prâxis* of wisdom can be seen as a fundamental perspective of Homo *sapiens*. Interestingly, the word 'sapiens' derives from a verb that means having taste, subtly sensing flavour and aromas (Serres and Latour 1995). Thus sapiens refers to tasting with the mouth and the tongue. When we say Homo sapiens, we should keep in mind that the origin of the notion of wisdom, or of discourse – man as speaking man – lies in the capacity to taste with the mouth, and with the sense of smell.

Interpreting practical wisdom as not only residing in language and intellect, but as embodied, experiential and situational action can be seen as part of the recent return to the body and to practice in organization and management studies (Küpers 2012b). This focus on embodiment and practices of practical wisdom as being embedded in praxis may serve as an antidote or inoculate against the danger of cognitive or intellectual bias and over-conceptualizing or over-hyping as well as instrumentalizing it. Moreover, the embodied experiences, reflections and actions within praxis can be seen as a prerequisite and media for *phrónêsis* and a corresponding morally committed practice. In this sense, committing to the 'happeningness' of praxis as a way of life helps to learn or to develop *phrónêsis* (Kemmis 2012) understood as a wise practice and proto-integral life-style. As such it moves between personal, situational and collective, encultured levels, while being conducive to the sustainable continuity and prosperity of the whole.

But what does *phrónêsis* as an embodied, variable, action-oriented practice mean in increasingly instrumentalized and institutionalized contexts and in the face of various structured constraints of professional practice?

Sowing Seeds in Hostile Ground

Practices in organizations and institutions are situated today on a 'hostile ground for growing *phrónêsis*' (Pitman 2012). This is a time of technocratic regimes, excessive managerialism, systems of surveillance and accountability discourses, in which professionals have numerous and frequently conflicting ruling bodies to which they are answerable. These constraining realities affect decision-making and other practices, often in unwise ways. Wisdom in such situated contexts does not unfold easily. It can often be derailed by temporal dynamics, for example the competing requirements of customers, enframing technology and production cycles, or suffer from the influence of dominant unwise or counter-wise logic.

Organizational contexts are not 'benign' (Brookfield 2010). They include psychodynamic factors such as denial and organizational defensiveness (Argyris 2008), and socio-cultural and structural-systemic obstacles and especially political processes and institutional dimensions. The political matrices of organizational settings with their often 'fraught coalitions' or compromises are unearthed by the circuitries of power and contextual power relationships (Clegg 2002), which suffuse them with meaning and signal some actions as possible and others as 'wise' to avoid in various moral mazes (Jackall 1988). For example, reflexive honesty articulated aloud may not prove a wise practice in organizational environments, which may at times appear to require and even reward deception (Shulman 2007).

Creating wise practice as part of *prâxis* needs to address these and other political and institutional issues in order to prepare the ground in which wisdom may grow. In other words, demands for *phrónêsis* need to be seen in light of extra-individual features (Kemmis 2005).

Accordingly, we suggest a *politically informed 'wisdom as practice' approach*, also for research, as discussed in the following, that would go beyond a reactive, moralizing sentimentalism. Instead, for such an approach the practicing of wisdom is bodily and reflectively intertwined in an individual's and group's relative power, freedom and responsibility, while considering enabling and constraining conditions of structures and systems. For example, practically wise judgements and decisions about what to do, why and by whom, take into account organizational, cultural and societal as well as ecological dimensions and contexts, in which practices are situated, framed and governed (Ibarra-Colado 2007).

Possibilities and limitations of applied wise practicing must be explored by looking into micro-political acting. Specifically individual and social strategies of retaining and developing power could be investigated as possible causes of failures in implementing wise dimensions in organizational and leadership practice.

Additionally, global and cross-company dimensions of practical wisdom could be investigated with regard to wiser forms of production, products and services as well as marketing and finance-related activities. For example, the status of wisdom in decisions about location of industry and outsourcing, as well as the problems of staffing cutbacks or labour displacement and corruption call for further exploration.

The leading-edge and best practices of mainstreaming wise practice would comprise the alignment with business objectives within overall company strategy and the integration across business entities and functional areas and the institutionalization by embedding strategies, policies, processes and systems into the fabric of the organization. At the same time this requires consideration of critical conditions like scale, transience and disparities, which infect the public perception of business and prompt questions about what the corporate future holds.

The challenge to integrate practical wisdom as a work in progress is in need of further analytical exploration, theoretical conceptualization and empirical investigation or evaluations (see Research Context section on p. 9).

But facing the concern about what good is theory if it is theorizing about a world that *no longer exists*, or is, at the very least, disintegrating, we need to ask and respond to critically radical questions like: what kinds of economics, businesses and organizations do we need in the twenty-first century and beyond to deliver and serve genuine sustainable development? What would wise leadership, followership, organizations and institutions look like that can lead into mindful presence and an integral future (Voros 2008)?

The Acceptance and Legitimization of Wisdom

If we can convincingly address the issues raised above, we will go a long way in getting wisdom accepted and legitimatized in organizational discourses and practices. This is particularly challenging in our current times and under present institutional conditions, which are so radically different to historical and especially Aristotelian epochs.

Aristotle's concept of *phrónêsis* rests on a vision of moral clarity and normativity that is in stark contrast to our prevailing moral pluralism, making contemporary agreement on the quality of *phrónêsis* challenging at least: Aristotle's ultra-conservative account of the role of leaders, the male elite governing the city-state (Kraut 2002), the status of supposed natural slaves and patriarchal masters, the subjugation of women. These and many more problematic issues typify Aristotle for some critics as the archetypal 'dead white European male' and exemplify outdated components of his system, such as his metaphysical biology, supposed first principles, moral essentialism and corresponding 'grand' claims for practical rationality (Ellett 2012). So how might *phrónêsis* be reinterpreted, understood, applied and extended in a world radically different to that of its progenitor? For example how to rethink virtue not as given or attributed by specific character traits or strength of particularly 'virtuous' individuals defined independently of specific contexts and practices in organizations (Weaver, 2006), but to develop a post-heroic, relational understanding and legitimizing virtuosity as part of interdependent moral agencies of individual and collective agents.

The poly-contextualism in today's co-evolution of society and organization relies on continuous legitimization in public reflective communication processes and within networks and partnerships involving conflicting perspectives (Holmstrom 2006). Organizing wisdom today must rest dynamically on democratic principles, often at odds with the travails and exigencies of political and power relationships (Butcher and Clarke 2002, Varman and Chakrabarti 2004). What does it imply to understand and interpret wisdom, like reflexivity, as a democratic value (Rosanvallon 2011) and valuable civic virtue? How can practical wisdom – legitimized by a deliberative democracy of dynamic civic society as vibrant area – be translated into corresponding democratic and participative organization and leadership (Raelin 2012)?

One reasonable approach is to accept that a deliberative and political conception of practical wisdom in organizations can be seen as part of an all-embracing responsibility. This then in turn calls for a proactive concept of societal involvement embedded in democratic mechanisms of politicization, communicative discourse, governance transparency and accountability (Scherer and Palazzo 2007). Furthermore, practical wisdom calls for reinventing or reforming civic institutions like universities, think tanks, research labs and so on, in ways in which these can develop and make informed and inclusive decisions, leading to deliberative action. Institutionally, wise processes need to be understood and connected with regard to governance systems which are ordering economic and societal transactions, organizing the 'cosmopolis' of our times. Concepts like Corporate Citizenship (Burchell and Cook 2006, Norman and Néron 2008, Crane et al. 2008) or post-traditional Corporate Governance (Mason and O'Mahony 2008) and a critical and integral understanding of Corporate Social Responsibility and sustainability (Küpers 2012a) are offered up to account for social embeddedness and legitimacy of wisdom.

However, there is a 'danger' of calling for *phrónêsis* and holding practitioners accountable for practical wisdom in contexts that may not support it. Moreover, there may be forces that actively mitigate against it. Practitioners may then also face a double bind, where they are blamed for a failure of agency at the personal level, when the issues are structural and systemic. Of course there is also the difficulty of dealing with administrative evil (Reed 2012), whereby otherwise well-intentioned individuals participate in systems that cause harm to innocent people. Likewise, organizational and ethical failures as well as when leadership goes wrong (Schyns and Hansbrough 2010) or becomes destructive (Einarsen, Aasland and Skogstad 2007) generate possibly unintended, but actual unwise processes and consequences.

Along with Bernstein (1986), we doubt that *phrónêsis* is always a possibility no matter how corrupt the existing practices are or the communities and institutions that sustain it. What can be done when the polis or community is itself corrosive or corrupt or not ready to cultivate and enact or indeed debases practically wise decisions, judgements and actions?

Most of the current assumptions of organizational and economic success and growth orientation are based on non-sustainable practices and unwise belief systems and practices. Realizing actual sustainability and actualized wisdom requires radical transformation. Radical here refers to not only translational or transactional moves, but on a very broad scale also involves deep change (Carroll 2004). Such delving into more profound changes and transformational moves while pursuing an uplifting vision systematically requires developing and using integral lenses, metatheoretically, methodologically and practically (Edwards 2009a, b, c).

For a genuine transformation towards practical wisdom in organization and leadership to take place, a radical re-orientation of meanings, values and practices as well as lives of individuals, organizations and societies needs to occur at both local and global levels. This re-evaluating may help to supplement or even supplant not only the business and performance reports by more 'green forms' of auditing, and 'Gross National Product' by alternative measures such as the 'Index of Sustainable Economic Welfare' (Daly and Cobb 1994) or 'Common Wealth' (Sachs 2008), but also objectives and reporting of business in terms of wholesome wealth and integral well-be(com)ing (Küpers 2005) for all stakeholders.

The extent to which the broader institutional environment of the market, corporate society and regulatory bodies reinforce, exasperate or alter the pressures and logic to introduce and practice practical wisdom within academic institutions, especially business schools, is an avenue of inquiry requiring further exploration.

Like social justice (Toubiana 2012) and other ethical orientations, practical wisdom is also exposed to hegemonic forces and pressures driving business programmes. For example, profit-driven business ideologies, the particular character of MBA programmes and bias toward quantitative research in business programmes might negate how faculty engage with, teach and research the meaning of wisdom. This all calls for an institutional redesign, and institutional work that creates, maintains and also disrupts institutions (Lawrence and Suddaby 2006).

As the future is not and will not be what it used to be, there is a need to develop shared visions of what a responsible, sustainable wise business and society would look like. What are adequate images, metaphors and stories, desirable values, maps and pathways and how can we subsequently determine appropriate ends and choose corresponding specific means? In other words, what world-views and corresponding wise practices and developments do we envision in 10, 20, 50 years ahead?

Finally, understanding the limitations of what we can do wisely and what cannot be tackled by practical wisdom allows cultivating non-resignative forms of an 'engaged letting-go'. To paraphrase an old proverb, with such an attitude we may learn to accept the things we cannot change, the courage to change the things we can and should, while deploying the wisdom to know the difference between the two. Realizing that one cannot practice a complete wisdom in relation to all possibilities prioritizes the need to move in the continuum of the wise and the wayward or foolish and even seeing wise qualities in the latter one. Actually, the deconstruction of the binary pair wisdom/foolishness allows considering an extended variety of concepts resulting from different sense-making strategies rooted in local theories of wisdom and seeing supplementary value in foolishness for organization studies and practices (Izak 2013). Accordingly, it seems to be wise to open up and allow *wisdom to be foolish*, thus developing a more integral understanding and practice of it means to be wise and what comprises wisdom practically.

Overall, cultivating a sense for not a frenetic, but *phrónêtic* utopia – a longing for wiser practices and wiser forms of civic community and organizational life – might enable citizens and members of organization to be guided by ideals, values and more long-term, sustainable orientations towards which to look and move; instead of acquiescing to shortsighted near-term solutions and impatient hyper-practicalisms. This may then open up ethical states as 'spaces for freedom' (Ricoeur 1997, 334); a freedom to engage wisely!

Research Context

For a long time, wisdom has slipped from the scholarly map and now we need new mappings for today and times to come. Accordingly, we see this handbook as part of an emerging wisdom research agenda, especially in the fields of organization and leadership. Pursuing and seeking to actualize the creative potentials of integral practical wisdom, this book aspires to contribute particularly to the contemporary epistemic and ontic odysseys in research and practice. Wisdom research provides various bridges to underestimated, neglected or forgotten knowledge and offers transformative passages between Scylla – the rocks of dogmatic modernity – and Charybdis – the whirlpool of dispersed post-modernity.

Research on wisdom moves in contested territory with competing interpretations and pathways. Critical research on practical wisdom allows for a better equipped and more experiential and reflexive journey. It encourages and fosters the art of mindful travelling into the enigmatic spheres and elusive and ambiguous issues of yet unknown possibilities. In particular it can help to understand ambiguities, dilemmas, paradoxes and even aporias as characteristics of the work and research on the multidimensional practice of wise and unwise organizing and leading. Such integral research on wisdom invites entering the *in-between* of embodied selves, groups and communities, their local cultures, organizations, institutions, regional realities and societies, natural environment and ecologies.

Research into practical wisdom needs to be further developed, explored, theorized and empirically studied in order not only for developing a more refined and comprehensive understanding but also to better inform the field of organization and leadership practice. Practical wisdom can also be informative as a corrective or complementary construct for other approaches conceptually and procedurally, as for example with limitations and problems in 'Positive Scholarship' research, like reality-polarization and time-frame circumspection (Gygax 2011).

For advancing wisdom research, we suggest some specific recommendations, which comprise careful conceptual framing, integration and methodological rigour and pluralism. This comprises clearing and avoiding conceptual (retrograde) slippages and debris through a more critical delineation of wisdom from closely related yet distinct constructs. Moreover, we must be able to deal with the varieties of wisdom that abound and seek integration (Walsh 2011).

Methodologically, a multilevel approach is required, which considers systematically various levels and orders of emergence of practical wisdom, and which moves and mediates simultaneously individual and collective spheres (Küpers and Statler 2008).

In other words, we need more complex and thoroughly worked-through theories and proto-integral frameworks that are methodologically pluralistic and cross-disciplinary. As a sapiential orientation transgresses methodological, disciplinary and sub-disciplinary boundaries, we call for cross-level analysis and greater inter-, trans- and post-disciplinary collaboration to approach the multidimensionality and contextual embedding as well as the interconnections of wisdom and its study. An integral understanding of wisdom requires joint and mutually enriching undertakings and the cooperation of different research traditions and perspectives as part of a post-paradigmatic, engaged *phrónêtic* social and organization science (Flyvbjerg 2001, 2008, Flyvbjerg Landman and Schram 2012).

Future wisdom research may be a kind of 'delicate theorizing', which is described by Gidley (2010) in her outlining of a post-formal-integral-planetary scholarship as 'consistently attending to the kindred theories that rub up against our cherished theories and methodologies', such that 'we keep them soft and alive rather than hard, rigid and mechanistic' as well as 'creating ongoing dialogue – rather than debate – with kindred theoretic approaches' (2010: 130). In essence, delicate theorizing is a reminder to attend to and recognize the Other by weaving a tenuous web of wisdom scholarship, making (tentative) connections among empirical research in the social and natural sciences, as well as connecting them to lived experiences individually and collectively.

A critical and integral approach towards practical wisdom needs to be open-minded in so far as the involved relations and phenomena as well as theories developed or used are not pocketed and categorically fixed, but respected in their specific and particular ways of articulation. Theoretical developments in wisdom research continue to emerge apace and empirical, especially longitudinal, studies are urgently required and called for with respect to a wider variety of wisdom-related processes and in collaboration with practice.

Qualitative and mixed-method research can and should be useful for exploring not only structural factors and processual conditions, but also non-rational, embodied, emotional, aesthetic and spiritual dimensions. The latter ones are particular relevant as they have been banned by traditional modernistic scientific paradigms and discourses, often trapped in materialistic scientism. For investigating situational practice and wisdom phenomena, we encourage more participant- and observation-based methodological approaches, such as action research, action learning, ethnography and case studies, as well as innovative advances like art-based practices (for example, McNiff 2008). As stated by Rooney and McKenna (2008: 717) in their plea for multi-method research designs, researchers involved in wisdom research 'must get their hands dirty in the field, standing shoulder to shoulder with practitioners, and they must do their research as wise research practitioners who are able to operationalize their imaginations, emotions, ethical sensitivities, and logics simultaneously to produce excellent research that can be transformational'. In this spirit we call and hope for wisdom-based research methods for doing wise research and further developing and realizing an acceptable *phrónêsiology*.

What we take from the contributions of this handbook is that wisdom research is ready to face and seize the challenges and opportunities inherent in thinking about and exploring wisdom in our times and for futures to come. Overall, the chapters here speak of an interest and openness that can invite or push wisdom research forward in the aforementioned directions. We hope our readers will share our enthusiasm about intensifying wisdom research along these spiraling lines and beyond!

Handbook of Practical Wisdom – Locating an Emerging Idea

As with most creative endeavours, this book is a result of a confluence of people, places and circumstances. It is essentially the editors' and authors' response to a definable lack in the business schools and academic institutions in which most of us work and the troubling conditions we observe and live with in the world at large.. Here we offer some of the backstory of this book.

The immediate roots of this book go back to 2010, when the co-editors began to discuss and plan a symposium on practical wisdom, held 4–6 December 2011 at Massey University in Auckland. We each had a number of contacts writing about or interested in the idea of practical wisdom and we believed the time was right to bring them together. Our goal was two-fold: one, to begin a network of like-minded academics and practitioners in which we could develop research into practical wisdom and related areas; and two, to publish a book based on the papers presented at the symposium. Both of these goals have come to fruition. The quality of the book has been greatly enhanced by the group of authors' extensive discussion and feedback on each of the papers presented at the symposium and the continuing reviews and revisions that the network continued to share.

The territory that this book covers offers a mapping that is a tentative outlining of some issues and aspects that warrant ongoing investigation and a forum for conversation among a group of scholars, largely based at Australasian universities. The fact that the majority of the authors are from Australia and New Zealand was not surprising, as this is where we are located and this is where the symposium was held.

Yet maybe there is more to it than this. Perhaps one reason for this geographically-bound emerging wisdom research has to do with the fact that Australasia is situated on the margin or periphery compared to the prevailing mainstream of (other Western) culture. Being located on the edge and living on the fringe of the world seems to be advantageous for somewhat non-conventional research like that on wisdom.

As much as wisdom research should be historically informed and should try to make a contribution to the contemporary world, it can also be interpreted as a kind of avant-garde movement. Researching conditions, potentials and implications of practical wisdom not only pushes the boundaries of conventional thinking and acting, but is also situated under a 'boundary condition', demarcating and delimiting traditional forms of organisation, leadership and business, while aspiring to a 'transboundary' orientation. Accordingly, wisdom research is not in the centre of academic institutions and practices and Australasia is not only geographically, but also metaphorically, a borderland.

In relatively undetermined borderlands, interpreted also as psycho-social territories of transition, seeming contradictions may be embraced and potentially become a creative force for new connections, for example between ideas and people, visions and enactments. Furthermore, the borderlands metaphor possesses and creates an atmosphere and has the 'power of sustainable engagement, a mixing and a blending that results in the emergence of novelty' (Tyler 2009: 532).

When here in New Zealand the sun rises just over the international dateline, the Australasians are the first to the future: hopefully, being situated so close to the future also opens up a prospect for research and practice of a living wisdom to come.

Personal Background and Motivation of Editors

Going further back, the book is the natural outcome of the editors' developing academic and life interests. Both editors have had a fairly extensive history with knowledge management (KM). One (David Pauleen) has been teaching KM at the graduate level since 2002. He quickly ascertained that KM was more than technology and information and over the years introduced a more holistic understanding of KM into the classroom drawing on his students' experiences in the workplace. He introduced reflective assignments into his post-experience Master's class and was somewhat surprised to find how much difficulty people in their 30s and 40s had reflecting on their work experiences and what they were studying in class, and applying this to future career scenarios. From this, he went on to develop ideas around Personal Knowledge Management, which he understood as the skills and knowledge needed for individuals to survive and thrive in turbulent environments. He soon realized that these needed skills and knowledge could naturally be understood as an entrée into a life based on wisdom. In his personal life, he began practicing Buddhist meditation at 19, which he has continued, with occasional shamanic and Taoist interludes, ever since.

The other editor (Wendelin Küpers) has a long-term interest in phenomenology, and inter- and transdisciplinarity as well as integral research. In his understanding, advanced forms of phenomenology and hermeneutic philosophy can contribute to reveal the capacity and relevance of practical wisdom through exploring the significance of the living body, embodiment and creative engagement in experiential practice and *prâxis*. In particular a phenomenology in the spirit of Merleau-Ponty is critical with regard to objectivistic or idealistic thinking and helps overcoming dualistic and dichotomist orientation also in relation to wisdom theory and practice. For him, phenomenological and hermeneutical understanding is itself a form of practical reasoning and practical knowing, thus closely connected to practical wisdom.

Being a cross-disciplinary traveller, he is interested in *bricolage*, building (living) bridges at the intersection of various territories and facilitating interrelation and interaction of researches in and between different territories. For him, practical wisdom research resonates and calls for crossing boundaries and thus invites cross-disciplinary inquiries. Furthermore, practical wisdom provides a proto-integrative potential; it serves as a reference point or medium for a more integral research. Correspondingly, he pursues research on relational and integral dimensions in organization and leadership or management as well as possibilities of responsibility and sustainability, which all lead towards exploring practical wisdom.

The Chapters

As editors, we naturally gave a lot of thought to the ordering of the chapters in the book. We thought about having separate sections on leadership, organization and business integration to reflect the book's title. Given the multifaceted nature of wisdom and the chapters at hand, this was not so simple. Most of the chapters, as would be expected for a subject such as this, link wisdom to leadership and organization: the linking of these partially or implicitly addresses integral business practice.

Rather than trying to divide the chapters into impossibly neat categories, we have decided to let the guiding ideas of each chapter flow in as natural a manner as possible. That said, the contents of the chapters mingles and interlinks, hence providing a recursive and reflective journey for the reader. To emphasize the reflective nature of this voyage, and to bridge between the reader and the an aspired practical nature of wisdom, we have asked the authors to provide a set of programmatic questions at the end of their chapters to invite further contemplation and perhaps 'activate' the chapters' messages or visions.

The book begins with a chapter by the co-editor Wendelin Küpers on 'The Art and Practice of Wisdom'. This contritution sets the stage for the book by providing an advanced phenomenological understanding of practical wisdom as a situated, embodied and relational 'inter-practice' as well as creative action in organization and leadership. A special emphasis is given to the aesthetic and artful dimensions of practical wisdom and it proposes a critical *phrónêsis* understood as a responsive and responsible *poiêsis*. Furthermore, moral perceptions and moral imaginations as well as artistic practices are described as *phrónêtic* capacities. Finally, this chapter offers some implications and perspectives on a professional artistry related to practicing wisdom.

The art and practice of wisdom is specifically embodied in the hermeneutic circle. In Chapter 2, *Phrónêsis in Action: A Case Study Approach to a Professional Learning Group*, Claire Jankelson shows how practical wisdom may be engendered by the application of a hermeneutic phenomenological approach when working with professionals engaged in PhD research in a management school. It is at this nexus of higher education, research and management that the manifestation of *phrónêsis* as practical wisdom may emerge. The chapter moves from description of experience to theoretical analysis and back again in a spiralling fashion, anticipating that clarity, comprehension and engagement best eventuate within a hermeneutic circularity.

In Chapter 3 Peter Case offers a non-Western perspective on the cultivation of embodied wisdom in Cultivation of Wisdom in the *Theravada* Buddhist Tradition: Implications for Contemporary Leadership and Organization. While very much present in the 'mundane' world of social human interaction, in this Buddhist tradition, wisdom, in the form of insight, may provide an entrée into a supra-mundane world. The chapter also draws comparisons between Buddhist wisdom and contemporary philosophical interest in the art of living, and suggests that Buddhism can contribute to the exploration of alternative ways of being and acting in organizations based on the reduction of egocentricity and development of a deeper sensibility with regard to the holistic or interconnected nature of all phenomena.

David Rooney's 'Being a Wise Organizational Researcher: Ontology, Epistemology and Axiology', Chapter 4, allows us to step back and look at the foundational basis of practical wisdom, particularly ontology and epistemology as elements of research as well as ontology and epistemology of practical and social practice wisdom. Going further, the chapter also discusses the benefits of doing organizational wisdom research that uses a wisdom-based methodology (*phrónêsiology*) and methods rather than traditional epistemology. The five core principles of Social Practice Wisdom are introduced and used as a framework for discussing what is involved in using *phrónêtic* research methods.

In Chapter 5, somewhat in contrast to Rooney's more conceptual chapter, Boyle and Roan, in The Paradoxical Nature of the Representation of Women in Management, point out some of the concrete inconsistencies and practical challenges that are still to be found in the organizational embrace of practical wisdom. The authors discuss why women remain under-represented in the top layers of many areas of upper management and show that while classifying women's wisdom as 'special' and 'different' may appear advantageous to women, there are also dangers in that women's wisdom is often classified as coming from the private sphere of nurturing and care and thus undervalued in organizations.

In an empirical approach in Chapter 6, 'Evaluating the Process of Wisdom in Wise Political Leaders Using a Developmental Wisdom Model', Biloslavo and McKenna draw upon contemporary psychological research to identify core assumptions about wisdom and then propose a model of wise leadership. They use a textual analysis of the lives and leadership of Nelson Mandela and Aung San Suu Kyi and conclude that these two leaders display high levels of performance in the four dimensions. The authors argue that the model provides a useful parsimonious account of the major factors contributing to wisdom and call for further testing.

In Chapter 7 Jay Hays offers an aspirational approach to motivated leaders in his contribution on 'Transformation and Transcendence for Wisdom: the Emergence and Sustainment of Wise Leaders and Organizations' by introducing a dynamic model that integrates transformational leadership, transformational learning and transformational organizational change (T^3) with transcendence and wisdom. The exploration and synthesis of the respective elements and their relationships significantly contributes to a practical and systemic understanding of the dynamics of learning and change and the potential for leader and organizational wisdom. Exercises are included and are designed to help readers operationalize and make the most of the theory, philosophy and principles of transformation and transcendence.

Intezari and Pauleen, in Students of Wisdom: An Integral Meta-competencies Theory of Practical Wisdom, Chapter 8, discuss how wisdom may be taught to business students and business people. They introduce an integral meta-competencies theory of wisdom, suggesting that wisdom is the manifestation of a person's cognitive and practical interactions with the real world, which can be fostered through the development of a set of meta-competencies. Some classroom strategies for developing these meta-competencies are proposed.

Subsequently, Bernard Kleimann in Chapter 9, 'University Presidents as Wise Leaders? Aristotle's *Phrónêsis* and Academic Leadership in Germany' connects university leadership with practical wisdom. The focus on the deliberation and decision-making processes of university presidents in contemporary German higher education renders revealing insights and effects as well as offers important lessons for leaders in other large organizations.

Finally, the book closes with a thoughtful contribution by Mark Edwards chapter on 'In Wisdom and Integrity: Metatheoretical Perspectives on Integrative Change in an Age of Turbulence', Edwards raises the paradox that organizations, managers and leaders today face in responding to the imperative for radical transformation while also safeguarding the welfare and the investments of their members and key stakeholders. This chapter considers the quality of wisdom that is concerned with this kind of discernment, in particular the role of integrity in holding together the many aspects of high-performance functioning. A typology is presented which describes different kinds of wisdom with its shadow sides and their relationships to types of environmental change and corresponding organizational responses. Finally, he offers some implications of the meta-theoretical conceptualizations for studies of organizational.

We view this handbook as a suitable platform and medium for reassessing and rearticulating more responsible ways of research and reflexivity, connecting to 'prâxis' in the field of organization and management research and beyond. In this spirit, the juxtapositions of the chapters in this book open a space for expressions of divergent perspectives as well as for encounter and dialogue. Rather than offering closures and final answers, we hope the contributions in this book invite further explorations, inquiries, and conversations.

Further Thoughts and Invitation by the Editors

Overall, the book tries to offer departure points or a sources for those engaging with and learning more about practical wisdom and its research. Moreover, as we would like to see the network of wisdom researchers grow we invite all those would like to be involved to get in touch with us. It is our intention to organise further symposia and we welcome the participation of all who are interested. Correspondingly, we hope to see these symposia result in further published books. To this end, Gower has been very supportive in agreeing to allow us to serve as series editors and publish a number of books on a range of issues fundamental to understanding and supporting the role of wisdom in organizational and management respectively leadership studies and practices. Therefore, we invite those of you who are interested in (co-)authoring chapters or (co-)editing a book to contact us with your ideas or proposals.

On the whole, we do hope that the handbook breathes new life into the ancient idea and potential of practical wisdom as we firmly see it placed at the forefront of responsible, ethical and sustainable organisation and management/leadership: a much needed approach at the dawn of the twenty-first century and the futures to come.

As a Chinese wisdom proverb says, 'Even a very long journey begins with a single step'. Baltes and Staudinger (2000: 133) add: 'And this step is more effective the more it is a step in the right direction'. They even state that 'In fact, if the directional movement is correct, such as is true for the direction and destination of wisdom, we can even afford slow progress.' (Ibid.).

In this sense and as a counterforce to 'over-rushing' knowledge-production, research on practical wisdom resonates with the 'slow science' movement, which not only follows a different pace, but proceeds with more deliberation and caution (The Slow Science Manifesto, 2010).

As the stoic Roman Marc Aurel said: 'It is better to move slowly along the right path than walk stridently in the wrong direction'. In accordance with this sentiment, we would like to invite researchers in the area of practical wisdom in organization and leadership to continue the exploration of and dialogue about possible understandings, approaches, interpretations, but also operationalization and practices of wisdom.

Practical wisdom can only be realized if research, organizations, its members and stakeholders as well civic and globalised society learn not only to aspire to, but actually co-create, design and live excellence in their local, interwoven relation-'ships'. Correspondingly, a timely and properly understood '-ship' moving through responsible and sustainable relations may then set out for a 're-evolution' of enacted practical wisdom at present while journeying towards wiser futures.

References

Alvesson, M. and Spicer, A. (2012). A stupidity base theory of organization.h *Journal of Management Studies*, 49(7), 1194–1220

Arnsperger, C., Goerner, S. and Brunnhuber, S. 2012. *Money and Sustainability: The Missing Link. Report from the Club of Rome*. Axminster: Triarchy Press.

Argyris, C. 2008. Organizational defenses: denials and denials of the denial, in *The SAGE Handbook of New Approaches in Management and Organization*, edited by D. Barry and H. Hansen. London: SAGE, 217–9.

Baltes, P.B. and Staudinger, U.M. 2000. Wisdom: a metaheuristic (pragmatic) to orchestrate mind and virtue toward excellence. *American Psychologist*, 55(1), 122–36.

Bernstein, R. 1983. *Pragmatism and Hermeneutics Beyond Objectivism and Relativism: Science, Hermeneutics, and Praxis*. Philadelphia: University of Pennsylvania Press.

Bernstein, R. 1986. *Philosophical Profiles: Essays in a Pragmatic Mode*. Cambridge: Polity Press.

Brookfield, S.D. 2010. *The Power of Critical Theory for Adult Learning and Teaching*. New York: Open University Press.

Burchell, J. and J. Cook, J. 2006 Confronting the corporate citizen: expanding the challenges of corporate social responsibility, *International Journal of Sociology and Social Policy*, 26(3/4).

Butcher, D. and Clarke, M. 2002. Organizational politics: the cornerstone for organizational democracy. *Organizational Dynamics*, 31(1), 35–46.

Carroll, J.E. 2004. *Sustainability and Spirituality*. Albany: SUNY Press.

Clegg, S. 2002. *Frameworks of Power*. London, UK: SAGE.

Crane, A., Matten, D. and Moon, J. 2008. *Corporations and Citizenship*. Cambridge: Cambridge University Press.

Crespo, R. 2008. 'The economic' according to Aristotle: ethical, political and epistemological implications. *Foundations of Science*, 13(3–4), 281–94.

Daly, H.E. and Cobb, J. 1994. *For the Common Good: Redirecting the Economy Towards Community, the Environment, and a Sustainable Future*. Boston: Beacon Press.

Dickens, C. 1859. *A Tale of Two Cities*. London: Chapman and Hall.

Edwards, M. 2009a. *Organizational Transformation for Sustainability: An Integral Metatheory*. London: Routledge.

Edwards, M. 2009b. An integrative metatheory for organisational learning and sustainability in turbulent times. *The Learning Organization*, 16(3), 189–207.

Edwards, M. 2009c. Visions of sustainability. An integrative metatheory for management education, in *Management Education for Global Sustainability*, edited by C. Wankel and J. Stoner. Greenwich: Information Age Publishing, 55–91.

Einarsen, S., Aasland, M.S. and Skogstad, A. 2007. Destructive leadership behaviour: a definition and conceptual model. *Leadership Quarterly*, 18(3), 207–16.

Ellett, F. 2012. Practical rationality and a recovery of Aristotle's 'phronesis' for the professions, in *Phronesis as Professional Knowledge: Practical Wisdom in the Professions*, edited by E.A. Kinsella and A. Pitman. Rotterdam: Sense Publishing, 14–33.

Flyvbjerg, B. 2001. *Making Social Science Matter: Why Social Inquiry Fails and How It Can Succeed Again*. Cambridge: Cambridge University Press.

Flyvbjerg, B. 2008. Phronetic organizational research, in *The Sage Dictionary of Qualitative Management Research*, edited by R. Thorpe and R. Holt. Los Angeles: Sage Publications, 153–55.

Flyvbjerg, B., Landman, T. and Schram, S. 2012. *Real Social Science – Applied Phrónêsis*. Cambridge: Cambridge University Press.

Gidley, J. 2010. Another view of integral futures: de/reconstructing the IF brand. *Futures: The Journal of Policy, Planning and Futures Studies*, 42(2), 125–33.

Gygax, M. 2011. Enriching the positive organizational behavior framework with wisdom. *International Journal of Business Research*, 11(2), 23–41.

Hall, S.H. 2010. *Wisdom: From Philosophy to Neuroscience*. New York: Knopf.

Hedberg, B., Nystrom, P. and Starbuck, W. 1976. Camping on seesaws: prescriptions for a self-designing organization. *Administrative Science Quarterly*, 21, 41–65.

Holmstrom, S. 2006. The co-evolution of society and organization, in *Organizational Legitimacy and the Public Sphere*, edited by S. Holmstrom. Roskilde: Roskilde University, 54–72.

Ibarra Colado, E. 2007. Future university in present times: autonomy, governance and the entrepreneurial university. *Management Revue*, 18(2), 117–37.

Izak, M. 2013. The foolishness of wisdom: Towards an inclusive approach to wisdom in organization *Scandinavian Journal of Management*, 29, 208–115.

Jackall, R. 1988. *Moral Mazes: The World of Corporate Managers*. New York: Oxford University Press.

Kellerman, B. (2004) *Bad Leadership: What it is, How it Happens, Why it Matters*, Boston: Harvard Business School Press.

Kemmis, S. 2005. Knowing practice: searching for saliences. *Pedagogy, Culture and Society*, 13(3), 391–426.

Kemmis, S. and Smith, T.J. 2008. Praxis and praxis development, in *Enabling Praxis. Challenges for Education*, edited by S. Kemmis and T.J. Smith. Rotterdam: Sense Publishing, 3–14.

Kemmis, S. 2012. Phronēsis, experience, and the primacy of praxis, in *Phronesis as Professional Knowledge: Practical Wisdom in the Professions*, edited by E.A. Kinsella and A. Pitman. Rotterdam: Sense Publishing, 147–62.

Kraut, R. 2002. *Aristotle: Political Philosophy*. Oxford: Oxford University Press.

Küpers, W. 2005. Phenomenology and integral pheno-practice of embodied well-be(com)ing in organizations. *Culture and Organization*, 11(3), 221–31.

Küpers, W. 2012a. Integral response-abilities for organising and managing sustainability, in *Business and Sustainability: Concepts, Strategies and Changes, Critical Studies on Corporate Responsibility, Governance and Sustainability*, Volume 3, edited by G. Eweje and M. Perry. London: Emerald, 25–58.

Küpers, W. 2012b. Embodied inter-practices of leader-ship. *Leadership*, Special Issue, The Materiality of Leadership: Corporeality and Subjectivity (forthcoming).

Küpers, W. and Statler, M. 2008. Practically wise leadership: towards an integral understanding. *Culture and Organization*, 14(4), 379–400.

Lawrence, T.B and Suddaby, R. 2006 Institutions and institutional work, in *Handbook of Organization Studies*, 2nd Edition, edited by S.R. Clegg, C. Hardy, T.B. Lawrence and W.R. Nord. London: Sage, 215–54.

Lipman-Blumen, J. (2005) *The Allure of Toxic Leaders: Why We Follow Destructive Bosses and Corrupt Politicians – and How We Can Survive Them*. New York: Oxford University Press.

Long, C. 2002. The ontological reappropriation of phrónêsis. *Continental Philosophy Review*, 35(1), 35–60.

Mason, M. and O'Mahony, J. 2008. Post-traditional corporate governance. *The Journal of Corporate Citizenship*, 31(Autumn), 1–14.

McNiff, S. 2008. Art-based research and the spectrum of possibilities, in *Handbook of the Arts in Qualitative Research: Perspectives, Methodologies, Examples, and Issues*, edited by J.G. Knowles and A.L. Cole. Thousand Oaks: Sage, 29–40.

Norman, W. and Néron, R. 2008. Citizenship Inc.: do we really want businesses to be good corporate citizens?, *Business Ethics Quarterly*, 18(1), 1–26.

Pitman, A. 2012. Professionalism and professionalisation: hostile ground for growing phronesis?, in *Phronesis as Professional Knowledge: Practical Wisdom in the Professions*, edited by E.A. Kinsella and A. Pitman. Rotterdam: Sense Publishing, 131–46.

Polanyi, K. 1944. *The Great Transformation*. New York: Rinehart.

Raelin, J. 2012. Dialogue and deliberation as expressions of democratic leadership in participatory organizational change. *Journal of Organizational Change Management*, 25(1), 7–23.

Reed, G. 2012. Leading questions: leadership, ethics, and administrative evil. *Leadership*, 8(2), 187–98.

Ricoeur, P. (1997). *From text to action: Essays on Hermeneutics II*. Evanston, IL: Northwestern University Press.

Rooney, D. and McKenna, B. 2008. Wisdom in public administration: looking for a sociology of wise practice. *Public Administration Review*, 68(4), 709–21.

Rosanvallon, P. 2011. *Democratic Legitimacy: Impartiality, Reflexivity, Proximity*. Princeton: Princeton University Press.

Sachs, J. 2008. *Common Wealth – Economics for a Crowded Planet*. New York: Penguin Press.

Sandel, M. 2012. *What Money Can't Buy: The Moral Limits of Markets*. New York: Farrar, Straus and Giroux.

Scherer, A.G. and Palazzo, G. 2007. Towards a political conception of corporate responsibility. Business and society seen from a Habermasian perspective. *Academy of Management Review*, 32(4), 1096–120.

Schyns, B. and Hansbrough, T. 2010. *When Leadership Goes Wrong: Destructive Leadership, Mistakes and Ethical Failures*. Greenwich, CT: Information Age Publishing.

Serres, M. and Latour, B. (1995) *Conversations on Science, Culture and Time*, trans. R. Lapidus. Ann Arbor: University of Michigan Press.

Shulman, D. 2007. *From Hire to Liar: The Role of Deception in the Workplace*. New York: Cornell University Press.

Sternberg, R.J. 2004. Why smart people can be so foolish. *European Psychologist*, 9(3), 145–50.

Stiglitz J. 2010. *Freefall: America, Free Markets, and the Sinking of the World Economy*. New York: W.W. Norton & Co.

The Slow Science Manifesto (2010), The Slow Science Academy, Berlin http://slow-science.org/

Toubiana, M. 2012 Business pedagogy for social justice? An exploratory investigation of business faculty perspectives of social justice in business education. *Management Learning*, 43(5), 1–22.

Tyler, J.A. 2009. Moving beyond scholar-practitioner binaries: exploring the liminal possibilities of the borderlands. *Advances in Developing Human Resources*, 11(4), 523–35.

Varman, R. and Chakrabarti, M. 2004. Contradictions of democracy in a worker's cooperative. *Organization Studies*, 25(2), 183–208.

Umphress, E.E. and Bingham, J.B. (2011). When employees do bad things for good reasons: examining unethical pro-organizational behaviors. *Organization Science*, 22(3), 621–640.

Ventura, M. 1993. *Letters at 3 AM: Reports on Endarkenment*. New York: Spring Publications.

Voros, J. 2008. Integral futures: an approach to futures inquiry. *Futures*, 40(2), 190–201.

Walsh, R. 2011. The varieties of wisdom: contemplative, cross-cultural, and integral contributions. *Research in Human Development*, 8(2), 109–27.

Weaver, G.R. 2006. Virtue in organizations: Moral identity as a foundation for moral agency. *Organization Studies*, 27, 341–368.

CHAPTER 1

The Art of Practical Wisdom: Phenomenology of an Embodied, Wise 'Inter-practice' in Organization and Leadership

WENDELIN M. KÜPERS

Introduction

We live in a world ridden with increasingly urgent planetary problems and unprecedented interrelated global and local challenges. Societally, politically and economically, our world is currently exposed to unprecedented levels of complexities and uncertainties characterized by instability, volatility and unexpected and disruptive change. The recent and ongoing global economic crisis with its failures of responsibilities (Küpers 2011a) and the threatening of natural and socio-cultural ecologies are among many more manifestations of a profound dis-integration and non-integral way of living. Underlying these and many further symptoms and realities are fundamental ontological and epistemological as well as ethical inadequacies and reductive understandings and orientations calling for a more sustainable integration.

The following chapter is based on the premise that re-considering practical wisdom and reviving the meaning of artful wise practices can be an apt medium for realizing such integral understanding and practice. Reasons for re-habitualizing this wisdom for our contemporary times and futures lie in its proto-integral and transformative potential on all levels, especially in organizations and leadership (Küpers and Statler 2008, Walsh 2011, 2012).

In particular, practical wisdom has the capacity to integrate virtuous good, practical and artful ways of life. In other words, wise practicing provides a medium for dealing with the ethics and pragmatics of everyday life, while developing and enacting a creative art of living well.

For developing and realizing such an integrative art, first this chapter will reconstruct Aristotelian ways of practical wisdom as *phrónêsis* (Φρνησις) that is as practical reasoning, knowledge and virtuous habit. For a more integral understanding then an advanced phenomenology of embodied practice of wisdom is developed. Phenomenological interpretations not only allow a critique of person-centred, cognitivist or mentalist orientations, but consider the materiality, embodied and responsive agency as well as dynamics of wisdom as an inter-relational and emerging process. For elaborating such processual understanding, this chapter next outlines specifics of a responsive 'inter-practice' of wisdom. This relational practicing of wisdom is then situated as one that is connected to creative action in the context of organization and leadership. Furthermore, based on aesthetic dimensions, I will develop a critical *phrónêsis* as a form of creative practice. For this approach towards a *poiêtic phrónêsis*, the roles of moral perception and moral imagination as well as artistic practices are discussed as *phrónêtic* capacities. Finally, the conclusion opens up perspectives on practical wisdom as professional artistry and raises some questions for the reader's further consideration.

In so far as this chapter has a message, it is that a phenomenological and a neo- and post-Aristotelian approach towards the living art of practical wisdom constitute an essential advance on conventional modes of thinking and practicing, organizing and leading towards a wiser praxis and more integral business.

Wisdom as Practical Knowledge and Virtuous Habit in *Prâxis*

Historically, after being part of oral traditions, wisdom has been most widely reflected in religious and philosophical writings (Birren and Svensson 2005, Osbeck and Robinson 2005). From cross-cultural perspectives it can be seen as diverse, but 'wholesome' knowledge (Assmann 1994). Taking the various historical and cultural forms, any critical re-interpreting of wisdom requires considering the historical, social, ethical and political conditions of its own operation (Long 2002), including the Aristotelian one, discussed in the following.

Classically, practical wisdom has been seen as one among other virtues, respectively encompassing the principal ones; as once you have practical wisdom you have all the virtues (Aristotle 1985). Moreover, exercising or striving to exercise moral virtues, to make them part of the habituated personal character (ethos), requires a certain form of practical wisdom.

The classical understanding of virtue (Greek: ἀρετή 'areté') refers to a form of enacted moral excellence. Its functioning has been ordered as a balance point or golden mean between deficiency and excess in order to find or create *eudaimonia* - translated as flourishing or happiness - individually and collectively.

Correspondingly, practical wisdom, interpreted as *phrónêsis* (φρόνησις), was defined by and from Aristotle onwards as a mind-oriented, intellectual virtue. Similar to the related character-oriented moral virtues, its task was to help in guiding decisions and action that serve the common good or enhance the societal well-being that is the quality of communal and responsible life in the polis.

As a concern for what is practically good in each here and now, *phrónêsis* focuses on making the 'right' use of knowledge and preferential choices or judgements for the prudentially doable actions of humans as rational, social and political animals. It works by determining the mean at which virtue aims and reflexively finding a proper balanced middle way between undesirable extremes, avoiding states that are 'too hot', experiencing the agitation of excess, as much as 'too cold', experiencing inert states of sterility and indifference (Aristotle 1985, 1998).

Importantly, this capacity depends on an openness to each situation and the ability to *perceive* as well as to have the appropriate *feelings* or desires about it, to *deliberate* on what is appropriate in specific circumstances, to value, to respond and to *act* adequately (Aristotle 1985, Schwartz and Sharpe 2006). Thus, *phrónêsis* incorporates and operates through the integration of various modes in relation to the world, including embodied, sensual and tacit knowing, intuition and emotions (Roca 2007). All of these modes are gained through gradually acquired experience (*empeiría*) and can be cultivated through practicing and deliberating with and for virtuous Others.

As much as *phrónêsis* is part of the very being of those practicing it, its actions are always constrained to some extent by fate, luck and contextual circumstances. Accordingly, wisdom is processed in a world of uncertainty and ambiguity, where cause and effect may not be clear-cut and in which the result of an act or decision cannot be predicted, while knowing that the political good is often 'irregular' and 'imprecise' (Lord 2002: 80). Understood more as a steady state than a final endpoint or final product, the aspiration of the practically wise (*phronimos*) is more an open process that is always moving toward the good as never-quite-achieved *telos*. This processual orientation calls for a continuous reappraisal of strategies for approaching virtuosity and goodness respectively the potential for the good in the particular (Gadamer 1982).

As it is bound up with lived situated experience, worldly *phrónêsis* has been differentiated by Aristotelian thinking from other forms of knowing and practices. Accordingly, *phrónêsis* is different from contemplative, transcendental wisdom (*sophía*) and from a theoretical and universal knowledge of abstract reasoning (*theoría*). These privileged forms of knowing are based on *epistêmê*, and on *nous* as intellectual intuition, for gaining knowledge about necessary and eternal first principles or first causes as the highest form of intelligibility, using formal logic and mathematical calculation, seeking the excellence of or participating in the divine. For a complete understanding of wisdom along *phrónêtic* dimensions, 'sophían elements', like cosmic and intuitive knowing, may also need to be included (Trowbridge and Ferrari 2011). Moreover, Baehr very recently (2012) showed convingly how theoretical and practical wisdom are conceptually and practically intertwined. On the competence level, theoretical wisdom as a cognitive competence can be interpreted as a component or mode of practical wisdom. In turn, theoretical wisdom sometimes aims at acting for the sake of deep explanatory understanding and thus can be seen as constituting one dimension or application of practical wisdom.

Furthermore, *phrónêsis* has been distinguished from a product-focused technical knowledge (*tékhnê*) and *poiêsis* as producing or making activities. *Tékhnê* knowledge refers to a particular 'knowing how to' as used in craft and art by applying a replicable skill or set of techniques to make artefacts based on an *eidos* (idea or a plan or design) to be deployed by an instrumental mindset. The end or goal of action in a *tékhnê*-focused orientation – and its corresponding realization through *poiêsis* as its making – is established before production begins. And *tékhnê* is used to figure out the procedure for using resources (*khresis*) and material transformation for useful or aesthetic goods. The worth of a *poiêtic* activity and its artefacts can only be judged by their effects and consequences that is how well they serve the intended purposes. In contrast, or supplementing the dominating calculative means-ends mentality of object- and consequence-oriented *tékhnê*, *phrónêsis* is concerned with actions that relate to the originary *prâxis* of human beings, and it is used for knowing how to live fully.

Thus, there are two kinds of practices: *poiêsis*, which is guided by *tékhnê*; and the more comprehensive *prâxis*, which is guided by *phrónêsis*. This *prâxis* is present not only in the execution of certain actions, but is always already given with existence itself, insofar as it constitutes its nature and precedes every particular action. As *phrónêsis* is used in and for *prâxis* as acting for the common good, it manifests a situated practical reasoning, knowledge and habit, which directs action for acting well (*euprâxía*) and living well (*éu zén*). Whilst calculating *tékhnê* is the knowledge that steers the activity of making (*poiêsis*), in which means and ends are distinguishable from one another, deliberating *phrónêsis* guides *prâxis* in a way by which the 'doing' that is practiced constitutes an end in itself: '*Poiêsis* Makes Things, *Prâxis* Makes Perfect' (Eikeland 2008: 122). While *tékhnê* can be conceptualized in terms of its 'possession' (being) and its 'application' (use or production), *phrónêsis* cannot be instrumentalized (Dunne 1993) because the good that is embodied in *phrónêtic* action is a combination of the motives of the agent and the action being done.

Activities based on integrity and practical judgement of how to become and act wisely in this particular moment, case and context are forming a *prâxis*, which has a value in itself. As *prâxis* integrates embodied experiences, reflection and actions, it is a condition of possibility of *phrónêsis* and its development (Kemmis 2012). Accordingly, '*phrónêsis* … is not a knowledge of ethical ideas as such, but rather a resourcefulness of mind that is called into play' when circumstances demand an intervention. It is a habituated disposition that has 'developed an eye … or a nose for what is salient in concrete situations' (Dunne 1993: 368, Aristotle 1985 1143b13, 1033, Eidinow and Ramirez 2012). Our moral commitments are disclosed by the situations this eye identifies as worthy of note, of responsive action and agendas pursued then in the course of life by *phrónêsis* as executive faculty.

Problematizing the discussed differentiations, according to Eikeland (2006, 2008), Aristotle's *prâxis*-orientation is in danger of becoming invisible by operating with simplified and mutually exclusive divisions between *epistêmê*, *phrónêsis* and *tékhnê*, and by conflating other distinctions. Ways of dichotomizing simply miss the complexity and richness of both Aristotle and the world confronting us. Therefore, the separation between *phrónêsis* and *poiêsis* especially needs to be problematized and a re-integration developed. Such integration requires seeing practical wisdom as embodied and a(i)esthetic practice as well as critically re-interpreting *phrónêsis* as itself being a responsive *poiêsis*.

Phenomenology of Embodied Practices of Wisdom – *Prâxis* and Flesh

Vital for any phenomenological understanding of wisdom is that it is not only a special form of empirical-analytic knowledge and that it cannot be adequately investigated sufficiently as merely cognitive competency or meta-cognitive capacity and expert knowledge used for judgements.

Acquiring and having intellectual knowledge and advanced cognitive functioning (Baltes and Smith 1990) is only one among other elements of becoming, enacting and transforming wisdom (Kitchener and Brenner 1990, Ardelt 2004, Baltes and Staudinger 2000, Hays Chapter 7) and depends on a coalition of multiple experiential factors.

Therefore, instead of a cognitive or mentally biased approach, a phenomenology of wisdom strives to overcome the neglect of bodily and dynamic dimensions involved. Rather, it conceives wisdom as an embodied practice, which is constituted and processed through experiential, affective, implicit, life-worldly dimensions (Küpers 2007). This orientation was already latently inherent in an Aristotelian understanding of *phrónêtic* thinking as an embodied reasoning, which makes use of bodily and imaginative forms of knowing (Polkinghorne 2004). Considering practical wisdom as a form and enactment of bodily processing implies seeing, interpreting, and realizing wise practicing as a medium of relational be(com)ing. Accordingly, it is bringing forth effects on the bodily situated, feeling, thinking, acting, self, others and inter-involved multiple parties (Yang 2008). In this sense, practical wisdom is more than a composite of personality characteristics, logos-based competencies or reflected knowledge bound to reductionist intellectualism or idealism.[1] Such interpretations would fail to adequately acknowledge the embodiment and situatedness of experience and its structural constraints that influence or deflect virtuous behaviours. Phenomenologically, all practices and practicing are embodied, that is they are mediated by bodily processes and forms of embodiment constitute and involve various modes of practical engagements (Küpers 2012). According to Merleau-Ponty (1962, 1995) our body is our very way of 'being-in-the-world' that is experiencing and belonging as well as being practical and communicatively situated in the everyday-life with Others. Accordingly, practice is built upon a pre-reflective, ambiguous 'ground' of primordial experiences and inter-corporeal relationships as well as expressive dimensions. As life-worldy practice is first and foremost embodied and practitioners embodied beings, they are both part of the world and coextensive with it that is constituting, but also constituted (Merleau-Ponty 1962). Consequently, the life-world is found meaningful primarily with respect to the ways in which practitioners perceive and act within it and which acts upon them (Crossley 1996). Importantly, 'embodiment' does not simply refer to bodies' physical manifestation, nor is the body merely a physico-perceptual thing or only a surface for inscription. Rather, being embodied means that practitioners are *dynamically*

---

1   Merleau-Ponty shows that alongside an empirical realism and materialism a rationalistic idealism or intellectualism are reductionist as they reduce live-worldly phenomena, perception and sensation either to the realm of matter or to that of ideas and judgements. While empiricism regards perception as grounded in sensation, intellectualism sees it as a function of judgement. What both empiricism and intellectualism lose sight of is the phenomenal field itself, the giving of the world to a situated bodily perspective that is neither merely sensory nor intellectual. Behaviourist-empirical and mental-idealistic explanations fail to explain the body because they assume the body must be understood as 'object' that is as a physiological corpus, passive receiver of sense impressions respectively, neuro-physiological mechanisms, nor as a 'subject' that is controlled by or treated as an extension of the mind. Instead, for a proper understanding Merleau-Ponty stresses that the body has both subjective and objective dimensions and it is (neither subjective nor objective as it is constituted in) the interchange between the two which constitute the phenomenal and living body and living experiences. Phenomenologically, perception is not simply the result of the impact of the external world sensory experiences (empiricist data gathering) on the body; for even if the body is distinct from the life-world it inhabits, it is not separate from it. Rather, there is only perception as it is lived in the world. Metaphorically speaking, there is no inner theatre of the mind where shows from the outside are projected, but perception is (via the body) in-the-world rather than (in) the mind. This implies that perceiver and perceived are (decentred and) relational beings participating in a perceptual field as a meaningful configuration. Perception is neither the integration of a set of impressions by a sensing, physiological organism nor the synthesis of a manifold of intuitions by a categorizing, judging psychological ego. Perception obeys neither a logic of the (purely) physical nor a logic of the (purely) psychical; it is neither a purely objective process, wherein we simply take in the world, nor a purely subjective process, wherein we simply constitute the world. Rather, perception occurs precisely between these two processes, in a phenomenal field; it operates within this field like a dialogue – between subject and object, knower and known, perceiver and perceived. This dialogue is characterized essentially by ambivalence, since each 'pole of perception' simultaneously informs, and is informed by, the other. Neither the subject nor the object has a fundamental primacy in perception; the only candidate qualified for such a designation is the phenomenal field itself. 'Perception is not something given but rather an openness for further determination, Perception gives not sensation but a hold on the world. The perceiving subject is open to new forms of expression, including science, which reflect back and even transform its original sense of the world' (Rouse 2004: 272). Furthermore, perception is based in and interrogates the world in or through acting, that is, in looking, listening and touching and so on.

incarnated in and mediate through mundane experiences, actions and passions, others and their environments in an ongoing, foremostly sensual and meaningful relation. Thus, the embodied practicing subjects, as well as their socio-cultural embodiment, are situated in a tactile, visual, olfactory and/or auditory way. Whatever they perceive, feel, think, intend or do, they are exposed to a synchronized field of interrelated senses and synaesthetic sensations (Merleau-Ponty 1962), processed through body-schemes and body-images as existential and transcendental structures of lived perception, knowledge and behaviour (Tiemersma 1989).

It is through an embodied living in the midst of a world of touch, sight, smell and sound that the practitioners reach what they perceive and handle in relation to others at work and are affected by these senses and sensations. Moreover, practitioners act or cope wisely or unwisely, while being situated spontaneously and pre-reflectively in accordance with their bodies and within their embodiment. For this reason, the embodied experience and practices are emerging within a genuine horizon on which they 'body-forth', thus projecting their possibilities into the world in which they are enmeshed. The lives of political leaders like Nelson Mandela or Aung San Suu Kyi are real-life examples of this kind of embodied wisdom (Biloslavo and McKenna Chapter 6).

Following an intentional and responsive orientation, the actor or agent within the sphere of (potentially wise) practice does not feel only 'I think', but also 'I relate to' or 'I do'. In other words, the atmosphere within which wise practices are situated is not only what people 'think about' it, but primarily what they '*live through*' with their 'operative intentionality' (Merleau-Ponty 1962: xviii) as a bodily, pre-reflexive, non-representational, but concrete spatial motility and situated responses. This responsiveness itself refers to a specific *answering practice* (Waldenfels 2008) within a 'responsive order' (Gendlin 1997). This implies that as a living body and being embodied, practitioners respond to meaningful questions, problems or claims posed to them through embodied conditions and embedding contexts. Correspondingly, practical wisdom has been interpreted as 'the capacity to recognize the essentials of what we encounter and to respond well and fittingly to those circumstances' (Fowers 2003: 415). However, what is meant by 'well' and 'fitting' is debatable and calls for critical reflection and dialogical negotiation. Thus, embodied practical wisdom is not only a discerning intellectual and virtue-oriented process of deliberating the means and reflecting the ends of contextually constrained actions. Rather, it also involves sensing, perceiving, making choices and realizing actions that display appropriate and creative responses under challenging circumstances through bodily ways of engagement. Practicing wisely arises from participation in embodied acts and responses of organizing its practice. In that it makes bodily relations and response primary, Merleau-Pontyian phenomenology provides an appropriate *práxis*-philosophy for a body-mediated understanding of practical wisdom. In contrast to mere doing, *práxis* refers to deliberately taking actions as they occur within a situated sphere, and being morally committed, and thus happens as an embodied conduct in connection to a 'held-togetherness' ('*Zusammenhang*') that is a dynamic Gestalt. This Gestalt refers to a relational whole, which is integrating parts of acting and enactment, while functioning as a medium in which lives interrelate. Thus *práxis*-Gestalts emerge in sayings, doings and relatings (Kemmis and Grootenboer 2008). For Kemmis (2012: 150), the happeningness of *práxis* is the embodied action itself, 'in all its materiality and with all its effects on and consequences for the cultural-discursive, material-economic, and social-political dimensions of our world in its being and becoming'. By considering these dynamically interrelated dimensions, which are preceding and grounding all theory of practice, Merleau-Ponty is offering an extended understanding of also socially wise practicing within a phenomenal co-present field. In particular, it allows for studying embodied practicing as joint, plural action and cooperation, processed through 'We-Mode' intentionalities and collective commitments (Tuomela 2007, Schmid 2009), enacted as 'We-can'.

The 'bodies-in-action' of wise *prâxis* is practically and constitutively engaged and serves as a medium in the disclosure of the world and in the creation and maintenance of meaning and signification. From a phenomenological perspective, not only is practicing embodied, but being embodied is always already a way of mediating the (potentially wise) practicing through lived situations. Within this situatedness, the living body mediates between internal and external, or subjective and objective, as well as individual and collective experiences and meanings of wise practices. This body-mediated performance coordinates the relations between individual behaviour, social relations, artefacts and institutions, particularly through language and communication as the expressive media of interrelation (Merleau-Ponty 1962).

Therefore, wise practices can be seen as a function and emergent process of a vividly bodily subject and a dynamic, social and systemic embodiment of realities, in which practitioners through and with their practices are interrelated and embedded, and thereby actively and passively take part in such processes. Correspondingly, wise practitioners and practices co-constitute each other, as they cannot exist separately, but are ontologically implicated as an embodied mutual involvement or co-entanglement. As an emerging process, practitioners and their practicing and practices are always already co-constituted and continuously influenced by primordial and pre-reflexive dimensions. These dimensions refer to how practices are co-created and continuously influenced by embodied pre-subjective and pre-objective capacities of experiential processes within what Merleau-Ponty calls the 'Flesh'.[2] This elemental mediating flesh refers to an incorporated intertwining and reversibility of pre- or non-personal with the personal and interpersonal dimensions. Serving as a common connective tissue, this flesh 'enables' phenomena to appear in the first place and processes a meaning that is woven through all levels of experience, preceding and making possible all particular horizons and contexts (Merleau-

2   This nexus of mediating flesh refers to a textile or common connective tissue of exterior and interior horizons (Merleau-Ponty 1995) and meaning that is woven through all levels of experience, preceding and making possible all particular horizons and contexts. As elemental being, flesh manifests as a kind of silent and invisible ontological fond out of which self, others and phenomena of leadership arise in reciprocal relations. Referring to a chiasmic, incorporated intertwining and reversibility of pre-personal, personal and interpersonal dimensions, Merleau-Ponty's indirect ontology of flesh allows the understanding of phenomena to be more profound and relational. With this relational understanding it becomes possible to approach what does not appear, and yet which is the very condition for appearance. Merleau-Ponty's philosophy of chiasmic flesh-in-betweenness with its reversibilities, criss-crossing and inter-corporeity provide the base for an ethos of relational leadership practice of 'be(com)ing'. This be(com)ing is processed through an constitutive difference (écart = gap, spacing, rift, dehiscence) in the fabric of experience. It refers to an opening which is like a separation-in-relation, a kind of 'separation-difference' that as a generative possibility makes perception and experience possible. Moreover, the wave, which flows within the sensing/sensed-being is inaugurated by contact with Others in the world. Sense encounters with the fleshly world are insertions of the world between a sensing and sensed body and its embodiment, like 'between two leaves' (Merleau-Ponty, 1995: 264). This manifests in the social world as an inter-mediating, open-ended soma-significative and dialogical exchange as chiasmic entwinement between embodied selves and others (Cataldi 1993). Correspondingly, flesh is yielding itself a sentience and sensory 'reflection' also with other sentient beings. As the chiasmic depth of flesh is constitutive of sensibility and affectivity, the affective configuration allows for a non-closure spiralling of verticality, non-representable presencing and expression. Merleau-Ponty's ontological interpretation of co-emerging flesh implies an explosion of being, a relational being that is indistinct from nature's coming-to-presence. His philosophy of chiasmic flesh-in-betweenness with its reversibilities, criss-crossing and inter-corporeity provide the dynamic base for an ethos of relational and integral be(com)ing as an un-, inter- and refolding.

Ponty 1995).[3] The ontological concept and carnal metaphor of 'flesh' expresses and allows associations with both the sensible and bodily commonality of beings and also the generative capacity of *being as becoming*. As a dynamic medium, this flesh inter-links the sentient and sensible body, through which in- and outside, passivity and activity enmesh. Thus, flesh refers to an original fabric that precedes what then becomes bifurcated into opposing categories, such as the 'subject' and the 'object' with its binary logic: as it is permeating all interrelated, interwoven things (Cataldi 1993), flesh serves as the common and generous source (Diprose 2002, Hancock 2008) and primordial participation of all beings.

Neither subjective or intersubjective, or objective dimensions of wise practice can be isolated from the process of intermediating embodied practicing. Viewing embodied practice as an entwinement between practitioner, practice and *prâxis*, the multi-folded spheres of practical wisdom can be considered together as a whole. This view also helps to conceive practice as interrelating perceptions, affects, feelings, meanings and actions as well as further intersubjective and objective material dimensions and conditions in a fluid, reversible and integrative fashion (Küpers and Edwards 2008).

Embodied 'Inter-practice' of Wisdom as Creative Action in Organization and Leadership

Following Merleau-Ponty's phenomenology of embodiment, human beings involved in organizations and leadership can be comprehended as 'body-subjects', whose embodied lived experience relationally connects them to their life-world in a particular time, space and socio-cultural context (Holt and Sandberg 2011). As such, they are embedded and comported intentionally and responsively towards a world which is already imbued with meanings. Respectively, their embodied experience opens up inexhaustible, meaningful possibilities. It is through their bodies that organizational members co-create a formation,

---

3   The polyvalent variegated open-ended term and metaphor of flesh is Merleau-Ponty's (1995) central ontological principle, which sustains his attempt to overcome traditional metaphysical dualisms as well as to expand and ontologise his concept of the lived-body. For him this body is signifying a polymorphous, open system, thus an ambiguous Being and foundation of the possibility of expression. The ontological concept and carnal metaphor of "flesh" expresses and allows associations to both the sensible and bodily commonality of beings and also the generative capacity of a difference-enabling being as becoming. Referring to the intertwining and reversibility of pre-personal, personal, inter- and transpersonal dimensions, Merleau-Ponty's ontology of flesh allows understanding phenomena more profoundly and relationally. Flesh refers to both the particular being and the more general element in which all beings and the world share, but with its indeterminate qualities cannot be reduced to the old notions of subject or object. Rather, flesh serves as the formative medium or milieu anterior or preceding the conceptual bifurcation into the 'subjective' and the 'objective' or other forms of dualistic categorising. Thus it allows a post-dualistic orientation, respectively critique of dualistic separations. As an inter-mediating realm, this flesh inter-links the pre-reflexive sentient and sensible body, through which in- and outside, passivity and activity enmesh. In this way, flesh refers to an original fabric that precedes what then become bifurcated into opposing categories, such as subject/object following a binary logic. As a universal dimensionality, the elemental Flesh subtends all other categorization and typicality (Weiss 1981). Not being a static totality or metaphysical identity, it is a process of incomplete difference-enabling Being as ongoing explosion tied to dehiscence as the manner in which the perceptual and meaningful horizon remain open, through differential progress and sedimentations of meaning (Weiss, 1981). Understanding flesh, as a kind of originary absence is what makes the presentation of being-present possible, but which never presents itself as such. Thus, it is 'non-space' of in-between, an 'écart', the gap, the separation, the differentiation between the touching and the touched, the seeing and the seen, mind and world, self and others. That gap, that space of corporeal difference, is the 'there is' within 'the Being that lies before the cleavage operated by reflection, about it, on its horizons, not outside of us and not in us, but there where the two movements cross' (Merleau-Ponty 1995: 95). There are farreaching implications of the fleshly embodied inter-be(com)ing and Merleau-Ponty's relational ontology for a processual understanding of organising (Küpers 2014).

through which their practicing and its meanings emerge as an experiential nexus (Schatzki 1996, Schatski, Knorr Cetina and Von Savigny 2001, Yakhlef 2010). Accordingly, practices in organizations are made up of a collection of embodied orientations, intentions, feelings, thoughts and activities related to equipment and tools as well as shared socio-cultural milieus. The latter includes also traditions, values, norms, procedures and routines and agencies of collaborating, performing practitioners, who are realizing joint practical purposes (Reckwitz 2002). A particular practice can take various forms, varying or morphing with changes in worldly situations and its structurations within specific altering margins and horizons. For this reason, practices are not singular and unitary, but multiple and contingent. Being implicated within various horizons, practices are not closed, but are evolving towards preliminary 'results'. As such they remain open, indeterminate and incomplete as well as being mutually related to other practices and social embodiments in the organization and beyond.

Connected to this relational process perspective and following Merleau-Ponty's phenomenology, practice can be interpreted as an 'inter-practice'. Based on a post-dual ontology of Flesh and 'inter-being' (Merleau-Ponty 2003: 208), such radicalized relational orientation understands wise practice and practicing in organizations as an emerging event.

The concept of inter-practice helps to reveal and interpret the interrelationship between being, feeling, knowing, doing, sharing, structuring and effectuating in and through *phrónêtic* action, both individually and collectively, as implicated in organization and in leader- and followership. Correspondingly, the concept of *phrónêtic* inter-practices can be used for inquiries into the negotiating interplay of the inherently entwined materialities, subjectivities, intersubjectivities and objectivities as they occur and are processed in organizational life-worlds. Embedded within the complexities of human and systemic pragmatics, wise embodied inter-practice of integrated business includes the experiential and social inter-actions of actors as well as institutionalized operations of organization ('incorporations') as collective agency.

Similar to the conceptualization of practice-configurations in a radical process-orientation (Chia and MacKay 2007), mediating inter-practices are not only a collection of purposeful activities of self-contained individual actors and material things. Rather, these relational practices are also pre-personal, personal and transindividual social and systemic events of emergent be(com)ings and meaning-giving complexes with specific agentic capacities. Such processual wise practices are modes of engagement with the inter-world of organizing and its in-tensions and ex-tensions in ongoing reconfigurations (Antonacopoulou 2008). Metaphorically, this practicing resembles more an iterative way-finding and dwelling, compared to a planned navigation and building. As such, it dares to enact strategies without design (Chia and Holt 2006), processing knowing while going, instead of knowing before going.

The corporeality, sociality and situatedness of inter-practice also renders possibilities for situated creativities and creative action (Joas 1996),[4] which introduces novel

---

4   As Joas in his pragmatist theory of situated creativity (1996) showed, corporeality together with situativeness and sociality reflect the embeddedness of actors. In particular, the concept of situation, as inherently meaningful and constitutive of agency, could be viewed as a 'suitable replacement for the means-ends schema as the primary basic category of a theory of action' (1996: 160). The situated creativity which resides and emerges through pre-reflective perceptions and social actions is based on a non-teleological interpretation of the intentionality of action through situatedness, body-schemes and primordial sociality of human life and, hence, human agency. Instead of starting with the teleological

possibilities in practical doing as well as provoking a variety of embodied, individual and social responses. Such embodied responding opens up concrete situated possibilities for practitioners as demonstrated by Chan (2005) in the context of practices of nursing.[5] Likewise, strategy as practice and strategic changes can be interpreted as creative responsive action (MacLean and MacIntosh 2012, Küpers, Mantere and Statler 2012).

Embodied practitioners, their own practices and the practicing of others are all inseparable and mutually implicated. Therefore, what practical wisdom 'is' can only be affirmed by pointing to the tendencies, doings and becoming of practices of various interacting wise practitioners and the specifics of their situated conditions and dynamic relationships. Importantly, inter-practices of wisdom in organizations are not only embedded in or exhibited by individual and social interactions or systemic operations, rather they are co-constituted, processed and effected through mediating and expressive a(i)esthetic and artistic dimensions.

A(i)esthetic Dimensions of Wisdom and Wise 'Inter-Practicing'

As mentioned before, conventionally the Aristotelian *phrónêsis*, as part of the realm of embodied *prâxis*, and the (tékhnê-guided) *poiêsis*, as the sphere of making or creating, have been understood as essentially different activities. Immanent action in *prâxis* is contrasted with transitive making or producing in *poiêsis* (Aristotle 1985)[6] or kinds of reasoning: one moral, the other in itself non-moral (Wall 2003, 2005) with different statuses of means and ends. Both *phrónêtic* immanent acting (in *prâxis*) and transitive,

---

assumption of given, antecedently fixed ends, and conceiving action as following choice of appropriate means, and the pursuit of those pre-established ends, a non-teleological conception operates differently. A creative situational orientation considers a quasi-dialogical relationship between action and pre-reflective contexts, and understands embodied acting as a response to a demanding situatedness, while also considering the sociality of action. Actions do not follow predefined or actual ends, but particular 'ends-in-view' as means of situated organizing (Dewey 1922). For Dewey the end-in-view is a plan or a 'hypothesis' that guides present activities and is to be evaluated by its consequences and revised throughout the activity guided by it. Thus, these ends-in-view are based on judgements and assumptions about the type of situation and the possible actions that flow from it. Conversely, the situation itself is not a fixed, objective 'given'. Situations are interpreted and defined in relation to capacities for action. Starting from the situation, action follows a series of various ends-in-views that remain relatively undefined at first, but are specified through ongoing reinterpretations and decisions about means. Actors test out and revise their courses of action as each end-in-view itself becomes a means for further ones. Means and ends do not form a transitive order in which one poses no obstacle to the other and serves solely to fulfil that single purpose. As means and ends flow in a continuous stream of chiasmic reversible organizing and are part of an elastic meaning-situation-nexus, the distinction between them is only an analytical and temporal one. As a situated creative action located in an indeterminate, unpredictable and uncertain world, practical wisdom serves as a means of deliberating foresight in the light of what may occur or reflects the realization of future possibilities, creating and enacting new ways of life destined for meaningful ends.

5   Chan (2005) shows how the integration of Aristotle's notions of phrónêsis and prâxis with Merleau-Ponty's ontological notions of intentional arc and maximum grip can open up situated possibilities for practitioners. The 'intentional arc' names the tight connection between the agent and the world, storing as dispositions to respond to the solicitations of situations in the world. The intentional arc ensures the unity of perception and action, of the senses and intelligence and of sensibility and motility and is a calling to act virtuously based on previous experience, meanings and local practices, whereas the maximum grip refers to the body's tendency to respond to these solicitations in such a way as to bring the current situation closer to the agent's sense of an optimal gestalt. As such, it negotiates equilibrium with one's environmental and material situation. Importantly, both function non-representationally and actions do not represent a goal, but are responsive practices.

6   All actions are both immanent and transitive except in the case of a fully immanent action (to think, to love). For example, when somebody works there are two results, that is, an 'objective' result, such as the product or service (transitive), and a 'subjective' result, such as the increase in ability or the self-fulfilment of the agent as well as the morality of the act (immanent). Aristotle says, 'we call that which is in itself worthy of pursuit more complete than that which is worthy of pursuit for the sake of something else' (1998 I, 7, 1097a 30–31).

poiêtic doing/producing operate with means and ends. However, the only standard of action in *prâxis* is the coincidence of the means with the end, that is, the self-referentiality and self-sufficiency of the action in *prâxis*. In other words, the end is attained as soon as the activity is undertaken (*prâxis* as present), while *poiêsis* is future-oriented; practicing of the act is itself the end, whereas production has an end outside of the *poiêsis*. Unlike autotelic *prâxis*, *poiêsis* is heterotelic, meaning that its end is a separate object, state or objective presumably achieved when using formally different external instruments and making them from external material has stopped. The distinction between *poiêsis* and *prâxis* is one between self-immanent action, that is, auto-production, in which the end is always already present and a future-leaning, open and incomplete *poiêtic* production. Following from these elementary cosmological and ontological assumptions, Aristotle and the scholarly exegesis of the 'Corpus Aristotelicum' explicitly denies the possibility of the mutual entailment between *poiêsis*-oriented artistic excellence and praxis-oriented *phrónêtic* wisdom.

Interestingly, before this separation and patriarchal ordering, wisdom and art were mythologically connected, as for example the goddess of wisdom Athena and then Minerva were also the goddesses of the arts and crafts and patronesses of creative humans. However, it seems that an artistic and a(i)esthetic recognition and integration of how to be wise or how to foster wisdom as the 'art of living' has been lost in the dominant discourses and practices of the Platonic, Aristotelian, Christian and then modernist Western world, characterized by the hegemony of Cartesian rationalism and Enlightenment traditions, in contrast to non-dual Eastern wisdom practices where wisdom and art are seen as interconnected (Case Chapter 3).

What would it mean to think that we can be practically wise in our actions insofar as we creatively do something *poiêtic*ally and aesthetically, including that which is not yet done? How can we conceive artful *poiêtic* craft and images of artistic excellence as co-constitutive basic ontological conditions of wise action in praxis (Machek 2011)? How can we make a bridge between the capacity of *phrónêtic* acting, which exists for the sake of intrinsic virtuous action, and the transitive, *poiêtic* creative doing and using? How can we connect Aristotle's *phrónêtic* ethics and action of being with a *poiêtic* practice of creative becoming (Aubenque 1963)?

To respond to these questions and to understand the creative inter-practice of wisdom, the mediating power of embodied 'a(i)esthetic' senses, affects and perceptions need to be considered and integrated into a *poiêtic phrónêsis*.

Etymologically deriving from the Greek *aisthesis*, a(i)esthetics comprises expressions that designate embodied sensation and perception taken as a whole, prior to the assignment of any cognitive or artistic meaning. The Greek verb *aisthanomai* denotes the capacity to perceive and to know through or by using the senses. Phenomenologically, art-related and aesthetic experiences are constituted by us as sensually based, embodied-perceptual, emotional-responsive and expressive-communicative relationships. A(i)esthetic knowledge and understandings come from perceptive bodily sensuous faculties of seeing, hearing, smelling, tasting and touching. Thus, all forms of a(i)esthetics require a full engagement and refinement of sensibilities in perception, feeling, thinking and acting in their interconnection. In this sense, having an a(i)esthetic experience means being sensually responsive to the pattern that connects (Bateson 1979). A(i)esthetic responses can then be followed by aesthetic interpretations, a(i)esthetic judgements and aesthetic communication (Küpers 2002), all carrying a transformational potential.

Body-mediated a(i)esthetics – like 'somaesthetics' (Shusterman 2008) – relates to immediate, non-discursive experiential and transformative processes. Therefore the value of a(i)esthetical processes and artefacts are part of the dynamic embodied activities that are perceived through interdependent relationships of 'feeling-thinking-doing' and then evaluated individually and collectively in a situation-specific way of assessing particular phenomena.

Thus *aiesthesis* as 'situational appreciation' serves as an attunement and alertness, rather than mastery or domination (Dunne 1993: 256). Even more, 'all deliberating ends in an *aisthesis*' (Heidegger 1997: 110), as *phrónêsis* as *aisthesis* is a look of an eye in the blink of an eye (*Augenblick*), a momentary look at what is momentarily concrete, which as such can always be otherwise' (Ibid.).

In *poiêtic phrónêsis*, embodied aiesthetics, feelings, knowledge and judgement hold together and inform each other. It is through aesthetically refined embodied experiences, situational awareness and bodily-mediated passion and emotional capabilities[7] that intuition, mindfulness and creative enactments of experimenting and amplifying experiences can be cultivated, all of which are required for realizing practical wisdom. Aiesthetic *phrónêsis* also involves being open to further experience, rather than resting content once it has achieved a satisfactory set of procedures. In this way, not only a rationally deliberating, moral subject, but the aiesthetically processed living affective, perceiving and responsive body and pathic, ecstatic and e-motional fleshly embodiments are the media for be(com)ing beautifully wise.[8]

---

7   It is noteworthy that Aristotelian wisdom and moral virtue are concerned not simply with knowing, willing and performing the right actions, but also with feeling the 'right' embodied feelings. As naturally endowed human beings can be trained to think and act properly, so can their emotions be educated and refined by habituation and discipline (Aristotle 1998). As wise and virtuous action is action according to the mean determined by right reasoning (*kata ton orthon logon*), so the feelings of the wise and virtuous seek the right mean (Aristotle 1998). According to Garrison (1997: 80), 'passion is part of practical reasoning; nothing is called into existence without it'. Passions provoke a reasoning that helps for example to form new ends and new ideas about shared moral lives. This reasoning process incorporates thinking 'about those desirable imaginative possibilities that morally ought to be actualized even though they are not here now and may never have been before' (Garrison 1997: 81). Passions evoked by the aesthetic help us to collectively tap into particular, concrete moral visions of how we as individuals wish to live and educate for future societies. Our passions inform and shape our moral thinking, and though these can always (like our reasoning) be flawed or simply wrong, they can be sources of reflective insight into moral conduct and meaningful moral lives (Abowitz 2007). Emotional capabilities connected to practical wisdom have been investigated as antecedents of organizational accountability in revolutionary change processes (Durand and Huy 2008). According to Côté, Miners and Moon (2006), wise emotion regulation involves: 1) setting an effective emotion regulation goal, 2) choosing an appropriate strategy to achieve that goal, 3) implementing that strategy effectively and 4) adapting emotion regulation over time.

8   Gadamer's treatment of *phrónêsis* emphasizes the openness of conversation and ongoing participation that may lead to processes for deliberating on the common good. According to Gadamer, *Bildung* is connected to notions of tact, judgement and taste for acquiring and intensifying sensitivity, subtlety and selectivity as well as a capacity for discrimination. They instance a practical knowledge of how to discriminate between good and bad, right and wrong, important and unimportant, beautiful and ugly and so on, as well as what to say and what not to say, what is appropriate and what is not. As much as they help us to see where lines are to be drawn, they also show how things go together. Aesthetic talents, in the Gadamerian sense 'the art of thinking beautifully' (Gadamer 1977/1986: 17), cannot solely be understood in conceptual terms. These talents involve certain 'finesses of mind' that include: playfulness, responsiveness and the capacity for improvisation; what MacIntyre (2000) described as delayed intentionality; self-understanding or self-recognition, which involves putting into question our historical consciousness through the use of our individual and collective memory, and using our sense of humour; and participation in festivals where we might experience community together, such as engaging in regularly scheduled conversations that consider our individual and collective values and well-being, or enacting celebrations of the partnerships themselves. Thus the personal and civic arts of phronesis, when practiced well, can be beautiful and phronesis is connected to 'the beautiful ethical life' (Gadamer 1977) enacting 'practical beauty' (Sandy 2011).

Critical *Phrónêsis* as and Through Responsive and Responsible *Poiêsis*

On the presented ontological base and outlined a(i)esthetic dimensions of wise inter-practices, the following discusses a critical *phrónêsis* as being itself a *poiêsis* and then discusses moral perception and imagination as creative *phrónêtic* capacities. For developing moral creativity and following Ricoeur's hermeneutical phenomenology a critical *phrónêsis* allows us to view practical wisdom as itself being *responsively poiêtic* (Wall 2005).[9] As such it is aiming for a delicate dialectical balancing of deontology (autonomous, intrinsic) and teleology (heteronomous extrinsic interests), universality and historicity as well as principles and situatedness.

Part of a more comprehensive hermeneutic endeavour into the poetics of the self and narrative identity, for Ricoeur poetic *phrónêsis* serves *both as means and an end in itself*: a means to creating narrative meaning (social creativity) that includes attention and recognition of others and otherness as well as social inclusivity as an end.[10] For example, *phrónêtic* awareness in an organization considers how to engage with others in ways that extend well beyond the issuing of instructions and the stipulation of ends (Tsoukas and Cummings 1997). In praxis there can be no prior knowledge of the right means by which we realize the end in a particular situation, for the end itself is only specified in deliberating about the means appropriate to a particular situation (Bernstein 1983). As we think about what we want to achieve, we alter the way we might achieve that. As we think about the way we might go about something, we change what we might aim at. There is a continual *interplay between ends and means*.

'Phrónêsis is poetic in that it implies at its very core the endless re-creation of concrete social relations' (Wall 2003: 337), by involving the self's dialectical capacity for 'creating or innovating ever more responsively inclusive social meaning' (Wall 2003: 334). Such a view is analogous to art and artisanship in that not only is the practically wise in many respects a poet but also that poetic practical wisdom 'has an end other than itself' (Wall 2008: 337) and generates newly re(con)figured narrative relations. Importantly,

---

9   According to Wall (2003), recent moral interpretations of *phrónêsis* fall into three broad categories: firstly, an *anti-utilitarian*, anti-technicistic practice of situated reasonableness focusing on *ends* (Dunne 1993). The second category is a *communitarian* application of shared values to particular situations, concentrating on *means* and application of already given moral 'truths' inherited from 'malleable' tradition. Judgements about good action are grounded here in larger communities of practice, that is, *poiêsis of ends* (Gadamer 1982; MacIntyre 1995), following the ethos of a 'socially teleological account' of the virtues. Finally, a third version gives concrete attention to human particularity, and a focus on *poiêsis of means* towards which practical wisdom should be directed (Nussbaum 1990). For example *literature* is seen as being a vital instrument for becoming a practically wise person, providing a unique and important education in what Nussbaum calls 'moral attention', that is, attention to the concrete particularities of actual persons and situations around us (1990: 162). For her, practical wisdom consists in *over-coming 'moral obtuseness'* and 'simplification' by sharpening, *through literary narratives, our capacities for 'moral perception', 'moral imagination', and 'moral sensibility'* (1990: 154, 164, 183–5; see also 1995). These *phrónêtic* capacities are for Nussbaum the *very end and completion of moral life as such. Moral wisdom consists precisely in attention, care and perception of human particularity.* Thus, poetics – especially as a literary means for great public and social catharsis – has the role in Nussbaum's ethics of a means to this *phrónêtic* end. Importantly, she emphasizes the need for poetic attention to the tragic and 'Fragility of Goodness': vulnerability, particularity, fortune, luck and changeability of the human moral situation (Nussbaum 2001: 5, 138).

10   Ricoeurian *phrónêsis* is one part within a larger hermeneutic investigation into questions of narrative and meaning that are quite explicitly poetic; inquiring the *poetical* role of imagening within the context his larger poetics of the will. Ricoeur's hermeneutics enables him to take up the concept of *phrónêsis* as a practice in which selves take the singularity or alterity of others into account. However, the end or goal of critical *phrónêsis* is never completed, but always to be pursued is an ever-greater 'mutual recognition' of self and other, while recognizing the *tragic nature of human* (finite and limited) *practice, action or existence itself, which is rendering poetic responses.*

these narrative relationships are qualified as advancing towards greater inclusivity and social participation on the basis of otherwise diverse and unrelated 'materials', that is, of narrative otherness (Wall 2005). Understanding others' perspectives is to understand how they might tell their stories, which itself requires a *phrónêtic* sensibility to the dialogical, temporal and contextualized nature of their lives. Practically, storytelling as a narrative practice has a significant history as a playful method for developing virtuous habits of practical wisdom (Statler and Roos 2007), especially in relation to strategy as practice (Roos, Victor and Statler 2004, Küpers, Mantere and Statler 2012). Poetically conceived, *phrónêsis* creates new narratives of life and new inclusivity, which engages with issues of power and conflicts as well as ambiguities, dilemmas and paradoxes as they appear in tragic differences and (moral) incommensurabilities in attempts to accomplish common goods. Living a wise life, also in relation to or as part of organizations, involves immersion in the messy discordances and tragedies of actual current life-worlds and embracing the task of forming together in a radically uncertain future. Based on considering the situated interplay and integration of means and ends in a critical poetic *phrónêsis* of narrative meaning and social inclusivity, it may be extended towards ecological meanings and systemic inclusivity, generating untold possibilities 'within the earth or humus' (Wall 2005: 192).

Practically, the *phrónêtic* poet's eye becomes the manager's eye when we think of managing as:

> ... the task of becoming aware, attending to sorting out, and prioritising an inherently messy, fluxing and chaotic world of competing demands that are placed on a manager's attention. It is creating order out of chaos. It is an art not a science. Active perceptual organization and the astute allocation of attention is a central feature of the managerial task. (Chia 2005: 1092)

Overall, *phrónêsis in praxis is poiêtically artful*; in enacting a quality of a flexible *poiêtic* improvisation (Polkinghorne, 2004), situated *poiêsis* is a *práxis* in that a(i)esthetic experiences and artistic creations are immanent and intrinsic actions respectively creations.

Figure 1.1 situates critical *poiêtic phrónêsis* in relation to other ways of knowing or being, orientations, foci and *teleos*.

Moral Perception, Moral Imagination and Artistic Practice as *Phrónêtic* Capacities

Practical wisdom requires processing deliberation and articulating judgements as a perceptive, sense-based, social and creative act and artistic practices as *phrónêtic* capacities. In particular, the development and exercise of wisdom involves an astute perception of (moral) situations, filtered through social interaction and imagination (Noel 1999), respectively projecting imaginative interpretation of current realities into new possibilities. As discernment in practical wisdom requires the perception of the contingent and changing situations and the particular, a priority is already given by Aristotle (1985) to the act of perceiving and the experiential. 'Practical insight is like perceiving in the sense that it is non-inferential, non-deductive; it is an ability to recognize the salient features of a complex situation' (Nussbaum 1990: 73). *Phrónêsis* requires and relates not only to acute perception (perspicacity), but also apperception.

Ways of knowing & being	Rationality / Orientation	Process / Focus	Teleos / Temporality
Theoría Epistêmê	Sophía	Theoretical Reasoning Contemplation	Truth/Enlightenment (timeless)
Prâxis Doing	**Phrónêsis**	Practical Reasoning Intrinsic Action / Process based & directed	Well-Being Common-Good Acting well (situational, here & now)
Creative *Inter-Practicing*	Critical **Poiêtic Phrónêsis**	Creative Processing In- & extrinsic Process & Product(ion)	Mediating *Praxis & Poíêsis* Creating well (situational, & transituational)
Poíêsis Making Khresis Using	*Tékhnê* calculative	Instrumental Reasoning Extrinsic Product(ion)	Producing well & Doing competently/ Optimal Usage (future-oriented, based on past experience)

Figure 1.1   Critical poetic *phrónêsis* in relation to other ways of knowing and being

The latter capacity refers to the ability to relate new experiences to previous experiences, in other words to recognize and reflect patterns in situations that facilitate understanding and resolution and to also frame or reframe them emotionally (Grint 2007). For example, wisdom in management can be conceived as being the 'ability to grasp the significance of many often contradictory signals and stimuli and to interpret them in a complete and integrative manner' (Malan and Kriger 1998: 249). In this way, practical wisdom can be connected to moral perceptions and moral imaginations (Abowitz 2007, Waddock 2009, Werhane 1999). While moral perception is our ability to see and comprehend a moral situation encountered in experience, moral imagination has been described as 'the ability in particular circumstances to discover and evaluate possibilities not merely determined by that circumstance, or limited by its operative mental models, or merely framed by a set of rules or rule-governed concerns' (Werhane 1999: 93). Thus both refer to a 'capacity to think of alternatives, to interpret situations beyond what is available to be known with certainty, and to formulate notions and ideas of ourselves and our worlds beyond what we currently experience or know as reality' (Abowitz 2007: 288). But the same is valid on a collective level, as practical wisdom refers to a community *éthos* in which the needs of others both internal to and external to the organization render the practices of the organization morally perceptive and guided.

Based on heightening awareness, enlivening aesthetic sensibilities provide and mediate somatic engagements and opportunities for individuals and collectives for sensing and seeing 'more' or differently, envisioning more intensively, perceptively and intersubjectively and responding correspondingly (Nussbaum 1990). Learning from artists and through artistic practices and aesthetic experiences, like staying with the senses, engaged detachment and imaginative free play, makes it possible to develop 'proto-wise' moral sensitivities for more sustainable and ethical organizations and leadership (Ladkin 2011). For example, as Steve Taylor and Donna Ladkin have shown (2009), arts-based methods in managerial development and leadership education are like transferences of artistic skills, projective techniques or the evocation of 'essence' and creating artefacts that might be connected or contrasted to practices of wisdom and leading or following in organizations. Likewise Sutherland (2013) showed how arts-based approaches leverage aesthetic experiences in leadership develop to generate non-logical capabilities needed to navigate and respond to uncertainties, ambiguities and complexities by affording aesthetic and reconfiguring work-spaces that generate memories with momentum that remain salient and in-formative for future professional practice.

While being sensually and aesthetically engaged, moral imagination also involves (self-) reflection that is, being able to step back from the situation and be aware of underlying processes and create design features. Therefore, complementing perceptual and imaginative *phrónêtic* capacities, an embodied deliberating reflexivity is required for an integral practice of wisdom. Practical reasoning is deliberative in that it takes into account local circumstances, addressing particulars and dealing with contingencies, exploring meta-cognitively possible solutions and their likely consequences, that is, trafficking and weighing trade-offs, aiming to arrive at good but imperfect decisions with respect to given circumstances.

Accordingly, *proto-integrally, perception, imagination and reason* can be combined in a 'good' aesthetic experience, as it should be in good moral reflection (Pendlebury 1995). Affective, sensual, artistic and aesthetically mediated reflective practices of wisdom can then be seen as a 'force' and embodied formation for initiating re-relating, and renegotiating alter-native, that is, 'other-birthly' ways of living. In other words, as part of a(i)esthetic and social performances, these forces and formations entail socio-cultural-political and ethical dimensions that invite leveraging the potential for a different more wise practicing.

With their irritating estranging effects, affective forms of art and artistic experiences can subversively question the status quo, bringing about a shift in embodied habitual patterns and mindsets and expressing new open-ended and refined senses of reality and possibility (Küpers 2005b). Aesthetic experience 'can contribute to the development of practical wisdom in organization to the extent that they provide an occasion to reflect critically on familiar forms of representation, discourses and thought' (Statler and Roos 2007: 160). Crossing boundaries and breaking or undermining rules, a(i)esthetic processes may alter the way that 'things' or entities are organized and managed unwisely.

A(i)esthetic practices mediate or create organizational life-worlds that are more wisely recognized as complex, colourful and vivacious, but also uncertain, questionable and indeterminate, as being manifest in *'negative capabilities' in sensu* Keats.[11]

---

11   He describes *negative capability* as openness for wonder: 'capable of being in uncertainties, mysteries, doubts without any irritable reaching after fact and reason' (Keats in Gittings 1970: 43). This 'being in uncertaint[y]' and state of intentional open-mindedness is a place between the mundane, ready reality and the multiple potentials of a more fully understood existence. It implies the capacity to sustain reflective inaction (Simpson, French and Harvey 2002) and to resist the tendency to disperse into actions that are defensive rather than relevant for transitional states and tasks. Not knowing what to do and tolerating ambiguities, paradoxes, uncertainties and complexities for being in the present moment is not only relevant for leadership practice (Simpson and French 2006) but in particular for transitions. Whereas positive capabilities enable us to make things happen fast and effectively, conversely negative capability is the capacity to wait without expectations and to hold back the tensions and pressure for solutions or quick fixes in response to problems and uncertainties. It is the very negating of habitual patterns of pressured action that allows the creative process its own rhythm and prevents premature closure. The root meaning of 'capable', like 'capacity' and 'capacious', is derived from

A(i)esthetic experience and process may be(come) wisely *transformative* (Hays Chapter 7), not only when new bodily states, feelings, thoughts, identities and actions are developed, but also as the experienced world reveals itself and acts upon one in new ways, particularly when control is relinquished and receptivity allowed. As a(i)esthetic transformations require and are processed by active doing and receptive undergoing: both people and groups with their worlds are mutually transformed. This process includes multifarious, ambiguous dimensions and the a(i)esthetic formations involved (Taylor and Hansen 2005), especially with regard to a transformational leadership and liminality in organizations (Küpers 2002, 2011b,c).

According to Rooney (Chapter 4), a 'social practice wisdom' not only acknowledges the intrinsic rewards and pleasures of wise action, it can articulate judgements aesthetically and creatively using imagination, style, design, appropriate genre and rhetorical skill or communicative excellence. The art of rhetoric is indeed a vital disclosing modality of political and a(i)esthetic *phrónêsis* (Farrell 1996, Holt 2006) that for effectiveness uses visualizing forms in organizations (Rämö 2011, Eidinow and Ramirez 2012). As wisdom is an embodied and situated practice, it is a social knowledge, presented in a public space or enacted socially. Therefore there are specific links to aesthetics and communication, that is, to the art of rhetoric (Farrell 1996, 1998) for moving people emotionally and rationally into action by giving emphasis to contested matters with the available means of persuasion (Mailloux 2004). As an enacting and disclosing practice (Holt 2006), this artistic enactment of wisdom through rhetoric is situated within conditions of uncertainty, where there is no possibility of appeal to final answers or steady states. Importantly, the fear of disrepute or shame, respectively trustworthiness and a public expression of prudent and just habituation relatively prevent a non-manipulative and non-exploitative use and consideration of moral concerns consequent on living within communities.

Conclusion – Practical Wisdom as Professional Artistry

Following *phrónêtic*, proto-integral and transformative interpretations, this chapter conceived practical wisdom phenomenologically as an embodied, emergent and responsive inter-practice, in relation to organizing and leading. Furthermore, some perspectives on a(i)esthetic, *poiêtic* and rhetorical forms for an embodied art of wisdom have been outlined. Based on these insights and applied to organizations and leadership, the *poiêtic*, artful qualities and dimensions of practical wisdom can be conceptualized as *professional artistry*. As embodied wisdom is processing by a non-rational tacit knowing and doing, it is integrally and relationally tied to an *artistry of practice* (Schön 1983, 1987),

---

the Latin word *capax*, 'able to hold much', thus referring to 'containing' or 'spacious', whereas the volume of a container is a measure of its internal 'negative' space. However, the 'negativeness' of this capability does not indicate negativity, deficiency or insignificance, but refraining from action which may facilitate change and transitions (French 2001). The active aspect of negative capability is to inhibit the patterns that perpetuate a controlling attitude. The focus is negative in the sense of negating what we know, leaving the space as emergent. The deeper aspect of the creative process gets a chance to operate when we open the space. Negative capability is both the ability to resist the inappropriate pressure for solutions and the capacity to hold creative tension. It requires considerable skill to remain detached enough to know, not only how, but also when to act – the ripe moment. Negative capability can create an intermediate space, a receptive state of intense and live waiting, attending to deeper patterns of meaning. Negative capability is relevant to organizational change management and transitions because it represents the ability to absorb and respond creatively to the emotional turmoil which can both arise from, and in turn cause, change and needs to be balanced with positive capabilities (French 2001).

operating in indeterminate zones of practice. Accordingly, the art of organizing and managing (wisely): 'reveals itself both in crucially important situations of uncertainty, instability and uniqueness and in those dimensions of everyday practice, which depend upon the spontaneous exercise of intuitive artistry' (Schön 1983: 240). As a practically habitualized incorporated disposition for acting, artistry strives towards what makes professional activity work at its best, and thus refers to a mastery state or condition that makes people perform tasks or functions well. The artistry of wisdom practices embodies kinds of reflections (Kinsella 2007) and actions. These are processed through ways in which the 'thinking bodies' (Burkit 1999) of practitioners interact with themselves, each other and their environment. Thereby they co-constitute the ways performances unfold. Furthermore, artistry requires sensibility, imagination, technique and the ability to make judgements about the feel and significance of the particular (Eisner 2002). Particularly, a judgement-artistry allows artful professional practitioners to make highly skilled micro-, macro- and meta-judgements that are optimal for the given circumstances (Paterson, Higgs and Wilcox 2006).

As a specific practicing within a shared tradition, a professional artistry involves a blend of practitioner qualities, attunement, knowledge, practice skills and creative imagination processes together with the ability to use them critically, intuitively and practically (Titchen and Higgs 2001).[12] Being more an activity-oriented than attitude-oriented practice, professional artistry is enacted in a mature performance that is characterized by virtuosity and excellence (Bourdieu 1990), for example in health practices (Titchen and Higgs 2008) or leadership processes (Kay 1994).

Professional artistry is processed and manifests in the creative ability to *play* (*Spiel*), understood as the hermeneutic practice of (reflexive) understanding, interpretation and enactment that is itself a form of *phrónêsis* from and of a particular situation and horizon (Gadamer 1982, Bernstein 1983). Play, like *phrónêsis*, is not the application of general principles to practical situations, but a living dialogue. As such it is always already mediated by the application of universality and particularity forming a practical, reasonable and participatory way of being.

A *poiêtic phrónêsis* enacts performatively through being responsively and creatively playful and in situations where aesthetic play becomes an organizing principle (de Monthoux and Statler 2008). In this sense, there is a close connection between practical wisdom and serious play (Statler 2005), especially for developing practically wise leader(ship) (Holliday, Statler and Flanders 2007).

Without discussing theoretical, methodological and practical implications in detail here (Küpers 2007, Küpers and Statler 2008), it seems important to be critically aware that practices of and research on wisdom and organization respectively leadership in a wise way is a challenging endeavour, entailing various tensions and ambiguities (Rooney, McKenna and Liesch 2010). For example, it remains important to consider ideological

---

12   According to Higgs, Titchen and Neville (2001), professional artistry involves a blend of qualities, skills and processes, particularly: practitioner qualities (for example, connoisseurship, emotional, physical, existential and spiritual synchronicity and attunement to self, others and events); and practice skills (for example, expert critical appreciation, ability to disclose or express what has been observed, perceived and done and meta-cognitive skills used to balance different domains of professional craft knowledge in the unique care of each patient, and to manage the fine interplay between intuition, practical reasoning and rational reasoning and between different kinds of practice knowledge). Creative imagination processes are imagining the outcomes of personalized, unique care interventions and creative strategies to achieve them.

and control linkages between ethics regarding wisdom and aesthetics or an anaesthetising a(i)esthetic craving in organizations (Kersten 2008).[13]

Nevertheless, organization and leadership research as well as inter- and transdisciplinary projects may benefit from the development of research methods based on wisdom or wisdom principles (Rooney and McKenna 2008, McKenna, Rooney and Boal 2009, Rooney Chapter 4, Jankelson Chapter 2) and contributing to a post-paradigmatic *phrónêtic*, 'real' and engaged social science (Flyvbjerg 2001) that relies on public deliberation, strives for 'adequation' in value-inclusive, collective decision-making and for which 'applied' means a focus on "bottom-up contextual and action-oriented knowledge" (Flyvbjerg, Landman and Schram 2012: 286). Furthermore, a theory and practice of wise leadership and organizations needs to be connected to education and learning (Intezari and Pauleen Chapter 8, McPherson 2005, Küpers 2013), especially experiential learning (Hays Chapter 7), by which social actors become virtuoso.

A truly integral practical wisdom embraces the body (embodied incorporated dimensions), mind (cognitive, logical, rational thought), heart (feelings, emotions, moods) and 'spirit' of individuals and collectives. Striving for integrity (Edwards Chapter 10) of being, knowing, doing and effectuating, this proto-integral orientation supports processes for achieving embodied authentic leadership (Ladkin and Taylor 2010) or relational authenticity in organizations. As such it contributes to accomplishing a genuinely worthwhile purpose that meets present and future needs sustainably and with this contributes to the well-be(com)ing of all members and stakeholders of organizations (Küpers 2005a). Such integrity-based 'wised-up' organizing and leading invites a radical re-thinking and raises critical questions. Some of those questions with regard to embodiment, leadership, organization research and the macro context will be presented in the following.

WISDOM AND EMBODIMENT

How can we bring the body and embodiment more mindfully back into practicing of organizations and leadership? What is incorporated in wise embodied organizational practices and in which ways? How can we think of organizations as incorporations and their leadership from an embodied point of view?

WISDOM AND LEADERSHIP

Along with asking what leadership is, enquire into what leadership is *for* (Ladkin 2010). For example, how can leadership contribute not only to maximizing economic and functional objects like efficiency, productivity and growth, but to optimal flourishing, entailing respect, integral health, happiness, dignity, ethical practices, service for others, holistic care (Leathard and Cook 2009) and the achievement of creative potentials and so

---

13   Kersten (2008) sensitizes us to critically take into account that practices of ethics, wisdom and aesthetics are shaped by their social, political and historical context, in theory and in experience. Our ideas of what is beautiful, true and good are bound by time and place and can serve political and ideological functions. They are closely linked to issues of identity formation and social control and they often reflect class, race, gender and cultural positioning and biases. She specifically problematizes aesthetic craving (see also Kateb 2000) by which people seek satisfaction in that they create a sense of beauty – form, style and colourfulness – culminating in certainties of meaningfulness while processing an unconscious aestheticism.

on as part of an integral understanding and practice? What would a wise leadership style comprise as a caring and meaningful executive function? What does wisdom displayed through leadership look like (Yang 2011)? In particular, how can a wise leader(-ship) develop the capacity for ontological acuity, that is, to discern, integrate and narrate various situated complexities and appropriated responses (McKenna, Rooney and Boal 2009, Biloslavo and McKenna Chapter 6)? How can leaders practice enlightened wise judgements, which consider consequences of decisions and actions in the light of how judgements affect the self, others, the organization and society at large, thus reflecting executive integrity, courage and careful concern for the common good (Bierly and Kolodinsky 2008), including asking whose good the common good is (Offe 2012)?

WISDOM AND ORGANIZATIONS

How should we understand the relationship and conflicts between (un-)wise individuals in an organization and (un-)wise forms of organizing in groups regarding (un-)wise structures and functions of organizations? What are the challenges, constraints or failures in seeking to become a wise organization? What enables and facilitates the emergence and flourishing of practical wisdom in individuals and organizations? How do we create conditions that help us to acquire wisdom through experience, that is, a cycling of observations and contemplation that leads to broader understandings of context, self-reflection and faith in doing the right thing and passion, that is, strength of belief to act (Bierly, Kessler and Christensen 2000)? How can wisdom, as an enacted complexity, become a means of heightening awareness, mindfulness, sensitivities, reflection and critical consciousness of individuals, groups and thus organizations? What conditions, resources and competencies, for example human, social, socio-cultural, infrastructural, financial and technological, are required for developing a wise organization? What would a 'wisdom atmosphere' (Meacham 1990) or 'culture of wisdom' (Jones 2005) look like?

Is the wise organization an aspirational state, or an intermittent state? How is or can wisdom and failures of its realization be recognized, researched and how is it possible to assess wisdom properly? Are there examples of 'wise organizations', and if so how can they be identified (Rowley and Gibbs 2008)? How can we situate wisdom conceptually and practically between the need for increasing and reducing complexity, complexifying and simplifying, inserting and eliminating uncertainties, opening up and establishing borders? How to nurture 'between-times' and 'between-places' in organizations for the co-creation of value and wisdom in different constellations (Berthoin Antal 2006)?

WISDOM AND MACRO CONTEXT

How can we deal with the dominant logos of *tékhnê* in our contemporary times and increasingly instrumentalized, institutionalized contexts of neo-liberal, neo-conservative regimes and structured, auditing constraints of professional practice, which impede practitioners' *prâxical* and *phrónêtic* capacities? What does it imply that there is a 'hostile ground for growing *phrónêsis*' (Pitman 2012), characterized by an increasing managerialism, systems of surveillance and accountability in the professions, in which professionals have numerous and frequently conflicting ruling bodies to which they are held accountable? Furthermore, is *phrónêsis* always a possibility no matter how corrupt the existing practices are or the communities and institutions that sustain it (Bernstein 1986)?

With its multifaceted modalities, wisdom carries tremendous potential for broadening, deepening and realizing more integral ways for current and future practices in leadership and organizations. Moreover, a timely professional artistry of wisdom – as part of the art of and way of living Hadot 1995) – becomes even more relevant for transforming today's personal, social, cultural, political and economic realities into a more equitable, peaceful and enjoyable existence and evolution. Practical wisdom and its actual practices may then provide a medium for a more artful leading and organizing, which are much in demand in our increasingly inter-co-dependent worlds.

It is hoped that this chapter contributes to the ongoing revitalization of practical wisdom as an integral and sustainable practice and medium for the emergence of relational realities of leadership and organizations, being part of or interceding a 'wisdom economy' characterized by 'Sapienism' (Murtaza 2011) and integral wise ecology of an 'Inter-Integralism' (Küpers 2012). Then indeed, with an enlivening art of wisdom, the vigilant Owl of Minerva may take flight and be wise, not retrospectively post-factum with twilight falling into dusk, spreading its wings only when civilizations are in decline, but early enough and towards a horizon which is opening for a dawn of possible sustainable futures to be-come.

References

Abowitz, K.K. 2007. Moral perception through aesthetics: engaging imaginations in educational ethics. *Journal of Teacher Education*, 58(Sept/Oct), 287–98.

Antonacopoulou, E. 2008. On the practise of practice: in-tensions and ex-tensions in the ongoing reconfiguration of practices, in *The Sage Handbook of New Approaches in Management and Organization*, edited by D. Barry and H. Hansen. London: Sage, 112–31.

Ardelt, M. 2004. Wisdom as expert knowledge system: a critical review of a contemporary operationalization of an ancient concept. *Human Development*, 47(5), 257–85.

Aristotle 1985/1998. *Nicomachean Ethics*. Indianapolis: Hackett.

Aristotle 1998. *Politics*. Indianapolis: Hackett.

Assmann, A. 1994. Wholesome knowledge: concepts of wisdom in a historical and cross-cultural perspective, in *Life-span Development and Behavior*, edited by D.L. Featherman, R.M. Lerner and M. Perlmutter. Hillsdale: Erlbaum, 187–224.

Aubenque, P. 1963. *La Prudence chez Aristote*. Paris: Presses Universitaires de France.

Baehr, J. 2012. Two types of wisdom. *Acta Analytica*, 27(2), 81–97.

Baltes, P.B. and Smith, J. 1990. Towards a psychology of wisdom and its ontogenesis, in *Wisdom: Its Nature, Origins, and Development*, edited by R.J. Sternberg. New York: Cambridge University Press, 87–120.

Baltes, P.B. and Staudinger, U.M. 2000. Wisdom: a metaheuristic (pragmatic) to orchestrate mind and virtue toward excellence. *American Psychologist*, 55, 122–36.

Bateson, G. 1979. *Mind and Nature: A Necessary Unity*. New York: Ballantine.

Bernstein, R. 1983. *Beyond Objectivism and Relativism: Science, Hermeneutics, and Praxis*. Philadelphia: University of Pennsylvania Press.

Bernstein, R. 1986. *Philosophical Profiles: Essays in a Pragmatic Mode*. Cambridge: Polity Press.

Berthoin Antal, A. 2006. Reflections on the need for between-times and between-places. *Journal of Management Inquiry*, 15(2), 154–66.

Bierly, P.E., Kessler, E. and Christensen, E. 2000. Organizational learning, knowledge and wisdom. *Journal of Organizational Change Management*, 13(6), 595–618.

Bierly, P. and Kolodinsky, R. 2008. Strategic logic – toward a wisdom-based approach to strategic management, in *Handbook of Organizational and Managerial Wisdom*. London: Sage, 61–88.

Birren, J.E. and Svensson, C.M. 2005. Wisdom in history, in *Handbook of Wisdom: Psychological Perspectives*, edited by R.J. Sternberg and J. Jordan. Cambridge: Cambridge University Press, 3–31.

Bourdieu, P. 1990. *The Logic of Practice*. Stanford: Stanford University Press.

Burkitt, I. 1999. Relational moves and generative dances, in *Relational Responsibility: Resources for Sustainable Dialogue*, edited by S. McNamee and K.J. Gergen. London: Sage, 71–9.

Cataldi, S.L. 1993. *Emotion, Depth and Flesh. A Study of Sensitive Space. Reflections on Merleau-Ponty's Philosophy of Embodiment*. Albany: The State University of New York Press.

Chan, G.K. 2005. Understanding end-of-life caring practices in the emergency department: developing Merleau-Ponty's notions of intentional arc and maximum grip through praxis and phronesis. *Nursing Philosophy*, 6(1), 19–32.

Chia, R. 2005. The aim of management education: reflections on Mintzberg's 'Managers not MBAs'. *Organization Studies*, 26(7), 1090–92.

Chia, R. and Holt, R. 2006. Strategy as practical coping: a Heideggerian perspective. *Organization Studies*, 27(5), 635–55.

,Chia, R. and MacKay, B. 2007. Post-processual challenges for the emerging strategy-as-practice perspective: discovering strategy in the logic of practice. *Human Relations*, 60(1), 217–42.

Côté, S., Miners, C. and Moon, S. 2006. Emotional intelligence and wise emotion regulation in the workplace, in *Individual and Organizational Perspectives on Emotion Management and Display*, edited by W.J. Zerbe, N.M. Ashkanasy and C.E.J. Härtel. Bingley: Emerald, 1–24.

Crossley, N. 1996. *Intersubjectivity: The Fabric of Social Becoming*. London: Sage.

Dale, K. 2005. Building a social materiality: spatial and embodied politics in organizational control. *Organization*, 12(5), 649–8.

Depraz, N. 2001. The Husserlian theory of intersubjectivity as alterology: emergent theories and wisdom traditions in the light of genetic phenomenology. *Journal of Consciousness Studies*, 8(6–7).

Dewey, J. 1922. *Human Nature and Conduct: An Introduction to Social Psychology*. New York: Modern Library.

Diprose, R. 2002. *Corporeal Generosity: On Giving with Nietzsche, Merleau-Ponty, and Levinas*. Albany: State University of New York Press.

Dunne, J. 1993/1997. *Back to the Rough Ground. 'Phrónêsis' and 'Techne' in Modern Philosophy and in Aristotle*. Notre Dame: University of Notre Dame Press.

Durand, R. and Huy, Q. 2008. Practical wisdom and emotional capability as antecedents of organizational accountability in revolutionary change processes, in *Emotions, Ethics and Decision-Making Research on Emotion in Organizations*, Volume 4, edited by W.J. Zerbe, C.E.J. Härtel and N.M. Ashkanasy. Bingley: Emerald, 311–32.

Durand, R. and Huy, Q. 2008. Practical wisdom and emotional capability as antecedents of organizational accountability in revolutionary change processes, in Wilfred J. Zerbe, Charmine E.J. Härtel and Neal M. Ashkanasy (eds) *Emotions, Ethics and Decision-Making Research on Emotion in Organizations*, Volume 4. Emerald Group Publishing Limited, 311–32.

Eidinow, E. and Ramirez, R. 2012. The eye of the soul: phronesis and the aesthetics of organizing. *Organizational Aesthetics*, 1(1), 26–43.

Eikeland, O. 2006. *Phrónêsis*, Aristotle, and action research. *International Journal of Action Research*, 2(1), 5–53.

Eikeland, O. 2007. Why should mainstream social researchers be interested in action research? *International Journal of Action Research*, 3(1+2), 38–64.

Eikeland, O. 2008. *The Ways of Aristotle. Aristotelian Phrónesis, Aristotelian Philosophy of Dialogue, and Action Research*. Bern: Peter Lang.

Eisner, E.W. 2002. From episteme to *phrónêsis* to artistry in the study and improvement of teaching. *Teaching and Teacher Education*, 18(4), 375–85.

Eikeland, O. and Nicolini, D. 2011. Turning practically – broadening the horizon. Introduction to the special issue. *Journal of Organizational Change Management*, 24(2), 164–74.

Eisner, E.W. 2002. From episteme to Phrónêsis to artistry in the study and improvement of teaching. *Teaching and Teacher Education*, 18(4), 375–85.

Farrell, T. 1996. Phronêsis, in *Encyclopedia of Rhetoric and Composition: Communication from Ancient Times to the Information Age*, edited by T. Enos. New York: Garland, 517–19.

Farrell, T.B. 1998. Sizing things up: colloquial reflection as practical wisdom. *Argumentation*, 12(1), 1–14.

Flyvbjerg, B. 2001. *Making Social Science Matter: Why Social Inquiry Fails and How It Can Succeed Again*. Cambridge: Cambridge University Press.

Flyvbjerg, B. 2006. Making Organization Research Matter: Power, Values and Phrónêsis, in Stewart R. Clegg, Cynthia Hardy, Thomas B. Lawrence and Walter R. Nord (eds), *The Sage Handbook of Organization Studies*, Thousand Oaks, CA: Sage, 370–373.

Flyvbjerg, B., Landman, T. and Schram, S. 2012. *Real Social Science – Applied Phrónêsis*. Cambridge: Cambridge University Press.

Fowers, B.J. 2003. Reason and human finitude. *The American Behavioral Scientist*, 47, 415–26.

Gadamer, H.-G. 1977/1986. *The Relevance of the Beautiful and Other Essays*, edited by R. Bernasconi. Cambridge: Cambridge University Press.

Gadamer, H.-G. 1979. Practical philosophy as a model of the human sciences. *Research in Phenomenology*, 9, 74–86.

Gadamer, H.-G. 1982. *Truth and Method*. New York: Continuum Press.

Garrison, J. 1997. *Dewey and Eros: Wisdom and Desire in the Art of Teaching*. New York: Teachers College Press.

Gendlin, E. 1997. The responsive order: a new empiricism. *Man and World*, 30(3), 383–411.

Gittings, R. (ed.) 1970. *Letters of John Keats*. New Delhi: Oxford University Press.

Grint, K. 2007. Learning to lead: can Aristotle help us find the road to wisdom? *Leadership*, 3, 231–46.

Hadot, P. 1995. *Philosophy as a Way of Life: Spiritual Exercises from Socrates to Foucault*. Oxford: Oxford University Press.

Hancock, P. 2008. Embodied generosity and an ethics of organization. *Organization Studies*, 29(10), 1357–73.

Heidegger, M. 1997. *Plato's Sophist*. Bloomington: Indiana University Press.

Higgs, J., Titchen, A. and Neville, V. 2001. Professional practice and knowledge, in *Practice Knowledge and Expertise*, edited by J. Higgs and A. Titchen. Oxford: Butterworth-Heinemann, 3–9.

Holliday, G., Statler, M. and Flanders, M. 2007. Developing practically wise leaders through serious play. *Consulting Psychology Journal*, 59(2), 126–34.

Holt, R. 2006. Principals and practice: rhetoric and the moral character of managers. *Human Relations*, 59(12), 1659–80.

Holt, R. and Sandberg, J. 2011. Phenomenology and organization theory, in *Research in the Sociology of Organizations*, edited by H. Tsoukas and R. Chia. Bingley: Emerald, 215–49.

Joas, H. 1996. *The Creativity of Action*. Chicago: The University of Chicago Press.

Jones, A.C. 2005. Wisdom paradigms for the enhancement of ethical and profitable business practices. *Journal of Business Ethics*, 57(4), 363–75.

Kateb, G. 2000. Aestheticism and morality: their cooperation and hostility. *Political Theory*, 28(1), 5–38.

Kay, R. 1994. The artistry of leadership: an exploration of the leadership process in voluntary not-for-profit organizations. *Nonprofit Management and Leadership*, 4(3), 285–300.

Kemmis, S. 2012. Phronēsis, experience, and the primacy of praxis, in *Phronesis as Professional Knowledge: Practical Wisdom in the Professions*, edited by E.A. Kinsella and A. Pitman. Rotterdam: Sense, 147–62.

Kemmis, S. and Grootenboer, P. 2008. Situating praxis in practice, in *Enabling Praxis: Challenges for Education*, edited by S. Kemmis and T.J. Smith. Rotterdam: Sense, 37–64.

Kersten, A. 2008. When craving goodness becomes bad: a critical conception of ethics and aesthetics in organizations. *Culture and Organization*, 15(2), 187–202.

Kinsella, E.A. 2007. Embodied reflection and the epistemology of reflective practice. *The Journal of Philosophy of Education*, 41(3), 395–409.

Kitchener, K.S. and Brenner, H.G. 1990. Wisdom and reflective judgment: knowing in the face of uncertainty, in *Wisdom: Its Nature, Origins, and Development*, edited by R.J. Sternberg. New York: Cambridge University Press, 212–29.

Küpers, W. 2002. Phenomenology of aesthetic organising: ways towards aesthetically responsive organisations. *Journal Consumption, Markets and Cultures*, 5(1), 31–68.

Küpers, W. 2004. Art and Leadership, in J.M. Burns, R.R. Goethals and G.J. Sorenson 2004. *Encyclopaedia of Leadership*. Thousand Oaks, CA: Sage, 47–54.

Küpers, W. 2005a. Phenomenology and integral pheno-practice of embodied well-be(com)ing in organizations. *Culture and Organization*, 11(3), 221–31.

Küpers, W. 2005b. Envisioning a refined existence between the sense of reality and the sense of possibility through a responsive encounter between art and commerce, in *Sophisticated Survival Techniques – Strategies in Art and Economy*, edited by M. Brellochs and H. Schraat. Berlin: Kadmos, 372–97.

Küpers, W. 2007. Integral pheno-practice of wisdom in management and organisation. *Social Epistemology*, Special Issue on Wisdom and Stupidity, 22(4), 169–93.

Küpers, W. 2011a. Integral responsibility for a sustainable practice in organisations and management. *Corporate Social Responsibility and Environmental Management Journal*, 18, 137–50.

Küpers, W. 2011b. Trans-+-form – transforming: transformational leadership for a creative change practice. *Leadership & Organization Development Journal*, 32(1), 20–40.

Küpers, W. 2011c. Dancing on the limen – embodied and creative inter-place as thresholds of be(com)ing: phenomenological perspectives on liminality and transitional spaces in organisations. *Tamara, Journal for Critical Organization Inquiry*, Special Issue on Liminality, 9(3–4), 45–59.

Küpers, W. 2012. Inter-integralism – critical perspectives on advanced and adequate phenomenology and 'pheno-practice' for integral research – or why phenomenology is more and different than an 'upper left' or 'zone #1' affair, in *True but Partial – Essential Critiques of Integral Theory*, edited by S. Esbjörn-Hargens. Albany: The State University of New York Press.

Küpers, W. 2013. Wisdom and learning – habituation of practical wisdom and embodied learning in organisations. *Journal of Organizational Change Management* (forthcoming).

Küpers, W. 2014. Embodied Inter-Be(com)ing – The contribution of Merleau-Ponty's relational Ontology for a processual understanding of Chiasmic Organising, in *Oxford Handbook of Process*

Philosophy and Organization Studies, edited by J. Helin, T. Hernes, D. Hjorth and R. Holt. Oxford: Oxford University Press (forthcoming).

Küpers, W. and Edwards, M. 2008. Integrating plurality – towards an integral perspective on leadership and organisation, in *Handbook of 21st Century Management*, edited by C. Wankel. London: Sage, 311–22.

Küpers, W. and Statler, M. 2008. Practically wise leadership: towards an integral understanding. *Culture and Organization*, 14(4), 379–400.

Küpers, W., Mantere, S. and Statler, M. 2012. Strategy as storytelling: a phenomenological exploration of embodied narrative practice. *Journal for Management Inquiry*, (21)3, 1–18.

Ladkin, D. 2010. *Rethinking Leadership, a New Look at Old Leadership Questions*. Cheltenham: Edward Elgar Publishing.

Ladkin, D. 2011. The art of 'perceiving correctly: what artists can teach us about moral perception. *Tamara – Journal for Critical Organization Inquiry*, 9(3–4), 91–101.

Ladkin, D. and Taylor, S.S. 2010. Enacting the 'true self': towards a theory of embodied authentic leadership. *Leadership Quarterly*, 21, 64–74.

Leathard, H.L. and Cook, M.J. 2009. Learning for holistic care: addressing practical wisdom (*phrónêsis*) and the spiritual sphere. *Journal of Advanced Nursing*, 65(6), 1318–27.

Long, C. 2002. The ontological reappropriation of *phrónêsis*. *Continental Philosophy* Review, 35(1), 35–60.

Lord, C. 2002. Bringing prudence back, in *Tempered Strength: Studies in the Nature and Scope of Prudential Leadership*, edited by E. Fishman. Oxford: Lexington Books.

Machek, D. 2011. The doubleness of craft: motifs of technical action in life *Prâxis* according to Aristotle and Zhuangzi. *Dao: A Journal of Comparative Philosophy*, 10(4), 507–26.

MacIntyre, A. 1985. *After Virtue*. London: Duckworth.

MacLean, D. and MacIntosh, R. 2012. Strategic change as creative action. *International Journal of Strategic Change Management*, 4(1), 80–97.

Mailloux, S. 2004. Rhetorical hermeneutics still again: or, on the track of phronēsis, in *A Companion to Rhetoric and Rhetorical Criticism*, edited by W. Jost and W. Olmsted. Wiley-Blackwell, 457–72.

Malan, L.C. and Kriger, M.P. 1998. Making sense of managerial wisdom. *Journal of Management Inquiry*, 7(3), 241–51.

McKenna, B., Rooney, D. and Boal, K. 2009. Wisdom principles as a meta-theoretical basis for evaluating leadership. *The Leadership Quarterly*, 20(2), 177–90.

McPherson, I. 2005, Reflexive Learning: Stages towards wisdom with Dreyfus. *Educational Philosophy and Theory*, 37: 705–18.

Meacham, J.A. 1990. The loss of wisdom, in *Wisdom: Its Nature, Origins, and Development*, edited by R.J. Sternberg. New York: Cambridge University Press, 181–211.

Merleau-Ponty, M. 1962/1996. *Phenomenology of Perception*. London: Routledge.

Merleau-Ponty, M. 1992. Texts and Dialogues, Princeton, NJ. Humanities Press.

Merleau-Ponty, M. 1995. *The Visible and the Invisible*. Evanston: Northwestern University Press.

Merleau-Ponty, M. 2003. *Nature*. Evanston: Northwestern University Press.

Monthoux, de, G.P. and Statler, M. 2008. Aesthetic play as an organizing principle, in *The Sage Handbook of New Approaches in Management and Organization*, edited by D. Barry and H. Hansen. London: Sage, 423–35.

Murtaza, N. 2011. Pursuing self-interest or self-actualization? From capitalism to a steady-state, wisdom economy. *Ecological Economics*, 70(4), 1–8.

Noel, J. 1999. Phronesis and phantasia: teaching with wisdom and imagination. *Journal of Philosophy of Education*, 33(2), 277–87.

Nussbaum, M.C. 1990. *Love's Knowledge: Essays on Philosophy and Literature*. New York: Oxford University Press.

Nussbaum, M.C. 2001. *The Fragility of Goodness: Luck and Ethics in Greek Tragedy and Philosophy*. New York: Cambridge University Press.

Offe, C. 2012. Whose good is the common good? *Philosophy and Social Criticism*, 1–20.

Osbeck, L.M. and Robinson, D.N. 2005. Philosophical theories of wisdom, in *Handbook of Wisdom: Psychological Perspectives*, edited by R.J. Sternberg and J. Jordan. Cambridge: Cambridge University Press, 61–83.

Paterson, M., Higgs, J. and Wilcox, S. 2006. Developing expertise in judgement artistry in OT practice. *British Journal of OT*, 69(3), 115–23.

Pendlebury, S. 1995. Reason and story in wise practice, in *Narrative in Teaching, Learning and Research*, edited by H. McEwan and K. Egan. New York: Teachers College Record, 50–65.

Pitman, A. 2012. Professionalism and professionalisation: hostile ground for growing phronesis? in *Phronesis as Professional Knowledge: Practical Wisdom in the Professions*, edited by E.A. Kinsella and A. Pitman. Rotterdam: Sense, 131–46.

Polkinghorne, D.E. 2004. *Practice and the Human Sciences: The Case for a Judgment-Based Practice of Care*. Albany: State University of New York Press.

Rämö, H. 2011. Visualizing the phronetic organization: the case of photographs in CSR reports. *Journal of Business Ethics*, 104(3), 371–87.

Reckwitz, A. 2002. Towards a theory of social practices: a development in culturalist theorizing. *European Journal of Social Theory*, 5(2), 243–63.

Roca, E. 2007. Intuitive practical wisdom in organizational life. *Social Epistemology*, 21(2), 195–207.

Rooney, D. and McKenna, B. 2008. Wisdom in public administration: looking for a sociology of wise practice. *Public Administration Review*, 68(4), 709–21.

Rooney, D., McKenna, B. and Liesch, P. 2010. *Wisdom and Management in the Knowledge Economy*. London: Routledge.

Roos, J., Victor, B. and Statler, M. 2004. Playing seriously with strategy. *Long-Range Planning*, 37(6), 549–68.

Rowley, J. and Gibbs, P. 2008. From learning organization to practically wise organization. *Learning Organization*, 15(5), 356–72.

Sandy, M. 2011. Practical beauty and the legacy of pragmatism: generating theory for community-engaged scholarship. *Interchange: A Quarterly Review of Education*, 42(3), 261–85.

Schatzki, T. 1996. *Social Practices: A Wittgensteinian Approach to Human Activity and the Social*. New York: Cambridge University Press.

Schatzki, T. 2001. Practice theory, in *The Practice Turn in Contemporary Theory*, edited by T. Schatzki, K. Knorr Cetina and E. Von Savigny. London: Routledge, 1–14.

Schmid, H.B. 2009. *Plural Action Essays in Philosophy and Social Science*. Dordrecht, Springer.

Schön, D. 1983. *The Reflective Practitioner*. New York: Basic Books.

Schön, D. 1987. *Educating the Reflective Practitioner*. San Francisco: Jossey-Bass.

Schwartz, B. 2011. Practical wisdom and organizations. *Research in Organizational Behavior*, 31(1), 3–23.

Schwartz, B. and Sharpe, K. 2006. Practical wisdom: Aristotle meets positive psychology. *Journal of Happiness Studies*, 7(3), 377–95.

Shusterman, R. 2008. *Body Consciousness: A Philosophy of Mindfulness and Somaesthetics*. New York: Cambridge University Press.

Simpson, P., French, R. and Harvey, C. 2002. Leadership and negative capability. *Human Relations*, 55(10), 1209–26.

Simpson, P. and French, R. 2006. Negative capability and the capacity to think in the present moment. *Leadership*, 2(2), 245–55.

Statler, M. 2005. Practical wisdom and serious play: reflections on management understanding, in *Sophisticated Survival Techniques / Strategies in Art and Economy*, edited by H. Schrat. Berlin: Kulturverlag Kadmos.

Statler, M. and Roos, J. 2007. *Everyday Strategic Preparedness: the Role of Practical Wisdom in Organizations*. Basingstoke: Palgrave MacMillan.

Sternberg, R.J. 1990. Wisdom and its relations to intelligence and creativity, in *Wisdom: Its Nature, Origins, and Development*, edited by R.J. Sternberg. New York: Cambridge University Press, 142–59.

Sutherland, I. 2013. Arts-based methods in leadership development: affording aesthetic workspaces, reflexivity and memories with momentum *Management Learning*, February 2013 44: 25–43.

Taylor, S.S. and Hanson, H. 2005. Finding form: looking at the field of organizational aesthetics. *Journal of Management Studies*, 42(6), 1211–32.

Taylor, S.S. and Ladkin, D. 2009. Understanding arts-based methods in managerial development. *Academy of Management Learning and Education*, 8(1), 55–6.

Tiemersma, D. 1989. *Body Schema and Body Image: an Interdisciplinary and Philosophical Study*. Amsterdam: Swets & Zeitlinger.

Titchen, A. and Higgs, J. 2001. A dynamic framework for the enhancement of health professional practice in an uncertain world: the practice-knowledge interface, in *Practice Knowledge and Expertise*, edited by J. Higgs and A. Titchen. Oxford: Butterworth-Heinemann, 215–25.

Titchen, A. and Higgs, J. 2008. *Towards Professional Artistry and Creativity in Practice in Health, Education and the Creative Arts*. Oxford: Blackwell, 273–90.

Trowbridge, R. and Ferrari, M. 2011. Sophia and *phrónêsis* in psychology, philosophy, and traditional wisdom. *Research in Human Development*, 8(2), 89–94.

Tsoukas, H. and Cummings, S. 1997. Marginalization and recovery: the emergence of Aristotelian themes in organization studies. *Organization Studies*, 18(4), 655–83.

Tuomela, R. 2007. *The Philosophy of Sociality*. Oxford: Oxford University Press.

Waddock, S. 2009. Finding wisdom within – the role of seeing and reflective practice in developing moral imagination, aesthetic sensibility and systems. *Journal of Business Ethics Education*, 7, 177–96.

Waldenfels, B. 2008. The role of the lived-body in feeling. *Continental Philosophy Review*, 41(2), 127–42.

Wall, J. 2003. *Phrónêsis*, poetics, and moral creativity. *Ethical Theory and Moral Practice*, 6(3), 317–41.

Wall, J. 2005. *Moral Creativity: Paul Ricoeur and the Poetics of Possibility*. New York: Oxford University Press.

Walsh, R. 2011. The varieties of wisdom: contemplative, cross-cultural, and integral contributions. *Research in Human Development*, 8(2), 109–27, Special Issue: Sophia and Phrónêsis in Psychology, Philosophy, and Traditional Wisdom.

Walsh, R. 2012. Wisdom: an integral view. *Journal of Integral Theory and Practice*, 7(1), 1–21.

Weiss, A.S. 1981. Merleau-Ponty's concept of the flesh as libido theory. *SubStance*, 30, 85–95.

Werhane, P. 1999. Justice and trust. *Journal of Business Ethics*, 21(2–3), 237–49.

Yakhlef, A. 2010. The corporeality of practice-based learning. *Organization Studies*, 31(4), 409–30.

Yang, S.-Y. 2008. A process view of wisdom. *Journal of Adult Development*, 15(2), 62–75.

Yang, S.-Y. 2011. Wisdom displayed through leadership: exploring leadership-related wisdom. *Leadership Quarterly*, 22(4), 616–32.

2 *Phrónêsis in Action: A Case Study Approach to a Professional Learning Group*

CLAIRE JANKELSON

Introduction

The writing of this chapter with a case study description aims to be faithful to the very theme of *phrónêsis* as practical wisdom. The work of Flyvbjerg (2002, 2004) suggests the paradoxical nature of arguing theoretically about a methodology. Moreover, with the subject matter, *phrónêsis*, of a practical nature, it seems apt to use tools of expression which suggest the content. Narrative description is used to disclose the background, rationale and some lived moments of a supervision group (hereafter called the Circle) with PhD candidates. The goal for the Circle is to stimulate the practice of the art and craft of embodied, situated and contextualized research. In this context, research itself becomes a practice for a professional group engaged in dialogue that grapples with making sense of, understanding and interpreting PhD researching practice.

A description of the Circle as it has evolved through a four-year cycle situates the case study. It names the concrete and actual events of the Circle and the experience and intentions of this supervisor (and author). It is hoped that the reader will appreciate the practice, the complexity and the value of the Circle, and perhaps through this detailed description be able to operationalize an equivalent environment or practice. Following the description are some of the overarching themes that arise from reflecting on them. It will be noted that these emergent themes cohere with the descriptors of *phrónêsis* that follow.

A discussion of *phrónêsis* as practical wisdom draws initially on Aristotle as explicated in his *Nicomachean Ethics* (1962). With the Circle operating within a hermeneutic framework, it is also apt to consider the attraction that two primary thinkers on hermeneutic phenomenology, Heidegger and Gadamer, had with *phrónêsis*. Both describe and directly connect their theories with Aristotelian *phrónêsis* and both compare 'practical wisdom' with Aristotle's other types of wisdom (Bernstein 1988, Palmer 1969).

The Circle is situated within a Management School at a University in Sydney, Australia. The participants are professionals who are engaged in doing PhD research and writing their theses, and the two supervisors.[1] It is therefore within candidates' relationships

---

1   The other supervisor is Dr Steven Segal, a senior lecturer at the university. The Circle was conceived and has been developed and facilitated by us both.

with management or professional practice, higher education and research that *phrónêsis* will be sought. Coherent with a case study framework, a narrative approach will be used to describe anecdotes of actions and dilemmas that offer examples of the occurrence of *phrónêsis* within the practice of the Circle.

Phrónêsis as practical wisdom is integrally connected with *prâxis*: a practice that goes beyond rules, that deliberates and takes all possible circumstances into account in order to do one's best (Kemmis 2011). Kemmis describes how *phrónêsis* arises out of *prâxis* as the wisdom that emerges out of experience. This study focuses on the practice rather than the theoretical development of research, management and learning within higher education. Each of these can be seen as a practice where the idea of practice is not defined simply in relation to the distinction of theory versus practice. Instead, practice is closer to the Greek term *prâxis*, which refers to human activity as a member of the society. As Coulter and Wiens (2002) describe, *prâxis* demands a particular kind of engaged, embodied and enacted judgement that links knowledge, virtue and reason. *Prâxis* can therefore be characterized as trying to act in the best way possible within the particular circumstances.

What is the nature of the knowledge or the knowing that emerges through the engagement within the Circle and how can it be said to be useful or add value for management candidates engaged in their PhD research? What is the nature of the dialogue between the candidates and how is this dialogue significant to the individual candidate and to the supervisors? When can one speak of *phrónêsis* occurring and how would such an occasion be identifiable? These are questions that this chapter will consider and respond to.

The chapter concludes with some reflections on the value of *phrónêsis* as a framework to evaluate the Circle. It offers pointers both about the movement of this chapter as transparently expressing the art and practice of *phrónêsis* and the Circle as '*phrónêsis-in-action*'. Finally, it reviews the generalizability of the work of the Circle in relation to the applicability of such a methodology to other practices, including within management and higher education.

Narrative Description of the Circle

The two supervisors who created the Circle have been teaching in academic institutions for decades, and have a keen interest in the educational and management learning opportunities that doing higher degree research in a management school can provide. One supervisor had been Director of Higher Degree Research and the other supervisor and author of this paper had completed her own PhD a number of years earlier with the inspirational support of a small group of three PhD candidates who met regularly and dialogued using a Bohmian style conversation.[2]

There was no blueprint for how this research circle would proceed. We were both anxious and excited at the idea of innovating a new form of learning within an academic institution, of offering PhD candidates another option. In preparation for first creating the Circle, the supervisors held conversations with one another and immersed themselves in the theory and practice of hermeneutics. Recognizing that researching

---

2   This refers to a form of dialogue that is non-hierarchical and a moment of silence is practiced between speakers; communication is self-directed in an inquiring rather than an advocating style while listening is paramount (Bohm 1990).

itself is intrinsically an extension of the researcher, we wanted to create an environment in which the drawing forth of intentionality and even methodology could transpire. It appeared that a hermeneutic phenomenological theoretical framework could support the intentions of reflecting on, learning and practising the art of research.

We had recognized how 'lost' many PhD candidates were and believed that that emotion of 'feeling lost' often contains the seeds that could be transformative to their research process. We knew that transformation can occur from learning how to be in question with your questions: a kind of embracing of that 'lostness'. The core idea was that research itself is a practice that requires a particular kind of perception and practice to manage. We believed that a 'good' research practice could translate into having a consequential PhD experience that may have an impact both on the research process and on candidates' professional management practices.

It is undeniable that the possibilities of such a conversation excited us as supervisors. Having myself conducted extensive research and taught the art and craft of research, I suspected that a group could offer a kind of window or extra perspective for each person that is unattainable by any other means. I felt challenged to nurture my perceptual, facilitatory and group communication skills that would enable each person's research practice to flourish.

Sessions are scheduled as monthly afternoon events. This frequency has continued and appears to be a good interval between sessions. Most of our candidates are professional management practitioners who are working either full or part time. The time they give up for the supervision group is considered precious and there have been challenges from candidates with regard to the group time being used for optimal results. Attendance at the group is completely voluntary.

Around 12 to 15 mature-age people are seated around a boardroom table, including the supervisors. The split of males to females is roughly equal. The mode of operating is respectful and friendly. As supervisors, we have created a plan and intention for structuring the session. This may include presentations, a group writing or conversational exercise such as setting goals for the year or individual spontaneous reflection on progress and problems experienced. Any topic can provide the yeast for reflection on researching.

We reiterate our intention, which is to create an environment within which candidates can 'be in' the practice of research and that it is from this experience of 'being-in' that the question or the phenomenon develops. This is the basis for reflecting upon and theorizing the research process.

As supervisors, we agree on most pedagogical and philosophical principles. Our disagreements often concern the relative amounts of time given for presentation and academic content compared with a more spontaneous or off-the-cuff type inquiry. The third hidden role in our disagreement is the academic institution. It calls for measurable outcomes and appropriate theorizing. What constitutes a 'good enough' session may be different for the three parties. We communicate openly with the group and with one another in deciding to change or reshape the direction the group is moving through.

It is complex to try to delineate the method that is used to facilitate the conversation. To call it a method is to lock it into a set of rules and procedures and yet it is so much more than that; there is no order to what we do; there is a dynamic responsiveness and attempt at sensitivity to what is unfolding by the group. We are often surprised at what actually transpires in the group. The most I can offer are a number of pointers that signify what we may do. I believe that were this piece to be written by the other supervisor or by the students themselves, they may describe something quite different.

Presentations in the Circle are encouraged to be on topics in progress or on topics that candidates are grappling with. Presentations may be methodological, related to actual content or on a topic related to the experience of doing research. Sometimes students use the session to hone their ideas as practice in anticipation of a more formal presentation.

Candidates drive their own presentation process by inviting questions and conversation. The group listens carefully with full attention. We listen for what has not been said, for what is perhaps missing. We listen for an internal logic and flow, for the resonance between the presenter and the content of their presentation. We listen for what the phenomenon is that is just behind or within the content; perhaps this is the context that is driving the content. Questions and comments build towards a shared understanding through the group interaction and collaboration. Connections are uncovered and discovered: these could be resonances of topics between candidates; applications to the Weltanschauung or the Zeitgeist; academic literature sources that support or contradict; archetypal or mythical connections.

As supervisors, we are both gatekeepers and drivers of the conversation. We are mindful of content and the nature of the relationships within the group, the irritations and the power play. We make an effort to keep bringing the conversation back to the details of the actual experience of what is being described. This may include: questioning the meaning of what is being stated; reaching into understanding the nature of what is described; noticing connections or similarities between speakers; fine tuning the theorizing; framing what is said in theory; appreciating the breadth and depth of the words and meanings and bringing this to attention; and seeking the context or background of what is described.

We are cultivating a careful and conscious practice: the appreciation of what is arising. Avoiding finding solutions or answers sometimes feels like trying to keep the door open when the wind is blowing hard. Perhaps the wind is the academic tradition that insists on closure, on finding answers, of compartmentalizing theory and practice. I notice my own tendencies to judge, to interpret, and to 'dismiss' a phenomenon by theorizing. The kinds of question that I often bring into my consciousness and sometimes share with the group include: what are we now learning or understanding about research? What does it mean to 'stand in' the phenomenon that is being spoken about? What else is being said here? What is underlying all of this?

Sometimes a particular kind of understanding just arises in the group. Smiles and nods and responses of 'yes' emerge as insights shoot across the room. There may be raised voices and even laughter. It appears that the time spent grappling has taken us to an unexpected conclusion. It is as though a kind of group-wisdom has occurred. What was not understood now makes sense! Furthermore, this understanding gives rise to new interpretation and theorizing. There is a natural next step as people recognize possible applications within their own theses. It appears that learning has transpired.

Challenges are not avoided and at the same time the rule of kindness applies. We are not seeking agreement with one another; nor are we seeking disagreement. We are each seeking our 'felt' response to the conversation as we try to continuously stay with the phenomena being addressed, allowing and inviting the grappling to take place.

A conversation about language explores how the complexity of the language of a theoretical system becomes a barrier to the theory. What is the experience of that barrier? And what is it like on either side of that barrier: is it a barrier or is it a protection? We grapple with the nature of language opening up, the nature of understanding and interpretation. Some argue that the language of hermeneutics poses a barrier to its understanding; others speak of the journey into the language as a journey of comprehension. Insight arises about being inside and being outside of your PhD, about the struggle, about finding your purpose.

Playfulness, banter and teasing are part of the culture of the group. In speaking of when and how creativity occurs, we lead to the nature of thoughts taking hold and letting go of one. We argue playfully about the nature of 'being in' a question and the nature of talking about 'being in' a question, about how the way into the hermeneutic circle is through a leap into the circle – and what does that actually mean? Some take the leap; others prefer the safety of the known. We are still learning what that means.

With four years behind us, we recognize that the Circle is making a difference for candidates. Some candidates appear to need less individualized input from supervisors. Relationships and support dyads and triads are being created. References are exchanged. Papers are being collaborated on. People turn up regularly for the Circle and appear enthusiastic about their research journeys.

Arising Themes

The above passage has described my experience as immediate perception of the Circle. This was written without interpretation or theorizing. In keeping with the method of phenomenology where conceptualization follows perception, the following themes represent a drawing out of some of the central features of the group experience that emerge seamlessly from the description. This pattern is similar to what transpires in the Circle where understanding and interpretation follow experience. It can be noted that these features capture many of the central concepts of *phrónêsis* as will be delineated in the next section, which articulates a theoretical overview of *phrónêsis*.

1) CULTIVATION OF PRACTICE

Participation in the Circle is not sporadic. Through regular attendance and regular reflection on how we participate in the nature of the Circle, it appears that we are actively cultivating our particular way of participating and thereby actively creating the very nature of the Circle. The nature of our participation in the circle is therefore evolving through both our experience of participation and the reflection on the experience, whilst being within the experience of the circle, regularly. Our practice is thereby being both nurtured and cultivated: a training ground!

2) PLAYFULNESS AND HUMOUR

These appear to be intrinsic to the life of the Circle. Whilst our primary task of learning about research and our primary methodology of phenomenology are both complex and engaging activities, a quality of lightness fuels the living nature of the Circle. This area is a balancing act with attendance to the 'right' amount of lightness. This can only be assessed from within the particular context.

3) RELATIONSHIP AND DIALOGUE

The dialogue is inclusive and an essential aspect of the life of the circle. We try to avoid dominance by a few, frequently inquire of those that have not been vocal and generally try to ensure that everyone participates without inhibition. The development of the dialogue is in itself a practice that is being cultivated. There have been negative behaviour patterns such as personal criticisms. The nature of the dialogue is frequently attended to through sharing reflections on the dialogue and relationships by the supervisors and often by the candidates themselves.

4) GRAPPLING AND UNCERTAINTY

As supervisors we are suspicious when the conversation is relaxed and logical. We are on the look-out for bringing the conversation back to experience, ensuring that theorizing is arising out of experience. Our understanding is that when we are 'on track', we are theorizing and interpreting. We are operating in the field of 'the known'. When there are levels of discomfort and grappling, it is a sign that we are 'off track'. This is the process that we wish to straddle: the continuous interaction of experience and theory. The 'not-knowing' of the outcome of the conversation takes each person into experience and it is out of the experience of grappling, an all-embracing experience that insight and learning often appear.

The four themes

Seen together, the above four themes offer a useful gauge with which to consider the effectiveness of a professional learning group. Without specifying exactly what each feature ought to reveal, they can be applied as a kind of meta-pattern in evaluating a specific group. Each feature can be applied and assessed after a group meeting with questions such as: 'What was the quality of the dialogue today?' A group will develop its own benchmarks according to its needs. The features can provide a reflexive opportunity for the group *prâxis*.

It can be noted that the above features suggest the generalizability of the nature of this work. The creation of an intersubjective learning environment operating with hermeneutic principles is best utilized with a group that is wishing to learn or work towards a particular intention. One key ingredient of critical significance is that each member of the group has a self-directed (autotelic) interest in building a particular practice or learning. This implies that such a group would not operate well through coercion. A practice with a hermeneutic phenomenological methodology is therefore best served where each participant is a 'professional', who is pursuing the understanding of some aspect of professional practice or research.

THE HERMENEUTIC CIRCLE

Whilst the Circle is called a hermeneutic circle, 'it is not to be reduced to the level of a vicious circle, or even a circle which is merely tolerated' (Heidegger 1962, section 32). The hermeneutic can usefully be considered as a process that creates the conditions for understanding to occur. It uses the engagement with an arising phenomenon (idea or experience) to understand a larger concept, thereby using the parts to get to the whole and the whole as a way of accessing the particularity of a concept. This is a dialectic process of recognizing how the whole contextualizes each of the parts in the process of continuously seeking to illuminate the phenomenon within its context (Higgs, Paterson and Kinsella 2012). Through this hermeneutic practice, preconceptions emerge and genuine understanding and interpretation is reached. This kind of underlying wisdom is a *'phrónêsis-*in-action' and the circle-like nature an essential aspect of enabling the understanding to occur!

This inquiry now puts the Circle aside and continues with building an understanding of the nature of *phrónêsis*. It begins with Aristotle's description and then a review of how Heidegger and then Gadamer have adopted the notion. Thereafter, I return to the Circle using specific anecdotes that suggest its application within organizational management practices and higher education.

Conceptualization of *Phrónêsis*: Aristotle and then Heidegger and Gadamer

Phrónêsis, interpreted as practical wisdom or knowing, arises within Aristotle's (1962) moral and political philosophy. It is distinguished primarily as being an activity of apprehension, the 'how' of knowing, that includes the theoretical (*sophía*), the practical (*phrónêsis*) and the technical (*tékhnê*) ways of knowing.

Sophía is translated as theoretical wisdom and is seen by Aristotle (1962) as the highest intellectual and philosophical excellence that people are able to reach. For the sake of distinction, *sophía* can be considered as wisdom, as it is commonly used.

Tékhnê can be translated as knowing the techniques that are required to operate well in the world. These are the rules and the skill set that can often be learnt in anticipation of the activity. The difference between *tékhnê* and *phrónêsis* is argued in relation to the debate as to whether medicine involves the knowledge of *tékhnê* activity or *phrónêsis* (Waring 2000). The debate itself will further thoughtfulness and deliberation about the practice of medicine and therefore, in itself, would be considered by Aristotle to be an ethical activity.

Aristotle describes *phrónêsis* as an ethical and an intellectual virtue. The essence of the virtues is that they are founded in activity, rather than in knowledge, and arise by being cultivated, exercised and practiced (Ladkin 2010). 'It is an adult trenchancy of insight into practical matters that is cultivated by training and experience' (Aristotle 1962: 1140b: 20).

Central to *phrónêsis* is the activity of deliberation about 'living well in general' or about the things which manifest our happiness in 'living well as a whole'. Thus the sense of 'doing well' is an essential concern of *phrónêsis*. Aristotle describes it thus: *phrónêsis* is a 'state grasping the truth, involving reason, and concerned with action about human goods' (1962: 1140b5). It implies further that the appreciation of 'doing well' is not according to externally created rules but rather the answers arise from within the context of the deliberating on what 'doing well' means. Hence community becomes integral in the development of *phrónêsis*.

More than this, *phrónêsis* is a particular kind of apprehension and autotelic action. The goodness of *phrónêtic* living is intrinsic; it does not aim at an end that is distinct from the activity (of living). *Phrónêsis* is an overall state of being and is inseparable from the kind of person one is.

The activity or actioning of *phrónêsis* is *prâxis*. *Prâxis* is guided by the purpose (intentionality) of *phrónêsis*. A person's action is considered to be *prâxis* if they are acting for the sake of acting rightly within the particular circumstances; that is, they are not following rules or acting for the purpose of a particular or external outcome (Kemmis 2011).

Phrónêsis, as a way of knowing, necessarily involves action and relationality, dialogue and deliberation (Ladkin 2010). Whether an action is *phrónêtic* depends on whether the person acts knowingly, chooses the act for its own sake and acts from a firm and unshakeable disposition. The example given by Aristotle (1962) is that the knowledge of the theory of moral philosophy will not result in moral behaviour. Whilst *phrónêsis* is concerned with universals, it must also recognize the particulars; it is practical, and practice is concerned with particulars. Apprehension, therefore, arises out of the deliberate (for its own sake) engagement in the particulars of the practice.

Heidegger's Transformation

Heidegger interprets the *Nicomachean Ethics* as ontology of human existence. Accordingly, the practical philosophy of Aristotle is a guiding thread in his analysis of existence (1962, 1995) according to which facticity names our unique mode of being in the world. Through his 'existential analytic', Heidegger recognizes that 'Aristotelian phenomenology' suggests three fundamental movements of life – *poiêsis*, *prâxis* and *theoría* – and that these have three corresponding dispositions: *tékhnê*, *phrónêsis* and *sophía*. Heidegger considers these as modalities of Being inherent in the structure of *Dasein* as being-in-the-world that is situated within the context of concern and care. According to Heidegger, *phrónêsis* in Aristotle's work discloses the right and proper way to be *Dasein*. This means that Heidegger sees *phrónêsis* as a mode of comportment in and towards the world, a way of orienting oneself and thus of caring-seeing-knowing and enabling a particular way of being concerned. While *tékhnê* is a way of being concerned with things and principles of production and *theoría* a way of being concerned with eternal principles, *phrónêsis* is a way of being concerned with one's life as action in relation to the lives of others and to all particular circumstances. This is the scope of *prâxis* (Smith 2003). For a rich discussion detailing the relationship between different ways of knowing and being, as well as the role of a critical *poiêtic phrónêsis*, please see Küpers (Chapter 1).

Phrónêsis is a disposition or habit which reveals the being of the action, while its deliberation is the mode of bringing about the disclosive nature of that action. In other words, deliberation is the way in which the *phrónêtic* nature of *Dasein's* insight is made manifest.

Weidenfeld (2011) argues that a number of Heidegger's meaningful activities are considered equivalent to Aristotle's *phrónêsis*. A particular situation is a primary determinant for *phrónêsis*. The 'in the practice' learning of practice is the preparation needed for doing the right thing in the appropriate moment and practice is learnt in the place that the practice happens. The concerns of for-the-sake-of-which (*worumwillen*) are guided by circumspection (*Umsicht*). Heidegger himself translates *phrónêsis* as *Umsicht* and 'for the sake of which' is *Dasein* itself. *Umsicht* points to the capacity for making sense of practical situations, which thereby become a phenomenological account of *phrónêsis*. 'Whenever we have something to contribute or perform, circumspection gives us the route for proceeding with it, the means of carrying it out, the right opportunity, the appropriate moment' (Heidegger 1962: 216).

An example is that of the teacher, who learns what is needed to be an effective teacher only in the classroom in front of students (situatedness). *Tékhnê* alone cannot create excellence in a teacher, and the idea of poor teaching does not eventuate because of poor technical skills alone. The discerning of what is required to be excellent and the embedding of those skills is through circumspection, which occurs through the experience of teaching. The knowledge does not arise in detached reflection, rather it is revealed through the experience and doing of teaching as a *phrónêtic prâxis*.

Heidegger's adoption of Aristotle's *phrónêsis* is broadened rather brilliantly by a further level of conceptualization. Because it is the person him or herself who is ultimately the judge or referral point about the relative benefit of the knowing how to act, Heidegger includes conscience (*Gewissen*) as further implicated in *phrónêsis*. In wishing to act well, one is concerned about one's own 'to-be' rather than another's assessment of acting well.

The aspect that appears most relevant to Heidegger's conceptualization of *phrónêsis* is that it concerns what is good for the resolute deliberator him/herself. Resoluteness is that which brings *Dasein* through the anticipation of its own possibilities to choose authenticity, thus it discloses possibilities of existence, the potential-for-being that each *Dasein* possesses.

Weidenfeld (2011) suggests that conscience is an extreme form of circumspection and is tied to the moment of vision. This is the moment which recognizes the unique features of the actual situation. Examples of this include humour where a situation shows up as funny; moments of insight or vision arise because of the 'resolute' individual that discloses them as such. Thus humour only makes sense in relation to the particular situation. Further, conscience respects the norms and behaviours that are particular to that situation. *Phrónêsis* discloses the concrete ways of being within a particular situation and it is this disclosure that gives rise to self-understanding. Within the hermeneutic dialogue process, disclosure arises through the reflection of 'being with the question'. For Heidegger, *phrónêsis* is a form of self-knowledge that is concerned with self-understanding and thereby connected to conscience and deliberation.

Overall, Heidegger shows how *phrónêsis* discloses the concrete possibilities of being in a situation, as the starting point of meaningful action, processed with resolution, while facing the contingencies of life. However, in spite of Heidegger's interpretation of Aristotle inspiring practical philosophy, his ontologization has been criticized as closing *prâxis* within a horizon of solipsistic decisions (Volpi 2007).

The Transition to Gadamer

In Gadamerian hermeneutics, *phrónêsis* is connected to practice whereby reflexive understanding itself is understood as a way of being through having ontological significance, and through being situated in a hermeneutic context. *Phrónêsis* is a kind of knowing that is conceptualized as an experience with both historical and dialectic meaning and as such, is more than a perceptual act of knowing. Such an act of knowing is like an encounter or an event (Palmer 1969).

Gadamer disagrees with Hegel's concept of experience whereby it involves a restructuring of awareness and a new object of knowledge is generated or born out of it (Palmer 1969). Rather, experience fulfils itself through the openness to experience (Gadamer 1984: 320): 'what is properly gained from all experience then, is to know what is. But "what is", here, is not this or that thing, but "what cannot be done away with"'. That which cannot be done away with includes tradition where tradition has the same meaning in experience as text has in relation to hermeneutics. We necessarily belong to a tradition; which exists before we do. We may or may not be conscious of it, but we always already find ourselves within a tradition which influences and shapes our existence and thinking. Historicality becomes significant, as historical thinking has to account for its own history. Similarly our thinking needs to take account of the traditions in which we find ourselves. Finding out about such a matter is a continuous process and as Gadamer says, we are always 'on the way' to such self-knowledge. In relation to the dialectic aspect of *phrónêsis*, Gadamer describes the concept of horizon as all that can be seen (or known) from a particular position or vantage point. Horizons are thereby both limited and finite and at the same time fluid and changing.

Gadamer describes *phrónêsis* as the action of opening oneself to the truth that speaks through tradition. *Phrónêsis* therefore serves as a model for hermeneutics as it is a mode of uncovering truth in action. Moreover, the way towards knowledge and the understanding of a horizon is a dialectical movement with another. Whilst each person is grounded in their own situation, each horizon is enlarged and enriched through a fusion of horizons between the speaker and listeners. It is through this dialogue that we gain knowledge of ourselves. As Sandy (2011: 275) suggests, 'Gadamer's treatment of *phrónêsis* emphasizes the openness of conversation, ongoing participation that may lead to friendship, and processes for deliberating on the common good'. Accordingly, he focuses largely on the communicative and the creative dimensions of practical wisdom.

Dialogue, Disruption and the Intersubjective Space

A senior manager in a large telecommunications organization embarked on his PhD preoccupied by the word 'stupid'. His sense of frustration was the extent of 'stupid' decisions taken in his workplace, including 'stupid' actions of some managers, the waste of money and time, general poor communication and, of course, the frustration of his inability to change the culture. As a group, we listened carefully to the candidate's experience. Focusing on the word 'stupid', we noticed the emotions that were arising and through the conversation built an understanding of how 'stupid' as a phenomenon manifests. In the process, we uncovered some powerful insights into the nature of being a manager, into the nature of the student himself and into the nature of the workplace.

Robert Romanyshyn, author of *The Wounded Researcher* (2007), names the experience of disruption that may lead to undertaking a PhD as a kind of wounding. He suggests that the linking with vulnerability actually cements the candidate to their topic. Romanyshyn describes this as a shift from the tough-minded neutral observer to the vulnerable observer.

Through the engagement in the Circle with his experience (of 'stupid'), the candidate faced his historicality: the traditions that he emerges out of, his work life expectations, personal ethics and the situatedness of the business of telecommunications companies. His horizon became known to himself and to the others. The dialectic of conversation meant that his horizon fused with others through being heard and understood. The historical and the dialectic aspects of the experience led to a transformation of the phenomenon and he is now reviewing management practice in relation to anomalies and paradoxes. Furthermore, 'anomaly' is not for him a detached but an embodied concept that describes a wide range of work experiences. The insights that have arisen and the action that has been adopted would have been unlikely without the dialectic with his actual experience. This is consistent with the Heideggerian proposition that to question is to be in question and thus the research questions emerge out of the way he is in question in the being in of his professional practice.

When meaning arises out of intersubjective communication that is orientated towards mutual understanding, it corroborates Habermas' (1971) term, 'intersubjective co-creativity'. Intersubjective agreement is the foundation of consensual scientific knowledge established between communicating individuals. This becomes like a mutual beholding where the experience of consciousness arises as a felt experience as a result of the encounter. Further, it is through this network of linguistically mediated interactions that self-knowledge emerges (Bernstein 1988).

Gadamer (1998) speaks of how a hermeneutic approach actually embraces perspective as the only way through which understanding is made possible. The concrete instance provides the access to understanding (also the part to access the whole or vice versa). A phenomenon such as 'stupid' would be disavowed in most academic environments. However, its expression provided a unique horizon for the candidate and the group. The continued deliberation on the phenomenon has given rise to new insight and action. The intersubjective environment provided the creative forum for the phenomenon to be described, understood and interpreted.

Management and Professional Practice

Whilst some candidates will pursue the PhD for professional promotion, especially an academic career, the majority of our candidates decide to do a PhD because of a sense of disruption, discomfort or curiosity within their professional lives as consultants or managers. They are driven by their particular experience of their practices, bringing a powerful intention of caring to their work and they therefore already have a kind of embodied knowledge that is more than they can tell or speak of. This is the source of their intentionality that appears to provide the grist for their entire thesis. Moreover, it is within their *prâxis* as professionals in the world of management that *phrónêsis* is sought. Due to space constrictions, I offer one anecdote which shows the shift to action that has resolution and conviction and arises out of self-knowledge. It reflects a significant shift in judgement with regard to a fundamental principle of his professional practice.

He has been an independent consultant project manager in information technology for over 20 years. He was troubled by the inhumane expectations that arise within a scientific approach to project management where every project is considered a failure. Through his research, which included the reflection on project management as a phenomenon from within project management, he has taken a 'hermeneutic turn' and reconfigured his ways of thinking about project management. He recently headed and completed a $15 million project for a major airline in record time (nine months) and maintained the best possible relationships within the work environment. The client was satisfied with the outcomes. He ran the entire project by using a hermeneutic rather than a positivist approach to project management. He describes how the first third of the project time was building relationships and clarifying the goals and objectives for the project. Furthermore, only when every stakeholder had reached agreement on the simple two-page document outlining the goals did the application begin.

This candidate has integrated a hermeneutic approach to his professional practice, and recognized the significance of careful listening and connection in order to operationalize a project effectively. He has broken from traditional practices and taken action that reflects his subtle or tacit knowledge of his profession.

Research: Embodied Knowing and Understanding

By wisdom – I mean an often ineffable knowing born of direct experience, a kind of intuitive pragmatism that works to the extent that it takes account of the whole. It is inclusive and invariably involves empathy and compassion. (de Quincey 2005: 36)

A senior army Officer is doing his PhD on leadership. He remembers the pictures of past war heroes that his father used to show him as a child and shows these same photos to the group. Then he speaks with some pain of his relationship with his father. He thereby situates and understands his passion and his pain that surround the phenomenon of leadership for him.

Through the engagement with his historicality, this candidate has arrived at a point of embodied knowing about leadership and his research that shapes his relationship with the phenomenon of leadership. The presence of the group assisted this candidate to connect with the moment of vision whereby the features of that situation could be clearly recognized.

For Gadamer, the desire to seek understanding is also the desire to be understood by another. Genuinely speaking one's mind is not simply about explication but rather encompasses the idea of relationship: of involvement with someone. This process of developing a point of view is a process of developing the not-yet-fully-understood aspects of your subject more clearly into focus. 'To reach an understanding with one's partner in a dialogue is not merely a matter of total self-expression and the successful assertion of one's point of view, but a transformation into a communion, in which we do not remain who we were' (Gadamer 1998: 341).

It is interesting to notice that the word *conscientia* means 'knowing with' others (de Quincey 2005). Thus, originally the word 'consciousness' implied a dialogic process. To be conscious means that two or more people are privy to the process of insight emergence.

Gadamer illuminates his clear dismissal of knowledge as merely conceptual data. The act of knowing is closer to the action of perception. 'There is no such thing as a method of learning to ask questions; of learning to see what needs to be questioned' (Gadamer 1998: 329). He says thinking gives rise to questioning and that all this transpires in the art of conducting real conversation. In this situation, knowing becomes a happening; it is an experience, a kind of real life understanding that arises in the moment which we may even call wisdom (Ibid.).

Management author Nonaka (2004) writes about organizational knowledge and its creation. Consistent with Gadamer (1998), he suggests that creative dialogues give rise to tacit knowledge and that this occurs through images (experience/perceptions) being shared through metaphorical processes and merging perspectives. He argues that authentic knowledge comes about through a spiralling movement between the explicit and the tacit dimensions of knowledge. Such knowledge is enriched and enlarged for individuals and organizations and gives rise to building a 'truly humanistic knowledge society' (Nonaka 2004: 197).

In his book *Radical Knowing*, de Quincey (2005: 58) says: 'Intention is an expression of who we are into the world – it is sourced in the self and then directed outward'. The human experience is central in the act of knowing, the awareness of one's individual horizons and the fusion with others.

Most of the candidates' professional lives and work, their *prâxis*, has been significantly affected through their engagement with the Circle. Through the action of the candidate coming to 'know' his or her subject through the practice of being in question with others, through the challenge of the dialogue, through the deliberations, their intentions achieve authority and validation.

When a group meets regularly there is the potential for each person to become a conduit for others' learning and knowing and thus an intersubjective space of knowing arises. To appreciate the effect of the Circle from a research perspective is best exemplified by candidates' comments in response to the question of what they appreciate about their experience of the Circle: *the positive and non-competitive environment; everything becomes relevant; embracing alternative ways of thinking; supporting individual ways of thinking and individual voices; deepening understanding of what it means to do research; the opportunity of listening and being listened to; the opportunity to practice silence, respect and spiritual ideas; the opportunity to share your stories – successes and celebrations; it offers a real emotional climate; I was doing someone else's thesis, now I'm doing my own.*

Higher Education: Towards a 'Gentle Empiricism'

Arthur Zajonc (in Palmer and Zajonc 2010), scientist and educator, expresses the goals of the educational process through situating education within the paradigm of the new sciences. Heisenberg's uncertainty principle, dating back to the 1920s, has long ago specified that the goal of research is no longer about nature itself, but rather about the researcher's investigation of nature. The researcher therefore necessarily becomes implicated in any research conducted. With the world not independent from the knower, the conscious human being is necessarily part of any findings and knowledge becomes more of an event than an object, with human experience at the forefront of what is found.

Gadamer would agree that the real work of researching is to extend experience and to use reason and reflection to find the possible interrelationships of experience. Goethe (in Bortoft 1996: 223) suggests that 'every object well contemplated opens a new organ of perception in us'. The capacity to approach the object of our attention, the phenomenon at hand, without distorting it or changing it requires gentleness, a kind of 'gentle empiricism' (*zarte Empirie*).

The greatest impediment to understanding a thing or phenomenon comes from the need to explain it in terms of something else. Explanation results in each thing becoming an instance or example that can analytically be seen to belong to a group, perhaps a bit more or less like that group. Understanding a phenomenon is a way of grasping it as a whole. Moreover, Wittgenstein (in Bortoft 1996) describes understanding as the seeing of the connections intrinsic to the phenomenon. He appreciates this kind of seeing as an imaginative capacity, operating beyond the senses, and demanding a particular level of engagement in the researcher to be receptive to the phenomenon in its wholeness. It is as though this imaginative sense fuels the ongoing inquiry creating what Zajonc (Palmer and Zajonc 2010: 94) refers to as a 'contemplative inquiry'.

In discussing the aspirations of education, Kemmis (2011) longs for the goals that the ancients in Aristotle's time had of bringing people to learn wisdom so that the world would be worth living in. Education was not geared towards the skills of a field of expertise. He suggests that education is best suited towards giving people the particular kinds of experiences that will lead them to wisdom. Moreover, practice-based approaches are best suited to this. Correspondingly, the Circle provides such a practice-based education and experience of *prâxis* within research and an academic institution!

Bernstein (1988) provides an engaging analysis of Gadamer's interpretation of Aristotle's *phrónêsis*. He offers an ultimate higher education compliment by suggesting that Gadamer himself has understood, interpreted and appropriated Aristotle's text. Furthermore, he suggests that Gadamer's interpretation is an exemplar of hermeneutical understanding and that Aristotle's analysis of *phrónêsis* serves as a model for hermeneutics; it is a mode of uncovering truth in action. As a hermeneutical understanding is itself a form of practical reasoning and practical knowledge, it is a form of *phrónêsis*! (Bernstein 1988).

There is little provided by the academic environment to prepare candidates for their actual experience of PhD research. It is a pathway that is fraught with an experience of learning that causes many candidates to stumble and fail. I suggest that this is more significant within the interpretivist paradigms where the dissertation path is mapped through the unfolding engagement. The hermeneutic dialectic process provides a kind of gentle empiricism where the learning is engaging and the candidate's needs for a satisfying higher education experience are sated. Over the years, my observation is that the mood of the group has become both lighter and also more considered. As a group, we judge less, respond slower and with greater deliberation. A new kind of respect appears to be developing: the respect for difference. In a letter to Bernstein (1988: 264), Gadamer comments on the non-exceptionality of conflict: '*Phrónêsis* is always the process of distinguishing and choosing what one considers to be right'. Perhaps as a group, in a higher education environment, incorporating a 'gentle empiricism', we are also learning judgement!

Conclusion

The appropriate Aristotelian dialectic on this case study could be: is the Circle good for the practice of research?; is the Circle good for the practice of higher education?; and is the Circle good for the practice of management? In response, Gadamer (1998: 319) may reply: 'the dialectic of experience has its own fulfilment not in definitive knowledge, but in that openness to experience that is encouraged by experience itself'. That none of the participants have dropped out of their PhDs or the Circle and that their enthusiasm for their research seems to increase are pointers to a conclusion that the experience of the Circle is itself satisfying. There is an active interest in continuing the conversation.

This chapter has been written in a way to be true to the spirit of *phrónêsis*: as experience, as practical and as dialectic between the author and the reader. I have chosen to write in a format that is not simply about observation or objective knowing. Rather, I have been confronted by what I write through standing within the experience of the content. My understanding and appreciation of the Circle has been stretched remarkably, as has my readiness to critique its action. 'Can wisdom be taught?' is a question that is often posed in academic circles. I notice that through the *prâxis* and the actual engagement with the Circle over four years, through the practice of writing and the continuous reflecting on the Circle, rich learning has occurred for myself as supervisor and educator. With Kemmis (2011: 13), I agree that wisdom cannot be taught and 'we can give people the kind of experiences that will lead them to wisdom. I think this is the key role of practice-based education'. Peculiar to the nature of wisdom is a kind of humility such that reflection on one's own actions as 'wise' is a particularly 'unwise' position. Furthermore, should we be graced by the presence of wisdom, it should not linger in consciousness for more than a fleeting moment, and even that may be too long! Thus, we can invite wisdom without specifically teaching it; we can aspire to wisdom and yet must avoid naming its presence in our own actions.

Moreover, with this in mind comes a question in relation to managers learning applied wisdom, with humility: given that leaders are called upon to develop excellence in judgement, could a practice with the goal of developing an understanding of *phrónêsis* be used beneficially with senior managers as a tool towards developing such judgement capacity?

Green (2009) suggests that the case study as a way of documenting professional practice could usefully be brought back into our attention as researchers and as practitioners. Moreover, this is not simply to rewrite more of the same case studies but rather to reconsider its usage in what he calls 'a qualitative, practice-theoretical mode of meta-analysis' (Green 2009: 15). This chapter has attempted to achieve a richly descriptive weaving of anecdote and narrative towards capturing a sense of the practice of the Circle. At the same time, using the lens of *phrónêsis* has offered layers of observation, understanding, interpretation and judgement to the analysis that has elevated the case and brought an insightful engagement. With other authors such as Polkinghorne (2007) and Flyvbjerg (2004), I believe that the use of case study to inquire into practice provides an invaluable resource.

One question that applies to the use of a professional learning group working with cases is: with the goal of discovering ways of thinking that did not previously exist, could it be that a professional learning group could surpass the capacity of a single manager to find creative solutions to arising issues?

Through the writing up of this case study, another question that begs consideration is the potential generalizability of the practice of a hermeneutic phenomenological dialectic approach within management practice and within academic environments. Whilst some consideration has been given to this topic throughout the chapter, it is useful to reiterate some of the preconditions. These may include: the topic is personally meaningful to all participants (intentionality); that each person participates without coercion (autotelic); and that participants are prepared for a disciplined inquiry where purpose and direction can be mutually created (intersubjectivity).

A further major consideration is the critical role of the facilitators or leaders of such a group. A manager working with their team would need to develop excellent facilitation skills and be open to collaboration especially in managing the intersubjective power dynamic. Having found that the most useful training for this role has been the collaboration and reflection between the two supervisors, I would suggest that two facilitators or managers could be valuable. Further, before beginning this work, potential members of the group would best be educated and prepared for the nature of this practice, as each person plays a vital role in its creation; actually each person takes up a leadership role. A question that comes to mind is: given that the practitioner dialogue described has a clear developmental or formative aspect for the individuals, could a learning group of the nature of the Circle be used to enhance or stimulate leadership capacity (or further develop leadership) for managers?

It may be the case that the corporate world and the academic environment remain too hierarchical and fixed in their patterns of learning and operating. However, as suggested by Titchen and Manley (2006), the process of transformation that could be achieved through working towards attaining *phrónêsis* could enable a kind of human flourishing to be considered a worthy goal in human learning processes. Given that learning is significant to management as it is in educational institutions, a question that begs further research is: how can *phrónêsis* be applied as a goal towards developing thoughtfulness and judgement and gearing our learning towards the 'good', as a goal for the society, the environment and the self?

References

Aristotle 1962. *Nicomachean Ethics*, translated with introduction and notes by Martin Oswald. Indianapolis: The Bobbs-Merrill Company.

Bernstein, R.J. 1988. *Beyond Objectivism and Relativism: Science, Hermeneutics, and Praxis*. Philadelphia: University of Pennsylvania Press.

Bohm, D. 1990. *On Dialogue*. Ojai: David Bohm Seminars.

Bortoft, H. 1996. *The Wholeness of Nature: Goethe's Way of Science*. Edinburgh: Floris Books.

Coulter, D. and Wiens, J.R. 2002. Educational judgment: linking the actor and the spectator. *Educational Researcher*, 31(4), 15–25.

De Quincey, C. 2005. *Radical Knowing: Understanding Consciousness through Relationship*. Rochester: Park Street Press.

Flyvbjerg, B. 2002. One researcher's praxis story. *Journal of Planning Education and Research*, 21(4), 353–66.

Flyvbjerg, B. 2004. Phronetic planning research: theoretical and methodological reflections. *Planning Theory & Practice*, 5(3), 283–306.

Gadamer, H.G. 1977. *Philosophical Hermeneutics*, translated and edited by D.E. Linge. Berkeley: University of California Press.

Gadamer, H.G. 1984. *Truth and Method*. New York: The Crossroad Publishing Company.

Green, B. 2009. Introduction: understanding and researching professional practice, in *Understanding and Researching Professional Practice*, edited by B. Green. Rotterdam: Sense Publishers, 1–18.

Habermas, J. 1971. *Knowledge and Human Interests*, translated by Jeremy Shapiro. Boston: Beacon Press.

Heidegger, M. 1962. *Being and Time*. Oxford: Blackwell.

Heidegger, M. 1995. *Aristotle's Metaphysics*. Bloomington: Indiana University Press.

Higgs, J., Paterson, M. and Kinsella, E.A. 2012. Hermeneutic inquiry: interpretation and understanding in research practice. *Contemporary Psychotherapy*, 4(1) [Online]. Available at: http://contemporarypsychotherapy.org/vol-4-no-1-spring-2012/hermeneutic-inquiry/ [accessed: 29 July 2012].

Kemmis, S. 2011. Pedagogy, praxis and practice-based higher education, in *Practice-Based Education*, edited by J. Higgs, R. Barnett and S. Billet. Rotterdam: Sense, 1–17.

Ladkin, D. 2010. Book Review on Olav Eikeland, The Ways of Aristotle: Aristotelian Phronesis, Aristotelian Philosophy of Dialogue, and Action Research. *Action Research*, 8(4), 444–8.

Nonaka, I. 2004. A dynamic theory of organizational knowledge creation, in *How Organizations Learn*, edited by K. Starkey, S. Tempest and A. Mckinlay. Thomson, London, 165–201.

Palmer, R.E. 1969. *Hermeneutics*. Evanston: Northwestern University Press.

Palmer, P. and Zajonc, A. 2010. *The Heart of Higher Education*. San Francisco: Jossey-Bass.

Polkinghorne, D.E. 2007. Language and meaning: data collection in qualitative research. *Qualitative Inquiry*, 13(4), 471–86.

Romanyshyn, R. 2007. *The Wounded Researcher*. Spring Journal Books, New Orleans.

Sandy, M. 2011. Practical beauty and the legacy of pragmatism: generating theory for community-engaged scholarship. *Interchange*, 42(3), 261–85.

Smith, D.L. 2003. Intensifying phronesis: Heidegger, Aristotle, and rhetorical culture. *Philosophy and Rhetoric*, 36(1), 77–102.

Titchen, A. and Manley, K. 2006. Spiralling towards transformational action research: philosophical and practical journeys. *Educational Action Research*, 14(3), 333–56.

Volpi, F. 2007. In whose name?: Heidegger and 'practical philosophy'. *European Journal of Political Theory*, 6(1), 31–51.

Waring, D. 2000. Why the practice of medicine is not a phronetic activity. *Theoretical Medicine and Bioethics*, 21(2), 139–51.

Weidenfeld, M.C. 2011. Heidegger's appropriation of Aristotle: phronesis, conscience, and seeing through the one. *European Journal of Political Theory*, 10(2), 254–76.

3 Cultivation of Wisdom in the Theravada Buddhist Tradition: Implications for Contemporary Leadership and Organization

PETER CASE

Introduction

Although by no means mainstream, there has been a growing interest in wisdom studies amongst Western scholars in recent decades.[1] This is an encouraging development in light of the general neglect of the concept, if not its outright eschewal, on the part of sciences and humanities which have been largely preoccupied with *rational* explanation and *cognitive* representation of human conduct in the post-Enlightenment period. Indeed, in the core discipline of philosophy, any serious inquiry into the *practical* dimension of wisdom, that is, study that extends beyond mere historical interest in the term, has largely been abandoned. This state of affairs is perhaps typified by John Kekes' terse essay on 'philosophy' in *The Oxford Companion to Philosophy* and his observation:

> *Although wisdom is what philosophy is meant to be a love of, little attention has been paid to this essential component of good lives in post-classical Western philosophy. It is perhaps for this reason that those in search of it often turn to the obscurities of oriental religions for enlightenment. (Honderich 1995: 912)*

The irony here is self-evident and the fact that this extract represents a significant proportion of the entire entry for 'philosophy' in Honderich's *Companion* also speaks subtextual volumes about the widespread disinterest in wisdom. Quite why Western scholarship has, in general, lost its appetite for philosophy in the practical sense – particularly in light of its central importance within classical understandings of knowledge and ethics – is an

---

1   For a comprehensive multidisciplinary bibliography of wisdom-related literature see Trowbridge (2010). For a recent review of literature and research developments within the discipline of psychology see Staudinger and Glück (2011).

intriguing and complex question that I shall not engage with directly in this chapter. For those interested, accounts of the development of Western knowledge offered by Hadot (2006) and Pieper (1999 [1952], 2007 [1966]) are highly instructive. Case, Simpson and French (2012) offer reflections on the denuding of theory in contemporary organization and leadership studies, and argue (Case, French and Simpson 2011) for the reinvigoration and reconnection of these fields with practical forms of wisdom.

My purpose in this chapter is to take up what Kekes rather uncharitably refers to as the 'obscurities of oriental religions' for further enlightenment on the theme of practical wisdom. I do not share Kekes' view that the religious and spiritual traditions of the orient are obscure; they only appear so to those with an orientalist (Said 1978) or ethnocentric attitude which permits them to overlook and dismiss the rich cultures in which these traditions have flourished and developed for centuries. Such a view also ignores the undeniable fact that, following a lengthy scholarly interest in oriental philosophy and religion on the part of Westerners, many of these traditions and their associated spiritual practices have now been 'imported' into Western cultures (for example, in Europe, North America and Australia) and have taken a firm root (see Batchelor 1994).

What can be learned about wisdom from non-Western and spiritual traditions, philosophies and related practices and what, furthermore, might be the implications for modes of organizing, leadership and organizational engagement? If one accepts a degree of universality within the human condition and the premise that aspects of leadership, organization and organizing are both transcultural and transhistorical, then it seems to me that a great deal can be learned from such non-Western traditions and philosophies. In this chapter, I shall focus attention exclusively on the conception of wisdom and its practical cultivation as advanced within the Theravada school of Buddhism (Gombrich 1988, Nārada 1980). The latter is a branch of Buddhism, dominant in contemporary Southeast Asia, whose genealogy can be traced, via its monastic order, directly back to Gotama (Gautama in Sanskrit, Skt. hereafter) Buddha some two and a half millennia ago. It is also one of the many traditions hailing from the orient that, through processes of migration, has been taken up by practitioners in the West (Batchelor 1994). Buddhism is of direct relevance to the theme of this book insofar as the cultivation of wisdom is, arguably, its principal raison d'être. My purpose is to outline the basic forms of wisdom embodied within the formal philosophical teachings of Theravada Buddhism and the course of training set out for those who wish to cultivate them (Nānamoli 1979, 1984). I base my contribution on 25 years of study and training in Buddhist meditation, some of which time was spent as an ordained monk. This chapter thus combines my practical interest in Buddhism with my professional interest in organization and leadership studies.

Buddhism (*Dhamma-vinaya*): A Brief Overview

My point of departure for this enquiry into Buddhist wisdom lies in ancient, non-modern history; namely, the spiritual teaching of Gotama Buddha, his founding of a monastic order and establishment of rules of training which inform monastic and lay life (Gombrich 1988). Siddhartha Gotama was born into a wealthy family in northern India, modern day Nepal, in c.563 BC. His father, Suddhodana, was a ruler of the Sāka clan and kingdom, and, accordingly, Gotama enjoyed a very privileged upbringing as a young prince. At the age of 28, however, confronted by the realities of death, disease and other forms of human suffering, he decided to renounce worldly life and become a wandering mendicant. After perfecting skills in concentration meditation and experiencing the deep tranquillity that this yielded, he was still dissatisfied and embarked, instead, on a series of ascetic practices (some of which brought him close to death). Following seven years of spiritual searching and maturation, he discovered what has become known as the 'Middle Way' between sensual indulgence and the austerities of self-denial. He was 35 years old when, it is said, he realized Enlightenment whilst sitting under a tree on the bank of the river Neranjarā near Gaya in modern Bihar (Nānamoli 1984, Nārada 1980, Rahula 1985).

Although initially reluctant to teach, Gotama discovered that he was able to assist others in coming to the same subtle insight that he had alighted upon and, subsequently, spent the remaining 45 years of his life wandering the Ganges valley teaching monks and lay people alike. What became known as 'Buddhism' began as *dhamma-vinaya* which, leaving aside nuances of translation and etymology, roughly means a 'path of discipline leading to insight'. Hundreds of his followers developed the wisdom of the Buddha (the 'Enlightened' one) and benefited not only from supra-mundane insight (which I shall discuss shortly) but also from Gotama's highly practical understanding of how to live a good and rewarding life. Having left this rich legacy, Gotama himself died at the age of 80 in c.483 BC.

Buddhism became a highly influential religion with variants and an international diaspora that saw the teachings spread north via Tibet to China, where it became *Chan*, then down into Japan where it gave rise to Zen (both *Chan* and *Zen* are phonetic adaptations of the Pali word *jhānam* – Skt. *dhyana* – meaning simply 'meditation'). While these latter traditions, known collectively as the Mahayana ('Greater Vehicle') schools, passed on the teachings using a mixture of Sanskrit and local languages, the earliest teachings were transmitted and preserved via the aural tradition of collective recitation within the Theravada monastic order. The Theravada tradition spread southward through India to Sri Lanka and the countries of Southeast Asia (Thailand, Myanmar, Laos, Cambodia and Vietnam).

Within these various Buddhist traditions – Mahayana, Zen, Theravada – there still exist living spiritual or mystical traditions whose teachers focus not so much on *religious* observance as on coming to realize the ultimate goal of the Buddha's teaching, that is, *nibbāna* (Skt. *Nirvāna*) or the cessation of the suffering associated with subjective attachments (see, for example, Kornfield 1977).

In approximately 80 BC, the oral teaching of the Theravada order was committed to script recorded on palm parchment by Sinhalese monks at a monastery called Aluvihara. Although the oral recitation of the *Dhamma* (the Buddha's teachings) persists to this day, the *Pali Canon* is now available in textual form in many languages. This *Canon* is arranged in three so-called 'baskets' (*tipitaka*) as follows: 1) the *Vinaya Pitaka* (numbering five books) which deals with the rules governing the monastic order and training; 2) the *Sutta Pitaka* (15 books) which record the Buddha's discourses to monks and lay people; and 3) the *Abhidhamma Pitaka* (seven books) which consists of a phenomenological and philosophical psychology which analyses consciousness and conditionality in extremely fine detail.

Pali is an Indo-Aryan language closely related to Sanskrit and now, rather like classical Greek and Latin in Europe, extinct as a spoken language except for its use in religious chanting, scholarly discussion and recitation of canonical teachings (Warder 2001). It is widely held that Magadhan, the language most likely spoken by the Buddha, was a Pali vernacular. Pali does not have an exclusive script (largely because of its oral origins) but has been transliterated in scripts that adopted the Buddhist religion, notably Sinhalese, Thai, Burmese, Lao and Cambodian. Nineteenth- and early twentieth-century Western scholars of Pali also undertook the task of rendering Pali into Latin script so that it would be accessible for wider Western readerships. The combined corpus of the *Pali Canon* stretches to over 40 bound volumes in English translation, many of them quite sizeable.

THE FOUR NOBLE TRUTHS AND THE EIGHTFOLD PATH

The purpose of following the Buddha's teaching as documented in the *Pali Canon* is to realize *nibbāna*, Enlightenment, and thereby to eradicate suffering. Common to all major forms of Buddhism – Theravada and varieties of Mahayana – are the core teachings of Gotama summarized as the four Noble Truths: 1) there is suffering (*dukkha*); 2) there is a cause of suffering, namely all forms of craving and attachment; 3) there is the cessation of suffering (*nibbāna* literally means 'extinction'); and 4) there is a path to the cessation of suffering, known as the Buddha's 'Eightfold Path'. With respect to the fourth and final Noble Truth, as its name suggests, the Eightfold Path contains eight path factors: right understanding, right thinking, right action, right speech, right livelihood, right concentration, right effort and right mindfulness. These are grouped into three sections as follows: *pannā* (wisdom), *sila* (ethical discipline) and *samādhi* (meditation). The classical Buddhist scholar Budhaghosa (c.400 AD) wrote a comprehensive compendium of the Buddha's teaching which classifies these three elements as 'paths of purification', that is, the 'purification of bodily conduct' through ethical discipline, the 'purification of mind' through meditative discipline and the 'purification of view' through insight and wisdom (Nānamoli 1979).

Two Forms of Wisdom

There are two forms of wisdom (*pannā* – Pali) acknowledged in the Theravada tradition (Nynatiloka 1972): mundane (that pertaining to everyday human and non-human worlds) and the supra-mundane (that pertaining to the phenomenological realm of meditation and insights deriving from meditative practice). With respect to the mundane universe, Buddhism recognizes truths and laws relating to the world as it is conventionally experienced: laws governing material physics, biological organisms and causality in these domains. Importantly, however, unlike Western philosophy it also asserts that there is a law governing the complex interrelationship between moral conduct and its results. This is known as the law of *kamma-vipāka* (action-resultant). *Kamma* (Skt. *Karma*) translates as 'action', while the result of action is *vipāka* (often in the West we mistakenly take *karma* to refer to the results of action, as in the phrase 'bad karma'). According to Buddhism, we inhabit a universe which is made up of interdependent conditioned and conditioning phenomena. Human actions of body, speech and mind form an integral part of this cosmic whole. Thus one's actions in what we might call a 'participatory universe' will have material and psychological consequences for oneself and others. In general terms, if one acts in a self-centred or self-interested manner, the *consequences* of these actions will rebound in negative and personally painful ways. By contrast, unselfish actions (those primarily motivated by and directed toward the welfare of others) will have pleasant results in the future. This law carries particular normative implications for how one should conduct oneself in the mundane world. The precepts for lay followers of Buddhism, for example, are aimed at minimizing and, ideally, eliminating what the Buddha colourfully referred to as the 'guilty dreads' that follow from unwise action.

So what would constitute wise ethical conduct? This is often framed in terms of the avoidance of unwise conduct rather than in terms of positive imperatives. It is concisely summarized, for example, in the five precepts which lay followers strive to keep, that is, undertaking the rules of training to abstain from: killing or harming living beings; taking that which is not given; wrongful or harmful speech; drinking alcoholic beverages or taking mind-altering drugs; and wrongful forms of sexual conduct (for example, promiscuity, rape, paedophilia). A lay person following a training in meditation typically takes on extra rules during a period of retreat (for example, abstaining from handling money), while monks and nuns have many more detailed rules to uphold. The latter range from those which can lead to expulsion from the order (such as killing a human being or making false claims about meditative attainments) through to minor rules that dictate, for instance, the way robes should be worn, how and when meals should be consumed and so forth.

The law of *kamma-vipāka* is, as the Buddha maintained, extremely complex and its intricacy is not at all easy to comprehend. However, he did set out some broad correspondences between choices of action and the kinds of results that might follow. Take, for example, the area of speech. Such acts as lying and deceitful speech, according to Buddhism, are likely to result in the perpetrator being perceived and treated as untrustworthy by others and also being prone to vilification and abusive speech: indulging in gossip or frivolous speech results in a person not being believed by others, while slander is likely to result in friendships ending without apparent cause. By contrast, unselfish action, such as generosity, leads to the acquisition of wealth; serving others in some capacity leads to one gaining a good reputation and so on. In other words, according to Buddhism, there is a moral economy to action and a form of natural justice that operates intrinsically within the universe.

The manner in which results (*vipāka*) of unwise action ripen is difficult to predict as it is bound up with many other non-*kammic* factors that act as past and present supporting conditions for any given action. Nonetheless, the general principles are, I suggest, open to subjective empirical observation. By striving to keep the precepts, for example, for a sustained period of time it is possible to observe, phenomenologically, whether or not one's well-being improves and also to discern the connection between acting wisely (according to these principles) and its subjective and intersubjective effects. Of course, such a claim is not open to *objective proof* according to the forms of criteria that are applied within Western empirical sciences but this, I contend, does not render it unempirical.

That there is subjective *benefit* from avoiding unwise action and pursuing 'the good' is precisely what makes *kamma-vipāka* a *mundane* matter within Buddhist cosmology. It is action, whether for good or ill, pursued with a sense of *subjective* purpose that ties the actor to the wheel of birth and death. We *produce* and *reproduce* ourselves as *subjects*, as it were, from moment-to-moment in the ethical volitions and choices we make with respect to thought, speech and action. This process of conditioned and conditioning interaction is represented in what is called the 'law of conditioned dependent origination' (*paticca-samuppāda*; Skt. *Pratītyasamutpāda*), which charts the co-relationship and causal interdependency between different elements of consciousness.[2] The experience of *agency* in the actions we pursue is what makes us worldly creatures subject to birth and death, not only in everyday life but also, in terms of Buddhist cosmology, from life-to-life through the process of rebirth.

I have chosen to focus primarily on ethical actions and their consequences, the *sila* or ethical discipline section of the Eightfold Path, on the assumption that readers unfamiliar with Buddhist philosophy will be able to relate and compare the principles to other ethical systems with which they are familiar and also to their own subjective experience. It should be pointed out, however, that mundane wisdom also plays an important part in the other two sections of the Eightfold Path, namely *pannā* – wisdom itself – and *samādhi* or meditation. For example, it is possible to gain proficiency in *samatha* (concentration) meditation and experience deep states of bliss and tranquillity. Such experiences are categorized as 'mundane' rather than genuinely 'spiritual' as, in themselves, they do not lead to a permanent release from suffering, or the craving and attachment which produces it. The experience is very pleasant while it lasts but the experience of mental and physical release is only temporary; once concentration can no longer be sustained, it ends and one is back in the everyday world of 'normal' consciousness.

What, then, is meant by supra-mundane wisdom within this tradition? In addressing this question we perhaps momentarily lose sight of the purpose of this book and its intention of exploring *practical wisdom*. Nonetheless, I shall endeavour to explain selective aspects of supra-mundane wisdom and also consider how, for those who pursue an experiential course of training in meditation, the resulting insights carry indirect practical implications for the way they apprehend and act in the world.

Unlike many modern Western philosophies of science which, in general, contrast propositional truth with falsity and observe a logical law of excluded middle (proposition p cannot coexist with not-p), Buddhism adopts a more nuanced approach to questions of veracity. It identifies three forms of truth corresponding to three forms of reality: 1) conventional truths (*vohāra-sacca* in Pali) that relate to consensus reality as socially conditioned and constructed; 2) so-called 'ultimate' truths pertaining to ultimate reality (*paramattha-dhammā*), which reduce human experience to constituent phenomenological events and processes of consciousness; and 3) *nibbāna* or *Nirvāna* (Skt.) which refers to an intuitive experience of truth and reality that transcends duality and representation (and, in so doing, is said to remove all the personal suffering that results from attachment to conventional things from a subjective position).[3] Although forms 2 and 3 are immanent in 1, Buddhism maintains that it makes no sense to conflate the three. Form 3 is literally unspeakable. It is beyond representational duality and therefore by definition ineffable – although it is defined as a *type of knowledge*. Investigation of form 2 through meditative discipline and practice reveals that the conventions of form 1 are illusory *at this level of enquiry*; that selves, authors, *personal* intention, trees, mountains, cars, organizations, management, critique, writing are not sustainable or meaningful categories in any *ultimate* or *absolute* sense. All that exists in form 2 are transient sensory phenomena, reducible to bare serial experiences of shape and colour, sound, taste, touch and a complex host of psychological concomitants (of which volition, feeling, perception and discursive thought would be discernible elements). Repeated and patient meditative observation

---

2   For a fuller account of *paticca-samuppāda* see Nānamoli (1979).

3   See *Nyanatiloka* (1972: 124–5); Bodhi (1993: 25–6).

of experience with respect to form 2 in time prepares the mind for a mystical realization of form 3 – *nibbāna* – which is the ultimate purpose of spiritual endeavour, according to Buddhist teachings.

The main vehicle for cultivating supra-mundane wisdom within the Theravada tradition is insight (*vipassanā*) meditation, sometimes also referred to as mindfulness meditation. Unlike concentration meditations that have tranquillity as their primary objective, insight meditation aims at working toward a deep understanding of *ultimate reality* (form 2, above) and its three intrinsic 'marks' or characteristics. These marks are: the transience of all sensory phenomena (*anicca*), their propensity to cause suffering (*dukkha*) if ignored, craved for, or pushed away and their interdependence or being void of an essential self (*anattā*). The development of 'right mindfulness', alongside a level of skill in concentration and balanced effort, is what permits experiential investigation of consciousness and its characteristics. In everyday waking consciousness the mind is generally so busy and caught up in a whirl of its own perceptions, thoughts, feelings and objects of desire that discerning how these elements of mind interact with one another is practically impossible. By concentrating and calming the mind to a level where physical and mental sensation is still present – where there are perceptions, feelings and occasional thoughts – it is as though these elements are 'slowed down' and can be examined with a degree of dispassionate clarity. Too little concentration means the mind is still subject to neurotic worries, petty concerns, desire for pleasurable experience and hatred of unpleasant experience, and hence cannot be *mindful* of events occurring in the psycho-physical system. Too much concentration means that the mind gets absorbed in tranquillity to the exclusion of anything else. It is also possible to wrongly (as opposed to rightly) concentrate the mind (for example, with too much effort) and end up with a headache or simply fall asleep during seated meditation practice.

The cultivation of mindfulness is not confined exclusively to seated practice. We might liken sitting meditation to a laboratory – a special set of conditions in which experience can be observed closely – but, to be effective, the discipline of mindfulness has to be extended into everyday living. Someone taking up this practice strives to be mindful as much as they possibly can as they go about their daily business, whatever that might be. It should also be added that successful development of these skills is only possible if one adheres to ethical disciplines and precepts. This is not a *moral* imperative as much as a *practical* requirement. Persistent unwise action in daily life destabilizes the mind to the point that it is unable to achieve the necessary basic level of calm and contentment necessary to *be mindful*.

Given time and application, the set of disciplines associated with mindfulness meditation can result in a series of insights. These insights are well documented in the *Pali Canon* and the voluminous scholarly commentary on it. The fact that the course of the meditative training follows a well-defined path that has been experienced by practitioners in many different cultures, speaking many different languages and across many generations would suggest that the patterns of experience and insight it produces are universal. What then, is the supra-mundane wisdom that this training yields? Without venturing too far into the technical descriptions (see Nānamoli 1979, Sayadaw 1965), there are certain transition moments which mark profound psychological shifts in understanding of the make-up of the world-as-experienced. Theravada Buddhism identifies four key turning points of this sort. Each so-called 'fruition moment' is deeper and more profound than the preceding one and each is reached through a portal of apprehending *one* of the three characteristics of conditioned reality – *anicca* (transience), *dukkha* (suffering) or anattā (non-self or interdependence). Each insight serves to weaken the grasp that the mundane world holds on the subject. For example, if one sees at a molecular level, as it were, that every possible experience is so transient that independent objects do not exist, then it becomes impossible to crave, hate or get attached to them. Similarly, if the self or subject is seen clearly and *experientially* (not merely intellectually) to be a social construction which does not exist independently of the conditions that produce it, then the mundane world has no purchase whatsoever on it; indeed, paradoxically, 'it' never existed in the first place. The self is apprehended as a fiction that can no longer be taken as seriously as it once was. In the words of Buddhaghosa: 'For there is suffering, but none who suffers; Doing exists although there is no doer; Extinction is but no extinguished person; Although there is a path, there is no goer' (Nānamoli 1979: 587).

The Buddha himself also made a similar observation concerning the nature of insight that leads to supra-mundane wisdom and release from subjective suffering:

> *In this world … substance is seen in what is insubstantial. [Sentient creatures] are tied to their psychophysical beings and so they think that there is some substance, some reality in them. But whatever be the phenomenon through which they think of seeking their self identity, it turns out to be transitory. It becomes false, for what lasts for a moment is deceptive. The state that is not deceptive is Nibbāna … With this insight into reality their hunger ends: cessation, total calm. (Saddhatissa 1994: 89)*

Implications for Contemporary Leadership and Organization

In this section I attempt to draw links between the cultivation of Buddhist wisdom and its implications for leadership and organization in the contemporary world. Given the challenging nature of this task, what follows is more an *outline* of future avenues of enquiry than a comprehensive analysis of the possibilities.

The kind of supra-mundane wisdom that *vipassanā* meditation produces is not, in and of itself, *practical* as much as it is a liberating form of *knowledge*. Nonetheless, someone who progresses with the Buddhist path of insight or, indeed, completes the course of training can expect to enjoy many practical benefits which, in turn, have implications for the way they interact with other beings (human and non-human) and the surrounding environment. In other words, supra-mundane wisdom carries implications for, and has an effect on, the mundane world. Having perfected their ethical discipline, such individuals, for example, would have no desire to harm others. In fact, they would be *incapable* of *intentionally* causing harm through acts of thought, word or deed. Instead, they would, from their own experience, have developed a deeply compassionate eye for the suffering of others and, within their own sphere of influence, seek to alleviate it in whatever way they were disposed or able. An Enlightened person, according to Buddhist teaching, has transcended the law of *kamma-vipāka* such that all of their *doing* (mental and physical) is 'karmically neutral'; 'Doing exists although there is no doer'.

Looking at the organizational world around us, one might think it highly desirable that such individuals take up positions of leadership, authority and responsibility. The practical problem that immediately presents itself, of course, is that only a minority of people are interested in Buddhism, fewer still take up the disciplines of meditation in a committed way and still fewer progress through the paths of insight. We might also be faced with the paradox posed by Plato (1995) in *The Republic*: that whilst it might be desirable for sages, in the guise of 'philosopher kings', to take up positions of influence within the *polis*, they, above all others, would have the wisdom precisely to eschew the mantle of such worldly responsibility. They might prefer to lead a more sheltered and reflective life. But this does not necessarily follow from pursuit of the Buddhist path. It could hardly be denied, for example, that the Buddha himself was a highly active and effective leader in the world. Not only was he a remarkably skilled and multilingual teacher, he also set up and ran what became, even during his lifetime, a major organization, that is, the *Sangha* or order of monks.

Gotama's monastic order, moreover, was quite revolutionary in the socio-political context of that region and time. Individuals of any caste ('Untouchable' to 'Brahmin') were permitted to take on the rules of monastic training and, in so doing, had to renounce the imperatives of social division associated with caste (Rhys Davids [1903] 1993). Seniority was (and, within the Theravada tradition, still is) based purely on length of time spent in the order. Thus a former Brahmin monk could well be junior to an Untouchable and so forth. The detailed rules of training, designed in large measure to promote harmonious community living, combined with this simple hierarchical principle resulted in the creation of an organization that has reproduced itself in successive generations and migrated across nations and continents.

There is, I suggest, a practical wisdom to the principles, structuring and processes of this organization which helps explain why it has enjoyed such longevity. While meriting a more in-depth study, from a leadership and organizational point of view there are intrinsic lessons to be derived from the remarkable fact that the Theravada order exists now in much the same form as it did when founded two and a half millennia ago. For example, the emphasis given to harmonious community living, care for others and mutual responsibility based on ethical disciplines might have much to offer in light of the post-material challenges of the current era. I am thinking, in particular, of the impending difficulties posed by eco-crises (the threats of anthropogenic climate change, depletion of natural resources, pollution, pressures on ecosystems, food and energy security challenges and so on). Learning to live with the basic requisites of life, as required within a Buddhist monastic community, may well become more widely germane to our own affluent societies as they struggle to address and accommodate increasing demands on natural resources and the environment. One consequence of cultivating Buddhist wisdom is knowing what it takes to *walk through the world lightly*, minimizing personal and collective demands on environmental resources and being *contented with little*. Whether such a transition in outlook can be effected on a wide scale within societies that are so enamoured of consumerism (including those growing economies in Asia that appear so eager to emulate the materialism of the West) is, of course, a politically fraught question. Nonetheless, it may be helpful to begin a debate within the community of wisdom studies scholars about the adaptation of the kinds of principles and possibilities I am seeking to introduce here with respect to leadership and organization.

There may also be useful connections to make between current academic and practitioner interests in the theme of responsible leadership (Maak and Pless 2006a, 2006b, Maak 2007, Waldman and Galvin 2008) and the corollaries of developing Buddhist wisdom. In part, this relates to previous points made about environmental sensibility but also to being 'other directed' and working to reduce the sense of individual *self-importance*. From a Buddhist point of view, many individual neuroses and pathologies stem fundamentally from an inflated and unwarranted sense of self-centredness and self-concern. This has been acknowledged in the leadership field by scholars who have explored the narcissism (Maccoby 2000) and psychopathology (Furnham 2010) of those in positions of power in organizations. It would also extend to the analysis of *collective* organizational pathologies viewed from a psycho-social perspective (Kets de Vries 2006, Kets de Vries and Miller 1984, Sievers 1994), where we might see cases of collective organizational narcissism. The cultivation of individual and collective wisdom, from a Buddhist point of view, involves directly confronting self-centredness and taking practical steps (for example, through ethical discipline and meditation) to erode narcissism in both its gross and subtle forms.

Buddhism, in general, has a reputation for encouraging tolerance and an ecumenical attitude toward spirituality. If we understand Buddhism as offering *one* path to wisdom (both worldly and supra-mundane) amidst a diverse range of alternatives, it can be seen as contributing to a wider discourse and set of practices which place importance on the cultivation of *philosophy* in the literal sense. Buddhist wisdom – of the forms outlined above – may be understood to be contributing to an increasing international groundswell of interest in the *art of living* (Foucault 1988, Nehamas 2000) and pursuit of *philosophy as a way of life* (Hadot 1995). That such concerns are beginning to be taken seriously is reflected in academic study of, for example, workplace spirituality (Lund Dean, Forniciari and McGee 2003, Giacalone and Jurkiewicz 2004) and 'authentic leadership' (Avolio et al. 2004). Though not without their critics, these areas of study and practice nonetheless represent serious attempts to explore alternative *ways of being and acting* in organizations: an endeavour to engage with approaches to workplace life that are more ethically robust and appreciative of the need for greater levels of corporate social and environmental responsibility. Buddhism, I suggest, has much to contribute to ongoing debates with respect to workplace spirituality and authenticity.

There are also ways in which Buddhism, in a qualified sense, articulates with the work of scholars who are revitalizing Western wisdom traditions (Rooney, McKenna and Liesch 2010, McKenna and Rooney 2007). There are, for instance, certainly parallels to be drawn between Buddhist forms of wisdom and the systems of virtue that emerged in Hellenic Greece in the fifth and sixth centuries BCE (Hadot 2002), but also important differences between the two sets of traditions. As Jullien (2004) has noted with respect to Taoist and Confucian philosophy when compared with that of the ancient Greeks, oriental philosophy generally shies away from the establishment of context-free, fixed or *ideal forms* of moral principle. In contrast to the ideals of virtue found in Aristotle's writing (Aristotle 1955), Theravada ethics – as we noted above – invites practitioners to live by 'rules of training' which act as a set of ethical heuristics to be applied intelligently within any given social context. A more fruitful comparison here might be with the Aristotelian notion of *phronesis*. Often translated as 'practical wisdom', *phronesis* entails the virtuous development of a worldly sensibility and astuteness that promotes responsible living and intelligent decision-making (Aristotle 1955). We should remember, however, that Buddhist ethics does not have as its ultimate purpose the pursuit of virtue as an ideal or end in itself. Indeed, as already pointed out, the culmination of training in *supra-mundane* wisdom is the transcendence of, or liberation from, ethics (see also Case and Brohm 2012).

One final set of implications that I think usefully follows from the discussion of Buddhist wisdom relates to current interests within organization and leadership studies in ontological approaches which acknowledge and work with holism and interconnectedness. The Buddhist exploration of 'ultimate truths' and experiential understanding of the interdependence of phenomena is paralleled by the intellectual pursuits of *process philosophy* (Whitehead 2004 [1920], Bergson 2007 [1911]) which, in turn, has influenced certain strands of post-structural philosophy (for example, Deleuze 1997, Latour 2005). These process-orientated philosophies are beginning to find traction in the writing of scholars working in the fields of organization studies (Cooper and Burrell 1988, Chia 1998, Tsoukas 2005) and leadership studies (Wood 2005, 2008, Wood and Ladkin 2008). Similarly, there are connections to be made between Buddhist wisdom and the Merleau-Ponty-inspired study of inter-becoming (Küpers 2014; Küpers and Weibler 2008), as well as with the concept of in-dwelling deriving from the work of Polanyi (Case and Gosling 2011). In a closely related line of enquiry, for example, Dian Marie Hosking has applied concepts from Mahayana Buddhism in her development of a 'relational constructionist' understanding of organizational and leadership processes (Hosking 2006, 2011). Others have drawn on Buddhist philosophy to augment social theory (Loy 2003) and organizational applications of complexity theory (Boulton 2011). Boulton (2011), for example, explores the close relationship between the ontology of contemporary quantum physics and those of Buddhism, arguing that this correspondence carries practical implications for complexity-informed modes of action research and organizational interventions.

Conclusion

In this chapter I sought to introduce and discuss Buddhist conceptions of wisdom as understood within the Theravada tradition. Buddhism is perhaps best understood as a way of life whose entire raison d'être revolves around the cultivation of both mundane and supra-mundane wisdom. As I attempted to explain, it is not possible to engage in the experiential task of meditation without simultaneously working on the practical dimension of ethics. In terms of the Eightfold Path, 'purification of understanding' (supra-mundane wisdom) cannot take place in the absence of 'purification of conduct' (taking scrupulous care to speak and act ethically) and 'purification of mind' (achieved through the disciplines of meditation). An appreciation of the law of *kamma-vipāka* (action and result) encourages followers to act wisely in the world, seeking to minimize harm to oneself, others and the wider environment. Insight (*vipassanā*) meditation is a technique that enables a mind which is sufficiently calm to explore the constituents and interrelationships between phenomena as these are manifest in consciousness. It 'slows down' the mind in such a way that complex and extremely rapid processes can be observed dispassionately. Pursuit of this technique can eventually lead to profound insights into the transience and interconnected nature of the universe which, in turn, becomes a gateway to apprehending the goal of Buddhism – *nibbāna*, or liberation from subjective suffering.

Having introduced the core concepts of Buddhist philosophy and practices which promote the development of mundane and supra-mundane wisdom, I then proceeded to offer some reflections on the potential implications that Buddhist wisdom has for the fields of organization and leadership studies. I suggested that an indirect effect of supra-mundane insight was the promotion of harmlessness in the world. The attitude or disposition of gentleness which Buddhist wisdom promotes, moreover, may usefully inform post-materialist debates concerning corporate social and environmental responsibility and sustainability. There are also potentially fruitful connections to be made with contemporary literature on responsible leadership, authentic leadership and workplace spirituality: literatures that, in diverse ways, are seeking to explore different modes of *being and acting in organizations*. Finally, I proposed that Buddhist supra-mundane wisdom has ontological implications for the way we conceive of organization and organizing. In this respect, I drew parallels with the ways in which process philosophy, complexity theory and strands of post-structural philosophy encourage students of organization and leadership to conceive of their fields of enquiry in holistic and interconnected ways. In common with these Western forms of ontology, Buddhism prompts us to move beyond a world populated by discrete objects into a realm of interdependency in which all phenomena are subject to complex processes of conditionality. The reflections I offer are only partial and provisional. My hope, however, is that introducing this discussion of Buddhist philosophy may not only be informative to those unfamiliar with its principles but will also yield fruitful lines of future enquiry within the field of wisdom studies.

References

Aristotle 1955. *The Nichomachean Ethics*, translated by J.A.K. Tomson. Harmondsworth: Penguin.

Avolio, B.J., Gardner, W.L., Walumbwa, F.O., Luthans, F. and May, D.R. 2004. Unlocking the mask: a look at the process by which authentic leaders impact follower attitudes and behaviors. *The Leadership Quarterly*, 15(6), 801–23.

Batchelor, S. 1994. *The Awakening of the West: The Encounter of Buddhism and Western Culture*. London: HarperCollins.

Bergson, H. 2007 [1911]. *Creative Evolution*. Basingstoke: Palgrave Macmillan.

Bodhi, B. 1993. *A Comprehensive Manual of Abhidhamma*. Kandy: Buddhist Publication Society.

Boulton, J. 2011. The complexity turn: narrative, science and utility. MPhil dissertation, University of Bath.

Case, P. and Brohm, R. 2012. Buddhist belief and living ethics: challenging business ethics, in *Belief and Organization*, edited by P. Case, H. Höpfl and H. Letiche. London: Palgrave Macmillan.

Case, P. and Gosling, J. 2011. Where is the wisdom we have lost in knowledge? A stoical perspective on personal knowledge management, in *Personal Knowledge Management*, edited by D. Pauleen and G. Gorman. Oxford: Gower, 17–42.

Case, P., French, R. and Simpson, P. 2011. Philosophy of leadership, in *Sage Handbook of Leadership*, edited by A. Bryman, D. Collinson, K. Grint, B. Jackson and M. Uhl-Bien. London: Sage, 242–54.

Case, P., Simpson, P. and French, R. 2012. From theoria to theory: leadership without contemplation. *Organization*, 19(3), 345–61.

Chia, R. 1998. *In the Realm of Organization*. London: Routledge.

Cooper, R. and Burrell, G. 1988. Modernism, postmodernism and organizational analysis. *Organization Studies*, 9(1), 91–112.

Deleuze, G. 1997. *Difference and Repetition*. London: Athlone Press.

Foucault, M. 1988. *The Care of the Self, The History of Sexuality, Volume III*. London: Random House.

Furnham, A. 2010. *The Elephant in the Boardroom: the Causes of Leadership Derailment*. Basingstoke: Palgrave Macmillan.

Giacalone, R.A. and Jurkiewicz, C.L. 2004. *Handbook of Workplace Spirituality and Organizational Performance*. New York: M.E. Sharpe.

Gombrich, R. 1988. *Theravada Buddhism: A Social History from Ancient Benares to Modern Colombo*. London: Routledge and Kegan Paul.

Hadot, P. 1995. *Philosophy as a Way of Life: Spiritual Exercises from Socrates to Foucault*, translated by Michael Chase. Oxford: Blackwell.

Hadot, P. 2002. *What is Ancient Philosophy?* London: Harvard University Press.

Hadot, P. 2006. *The Veil of Isis: an Essay on the History of the Idea of Nature*, London: Harvard University Press.

Honderich, T. 1995. *The Oxford Companion to Philosophy*. Oxford: Oxford University Press.

Hosking, D.M. 2006. Discourses of relations and relational processes, in *Relational Perspectives in Organization Studies*, edited by O. Kyriakidou and M. Ozbilgin. Cheltenham: Edward Elgar, 265–77.

Hosking, D.M. 2011. Telling tales of relations: appreciating relational constructionism. *Organization Studies*, 32(1), 47–65.

Jullien, F. 2004. *A Treatise on Efficacy*. Honolulu: University of Hawai'i Press.

Kets de Vries, M. 2006. *The Leader on the Couch: A Clinical Approach to Changing People and Organizations*. London: Wiley.

Kets de Vries, M. and Miller, D. 1984. *The Neurotic Organization: Diagnosing and Changing Counterproductive Styles of Management*. San Francisco: Jossey-Bass.

Kornfield, J. 1977. *Living Buddhist Masters*. Kandy: Buddhist Publication Society.

Küpers, W. 2014. Embodied Inter-Be(com)ing – The contribution of Merleau-Ponty's relational Ontology for a processual understanding of Chiasmic Organising, in *Oxford Handbook of Process Philosophy and Organization Studies*, Jenny Helin, Tor Hernes, Daniel Hjorth, Robin Holt, (eds) Oxford: Oxford University Press (forthcoming)

Küpers, W. and Weibler, J. 2008. Inter-leadership: why and how should we think of leadership and followership integrally? *Leadership*, 4(4), 443–75.

Latour, B. 2005. *Reassembling the Social: an Introduction to Actor-Network-Theory*. Oxford: Oxford University Press.

Loy, D. 2003. *The Great Awakening: a Buddhist Social Theory*. London: Wisdom.

Lund Dean, K., Forniciari, C. and McGee, J. 2003. Research in spirituality, religion, and work: walking the line between relevance and legitimacy. *Journal of Organizational Change Management*, 16(4), 378–95.

Maak, T. 2007. Responsible leadership, stakeholder engagement, and the emergence of social capital. *Journal of Business Ethics*, 74(4), 329–43.

Maak, T. and Pless, N.M., editors. 2006a. *Responsible Leadership*. London: Routledge.

Maak, T. and Pless, N.M. 2006b. Responsible leadership in a stakeholder society: a relational perspective. *Journal of Business Ethics*, 66(1), 99–115.

Maccoby, M. 2000. Narcissistic leaders: the incredible pros, the inevitable cons. *Harvard Business Review*, 78(1), 69–77.

McKenna, B. and Rooney, D. 2007. Wisdom in organisations: whence and whither. *Social Epistemology*, 21(2), 113–38.

Nānamoli, B. 1979. *The Path of Purification: Visuddhimagga, by Bhadantacariya Buddhaghosa*. 4th edition. Kandy: Buddhist Publication Society.

Nānamoli, B. 1984. *The Life of the Buddha: As It Appears in the Pali Canon*. 2nd edition. Kandy: Buddhist Publication Society.

Nārada, M.T. 1980. *The Buddha and His Teachings*. 4th edition. Kandy: Buddhist Publication Society.

Nehamas, A. 2000. *The Art of Living*. London: University of California Press.

Nyanatiloka 1972. *Buddhist Dictionary: Manual of Buddhist Terms and Doctrines*. Colombo: Frewin.

Pieper, J. 1999 [1952]. *Leisure: The Basis of Culture*. Indianapolis: Liberty Fund.

Pieper, J. 2007 [1966]. *The Four Cardinal Virtues*. Notre Dame: University of Notre Dame Press.

Plato 1995. *The Republic*. Harmondsworth: Penguin.

Rahula, W. 1985. *What the Buddha Taught*. London: Gordon Fraser.

Rhys Davids, T.W. 1903 [1993]. *Buddhist India*. Delhi: Motilal Banarsidass Publishers.

Rooney, D., McKenna, B. and Liesch, P. 2010. *Wisdom and Management in the Knowledge Economy*. London: Routledge.

Said, E. 1978. *Orientalism*. Harmondworth: Penguin.

Saddhatissa, H. 1994. *The Sutta-Nipāta*. London: Curzon.

Sayadaw, M. 1965. *The Progress of Insight*. Kandy, Sri Lanka: Forest Hermitage.

Sievers, B. 1994. *Work, Death, and Life Itself: Essays on Management and Organization*. Berlin: De Gruyter.

Staudinger, U.M. and Glück, J. 2011. Psychological wisdom research: commonalities and differences in a growing field. *Annual Review of Psychology*, 62, 215–41.

Trowbridge, R. 2010. A wisdom bibliography. [Online]. Available at: http://www.wisdompage.com/introwis04.html [accessed 3 April 2012].

Tsoukas, H. 2005. *Complex Knowledge: Studies in Organizational Epistemology*. Oxford: Oxford University Press.

Waldman, D.A. and Galvin, B.M. 2008. Alternative perspectives of responsible leadership. *Organizational Dynamics*, 37(4), 327–41.

Warder, A.K. 2001. *Introduction to Pali*. 3rd edition. Oxford: Pali Text Society.

Whitehead, A.N. 2004 [1920]. *The Concept of Nature*. Cambridge: Cambridge University Press.

Wood, M. 2005. The fallacy of misplaced leadership. *Journal of Management Studies*, 42(6), 1101–21.

Wood, M. 2008. Process philosophy, in *Dictionary of Qualitative Management Research*, edited by R. Thorpe and R. Holt. London: Sage, 171–3.

Wood, M. and Ladkin, D. 2008. The event's the thing: brief encounters with the leaderful moment, in *Leadership Perspectives: Knowledge into Action*, edited by K. Turnbull James and J. Collins. Houndmills: Palgrave Macmillan, 15–28.

4 *Being a Wise Organizational Researcher: Ontology, Epistemology and Axiology*

DAVID ROONEY

Introduction

The fundamentals of ontology, epistemology and methodology matter in wisdom research for two important reasons. One is that researchers need to understand at a fundamental level the nature of practical wisdom (also called *phrónêsis*) if they are to sensibly discuss and create insights about its nature and understand how to ground those insights in organizations. The other is that organizational wisdom researchers might be advised to consider adopting integral, practical wisdom-based (*phrónêtic*) methodologies, rather than traditional epistemic methodologies in their own work. Central to this methodological project is integrating ontology, epistemology and axiology. Understanding how epistemology, ontology and axiology can be integrated has much to tell us about applying? *phrónêtic* methodology in research. More broadly, social science and humanities, henceforth social and organizational science research needs a revitalization to better and more effectively address our turbulent and struggling world in which wise practice is urgently needed. Integral, wisdom-based research methods can help to facilitate this revitalization. This chapter therefore is as much about the fundamentals of developing and grounding social practice-based theories of organizational wisdom as it is about how management and leadership research can matter in the twenty-first century.

At its core, this chapter proposes that Social Practice Wisdom (SPW) (Rooney, McKenna and Liesch 2010), understood as an extension and update of Aristotle's practical wisdom, is a sound basis for using wisdom theory and research in organizational practice:

1. SPW is grounded in everyday practices, histories, values and assumptions that define cultures and the possibilities for social agency;
2. SPW links micro social practices with meso- and macro- discourses, and is therefore concerned with *prâxis*, social relations and culture;
3. SPW is an individual and collective competence in the art of living in particular times and places;
4. SPW draws on and appropriately integrates reasoning, subjectivities, transcendence,

virtues, aesthetics and other practical skills to create equanimity and dispositions to achieve excellences in and through personal and interpersonal activity; and

5. these excellences are evident in the ability to discern and create short- and long-term well-being for oneself and the greater good. SPW therefore requires deep understanding of the conditions of living and great social, ethical and political skill.

For much of the chapter, I will move freely between practical wisdom and SPW, emphasizing SPW when it provides better guidance than practical wisdom does. The chapter begins with brief discussions of what ontology and epistemology mean and how they are deployed in social and organizational research. I then examine what wisdom theory says about wisdom's ontology and epistemology and, finally, I consider the idea of integral wisdom-based (*phrónêtic*) methods in organizational studies research that can help facilitate wisdom research in organizations and wise research institutions.

Ontology and Epistemology

It is important to say what ontology and epistemology mean because they are intimately linked to understanding the capacities that practical wisdom provides, and to deciding how to research them. In simple terms, 'Ontology investigates the fact, nature and modal status of being' (Jacquette 2002: 275). In traditional Western philosophy, ontology tends to assume things have a fixed, true state of being. Ontology also assumes that things are connected somehow to other things and that describing those connections is important. Since the postmodern turn in social science, some scholars argue that the traditional ontology of being should be replaced by ontology of becoming (Chia 1996). In this view, the erroneous assumption of the fixed, unchanging nature of reality is replaced by ontology that says empirical reality is always changing. In the extreme relativist case this ontological position is taken to mean that reality is so fluid that there is actually no possibility of finding an empirical reality and therefore no truth. For some scholars reality exists only as a construct in each individual's mind and there are as many realities as there are minds. Moral relativism, based on the assumption that there is no universal truth, is also a feature of the extreme postmodern position.

A non-Western view of ontology is interesting to consider. Buddhism (see Chapter 3), which is very concerned about the relationship between the mind and reality, provides such a view. Here ontology and epistemology are, as they should be, overlapping concepts. As Peter Case shows elsewhere in this book, having a highly refined ontology and epistemology is central to Buddhist versions of enlightenment (wisdom) because one needs to see what is true and real behind the cognitive and sociological noise of everyday life. Buddhist ontology is interrelational and process-based, and is an ontology of becoming. That truth has a pre-eminent place in its epistemology is an important point (Laumakis 2008). Moreover, the core texts of Buddhism call for an empirical, scientific (analytical), (transcendentally) pragmatic, therapeutic, egalitarian and individual (but not selfish) approach to living (Smith and Novak 2003) that eschews moral relativism. Buddhist empiricism though is non-dualistic, it collapses opposites (dualities, binaries, dichotomies), and sees interdependence and interpenetration as fundamental ontological features of reality (Smith and Novak 2003). This view of wisdom is relational in the sense of values-based social relations but also in the sense that ontology, epistemology and axiology (theory of value and ethics) must integrate with each other because they are interdependent.

Epistemology is concerned with how to create knowledge and how to decide what counts as knowledge. Traditionally, the term implies that we have rigorous and authoritative ways of creating true knowledge, but more recently the totalizing notion of authoritative truth is slightly weakened in orthodox epistemology by saying that what counts as knowledge are 'justifiable' beliefs that are actionable (Welbourne 2001). This weaker epistemology still assumes that what counts as knowledge is created in rigorous ways and by authoritative people and is justifiable and actionable because the knowledge is instrumentally reliable. In a knowledge economy, knowledge is usually assumed to be important when it is economically instrumental for economic, political and intellectual elites (Rooney 2005, Rooney et al. 2003).

A more useful approach to epistemology in contemporary social science begins with social construction of knowledge theory. Berger and Luckmann (1966) led this approach in the 1960s by pointing out that we come to accept knowledge or truth within social contexts and through social interaction. This knowledge may or may not have a reliable connection to reality though. Thus, Kusch (2002) has strenuously criticized his colleagues in philosophy for inadequately catering for context and the role of social agreement in creating what is taken to be knowledge. Kusch is critical of epistemologists for ignoring the role of power and culture that can maintain untruths in the status of knowledge; for example, the historical beliefs that the earth is flat and the sun orbits the earth. Lakoff and Johnson (1980), Foucault (1972), Latour (2005) and Fuller (1988) are also among those who have accounted for the role of cultural assumptions, metaphor, linguistic artefacts or texts and discourse in how knowledge is produced, legitimized and then acted on 'as if' the legitimized knowledge is true. Foucault in particular raises questions about the political economy of knowledge and asks which authorities are able to say what counts as knowledge, what social or power relations enable the authorities to decide what counts as knowledge and whose interests the sanctioned knowledge serves.

These more naturalistic epistemological approaches show how knowledge is part of day-to-day life, what its political economy is like as well as how it shapes the way we think and act. This kind of epistemology is more useful to organizational practical wisdom research than the more asocial traditional philosophical approaches. It is important to say that although some postmodern scholars (e.g. Gergen and Thatchenkery 2004) invoke notions of socially constructed knowledge or realities to support their claims about the impossibility of truth, many social constructionists are not postmodernists. Berger and Luckmann, for example, do believe in the existence of an independent and empirically accessible reality and truth as well as reject (postmodern) relativism. Having made these general comments, it is time to more directly consider ontology and epistemology in relation to describing wisdom's nature.

Wisdom's Ontology

Wisdom is still a new concept in organizational research, but it is now attracting increasing attention (Bierly and Kolodinsky 2007, Meeks and Jeste 2009, Schwartz and Sharpe 2010, Spiller et al. 2011, Yang 2011, Rooney and McKenna 2007). Mumford (2011), for example, sees wisdom as an important new branch of leadership research, and Kessler

(2006) argues for wisdom's importance to management. One aspect of wisdom's newness to organizational research is that very little theory development has been done on it at an organizational level. So this book and the wisdom symposium (See Küpers and Pauleen, Introduction) it springs from are important vehicles for creating a conceptual base and a community of practice that can address these shortcomings. In this section, I first discuss wisdom theory in general. Following that discussion I consider psychological definitions of wisdom, Aristotle's practical wisdom and SPW with its sociology as an integral system.

Contemporary research into wisdom is dominated by two psychological schools. One of these is Robert Sternberg's Balance Theory School and the other is Paul Balte's so called Berlin School of Wisdom research. Baltes and Staudinger (2000) see knowledge, values and judgement as forming the foundation for wisdom. They say that wisdom is that which coordinates knowledge and judgements about the 'fundamental pragmatics of life'. Wisdom therefore consists of: 1) strategies and goals involving the conduct and meaning of life; 2) limits of knowledge and uncertainties of the world; 3) excellence of judgement and advice; 4) knowledge with extraordinary scope, depth and balance; 5) the search for a perfect synergy of mind and character; and 6) balancing the good or well-being of oneself and that of others (Baltes and Staudinger 2000). An important focus in this model is cognitive integration. What is also important about much of the work done in the Berlin School is that it often comes from research in life-span psychology that develops understandings about how cognition and behaviour change as people develop with age (Richardson and Pasupathi 2005, Staudinger and Pasupathi 2003). Experience is a concern here, and, by extension, the reflexive integration of experience with knowledge and behaviour. Going further, it is important to acknowledge that values must integrate with knowledge, experience and behaviour (Ardelt 2003) in wisdom. In this vein, Csikszentmihalyi and Rathunde (1990: 29–7) see wisdom as a meme that carries important social and cultural meanings relatively unchanged across generations implying, very importantly, that wisdom is a property of culture.

Sternberg promotes a Balance Theory of wisdom. In this theory, wisdom balances the intrapersonal, interpersonal and extrapersonal over the long and short terms to achieve a balance among adapting to existing environments, shaping existing environments and selecting existing environments (Sternberg and Ben-Zeev 2001). The word 'balance' might better be replaced by the phrase 'balancing, weighing and discerning'. Sternberg is adamant that IQ is not the most critical component of wisdom. Indeed, he argues that knowledge, intelligence and creativity can all be put to unwise, even evil purposes (Sternberg 2003, 2010). The key point for Sternberg is that wisdom contributes to the greater good; it contributes to the community, to humanity and to the planet. There is similarity here to Aldwin's (2009: 3) definition of wisdom: "wisdom is a practice that reflects the developmental process by which individuals increase in self-knowledge, self-integration, nonattachment, self-transcendence, and compassion, as well as a deeper understanding of life. This practice involves better self-regulation and ethical choices, resulting in greater good for oneself and others".

The core of Aristotle's (1984) practical wisdom is ethicality and the ability to virtuously create well-being (*eudaimonia*, human flourishing). Aristotle also presents an epistemology and ontology that is somewhat similar to critical realism (Bhaskar 1975), Berger and Luckmann's (1966) idea of socially constructed knowledge and has significant overlap with Buddhist views (see Chapter 3). To reiterate, this is where an empirical reality exists, but the human capacity to understand that reality is incomplete such that we require judgement, imagination, creativity, insight and other forms of transcendent understanding to deal wisely with that reality. For Aristotle, practical wisdom occupies a higher place than contemplative wisdom (*sophía*) because it is anchored in *prâxis*, which is where well-being is created and experienced. *Prâxis* is usually seen as being about translating theory into practice, but it means much more than that for Aristotle. Dunne (1997: 10) points to the Aristotelian idea that *prâxis* is about 'conduct in a public space with others in which a person, without ulterior purpose and with a view to no object detachable from himself, acts in such a way as to realize excellences that he has come to appreciate in his community as constitutive of a worthwhile way of life'. This, of course, entails more than mechanically translating theory into practice. It also considers and speaks to values and the social, cultural, political and economic context within which we live and perform wise practices; Aristotle's is a relational and practice theory of wisdom. Aristotle's social philosophy and *phrónêsis* foreground values and appropriate dispositions that regulate practice (Eikeland 2008).

To me, the sum of our present knowledge of wisdom says that because wisdom is ultimately situated practice, wise thinkers and actors must integrate thoughts and judgements about what ought to be done within the contingencies of the situation. Furthermore, this situation has a sociology or culture that might either help or hinder wise practice and that behaviour that creates well-being (not only wise thoughts) is the assessable outcome of wisdom. An important point here is that a wise person actually makes an ethical long-term difference to humanity and the planet. From an organizational research perspective, what is most needed are sociological and social psychological explanations of wisdom that traverse and integrate the micro= (individual), meso= (organizational) and macro= (external/global) levels and discursive processes of wise practice.

SOCIAL PRACTICE WISDOM

I move now to my own recent work with colleagues Bernard McKenna, Peter Liesch and Hannes Zacher, which focuses on SPW. SPW tries to contribute to the well-being or human flourishing in organizations and is grounded in everyday practices. It acknowledges histories, values, power, assumptions, cultures and the possibilities they present that help or hinder wise social practice. SPW links micro organizational practices with meso= and macro= discourses and practices. Therefore, SPW is grounded in *prâxis*, social relations and discourses. We have adopted the SPW approach because we want to be clearer than Aristotle and wisdom psychologists about the discursive sociological and social psychological elements of practical wisdom and the reciprocal interactions between macro- and meso-level structures and processes with the micro (individual). What this approach also implies is that we do not want to simply 'purify' Aristotelian *phrónêsis* or argue about its exact meaning; we will leave that task to real philosophers. We simply use Aristotle as a starting point for research and recognize that the world we experience today is not the same world of Aristotle. To be clear, we also suggest that wisdom can be facilitated or hindered by an organization's culture, structure and discourse.

Integral Grounded Wisdom, Integral Research

Csikszentmihalyi and Rathunde (1990: 31) say that wisdom's role is to replace narrow, fragmented and intellectually aloof accounts of reality with holistic or 'metasystemic awareness'. This stance or orientation suggests that an integral systemic view of the world is important for wisdom. It is useful to hypothesize why wisdom is a system so that its dimensions can be explored and to inform research designs. Küpers and Statler (2008) begin to shed light on the multidimensional and –level, systemic view of wisdom by focusing on the idea and concept of integral practical wisdom (Figure 4.1).

Consciousness, sociality, culture, history, behaviour, practice, competence and performance are, rightly, part of this model. Wisdom is situated and temporal, it is individual and collective, and it is abstract and concrete at the same time. At the phenomenological first-peson level this approach demands considering extraordinary affective, cognitive and behavioral or action-related complexities in the work that wisdom processes or wise people do. At social and organizational levels it represents an equally complex, situated, institutional, performative, ethical accomplishment and interplay. Individually and collectively, this view of wisdom delivers a very dynamic, even unstable or stochastic 'construct' and process. Somehow all these complexities must be integrated or cohere to be what is wise, which is no easy task. This also means that researching wisdom is challenging and fraught. Given these challenges, wisdom research might best be done using wisdom-based methods.

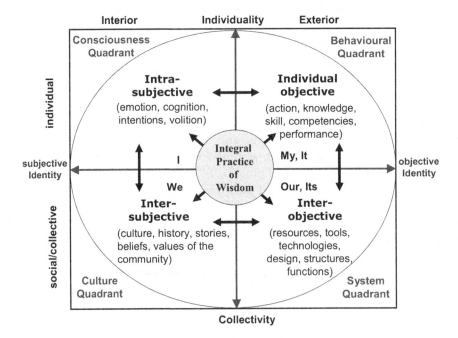

Figure 4.1   Multidimensional and multilevel integral practice of wisdom

Epistemology or *Phrónêsiology*? Researching Integral Practical Wisdom

Given the discussion above, the questions that arise now are how do we pursuit research practical wisdom as well as how can research methods be shaped by practical wisdom (*phrónêsis*) theory to replace epistemology with *phrónêsiology*? The reason why researchers should do something practically wise is to more effectively address global poverty and conflict, restore planetary sustainability, root out destructive business practices such as those that precipitated the global financial crisis of the first decade of this century, secure food and water supplies for everyone and cast out of power authoritarian and wicked political leaders. These are all goals that social science can and should engage effectively with.

THE BASIC PROBLEM OF RESEARCH: FROM KNOWLEDGE TO WISDOM

Before considering methodology and methods, I want to consider further why wisdom matters for research and why contemporary research should change. We owe a debt of gratitude to Nicholas Maxwell here, and so I begin with his value proposition.

Because enquiry (research) aims to enhance the quality of human life, it is damagingly irrational and unrigorous, for enquiry to only give intellectual priority to the task of improving knowledge rather than improving life. Rather, intellectual priority needs to be given to the task of articulating our problems of living, and proposing and criticizing possible solutions, namely possible human actions (Maxwell 1984: 2–3).

The blunt message here is that researchers claiming their job is done when they have contributed to the stock of knowledge are selling research short. Research needs actively and directly to do something to change positively the conditions in which we live. This is the same aim that practical wisdom has, and as Maxwell (1984: 118) says, wisdom's main questions can be summed up as pointing to a way of apprehending life by asking '[w]hat is the good life? How ought we live it? What is of genuine value in life and makes a positive difference and how is the good life achieved?'

PHRÓNÊSIOLOGY, NOT EPISTEMOLOGY: WISE METHODOLOGY

Social research can rise to the challenge of developing new research knowledge of wisdom and developing wisdom-based research methodologies: we have the plurality of ontologies, epistemologies and methods to do it, and we have some useful interdisciplinary research models.

To provide a simple starting point for developing *phrónêsiology* and *phrónêtic* organizational research methods, I present the SPW five core principles of wise practice that McKenna, Liesch, Boal and I have developed (McKenna, Rooney and Boal 2009, Rooney and McKenna 2008, Rooney, McKenna and Liesch 2010).

1) Wisdom is based on reason and observation

Wisdom uses observations leading to sound inferences and deductive explanations, as well as enabling salience and truth-value to be evaluated, while allowing for an intelligent balance between reasonable doubt and justifiable certainty about knowledge claims, including self-critique.

2) Wisdom incorporates non-rational and subjective elements into judgement

Wisdom uses sensory and visceral abilities, including insight, imagination and mindfulness in making judgements that are not bound absolutely to the rules of reason in ways that draw on upon experience, including learning from mistakes, facing challenges and enduring hardships, and in ways that understand the contingency of life and circumstance.

3) Wisdom is directed to authentic humane and virtuous outcomes

Wisdom uses virtue and is humble, tolerant and empathetic, is founded on the authentic expression of good character and good desires and values long-term good over short-term expediency.

4) Wisdom is articulate, aesthetic, and intrinsically rewarding

Wisdom can articulate judgements aesthetically and creatively using imagination, style, design, appropriate genre and rhetorical skill, and acknowledges the intrinsic rewards and pleasures of wise action and also of knowledge and contemplation for their own sake in bringing about harmony and happiness.

5) Wisdom is practical

Wisdom is prudent and practical, displaying a sensible worldliness leading to *eudaimonia*.

It is useful to consider each principle in turn because each of these has a role in wisdom-based research practices. An important part of doing this is to illustrate the capacity for each of the five principles to interconnect, overlap and collapse into each other, as well as to create tensions and conflict through their interactions while still occupying analytically distinguishable roles. Although the above principles are essentially Aristotelian, in the discussion below I will amplify those principles with input from contemporary research findings to better understand the dynamics that may be important for empirically accessing organizational wisdom and designing *phrónêtic* research. An integral approach should acknowledge biology. As the *Bhagavad-Gita* says: 'The sage performs his [sic] action dispassionately, using his body, mind and intellect, and even his senses, always as a means of purification' (Lord Krishna 1935: 5).

1) Reason and Observation

Aristotle was one of the main architects of rational, empirical knowledge production. Logic, systematic or organized empirical research, and abstract reasoning were important elements of his philosophical system. It is hard to agree with the idea that systematic empirical research and intellectually disciplined thinking have no role to play in producing knowledge or wisdom. We may hesitate at this statement and say that there must be more to wisdom than just rationalism, but 'reliable' knowledge of this sort is surely important to one degree or another. Engineers who build the bridges, aircraft and high-rise buildings need this kind of knowledge so that we can all live safely. Moreover, wisdom must identify any durable and reliable knowledge that we can depend on.

2) Subjective and Transcendent

We may have an innate capacity for logical reasoning but it is possible to overstate the importance of rationality in Aristotle's philosophical system by turning it into an ideology, and by ignoring other aspects of Aristotle's theory of practical wisdom that include subjective and transcendent elements.. Of course, as Wendelin Küpers shows in Chapter 1, subjectivies, intersubjectivities and transsubjective dimensions in interpractices are major components of a more integral understanding of wisdom. An important part of wisdom is that knowledge or meaning and understanding is developed from acting in the everyday world. In other literatures (e.g. Nelson and Winter 1982) this is called knowing-by-doing or experiential learning. Much of the value of this knowledge is born in its subjective, discerning, imaginative nature. Judging, weighting and discerning in moment-to-moment activities are largely felt and subjective. Discerning what is the most relevant or important information and knowledge upon which to make a difficult decision matters when we need to avoid paralysis and to actively make and then enact wise decisions. Subjective evaluations of what matters, what is good, what is right, what is valuable, what is fair, what is possible and so on are fundamental to wise judgement.

Importantly, it is the subjective-discerning-imaginative ability in us that enables us to step over gaps in knowledge, and to create new ideas and new possibilities without having to observe an empirical incarnation of an imagined, non-existent reality. This is a practical problem-solving and survival ability, and it is imagination, not pure logic, that is the supreme human evolutionary achievement. Recent neuroscience research (Dijksterhuis et al. 2006) suggests that it is not always best to deliberate rationally and that using a 'deliberation-without-attention' process can produce better choices. That is, by not using conscious reasoning but by using unconscious capacities like intuition, emotions and feelings, people can make more satisfying choices. Emotions are critical in motivating us to solve problems, and assist the process of retrieving from memory appropriate knowledge and modes of analysis that underpin reason (Damasio 2000, Rolls 2012). Subjective-imaginative capacity is not just important for its creativity; it also makes possible sophisticated communication capacities, empathy, ethicality and culture (Gebser 1985). (Moral) Imagination makes civil society possible, even if it also produces malevolent creativity in, for example, crime and warfare. Reason and subjectivity need to find complementary ways of working together.

Wisdom-based research methods have a place for reason and abstract propositional knowledge, along with subjectivity. An important point I am leading to here is that subjective and objective versions of reality both exist but are not opposites; they co-exist in a dialectical relationship even if they never quite correspond to each other (Berger and Luckmann 1966). Wisdom-based research methods themselves are, in part, a way of socially constructing knowledge grounded in observation and interpretation of empirically real processes, places and people. In the SPW framework, researchers are asked to reason, interpret, imagine and create. Socially and phenomenologically sterile positivistic formalism is too reductive and limiting for wisdom.

Similarly, that we are capable of subjective transcendence that leads to creativity and insight is not enough for wisdom. As has already been mentioned, each of these things can be put to antisocial and unwise use. Creativity and insight can, for example, be used by a salesperson to trick you into buying something you do not need and cannot afford (Sternberg 2010).

3) Virtue

Thus, virtue, including intellectual virtue and character, is central to Aristotle's philosophical system including his theory of practical wisdom. Virtue is important because, as I say above, the human mind and society are capable of enabling unwise and antisocial behaviour as much as wise behaviour. For Aristotle, practical wisdom does not exist without goodness, compassion, generosity, altruism, empathy, sympathy, humility, moral courage or cooperation. Fortunately, and underpinning the philosophical imperative for virtue, evolution has equipped humanity with the neural apparatus and possibility to be 'naturally' capable of altruism, of being other-focused, generous and social (Hall 2010). Going further, Hauser (2008) argues that humans have an inbuilt capacity for moral instinct based on what he calls a hidden moral grammar, which his research shows is closely linked to the emotional centres of the brain. Similarly, Becker, Cropanzano and Sanfey (2011: 945) conclude that neuroscience indicates that fairness has a biological basis and that being fair is intrinsically rewarding. Furthermore they showded that 'fairness perceptions emerge from oral intuition and emotional responses rather than from cognitive consideration of economic efficiency or deontological principles' (Becker, Cropanzano and Sanfey 2011: 945).

Maxwell (1984: 63) argues that objective, rational social science encourages manipulation of people through its findings and 'requires people to be obediently incapable of innovative thought and action'. Such tendencies have caused concern about intellectual authoritarianism. Returning to the earlier discussion of traditional epistemology, it is clear that one of its core values is an officially sanctioned intellectual authority that is beyond question. Intellectual authoritarianism or 'intellectual Taylorism' (Zijderveld 1974: 74–8) where 'substance is superseded by form, material by method, essence by function, reality by abstractions' is at odds with wise practice. The drive for technocratic solutions to life's problems through totalizing and authoritarian positivism have been demonstrated to be damaging (McKenna and Graham 2000). In a knowledge economy, technocracy offers easy promises, often in the form of management fads, which appeal to impulses that so many in business cannot resist, thus creating normative mass foolishness. It is reflexive virtue that translates imagination and reason into the building blocks of practical wisdom or SPW, and this requires deliberate practice (Ericsson, Krampe and Clemens 1993). Thus, elements of sociality like our sense of a shared human condition with others, reciprocity and moral obligation (Berger and Zijderveld 2009) must then go on to result in virtuous social practice.

Wisdom-based research is necessarily concerned with character, values and ethics, and must add axiology to ontology and epistemology in its methodological foundations. Each of these must integrate with each other coherently and meaningfully.

4) Aesthetics

An important point to make in relation to aesthetics is that contemporary neuroscience is now developing a clearer picture of the role of emotions in cognition. Emotions are now understood to be a critical component of reasoned thinking and all kinds of problem-solving and decision-making and I argue that emotion is central to the aesthetic practices of wisdom. Rationality and emotions are better seen as two sides of the same coin. Values-free and unemotional researchers are not part of wisdom-based research, even if wisdom is not an emotional and values free-for-all. Equanimity would replace values-free and unemotional research mindsets. For the purposes of this chapter, I use the term 'aesthetics' in a particular SPW way. I do not use it in the traditional philosophical sense it has today of being about informed or sophisticated appreciation or consumption of works of art and beauty. I use it in a communicative and social practice sense that identifies expressivity, equanimity, satisfaction and reward as important to wisdom. The interpretation of Aristotle's use of the term aesthetics in relation to practical wisdom that my colleagues and I make (Rooney, McKenna and Liesch 2010) is that it is the creative 'art of living' with special reference to communicating difficult-to-convey ideas in everyday social practice, and communicative excellence that creates value for oneself and others. How do you express a wise idea so that it inspires or persuades others to undertake difficult actions to bring about positive change in the world? It is undeniable that satisfaction, pleasure, beauty, emotions and creativity are important components of Aristotle's aesthetics, but that aesthetic activities also teach, elicit reflection and enhance emotional intelligence is critical to practical wisdom. Thus, intrinsically rewarding practices, like meditation, that access and re-evaluate subconscious schemas are also part of wisdom's aesthetics because they create equanimity as well as reorganize difficult to scrutinize and dysfunctional subconscious processes that detract from wise practices. These are the foundations of the critical micro social skills needed for SPW.

Communication is essential to social practice as there is no such thing as society if there is no communication. In SPW, aesthetics is a central part of what weaves reason, transcendence and virtue together to be deployed or expressed as wise social practice. Collins (1998: 379–81), in his epic, *The Sociology of Philosophies*, says that networks of personal contacts that pass 'emotional energy (passion, motivation) and cultural capital from generation to generation' are critical features of intellectual evolution. Elaborating this point, Collins states that what is also relevant within these networks is that there are always tensions between competing ideas or explanations of reality. He argues that 'interaction rituals' are important processes in sustainable intellectual change if they keep intellectual networks open to new ideas and, very significantly, are open to debate about competing ideas as they engage with those tensions. Communicative excellence in SPW therefore brings a focus to communicational 'discourse' and its role in opening admission of new ideas. This focus explicitly includes the expressive, encompassing the presentational, rhetorical, political and institutional processes that are at play. Socrates, Aristotle and Buddha were excellent communicators and teachers who understood something about the theatre and art of an open pedagogy.

Empathy, altruism, compassion and love, for example, are central to Western and Eastern explanations of wisdom and they are impossible without emotion and mean little if they are unexpressed. If wisdom's emotions are virtuous, then emotional regulation is a vital part of wisdom. Indeed, there is a growing consensus among scientists that emotional regulation is one of the most foundational components of moral reasoning and discernment (Hauser 2008). In important ways, wisdom is irreducibly a product of human hearts and micro-level social action. Passion and emotion are researchable in wisdom-based research but they are also important and positive elements of a researcher's motivations and their moral compass. It is also important that the research itself is aesthetic: that it effectively communicates difficult-to-communicate ideas that create valuable change, and which contribute to equanimity, to compassion, to positive emotional energy.

5) Practical

Within practical wisdom, the word practical does not mean short-term convenience or ease, or simple instrumentality, as it tends to mean in contemporary parlance. Practical, in a practical wisdom sense, is linked to a philosophy of wisdom that is about learning to live, see, experience, value, participate and create (Maxwell 1984). To be practical is to be able to navigate the challenges of thoughtfully and mindfully acting in social life; it means creating long-term well-being through *prâxis*. In this sense, practical wisdom is a 'way of being' that is often far from easy and convenient. The convenient and short-term instrumentality of the finance industry's unregulated and under-scrutinized financial practices that led to the global financial crisis was certainly not practically wise.

Practical necessarily means dealing with politics and being political (Eikeland 2008). The political (purpose, intention, strategy, power) elements of sociality are inevitable and cannot be eliminated. 'Politics, to Aristotle, is not something that can be done by abstracting general principles and running things predictably. It is not a form of social engineering. Political science, is a demonstration of practical wisdom, rather than craft' says Spicker (2011: 13). Wise political action and wise use of power is possible and meaningful. This is the politics that has the strength, courage and insight of wise convictions, the expressive capacity to persuade in honest and non-coercive ways and the long-term vision for sustainability that bestows fairness and well-being despite the uncertainty, hardship and ambiguity of life. A wise thinker and actor with no sense of social purpose and who refrains from channelling their wisdom into positive social action that results in well-being is not practically wise.

In business schools, practical often means concrete, recipe book, atheoretical teaching. Concrete facts are important to wisdom; however, as the scale of social systems increases from tribe, to town, to city, so increase the logistics of problem-solving as 'divisions of class, work, skill, culture and values grow' (Maxwell 1984: 84). On top of this social complexity, distance and size also influence the level of abstraction that we must create to deal with organizing social life (Lakoff and Johnson 1980, Rooney et al. 2010). Small communities experience social reality as very concrete with important aspects of life close at hand and easy to identify. Large communities provide a more abstract experience as many important aspects of life are remote in social, psychological and physical distance (Zijderveld 1974: 48–9):

> *Modern society is an essentially abstract society which is increasingly unable to provide man [sic] with a clear awareness of his identity and a concrete experience of meaning, reality, and freedom. This abstract nature of society is caused primarily by its pluralism, i.e. by its*

segmentation of its institutional structure ... As a result of this pluralism society has lost ... much of its existential concreteness.

Today, many of the cues for social action are abstract and independent-of-context rules or generalizing propositions. Remote bureaucracies run by people we do not know or recognize, and rules or regulations devised by politicians, whom we know only from the daily cascade of sound bites are common. Social isolation, disengaged lives, alienation and remote corporate and political power elites are all part of the abstract tone and atmosphere in contemporary life presenting particular challenges for wise practice and for making social science research matter. Context-independent abstraction plays many important social, political and economic roles and cannot be ignored or banned. Wisdom's aesthetics are important for ameliorating abstraction's negative side and reification in order to ground practice in particular contexts.

Abstraction can lead to what Marx called 'false consciousness', reification or mistakes in thinking and conceiving, as well as fetishism: for example, treating abstractions as if they are real and concrete, and where abstractions become archetypes for reality (Zijderveld 1974: 50–52). Reification is one of the problems that theorizing and generalizing research has helped produce. Reification means that sometimes facts do not matter as much in everyday activities anymore. If there is a discrepancy between theory and reality, it is reality that is sometimes blamed for being wrong. In a study performativiy in the Chicago Stock Exchange, MacKenzie (2001, 2009, MacKenzie and Millo 2003) showed, how reality changed to fall in line with economic theory. SPW may be situated, but must cope with both the concrete and abstract elements attached to situations. Understanding theory, theoretical literacy, including metatheoretical knowledge, is of growing importance. Practical wisdom and SPW use theory but acknowledge its limits. Specifically, wisdom (research) rejects reification and in many ways revisits familiar structure and agency questions including Giddens' (1984) and his mission to avoid the structure–agency, and micro–macro dualities. *Phrónêtic* research must avoid reification of its findings as well as turning its community of researchers into a reified and reifying cognitive community (Zima 2007).

Which Phrónêtic Methods?

It is liberating to consider the possibility of wisdom-based social science methods for organizational research (Rooney and McKenna 2008). Flyvbjerg (2001: 33) points to ethnomethodology and discourse analysis as providing inspiration for his *phrónêtic* social science methods. In particular, Flyvbjerg considers the double hermeneutic problem in social research. He says that the human condition is difficult for humans to research because humans are idiosyncratic reflexive interpreters of themselves, their social contexts and day-to-day activities, and can purposively change their behaviour. In other words, purely objective research of humanity by humans is impossible. This is one of the central problems in the history and philosophy of social science and it deflates notions of pure rationality and pure objectivity in social science. It is for this very reason that Flyvbjerg rejects the idea that research models used in natural science are appropriate for social science. As mentioned before, Foucault (1970) put this problem at the centre of his work on knowledge, power and discourse where he sees human action as essentially a process of meaning-giving.

Dreyfus and Dreyfus (1986) provide a critical extension for Flyvbjerg's views on the practice of using *phrónêtic* methods. They are concerned with how experts do their work by not working strictly to rules and procedures. Flyvbjerg (2001: 34) says:

> *Acquisition of researchers' basic skills is no different from other skills. Researchers do not need to be able to formulate rules for their skills in order to practice them with success. On the contrary, studies show that rules can obstruct the continuous exercise of high-level skills. There is nothing which indicates that researchers at expert level – those who have achieved genuine mastery in their field – pursue mainly context independent rules.*

Flyvbjerg also argues that rules can obstruct the continuous exercise of high-level skills. Tacit knowledge, intuitive feel and practical consciousness really matter to expert work, including social science research. *Phrónêtic* social science research is therefore not done strictly to a formula.

Grounding Research

Flyvbjerg's (2001) contribution is to carefully bring a focus on values and power to *phrónêtic* research. He argues that *phrónêtic* research balances instrumental rationality with value-rationality and that it is important to investigate the particular, rather than exclusively focus on the generalizable and abstract. Ethnomethodology and case studies have particular importance in this version of *phrónêtic* research. Flyvbjerg's *phrónêtic* research begins with values-focused questions: 1) Where are we going?; 2) Is this desirable?; and 3) What should be done? Methodologically, he argues for the importance of getting close to reality, but without 'going native' and in doing so emphasize the little things as they occur in local micro practices. He is at pains to urge researchers to observe practice before discourse because what people do actually carries more detail than what is eventually filtered through their words. Studying particular cases is important as practices are always influenced by situations and context-dependent judgements and these are best accessed in the field where people conduct their normal activities. Research should be about and part of a dialogue with a polyphony of voices. This resonates with Eikeland's (2008) view that central to *phrónêtic* research is dialogue. All this is good advice for grounding practical wisdom and its research in organizations.

Research designs include action research, case studies, ethnomethodology, grounded theory, phenomenography and transpersonal or mindfulness approaches (Charmaz 2006, Eikeland 2008, Flyvbjerg 2011, Davis 2003). Within such designs, qualitative and quantitative methods are both admissible. Multi-method designs are particularly relevant. Methods of data collection can vary and include critical incident research, historical studies, participant and observational studies, in-depth interviewing and reflexive or transpersonal methods such as those seen in positive and transpersonal psychology (see Walsh 2011 for an accessible introduction and overview of integral, transpersonal and mindfulness wisdom practices and contemplative disciplines). More attention could be paid to psychotherapy techniques in organizational wisdom research data collection. Self-awareness techniques such as used in cognitive behaviour therapy (see Walsh 2011 for a discussion of how therapeutic approaches that improve 'psychodynamics' can aid integration for wisdom in individuals), and mindfulness and acceptance-based therapy techniques may be useful for grounding wisdom in organizational behaviour. Of course, scenario or dilemma thinking-out-loud analyses as they are used in the Berlin wisdom research paradigm are already well established. I also see good uses for experimental inter-disciplinary designs in which wisdom researchers collaborate with neuroscientists, and also in role-play methods and intervention studies.

Extending Flyvbjerg, I argue that organizational climate and culture and other meso-(organizational) level phenomena like shared narratives should be part of *phrónêtic* organizational research. Organization-level conditions have to create spaces in which wise people and practices can be fostered and maintained so that SPW can take hold.

PHRÓNÊTIC RESEARCH INSTITUTIONS

What Flyvbjerg has not attempted to do is to map the inter-folding of *phrónêtic* research practices with the institutions in which research occurs, namely universities (Eikeland 2008). This has to be part of an integral approach to *phrónêtic* research. A useful starting point for discussing this inter-folding of research and institutions is Collins (1998). He describes three processes that shape intellectual creativity: 1) economic-political structures, which in turn shape 2) the organizations which support intellectual life, and these in turn allow the build-up of 3) networks among participants in centres of attention on intellectual controversies, which constitute the idea-substance of intellectual life.

Going further, Collins (1998: 333) shows that it is change to the organizational base that is most important. '[I]nnovative practices come from a long-term change in the organizational base, the full ideological ramifications of what has transpired do not emerge for many decades', and where those organizational changes cause the relationships between competing schools of thought to change, it promotes creative outputs. On top of all this, networks of personal contacts that pass 'emotional energy (passion, motivation) and cultural capital from generation to generation' and within contemporaneous social networks are critical to supporting intellectual change. What is also important, says Collins, is rivalry between points of view, absence of imposed single orthodoxies, tolerant scepticism and that the leading thinkers are involved in creating organizational transformations of the modes of intellectual production (Ibid.: 379–81). Organizational wisdom researchers can position themselves to bring about organizational change to universities away from current bureaucratic knowledge factories to adopting wisdom models, as has happened at the University College in London (Maxwell 2012). To illustrate the point, Collins points out that for example Greece and China both had periods in their histories of great intellectual success and failure. During their periods of great intellectual and cultural development as well as economic growth and flourishing, says Collins (1998: 146), 'the precipitating conditions involved political pluralism, the cosmopolitanism of commercial development and literacy, and a breakdown of traditional religious practices'. Landes (1998) has also shown that national level intellectual and economic declines result from becoming closed, anti-pluralistic and retreating from cosmopolitanism. Again reification of the intellectual apparatus of nations leads to redundancy.

As argued before, *phrónêtic* research must be integrated with politics. Berger and Zijderveld (2009) suggest that passion and conviction, rather than fanaticism, are possible and desirable in achieving the good life. In consonance with Collins and Landes, Berger and Zijderveld (2009) argue that a middle position between fundamentalism and relativism is important and that it requires: 1) openness to new ideas including an understanding of how values, norms and knowledge change; 2) acceptance that doubt has a positive role in the community of scholars; 3) to accept 'others', those who do not share our world-view without categorizing them as enemies; 4) developing and maintaining institutions of civil society that enable peaceful debate and conflict resolution; and 5) acceptance that choice is not only an empirical fact but morally desirable. This formulation should also apply in respect of social and organizational science methods, advocating for overcoming the black and white schisms between qualitative and quantitative method.

The politics of moderation steers clear of both relativism and fundamentalism. Yet it can be inspired by real passion in defence of the core values that come from the perception of the human condition that we have tried to describe in this chapter. "Our praise of doubt in no way detracts from such passion" (Berger and Zijderveld 2009, p. 166) because healthy doubting maintains intellectual openness.

We can also apply this schematic to universities to understand what causes research to run out of steam, as is increasingly thought to be happening to management research (for example, Alvesson and Sandberg, (2013); Buckley 2002).

Conclusion

Grounding wisdom research means positioning or locating it in everyday practice, in particular situations, with particular people, at particular times. It also means grounding researchers and research practices. Practical wisdom cannot, by definition, not be part of the *prâxis* of everyday life because it is performative, relational and communicative or dialogical (Eikeland 2008).

Phrónêsis must take into consideration where others are, emotionally, intellectually and in reltion to their attitudes and skills, in trying to find the right decisions or things to do, but it cannot use these circumstances manipulatively. It must know how to deal with egotistical, strategic and manipulative behaviour in others without itself becoming like this, but also without simply being subdued by it or letting such behaviour prevail in others and in general (Eikeland 2008).

Universities need to transform and reinvent themselves to create facilitative spaces for wise(r) research. Accordingly wise research calls for grounding the institutional frameworks for research. Researchers have to bring these institutional changes about, not near-sighted university managers. More open and pluralistic universities and business schools with less gratuitous competition, less reified managerialism and less identity politics are needed. Universities have to contribute to improving life, rather than privileging contributingto the total count of publications in ranked journals.

As practitioners, wise researchers and (wiser) research institutions will be characterized by a tolerance of ambiguity, flexibility, independence and open-mindedness. The research itself is marked by conceptualizing a situation broadly, asking unexpected questions, making remote associations, seeing unexpected links, finding problems, restructuring problems, generating solution criteria and communicating a situation to others in an accessible and meaningful and usable way. There are good reasons for being optimistic about the potential for wise practice to grow.

A final reflection is that despite the Aristotelian foundations of my work, I would like to see more non- or post-Aristotelian-based research on organizational wisdom. Kant, for example, is largely ignored despite his focus on practice. Non-theistic religious or spiritual accounts of wisdom and wise practice, like Buddhism, are only just being opened to the gaze of organizational wisdom scholars and we need more of it. Furthermore, I particularly recommend Mark Edwards' chapter (Chapter 10) for its acknowledgement of the dark side of wisdom, which must not be ignored, lest wisdom research becomes nothing more than a convenient rest-home for people who simply advocate for a supposed 'nice' world.

My departing questions are:

1. What is it that wisdom scholars in organisation and management studies can do using their perspectives that is better than other scholars in, for example, judgement, knowledge, decision-making and similar research areas?
2. What is the value to society of organizational (wisdom) research and do our research practices deliver that value?
3. How can researchers (academics) drive universities to become wiser institutions in the service of the public, rather than let university managers continue to drive change?

References

Aldwin, C.M. 2009. Gender and wisdom: a brief overview. *Research in Human Development*, 6(1).

Alvesson, M. and Sandberg, J. 2013. Has management research lost its way? Ideas for more imaginative and innovative research. *Academy of Management Review*, 50:1, 128–52.

Ardelt, M. 2003. Empirical assessment of a three-dimensional wisdom scale. *Research on Aging*, 25, 275–24.

Aristotle 1984. *Nicomachean Ethics*, translated by H.G. Apostle. Grinnell: The Peripatetic Press.

Baltes, P.B. and Staudinger, U.M. 2000. A metaheuristic (pragmatic) to orchestrate mind and virtue towards excellence. *American Psychologist*, 55(1), 122–36.

Becker, W.J., Cropanzano, R. and Sanfey, A.G. 2011. Organizational neuroscience: taking organizational theory inside the neural black box. *Journal of Management*, 37(4), 933–61.

Berger, P.L. and Luckmann, T. 1966. *The Social Construction of Reality: a Treatise in the Sociology of Knowledge*. New York: Doubleday.

Berger, P.L. and Zijderveld, A.C. 2009. *In Praise of Doubt: How to Have Convictions Without Becoming a Fanatic*. New York: HarperOne.

Bhaskar, R. 1975. *A Realist Theory of Science*. Sussex: Harvester Press.

Bierly, P.E. and Kolodinsky, R.W. 2007. Strategic Logic: Towards a Wisdom-Based Approach to Strategic Management, in *Handbook of Organizational and Managerial Wisdom*, edited by E.H. Kessler and J.R. Bailey. Thousand Oaks: Sage, 61–88.

Buckley, P. 2002. Is the international business research agenda running out of steam? *Journal of International Business Studies*, 33, 365–73.

Charmaz, K. 2006. *Constructing Grounded Theory: A Practical Guide Through Qualitative Analysis*. London: Sage.

Chia, R. 1996. The problem of reflexivity in organizational research: Towards a postmodern science of organization. *Organization*, 3:1, 31–59.

Collins, R. 1998. *The Sociology of Philosophies: a Global Theory of Intellectual Change*. Cambridge, MA: Belknap.

Csikszentmihalyi, M. and Rathunde, K. 1990. The psychology of wisdom: an evolutionary interpretation, in *Wisdom: Its Nature, Origins, and Development*, edited by R. Sternberg. Cambridge: Cambridge University Press, 25–51.

Damasio, A. 2000. *The Feeling of What Happens: Body, Emotion and the Making of Consciousness*. London: Vintage Books.

Davis, J.V. 2003. An overview of transpersonal psychology. *The Humanistic Psychologist*, 31:2–3, 6–12.

Dijksterhuis, A., Bos, M.W., Nordgren, L.F. and van Baaren, R.B. 2006. On making the right choice: the deliberation-without-attention effect. *Science*, 311(5763), 1005–7.

Dreyfus, H. and Dreyfus, S. 1986. *Mind Over Machine: The Power of Human Intuition and Expertise in the Era of the Computer*. New York: Free Press.

Dunne, J. 1997. *Back to the Rough Ground: Practical Judgement and the Lure of Technique*. Notre Dame: University of Notre Dame Press.

Eikeland, O. 2008. *The Ways of Aristotle: Aristotelian Phronesis, Aristotelian Philosophy of Dialogue, and Action Research*. Bern: Peter Lang.

Ericsson, K.A., Krampe, R.T. and Clemens, T.-R. 1993. The role of deliberate practice in expert performance. *Psychological Review*, 103, 363–406.

Flyvbjerg, B. 2001. *Making Social Science Matter: Why Social Inquiry Fails and How It Can Succeed Again*, translated by S. Sampson. Cambridge: Cambridge University Press.

Flyvbjerg, B. 2011. Case study, in *The Sage Handbook of Qualitative Research*, edited by N.K. Denzin and Y.S. Lincoln. Thousand Oaks: Sage, 301–16.

Foucault, M. 1970. *The Order of Things: an Archaeology of the Human Sciences*. London: Tavistock.

Foucault, M. 1972. *The Archaeology of Knowledge*, translated by A.M.T. Sheridan Smith. London: Tavistock.

Fuller, S. 1988. *Social Epistemology*. Bloomington: Indiana University Press.

Gebser, J. 1985. *The Ever Present Origin*, translated by N. Barstad and T.A Mickunas. Athens: Ohio University Press.

Gergen, K.J. and Thatchenkery, T.J. 2004. Organization science as social construction: postmodern potentials. *Journal of Applied Behavioral Science*, 40(2), 228–49.

Giddens, A. 1984. *The Constitution of Society*. Berkeley: University of California Press.

Hall, S.S. 2010. *Wisdom: From Philosophy to Neuroscience*. Brisbane: University of Queensland Press.

Hauser, M.D. 2008. *Moral Minds: How Nature Designed Our Universal Sense of Right and Wrong*. London: Abacus.

Jacquette, D. 2002. *Ontology*. Chesham: Acumen.

Kessler, E.H. 2006. Organizational wisdom: human, managerial, and strategic implications. *Group and Organization Management*, 31(3), 296–99.

Küpers, W. and Statler, M. 2008. Practically wise leadership: toward an integral understanding. *Culture and Organization*, 14(4), 379–400.

Kusch, M. 2002. *Knowledge by Agreement: The Program of Communitarian Epistemology*. Oxford: Oxford University Press.

Lakoff, G. and Johnson, M. 1980. *Metaphors We Live By*. Chicago: University of Chicago Press.

Landes, D.S. 1998. *The Wealth and Poverty of Nations: Why Some Nations Are So Rich and Some So Poor*. London: Little, Brown and Company.

Latour, B. 2005. *Reassembling the Social: an Introduction to Actor-Network-Theory*. Oxford: Oxford University Press.

Laumakis, S.J. 2008. *An Introduction to Buddhist Philosophy*. Cambridge: Cambridge University Press.

Lord Krishna 1935. *The Bhagavad Gita*, translated by S.P. Swami. The Big View.

MacKenzie, D. 2001. The big, bad wolf and the rational market: portfolio insurance, the 1987 crash and the performativity of economics. *Economy and Society*, 33(3), 303–34.

MacKenzie, D. 2009. *Material Markets: How Economic Agents Are Constructed*. Oxford: Oxford University Press.

MacKenzie, D. and Millo, Y. 2003. Constructing a market, performing theory: the historical sociology of a financial derivatives exchange. *American Journal of Sociology*, 109(1), 107–45.

Maxwell, N. 1984. *From Knowledge to Wisdom: a Revolution in the Aims and Methods of Science*. Oxford: Basil Blackwell.

Maxwell, N. 2012. How universities can help humanity learn how to resolve the crises of our times – from knowledge to wisdom: the University College London experience, in *Handbook on the Knowledge Economy, Volume II*, edited by D. Rooney, G. Hearn and T. Kastelle. Cheltenham: Edward Elgar.

McKenna, B. and Graham, P. 2000. Technocratic discourse: a primer. *Technical Writing and Communication*, 30(3), 219–47.

McKenna, B., Rooney, D. and Boal, K. 2009. Wisdom principles as a meta-theoretical basis for evaluating leadership. *The Leadership Quarterly*, 20(2), 177–90.

Meeks, T.W. and Jeste, D.V. 2009. Neurobiology of wisdom: A literature overview. *Archives of General Psychiatry*, 66(4), 355–65.

Mumford, M.D. 2011. A hale farewell: the state of leadership research. *The Leadership Quarterly*, 22(1), 1–7.

Nelson, R. and Winter, S. 1982. *An Evolutionary Theory of Economic Change*. Cambridge, MA: Belknap Press.

Richardson, M.J. and Pasupathi, M. 2005. Young and growing wiser: wisdom during adolescence and young adulthood, in *A Handbook of Wisdom: Psychological Perspectives*, edited by R.J. Sternberg and J. Jordan. Cambridge: Cambridge University Press, 139–59.

Rolls, E.T. 2012. *Neuroculture: On the Implications of Brain Science*. Oxford: Oxford University Press.

Rooney, D. 2005. Knowledge, economy, technology and society: the politics of discourse. *Telematics and Informatics*, 22(3), 405–22.

Rooney, D. and McKenna, B. 2007. Wisdom in organizations: whence and whither. *Social Epistemology*, 21(2), 113–38.

Rooney, D. and McKenna, B. 2008. Wisdom in public administration: looking for a sociology of wise practice. *Public Administration Review*, 68(4), 707–19.

Rooney, D., McKenna, B. and Liesch, P. 2010. *Wisdom and Management in the Knowledge Economy*. London: Routledge.

Rooney, D., Hearn, G., Mandeville, T. and Joseph, R. 2003. *Public Policy in Knowledge-Based Economies: Foundations and Frameworks*. Cheltenham: Edward Elgar.

Rooney, D., Paulsen, N., Callan, V.J., Brabant, M., Gallois, C. and Jones, E. 2010. A new role for place identity in managing organizational change. *Management Communication Quarterly*, 24(1).

Schwartz, B. and Sharpe, K.E. 2010. *Practical Wisdom: The Right Way To Do The Right Thing*. New York: Riverhead Books.

Smith, H. and Novak, P. 2003. *Buddhism: A Concise Introduction*. San Francisco: Harper.

Spicker, P. 2011. Generalisation and phronesis: rethinking the methodology of social policy. *Journal of Social Policy*, 40(1), 1–19.

Spiller, C., Pio, E., Erakovic, L. and Henare, M. 2011. Wise up: creating organizational wisdom through an ethic of Kaitiakitanga. *Journal of Business Ethics*.

Staudinger, U.M. and Pasupathi, M. 2003. Correlates of wisdom-related performance in adolescence and adulthood: age-graded 'paths' toward desirable development. *Journal of Research on Adolescence*.

Sternberg, R.J. 2003. *Wisdom, Intelligence and Creativity Synthesized*. Cambridge: Cambridge University Press.

Sternberg, R.J. 2010. The dark side of creativity and how to combat it, in *The Dark Side of Creativity*, edited by D.H. Cropley, A.J. Cropley, J.C. Kaufman and M.A. Runco. Cambridge: Cambridge University Press, 316–28.

Sternberg, R.J. and Ben-Zeev, T. 2001. *Complex Cognition: The Psychology of Human Thought*. New York: Oxford University Press.

Walsh, R. 2011. The varieties of wisdom: contemplative, cross-cultural, and integral contributions. *Research in Human Development*, 8(2), 109–127.

Welbourne, M. 2001. *Knowledge*. Chesham: Acumen.

Yang, S.-Y. 2011. Wisdom displayed through leadership: exploring leadership-related wisdom. *The Leadership Quarterly*, 22(4), 616–32.

Zijderveld, A.C. 1974. *The Abstract Society: A Cultural Analysis of Our Time*. Harmondsworth: Pelican Books.

Zima, P.V. 2007. *What is Theory: Cultural Theory as Discourse and Dialogue* London: Continuum.

5

'Wise Women or Caring Women': the Paradoxical Nature of the Representation of Women in Management

MAREE BOYLE AND AMANDA ROAN

Introduction

A paradox arises for those studying the persistence of the under-representation of women in senior areas of management and leadership. On the one hand it seems advantageous to present the many qualities and talents women can bring to the workforce as highly desirable. However, this promotion of women's qualities has led to a process of quarantining women as 'special' or 'different' that in turn may have led to a hierarchical layering of these very talents. The recent academic focus on wisdom as a desirable characteristic for a leader and decision-maker (Mumford 2011, Rooney, McKenna and Liesch 2010) raises a number of salient questions regarding women's under-representation. Does the under-representation of women in senior management mean that women lack wisdom or do women bring a different form of wisdom, which remains undervalued and underutilized? In this chapter, we examine these questions.

Despite decades of legislative activity, considerable gender segregation persists within many advanced Western economies, and although there have been significant increases in the numbers of women in management, women remain hugely under-represented in corporate boardrooms and at executive and CEO level. For example, in Australia women chair four boards and hold 14 per cent of board directorships in ASX200 companies' positions (EOWA 2012).

Although Oakley (2000) refers to the lack of women in senior management as a concern for business ethics and thus human rights, much of the contemporary work in gender equity recognizes what Bailyn and Harrington (2004) refer to as the 'dual agenda' of improving gender equity and gender-related organizational problems while simultaneously meeting the immediate and practical needs of organizational outcomes. This agenda has also been presented as the 'business case' for managing diversity (see Lorbiecki and Jack 2000). Arguments for the 'business case' have included promoting diversity in decision-making and creativity and even the humanizing of upper levels of management and the boardroom (Bilimoria 2000, Schwartz 1980, Frenier 1996, Tanton 1994, Huse 2007, Huse and Solberg 2006). Valuing and fostering the innate characteristics of women and minority groups therefore becomes an organizational imperative and it is reasonable to assume that this could be extended to the concept of wisdom. Most arguments therefore become centred on issues of 'equality', 'similarity' or 'difference'.

Much of the research into women in management and leadership has emerged from liberal feminist approaches. This literature has tended to examine psychological variables and sex/gendered differences in behaviour as illustrated through traditional organizational concepts such as leadership and management (Calas and Smircich 2006). Much of this literature focuses on individualistic 'deficits' such as self-efficacy or barrier issues such as lack of mentoring, poor business networks, lack of the required experience for senior positions and inadequate financing (Still and Chia 1995, Still and Souter 1996). The work of gender-cultural feminists also emphasizes women's difference. For example, Gilligan's (1982) work argued that women and men have different concepts of justice and morality, while Noddings (1984) emphasized a feminine ethics of care as not just different from, but better than a masculine ethics of justice (Calas and Smircich 2006). Subsequently women's difference and 'feminine qualities' have been featured in management literature as 'special' and 'value adding' within an organizational context. Examples of this work can be found in various examinations of women in leadership that have demonstrated that women leaders bring a more relational, interactive and participative style to leadership and management (Marshall 1984, Rosner 1990, Alimo-Metcalf 2010). Fondas' (1997) analysis of mainstream management textbooks found that these promote the new work modalities required for an increasingly competitive world needing leaders and managers who can 'reorient themselves toward a new role of coordinating, facilitating, coaching, supporting, and nurturing their employees' (Ibid.: 258–9). She argues that new schools of management thought indeed redefined management work with characteristics traditionally defined as feminine in our culture while failing to name these as such. Deeper examination of promoting 'female' qualities highlights the paradoxical nature of promoting women's 'special' wisdom but also brings possibilities for further exploration. Paradox can be explained as 'the simultaneous presence of contradictory even mutually exclusive events' (Cameron and Quinn 1988: 2). Lewis (2000) maintains that the complexity of contemporary organizational life which is driven by fast-paced technological and increasing workforce diversity leads to many divergent and contradictory experiences. Paradoxes are said to bring about defensive behaviours (Vince and Broussine 1996) in actors and produce tensions capable of driving change (Lewis 2000). We argue that popular and academic work that promotes the value of these 'female' qualities rarely note the hierarchical status that exists within organizations and the boardroom, nor do these characteristics define success in competitive organizational structures (Grant 1988, Pesonen, Tienari and Vanhala 2009).

The second problem in the promotion of women's special qualities also stems from the proposition that these valuable 'female' qualities emanate from and are still highly associated with women's caring and nurturing role. This literature often calls on women to make a judgement that is both rational and value laden (that is, balance the rational economic necessity of paid employment with the values of nurturing and caring) (Hakim 1995, 2000, 2003). With these controversies in mind, we argue that dangers exist in treating wisdom as a gender-neutral concept and in defining women's wisdom as 'special'. We attempt to reconcile these positions.

Wisdom: A Gendered Concept?

Despite the recent flurry of research in the area, defining wisdom remains problematic. Recent research into wisdom and leadership has also aimed at examining the dimension of wisdom as individual differences (Ardelt 2003, 2004, Sternberg 2003, Sternberg and Jordan 2005), while other psychology-based approaches have been concerned with cognitive and moral development (Piaget 1969, 1971, Kohlberg 1969, 1981). Other research streams remain deeply rooted in the philosophical tradition of Aristotle (see McKenna, Rooney and Leisch 2010). One common theme in much of the contemporary management literature on wisdom has been an attempt to identify the characteristics and dimensions of wisdom so that it may be fostered in organizational and public life (McKenna, Rooney and ten Bos 2007, Rooney and McKenna 2007).

Grant (1988) draws on Jane Baker Miller's (1976) work *Towards a New Psychology of Women* to demonstrate the complex and paradoxical nature of ascribing male/female qualities or characteristics. Grant (1988) points out that although biology has played a part, it is mostly women's experience in the family, the community (the private sphere) and their place in economic and political structures that have led to the development of 'feminine' qualities. Over two decades ago she noted, 'the very qualities that are elucidated are those that are least important for success as it is currently defined in such organizations' (Grant 1988: 63).

The other issue that has emerged from the literature on wisdom concerns the ability to measure or operationalize wisdom. For example, Ardelt's (2003) model shows that the practice of wisdom involves cognitive, reflective and affective personality characteristics. This model has been empirically tested and the results, especially in terms of the gendering of wisdom, are instructive. Gluck, Strasser and Bluck (2009) indicate that there needs to be a differentiation between professional expertise and expert knowledge and that these are key measures of wisdom. Most empirical studies conclude that there are few differences between how wise men and women are perceived. However, the key difference that does emerge is what Gluck, Strasser and Bluck (2009) identify as different views of wisdom in terms of related experiences in real life that may be construed as more 'gendered'. For example, 'wise' women are more likely to cite relational and interpersonal examples to demonstrate their wisdom than wise men. Conversely, wise men are more likely to identify knowledge of philosophy and expert knowledge as demonstration of their wisdom.

Nomination studies indicate that wise women may be more associated with 'helping others' whereas wise men are associated with deep thinking and political activity. Aldwin (2009) states that there are some intriguing hints that the pathways through which men and women develop wisdom and morals may differ, while Gluck, Strasser and Bluck's (2009) autobiographic study asking for descriptions of wise acts found that women's understanding of wisdom is more inclusive of affective events than men and they reported a higher percentage of events related to children, death and illness and self-transformation This exposes another great paradox of contemporary working life in that caring and nurturing roles are more likely to be seen as hindering the exercise of leadership in management in terms of being present, making decisions and exercising control in organizations.

The notion of feminine wisdom as described by Lustgarten (2007) also addresses the absence of women leaders' wisdom as a defining characteristic within both the scholarly and practice literature on leadership. Lustgarten argues that although women have made significant strides in accessing leadership positions, they have not yet arrived at a position where they are successfully recognized as leading through the expression of their own values based on their own authentic wisdom. Women leaders need to find their 'wise' voice in the face of a dominant culture if they are to have a sense of their own authenticity. In other words, leadership without feminine wisdom costs women their authenticity. However, it is worth noting that perhaps there needs to be a similar study conducted with men who are leaders in relation to their 'authentic' voice. In summary, the literature to date indicates that the strength of women's leadership is gained through relational and interpersonal practice.

Leaders, Managers and *Phrónêsis*

For the purposes of this paper we rely on Aristotle's original definition of wisdom, which is applied in a reasoned and true state of capacity within both broad and situated contexts to act with regard to human goods (Aristotle 1998: 1140). We use this to inform a contemporary definition as developed by Ardelt, Gluck, Levenson, Strasser and Aldwin (see Aldwin 2009), which integrates the *sophía* and *phrónêsis* aspects of wisdom and emphasizes the social justice and moral development aspects that they feel have been neglected in modern studies of wisdom.

In the *Nichomachean Ethics* (1967), Aristotle suggests that there are three kinds of knowledge associated with wisdom: *epistêmê* (necessary and universal knowledge), *tékhnê* (technical knowledge – knowledge of procedure) and *phrónêsis* (practical wisdom). For the purposes of this paper we will focus on *phrónêsis*, which is also known as either practical or prudential wisdom. The aim of *phrónêsis* is to adjust knowledge to the peculiarity of local or situated circumstances. *Phrónêsis* is characterized by perceptiveness with regard to concrete particulars, and is as much a way of knowing as it is a kind of knowledge, which is also embodied and habitualized knowledge (Dunn 1993). Above all, *phrónêsis* is considered to be a form of moral knowledge that provides guidance about the particular and the situated when we need to act in a given situation (Gadamer 1994).

Aristotle, however, implied that *phrónêsis* is always related to the 'good' and is thus divorced from the issue of power. Arguments about the meaning of *phrónêsis* also indicate that as a form of moral discretion, prudential wisdom cannot be learned, and that prudential leadership is not associated with utopian thought (Grint 2007). Statler, Roos and Victor (2007) also infer that leaders deficient in practical wisdom are more likely to succumb to hubris as a leadership style.

This brief overview of practical wisdom points toward several important considerations of how wisdom-based leadership and management practice may benefit or hinder women leaders and managers. As wisdom in management is not explicitly recognized as a gendered process, there is very little critical discussion or analysis within the nascent wisdom in management literature that specifically relates to women, management and leadership. We contend that this omission needs to be addressed by bringing together feminist approaches to female wisdom and discussion about the 'business case' for increasing women's participation and the diversity of approaches that women may bring to leadership positions.

Biloslavo and McKenna (Chapter 6) state that wisdom must be understood within a given socio-cultural context as a practice socially orientated to authentic, humane and virtuous outcomes. This statement invites questions: do virtuous outcomes differ when seen from the woman's standpoint?; and what outcomes (practical applications) are valued within the social world of the organization where rational and substantive outcomes are highly valued?

If indeed relational qualities such as caring and empathy and 'self-transcendence' (Kohlberg 1973), which Levenson (2009) describes as involving compassionate understanding of others, are important qualities of leadership and bring an important ethical foundation to organizations, we begin to encounter the paradoxes of women, leadership and work. The literature on wisdom makes reference to occupations such as midwifery and counselling as spaces for the exercise of practical wisdom (Price and Price 1997) yet they remain largely feminized occupations with a lower monetary value than many other professions.

We now draw upon the works of Dorothy Smith and Carole Gilligan to assist in illuminating the problems inherent in the gendering of practical wisdom.

Women's Wisdom or a Gendered Ethic of Care? The Influence of Dorothy Smith and Carol Gilligan

In the works of both Dorothy Smith and Carole Gilligan, we see much reference to how wisdom is gendered. For example, Smith pays close attention to how women's knowledge is situated as *phrónêsis*, as one of the Aristotelian concepts of wisdom. In particular, Smith's recent public work, with a focus on knowledge formation processes, emphasizes strongly the need to exalt the practical form of wisdom that is often anathema to the rational, 'objective' masculinized wisdom that dominates the neo-liberal, corporate world. Smith is simultaneously critiquing the hierarchical layering of what constitutes wisdom as well as the very process through which knowledge is constructed and disseminated. Smith's (1987) central concept of bifurcated consciousness illustrates how *phrónêsis* is considered a second tier or subordinate form of wisdom, for it is the kind of wisdom, according to Smith, at which women excel. Bifurcated consciousness is concerned with the disconnection and contradiction between a woman's life as a woman, or a woman's lived experience, and the objective abstracted, theoretical world in which she must operate as a public person. It assists in illuminating a woman's struggle to negotiate two disparate worlds: dominant knowledge concepts versus lived experience. According to Smith, this struggle represents a unique 'standpoint' of women, as the oppressed.

Smith also infers that the alienation that stems from this form of consciousness often leads to a deprivation in the ability to speak publicly. In other words, Smith is suggesting that women still do not have access to the *authority* to speak, which is one of the cornerstones of being considered 'wise', at least in today's global economy. Therefore, Smith (1990) challenges the idea that the governance of the abstract conceptual model of thinking and decision-making can always be located outside historical, material and social relations. She argues that knowledge stems from practice, is always both situated and relational and is fully embedded within specific historical material systems of power relations. In other words, Smith is stating that 'true' wisdom comes not from the *local* or situated context, but rather from the *extralocal*, with knowledge emanating from the *local* context considered inferior. Therefore, Smith's work suggests that the subordination of *phrónêsis* as a valid kind of wisdom is heavily gendered, and that women's ability to engage in *phrónêsis* needs recognition along with other forms of wisdom.

Gilligan, in her seminal work on gender and moral development (1982), found that men and women use fundamentally different approaches to moral decision-making. She argues that the male approach to moral theory is based on the idea that individuals have certain basic rights that one has to respect. By contrast, the women's approach is based on the notion that people have responsibilities to others, and, hence, imposes an imperative to care for others. Gilligan argues that the male approach has been viewed as superior, as the women's perspective is not taken as seriously, and therefore seen as less intellectually developed. In an organizational sense, to be wise, one had to adhere to the rational, male organizational norm (Acker 1990). Like Smith, she documents how theories of moral development have found women in deficit, and have not recognized the possibility that there may be a unique women's approach. According to Gilligan, the male approach, the *justice* orientation, views morality as a question of individuals having certain basic rights. One has to respect the rights of others, and, in doing so, morality imposes restrictions on what people do. On the other hand, the female approach to morality, the responsibility orientation, involves a responsibility towards others, and an imperative to care for others.

In relation to the paradox of gender and wisdom, both Smith and Gilligan become involved in the same dilemmas. First, both acknowledge and actively promote the possible existence of differences between men and women in relation to wisdom, knowledge construction and dissemination and moral development. This kind of approach has been very influential in the feminization of management literature, where a woman leader is often scrutinized for her ability to use her special knowledge and power as a woman. Second, both implicitly acknowledge that women have superior *phrónêsis*, a mastery of practical and situated knowledge. This kind of belief has also become extremely popularized, with the emergence of interest in the spirituality of organizations. Examples of this include the rise of the 'wise woman' movement, which is heavily steeped within an essentialist notion of female spirituality, wisdom and power. The 'divine feminine' is now becoming a popular topic for leadership and management consultants, where women are encouraged to draw upon their inner, essential feminine power to improve their position within the public world (see for example Schaaf, Hurty and Cheen 2011).

To assist in explaining the absence of women being seen to publicly engage the creation of wisdom, we draw upon the modernist notion of the gendered division between the public and private domain (Oakley 1976, Walby 1986). Until quite recently in history, most women were discouraged and even banned from seeking and developing wisdom as exemplified in organizational leadership through both formal and informal means (see Milkman 1976, 1983, Crompton 1986, 1987). Even when women did attend formal institutions, it was not until the twentieth century that women formally gained knowledge in co-educational settings. This can be illustrated through the struggle for professional recognition of the practice of midwifery. Here women were often classified as having, and indeed argued that they had, 'special knowledge', while the scientific practice of obstetrics was seen as a male domain (Oakley 1976, Witz 1992). Ford-Grabosky (2002) claims that before the twentieth century 'wise' women, often wrongly assumed to be pagan priestesses or practitioners of Wicca, were often persecuted and vilified. These women often were keepers of knowledge that was viewed as dangerous to the status quo. Private wisdom was gained through folklore and oral tradition, often metaphysical and spiritual beliefs and practices passed on from mother to daughter It is interesting to note that much of what has been written about women and wisdom in recent years has been within the context of spirituality, formal religion and new age beliefs and practices, and not within the context of the public sphere. While women have much greater access to the gaining and expression of public wisdom, many women are still discouraged from exhibiting public wisdom, and their sources of private wisdom are still not fully acknowledged as legitimate.

Smith's (1987, 1990) conceptual framework, which includes notions of extralocal relations of ruling and bifurcated consciousness, is very useful for helping to understand the paradox of gendered wisdom within organizations. Smith's (1990) term 'relations of ruling' involves society being divided into the local and the extralocal. While the local domain incorporates the everyday and the mundane aspects of social life, the extralocal domain relates to complex organizations that are organized by rules of impersonality, logic and objectivity. Smith asserts that the tools of the relations of ruling such as texts, documents and formal processes of the extralocal, lead to a denigration of the everyday or local world. Smith (1987) and others have documented that the local domain and knowledge/wisdom that emanates from this domain is largely the world and work of women.

THE ETHICS OF CARE

One area where feminist scholars seek to demonstrate the potential of the relational as well as the rational is the 'ethics of care' (Noddings 1984, Held 2005, Slote 2007, Robinson 2011). Indeed, Held (2005) and Slote (2007) claim that the ethics of care has been one important result of Carol Gilligan's (1982) work on women's moral reasoning. Recent work on the ethics of care places it as a distinct moral theory not to be simply added to or included in other influential moral theories. One of the key features of the ethics of care is that it attempts to reconceptualize the traditional notions about the public and private spheres. As Held (2005) infers, the ethics of care addresses rather than neglects moral issues arising in relations among the unequal and dependent, but that such relations are also often laden with emotionality and an involuntary sense of duty. These attributes apply not only in the household but in the wider society as well. Feminist scholars have now examined the ethics of care beyond family and social relations to local, national and global politics, arguing that it has implications for global security and peace (Ruddick 1989, Held 2005, Robinson 2011). Those promoting the ethics of care do not confine its values to those of women but note that women as traditional carers are more likely to demonstrate such ethics. The ethics of care is seen as a counter-view to a society 'dominated by conflict, restrained by law and preoccupied by economic gain' (Held 2005: 12).

Feminine Wisdom in the Twenty-first Century

This short review of the scholarly work of Smith, Gilligan and others brings stronger weight to the arguments that women can bring special qualities to organizations and their leadership through difference in terms of moral reasoning and relational abilities, yet the paradoxical nature of gender and wisdom within the context of management and leadership brings opportunities for change. In relation to implications this discussion has for the establishment of more effective gender equity within organizations, and to highlight some of the deficiencies in the simplistic nature of the 'business case', we present a set of questions in relation to 'feminine' wisdom in the hope that these can deepen discussions around the valuing of the relational, and personal practice of caring.

Conclusion

COMPREHENSIVE WISDOM: DOES IT EXIST?

Our discussion of *phrónêsis* as being simultaneously an inherently feminine as well as a second-tier attribute points towards the challenge of reifying the feminine: for example, women who are recruited into management positions on the basis of their 'caring and feminine' qualities often find themselves within an organizational culture that rewards epistemic or rational wisdom. Thus, the decision-making abilities of female leaders and managers may be put under greater scrutiny as the organizational culture in which they operate may not consider them *comprehensively* wise.

REPRESENTING WOMEN'S WISDOM AS 'SPECIAL': IS THIS A PROBLEM?

We believe that there are also implications regarding the types of education, training and mentoring that women leaders both seek out for themselves and that they can access at the organizational and industry level. Many current leadership programmes for women focus on a dominant perception of wisdom, thus reducing the likelihood of women receiving a more full-bodied and comprehensive grounding in the development of wisdom. Many programmes are based on the erroneous notion that most women are naturally 'good', 'virtuous' and leading through a caring ethic framework, and that most men are naturally deficient in the ability to lead in the same way. This makes it unlikely that women or men will develop the self-knowledge they need to improve their managerial and leadership qualities and abilities.

We also contend that this may have consequences for how women view themselves and other women as leaders and decision-makers. If women assume that they and other women will always possess a 'special wisdom', this may provide significant challenges for how individual women managers mentor other women, particularly in male-dominated organizations and industries (Roca 2007).

CAN PRACTICAL WISDOM AND POWER AND PRESTIGE COEXIST?

The scholarly and popular literature on wisdom does tend to infer that women are now 'too' wise to fully engage with activities in the public world such as high-level management, and that they are more likely to make decisions based on a morality steeped in virtues of communal responsibility rather than organizational imperative (Hammer 2002). We suggest that while this perspective has always applied to women, it is very rarely applied to men. The implication here is that, to fully understand how to engage in practical wisdom, one must be able to step back from the demand of power, prestige and material acquisition, and embrace (if only momentarily) communitarian values and ideas during the decision-making process. We contend that, particularly in relation to the work-life balance literature, there is an implicit assumption that men are almost incapable of successfully engaging in practical wisdom, let alone becoming expert at it. As Hammer (2002) argues, wise people are becoming increasingly difficult to find, as 'wise' managers, both men and women, choose not to work in a contemporary managerial environment where work-life balance is poor, and ethical and moral decision-making is often compromised.

Beyond a Gendered Practical Wisdom

In summary, there is a strong case for valuing the relational and personal aspects of wisdom, particularly when applied to leadership and management in organizations. Despite the appeal for women hoping to obtain these positions, we question the idea that practical wisdom should be considered an innately feminine attribute, particularly in relation to the recruitment and selection of women managers and leaders (Case and Gosling 2007). Historically, women were considered 'unwise' either by virtue of their biological status, social invisibility or because they were possessors of 'womanly' or 'special' wisdom, imbued with intuitive ability and connected to an ancient 'wise women' tradition (Ford-Grabosky 2002). The implication here is that when women are wise, it is a kind of wisdom that is not public or celebrated, for it is concerned with matters of the private rather than the public domain. The works of Gilligan and Smith outline some of the reasons why there is a constant challenge to women regarding their credibility as creators of wisdom within extralocal domains. The exposure of this paradox offers avenues for further research. At a theoretical level this discussion shows the potential contribution of feminist scholars to the understanding of wisdom in organizations. At a theoretical and practical level, recent work that has attempted to operationalize the ethics of care in the public sphere offers a platform for researching relational issues. The current surge of research in wisdom in leadership and management also offers the opportunity for a 'business case' for practical wisdom which in contrast to the business case on diversity could be based on inclusion rather than difference. Further research aimed at understanding the complexity of the paradoxical nature of wisdom within organizations will help to address the inequities and asymmetries that stem from this paradox.

Reflective Questions

1. This chapter has raised the issue of female characteristics being mooted as a valuable resource in organizational leadership and part of the 'business case' for diversity in organizations. Do you think this is a legitimate assertion? Reflect on women leaders you are familiar with and whether they bring something special to their organizations.
2. Fondas (1997) notes that 'coaching, supporting and nurturing' are promoted as important elements of management and leadership styles in the work modalities of the twenty-first century. Consider whether this represents the feminine in organizational life. How can these be fostered?
3. Taking the stance that 'caring' and 'nurturing' can foster practical wisdom, we note that the performance of nurturing and caring can also form barriers to full

participation in organizational life. Reflect on this paragraph and develop ways of dealing with this paradox.

4. How can the ethics of care be incorporated into our understanding of wisdom?

5. At the end of the paper we offer three questions in relation to women and the practical application to wisdom in organizations. How can these inform a more inclusive practice of leadership in organizations?

References

Acker, J. 1990. Hierarchies, jobs, bodies: a theory of gendered organizations. *Gender and Society*, 42(2), 139–58.

Ackrill, J. (ed) 1987. *A New Aristotle Reader*. Oxford: Clarendon Press.

Aldwin, C.M. 2009. Gender and wisdom: a brief overview. *Research in Human Development*, 6(1), 1–8.

Alimo-Metcalfe, B. 2010. An investigation of female and male constructs of leadership and empowerment. *Gender in Management: an International Journal*, 25(8), 640–648.

Ardelt, M. 2003. Empirical assessment of the three-dimensional wisdom scale. *Research on Aging*, 25(3), 275–324.

Ardelt, M. 2004. Wisdom as expert knowledge system: a critical review of contemporary operationalization of an ancient concept. *Human Development*, 47(5), 257–85.

Aristotle 1967. *The Ethics of Aristotle, The Nicomachean Ethics*, translated by J.A.K. Thompson, revised by Hugh Trednnick. New York: Penguin Classics.

Bailyn, L. and Harrington, M. 2004. Redesigning work for work-family integration. *Community, Work and Family*, 7(2), 197–208.

Baker Miller, J. 1976. *Towards a New Psychology of Women*. Boston: Beacon Press.

Bilimoria, D. 2000. Building the business case for women corporate directors, in *Women on Corporate Boards of Directors*, edited by R.J. Burke and M.C. Mattis. Dordrecht: Kluwer Academic, 25–40.

Calas, M. and Smircich, L. 2006. From the women's point of view ten years later: feminist approaches to organization studies, in *Handbook of Organization Studies*, edited by S. Clegg, C. Harding and R.W. Nords. London: Sage, 284–346.

Cameron, K.S. and Quinn, R.E. 1988. Organizational paradox and transformation, in *Paradox and Transformation: towards a Theory of Change in Organizational Management*, edited by R.E. Quinn and K.S. Cameron. Cambridge, MA: Ballinger, 1–18.

Case, P. and Gosling, J. 2007. Wisdom the moment: pre-modern perspectives on organizational action. *Social Epistemology*, 21(2), 87–111.

Crompton, R. 1986. Women and the service class, in *Gender and Stratisfaction*, edited by R. Crompton and M. Mann. Cambridge: Polity Press, 119–36.

Crompton, R. 1987. Gender status and professionalism. *Sociology*, 21(3), 413–28.

Dunn, D.S. 1993. Integrating psychology into the interdisciplinary core curriculum. *The Teaching of Psychology*, 20(4), 213–18.

Equal Opportunity for Women in the Workplace Agency 2012. *Gender in the Workplace Statistics 2012* [Online: Australian Government]. Available at: http://www.eowa.gov.au/Information_Centres/Resource_Centre/Statistics/Stats_At_A_Glance_Jul_2012.pdf [accessed: 13 June 2012].

Fondas, N. 1997. Feminization unveiled: management qualities in contemporary writings. *Academy of Management Review*, (22)1, 257–82.

Ford-Grabosky, M. 2002. *Sacred Voices: Essential Women's Wisdom through the Ages*. New York: Harper Collins.

Frenier, C. 1996. *Business and the Feminine Principle: The Untapped Resource*. Oxford: Butterworth Heinemann.

Gadamer, H.G. 1994. *Literature and Philosophy in Dialogue: Essays in German Literary Theory*, translated by R.H. Paslick. New York: State University of New York Press.

Gilligan, C. 1982. *In a Different Voice*. New York: Harvard University Press.

Gluck, J., Strasser, I. and Bluck, S. 2009. Gender difference in implicit theories of wisdom. *Research in Human Development*, 6(1), 45–59.

Grant, I. 1988, Women as managers – what they can offer organizations. *Organizational Dynamics*, 16(3), 57–63.

Grint, K. 2007. Learning to lead: can Aristotle help us find the road to wisdom? *Leadership*, 32(2), 231–46.

Hakim, C. 1995. Five feminist myths about women's employment. *The British Journal of Sociology*, 46(3), 429–55.

Hakim. C. 2000. *Work-Lifestyle Choices in the 21st Century: Preference Theory*. Oxford: Oxford University Press.

Hakim. C. 2003. A new approach to explaining fertility patterns: preference theory, *Population and Development Review*, 29(3), 349–74.

Hammer, M. 2002. *The Getting and Keeping of Wisdom: Inter-Generational Knowledge Transfer in a Changing Public Service*. Ottawa: Research Directorate, Public Service Commission of Canada.

Held, V. 2005. *The Ethics of Care: Personal, Political and Global*. Oxford: Oxford University Press.

Huse, M. 2007. *Boards, Governance and Value Creation*. Cambridge: Cambridge University Press.

Huse, M. and Solberg, A.G. 2004. Gender-related boardroom dynamics: how Scandinavian women make and can make contributions on corporate boards. *Women in Management Review*, 212, 113–30.

Kohlberg, L. 1969. *Stage and Sequence: The Cognitive-Development Approach to Socialization*. Chicago: Rand McNally.

Kohlberg, L. 1981 *The Meaning and Measurement of Moral Development*. Thousand Oaks: Sage.

Levenson, M.R. 2009. Gender and wisdom: the roles of compassion and moral development. *Research in Human Development*, 6(1), 45–59.

Lewis, M. 2000. Exploring paradox: towards a more comprehensive guide. *Academy of Management Review*, 25(4): 760–776.

Lorbiecki, A. and Jack, J. 2000. Critical turns in the evolution of diversity management. *British Journal of Management*, 11(1) (Special Issue), S17–31.

Lustgarten, R.S. (2007) *Women's Wisdom in Leadership*. Fielding: Fielding Graduate University.

Marshall, J. 1984. *Women Managers: Travellers in a Male World*. Chichester: Wiley.

McKenna, B., Rooney, D. and ten Bos, R. 2007 Wisdom as the old dog ... with new tricks. *Social Epistemology*, 21(2), 83–6.

Milkman, R. 1976. Woman's work and economic crisis: some lessons from the Great Depression. *Review of Radical Political Economy*, 8(1), 73–87.

Milkman, R. 1983. Female factory labour and industrial structures: control and conflict over 'woman's place' in auto and electrical manufacture. *Politics and Society*, 12(2), 159–203.

Mumford, M.D. 2011. A hale farewell: the state of leadership research. *The Leadership Quarterly*, 22(1), 1–7.

Noddings, N. 1984. *Caring: A Feminine Approach to Ethics and Moral Education.* Berkeley: University of California Press.

Oakley, A. 1976. Wisewoman and medicine men: changes in manufacturing of childbirth, in *The Rights and Wrongs of Women*, edited by J. Mitchell and A. Oakley. Harmondsworth: Penguin, 17–55.

Oakley, J.G. 2000. Gender barriers to senior management positions: understanding the scarcity of female CEOs. *Journal of Business Ethics*, 27(4), 321–34.

Pesonen, S., Tienari, J. and Vanhala, S. 2009. The boardroom gender paradox. *Gender in Management: An International Journal*, 24(5), 327–45.

Piaget, J. 1969. *The Mechanisms of Perception*. London: Routledge and Kegan Paul.

Piaget, J. 1971. *Biology and Knowledge: An Essay on the Relations between Organic Regulation and Cognitive Process*. Chicago: University of Chicago Press.

Price, A. and Price, B. 1997. Making midwifery decisions. *The Modern Midwife*, 7(10), 15–19.

Robinson, F. 2011. *The Ethics of Care: A Feminist Approach to Human Security*. Philadelphia: Temple University Press.

Roca, E. 2007. Intuitive practical wisdom in organization life. *Social Epistemology*, 21(2), 195–207.

Rooney, D. and McKenna, B. 2007. Wisdom in organizations: whence and whither. *Social Epistemology*, 21(2), 113–38.

Rooney, D., McKenna, B. and Liesch, P. 2010. *Wisdom and Management in the Knowledge Economy*. London: Routledge.

Rosner, J.B. 1990. Ways women lead. *Harvard Business Review* 68(6), 119–215.

Ruddick, S. 1989. *Maternal Thinking; Towards the Politics of Peace*. Boston: Beacon Press.

Schaaf, K., Hurty, K.S. and Cheen, G. 2011. *Women, Spirituality, and Transformative Leadership: Where Grace Meets Power*. Woodstock: Skylight Paths Publications.

Schwartz, F.N. 1980. Invisible resource: women for boards. *Harvard Business Review*, 58(2), 16–18.

Slote, M. 2007. *The Ethics of Care and Empathy*. Hoboken: Taylor & Francis.

Smith, D. 1987. *The Everyday World as Problematic: A Feminist Sociology*. Boston: NorthEastern University Press.

Smith, D. 1990. *The Conceptual Practices of Power: A Feminist Sociology of Knowledge*. Toronto: University of Toronto Press.

Statler, M., Roos, J. and Victor, B. 2007. Dear Prudence: an essay on practical wisdom in strategy making. *Social Epistemology*, 21(2), 151–67.

Sternberg, R.J. 2003. *Wisdom, Intelligence, and Creativity Synthesized*. New York: Cambridge University Press.

Sternberg, R.J. and Jordan, J. (eds) 2005. *A Handbook of Wisdom: Psychological Perspectives*. New York: Cambridge University Press.

Still, L.V. and Chia, W. 1995. *Self-Employed Women: Four Years On*. Working Paper No. 1, Women and Leadership Series. Perth: Edith Cowan University.

Still, L.V. and Souter, G. 1996. Sources of assistance for small business: from start-up to operations, in *Changing Business Relationships, Small Business Growth and Other Challenges Proceedings*, edited by B. Gibson, R. Newby and R. Morris. Joint SEAANZ and IIE Small Enterprise Conference. University of Newcastle Institute of Industrial Economics: Newcastle, Australia, 227–34.

Tanton, M. 1994. *Women in Management: Developing a Presence*. London: Routledge.

Vince, R. and Broussine, M. 1996. Paradox, defense and attachment: accessing and working with emotions and relations underlying organizational change. *Organization Studies*, 17(1), 1–21.

Walby, S. 1986. *Patriarchy at Work*. Cambridge: Polity Press.

Witz, A. 1992. *Professions and Patriarchy*. London: The International Library of Sociology.

6 *Evaluating the Process of Wisdom in Wise Political Leaders Using a Developmental Wisdom Model*

ROBERTO BILOSLAVO AND BERNARD MCKENNA

Introduction

Wise leadership is increasingly attracting attention in organizational, management and leadership literature (Mumford 2011). However, the notion of wisdom is still diverse and ambiguous. Determining what constitutes wisdom turns us in the directions of psychology and philosophy: Rooney, McKenna and Liesch (2010) claim that there is considerable overlap between Aristotelian philosophy and the work of contemporary wisdom psychological theorists. While some may find it inappropriate, incommensurate, even disturbing to attempt to measure a concept like wisdom because of its ineffable and transcendent quality (Case and Gosling 2007), there is considerable evidence to show that people believe that they 'know' wisdom when they see it (Pasupathi and Staudinger 2001). We propose, then, that to attempt to find human characteristics that might predict the likelihood of wisdom is not an inappropriate practice. For example, most would agree that a reasonable level of intelligence and knowledge is needed to be wise, although all the major wisdom theorists (Sternberg, Berlin School, Ardelt and so on) would strongly argue that it is a necessary, but not sufficient, condition.

So far, six significant empirical researchers or research groups have tried to identify and measure the dimensions of wisdom: Sternberg, Ardelt, Greene and Brown, Webster, Limas and Hansson and the Berlin School. There is considerable overlap among the concepts (Biloslavo and McKenna 2011): intelligence (fluid and crystallized), tolerance of uncertainty, reflexive life experience, ethics and altruism, emotional regulation and understanding are relatively uncontested. The Berlin wisdom paradigm, based primarily on the work of Baltes (Baltes and Smith 1990, Baltes and Staudinger 2000) using an explicit theoretical approach, sees wise people as displaying 'expert knowledge in the fundamental pragmatics of life that permits exceptional insight, judgment, and advice about complex and uncertain matters' (Baltes and Smith 1990: 95).

We provide a developmental model of wisdom based on four dimensions –cognition, conation, affect and morality – in order to see whether these dimensions are likely to capture the concepts contained in the six empirical approaches above. By providing three levels (formal, systematic and metasystematic) at which these dimensions manifest, the model provides an ontogenetic framework of wisdom development, although there is no necessary link between wisdom and age after early adulthood. Because our model is prototypical, our intention is to test it by evaluating whether two outstanding political leaders whom many would regard as being wise display the metasystematic criteria. We selected Nelson Mandela and Aung San Suu Kyi as our subjects because they are demonstrably wise, having displayed an essential characteristic of Aristotelian wisdom, namely *eudaimonia*, an altruistic commitment to human flourishing (Nussbaum 1994). We will subject extracts from their (auto)biographies (Kyi 1991, Mandela 1994) to textual analysis using a priori concepts derived from the four dimensions of our model. In this way, we hope to provide some degree of construct validity that could guide future research.

Short Overview of the Wisdom Concept

Attempts to define wisdom in Western culture date back as far as the Mesopotamian records of the third and second millennia BC. They are also found in Egyptian texts, in ancient Roman and Greek scholarship and in Judaeo-Christian religions, as well as Confucianism and Buddhism. Because of the numerous definitions and multidimensional nature of wisdom, there are various empirical measures. We can probably agree that, although there are some agreed universal principles of wisdom, its enactment and recognition must be contextual, or, to use Yang's (2008) term, 'a process view of wisdom'. Rooney, McKenna and Liesch's (2010) survey of the philosophy of wisdom from ancient to modern times and contemporary psychological literature led them to derive five principles of wisdom: 1) wisdom is based on reason and observation; 2) it incorporates non-rational and subjective elements into judgement; 3) it is directed to authentic humane and virtuous outcomes; 4) it is articulate, aesthetic and intrinsically rewarding; and 5) wisdom is practical. Elements of these wisdom principles are evident in other literature. For example, management theorists Malan and Kriger (1998: 249) conceive wisdom as being the 'ability to grasp the significance of many often contradictory signals and stimuli and to interpret them in a complete and integrative manner'. Another management scholar, Vaill (1998), similarly sees wisdom as a capacity to deal with uncertainty, a way of reflecting and living in constantly changing situations.

Among the psychological approaches to wisdom, Sternberg and the 'Berlin School' (for example, Baltes, Staudinger) have developed more elaborated notions of wisdom than other empiricists. Sternberg's (1998, 2003, 2004, 2005) definition of wisdom includes the exercise of successful intelligence and creativity, with the intermediation of values, in order to attain general welfare by striking a balance between intrapersonal, interpersonal and extrapersonal interests in the short and long term. All of this enables people to maintain a balance between adjusting to the existing environment, changes therein, or the choice of a new environment (Sternberg 2003). Thus, Sternberg sees wisdom not as prioritizing personal interests, but as balancing out different personal interests (intrapersonal aspect) with the interests of other people (interpersonal aspect) and with other aspects of the environment in which somebody lives (extrapersonal aspect). In testing wisdom, seen as 'an expert system dealing with the meaning and conduct of life'

(Baltes and Staudinger 2000: 124), the Berlin School uses an explicit theory approach: that is, constructions of wisdom as devised by expert theorists and researchers rather than laypeople. However, this has been criticized by some (Ardelt 2004) for emphasizing advanced cognitive functioning. Kunzmann and Baltes (2003: 294–5) disagree, asserting that wisdom is characterized by 'excellence in mind and virtue and ... excellence in the conduct and meaning of life'.

The 'fundamental pragmatics of life' (Pasupathi, Staudinger and Baltes 2001: 351) that underlie the Berlin School's definition of wisdom include 'insight into the social nature and incompleteness of human existence, the variability of life goals, knowledge about oneself and the limits of one's knowledge, and insight into how knowledge is translated into behaviour' (Staudinger and Pasupathi 2003: 240). They also differentiate between cognitive mechanics and cognitive pragmatics of the mind (Baltes and Kunzman 2003, Kunzman and Baltes 2003), which can be understood as the distinction between fluid intelligence and crystallized intelligence (Baltes, Smith and Staudinger 1992) as devised by Horn and Cattell (1967). There are multiple forms of intelligence, probably more than two, as Sternberg et al. (2000) strongly claim. Fluid intelligence, the ability to perceive relationships without previously being taught, is 'an expression of the level of complexity of relationships which an individual can perceive and act upon when he [sic] does not have recourse to answers to such complex issues already stored in memory' (Cattell 1971: 115). That is, it is abstract reasoning that is independent of learning, experience and education. By contrast, crystallized intelligence, built on experience and learning, comprises 'complex, acquired abilities, in the form of high-level judgmental skills' (Cattell 1987: 139). While fluid intelligence peaks between 30 and 40 years of age, crystallized intelligence grows with age (Schaie 2005). Thus, it is likely that our use of different types of intelligence varies over our lifetime. The accumulation of crystallized intelligence is also important in mentoring situations because older people's level of crystallized intelligence is related to their openness to experience (Zimprich, Allemand and Dellenbach 2009), which makes them more likely to have encountered and dealt with various situations met by younger or less experienced people.

Clearly, then, wisdom is closely linked to knowledge and intelligence. But what wisdom philosophers and psychologists tell us is that wisdom requires much more than mere knowledge or modes of cognition. Schwaninger (2006) sums up most of this thinking by positing wisdom as knowledge and understanding of a higher quality, which contains both an ethical and an aesthetic dimension. From a knowledge perspective, being wise requires knowing what one knows and does not know, what it is possible to know and what it is not possible to know at a given time and place (Sternberg 2003). Furthermore, a wise person is also able and willing to use the appropriate knowledge in accordance with the needs of all who will be affected by the consequences of an action such as stakeholders.

Other aspects of wisdom have been developed by various writers. Wisdom must be practical and applied, as Aristotle insisted. Beck (1999) stresses that wisdom consists of not just knowledge (understanding truth) but also action (doing good). This can also be understood as embodiment (Yang 2008: 65). To know what is right, yet not to do it, or to do what is right without knowing that it is right, is not wisdom: in other words, there must be more than moral cognition. Wisdom is built on values that sustain good community. While wisdom includes knowledge, it also reaches further and comprises 'value judgments ... in order to create better conditions of life, better institutions, habits and social relations' (Maxwell 1984: 66). Wisdom, in contrast to the present concern with ephemerality and short-termism, takes account of the long-term implications and consequences of our actions: wisdom is 'the ability to comprehend and evaluate the long-term consequences of behaviour' (Ackoff 1996: 29). Birren and Fisher (1990) share with Sternberg the notion of wisdom as a balance. They see balance as 'opposing valences of intense emotion and detachment, action and inaction, and knowledge and doubts' (326). According to Birren and Fisher (1990: 325), wisdom integrates 'the affective, conative, and cognitive aspects of human abilities in response to life tasks and problems'.

To sum up, wisdom must be understood within a given socio-cultural context as a socially oriented practice directed to authentic, humane and virtuous outcomes. Wisdom must incorporate reason and knowledge using fluid intelligence and crystallized intelligence. But it must also incorporate non-rational and subjective elements when making judgements. It must be articulate and aesthetic. But it must above all be practical. Wisdom provides a capacity to deal with uncertainty, mutability and ineffability. The wise person must be intelligent and creative in different ways. The wise person is committed to humane values, and must balance personal interests with those of others, as well as long- and short-term interests. The wise person is adaptable, but not capricious or vacillating. Therefore we can conclude that to be distinctively wise, one must achieve high levels of personal development, which includes development in cognitive, conative, affective and moral domains.

Short Overview of the Empirical Measurement of Wisdom

Attempting to measure all of these elements is fraught with considerable complexity. The Berlin School, Sternberg and a number of other US empirical researchers have attempted to measure wisdom. The Berlin School use a think-aloud technique in which participants are asked to respond to a hypothetical problem or a personal reflection, with the responses being assessed by trained raters according to general (GW) or personal wisdom (PW) criteria. A number of US researchers have attempted to measure wisdom using self-assessment surveys. Monika Ardelt (2003, 2011) uses a Three-Dimensional Wisdom Scale (3D-WS) to test for cognitive, reflective and affective dimensions. Jeffrey Webster (2007) tests for five dimensions: critical life experiences, reminiscence/reflectiveness, openness to experience, emotional regulation and humour. Scott Brown (Greene and Brown 2009) tests for six dimensions: self-knowledge, understanding of others, judgement, life knowledge, life skills and a willingness to learn. Sternberg (2003) mostly uses scales to test for reasoning ability, sagacity, learning from ideas and the environment, judgement, expeditious use of information and perspicacity but also uses 'expert' analysis of responses (Sternberg, Wagner, Williams and Horvath 1995).

The five most commonly shared dimensions among all these theorists are: tolerance of divergent values; tolerance of ambiguity and uncertainty; self-insight; emotional understanding and emotional regulation; and sound levels of crystallized and fluid intelligence. These are consistent with the four domains of personal development in our model: cognitive, conative, affective and moral as outlined in Table 6.1. More specifically, the cognitive domain requires fluid and crystallized intelligence. Values tolerance is included as a cognitive as well as moral dimension because it requires more than a tolerant disposition. True values tolerance involves sagacity of which listening to all sides is a component (Sternberg 1990). The cognitive capacity to use relativistic and dialectical reasoning is crucial to sagacious judgement (Kramer 2000). According to Kriger and Malan (1993: 396), the wise manager needs to 'develop more tolerance for opposing worldviews and ways of exploring organizational issues'. In each of these instances, values tolerance involves a cognitive capacity to evaluate and perceive a situation from an unfamiliar cognitive framework, and thus involves high levels of cognition. Similarly, the capacity to tolerate ambiguity and uncertainty requires not just sufficient cognitive capacity to make judgements based on uncertain or changing assumptions (Ardelt 2011), but also a resolution to stay the course in such circumstances, which is a feature of conation. Self-insight is a requirement for any person to accept that they acted wrongly, which is fundamental to moral development. Finally, the affective domain clearly involves empathy (Ardelt 2011) and emotional regulation (Webster 2007).

Table 6.1   Four domains of personal development and five dimensions of wisdom

Five Dimensions of Wisdom	Four Domains of Personal Development
Values tolerance	Moral and cognitive
Ambiguity and uncertainty tolerance	Conative and cognitive
Self-insight	Moral
Emotional understanding and emotional regulation	Affective
Fluid and crystallized intelligence	Cognitive

The Developmental Wisdom Model

The developmental wisdom model proposes that wise action comprises the synthesis of these dimensions at a metasystematic level. The dimensions are informed by Piaget's (1969, 1971) theories of cognitive development, Kegan's (1982, 1994) constructive development theory, Kohlberg's (1969, 1981) model of moral development and Huitt and Cain's (2005) study of conation. Because of the 'universal' nature of its stages, the nonlinear nature of task performance and the sequence from lower order actions, Commons' (2008, Commons et al. 1998) model of post-formal levels of development is used. This Model of Hierarchical Complexity (MHC) specifies 14 orders of hierarchical complexity and their corresponding stages. Commons incorporates four post-formal stages (11–14): systematic, metasystematic, paradigmatic and cross-paradigmatic. We posit that the borderline level of development for wisdom development is the metasystematic stage as this presents 'a deep structural shift in basic premises of thought, feelings, and actions ... a shift in consciousness that dramatically and permanently alters our way of being in the world' (Morrell and O'Connor 2002: xvii).

Wisdom can be judged only through the actions of individuals; otherwise it is not wisdom, but something else (for example, wise thoughts). Individual actions (that is, behaviours) are, however, predicted by personal characteristics, which, since Plato and Aristotle, have been divided into three core psychological functions: motivational, affective and cognitive (Musek 2003). A person with their conative dispositions and cognitive abilities regulates their relationship with the environment by either adjusting to it or actively transforming it in accordance with their own perceptions of competency and effectiveness (that is, the concept of self-efficacy). This process takes place through setting and achieving goals, derived from the person's needs and desires. The performances achieved as well as actions taken are judged based on the moral standards of the person. Most importantly, motivational events are regularly accompanied by the appropriate emotions. Occurrence of needs we usually experience as emotional stress and frustration, while their satisfaction we experience as positive emotions of pleasure, relaxation and satisfaction. Similarly, motivational activities are monitored by our cognition. A need starts to work only when it is perceived. Without cognition we would not be able to search and detect motivational goals that guide our motivated acts. Therefore, the motivation itself takes place at the affective and cognitive levels. Because we emotionally experience motivational goals, they can direct our actions (that is, they either attract or repel us). However, cognitive elements represent an essential part of emotional response. Without them we would feel just an emotional arousal, but not the real content of emotional experiences. We can see how emotional experience is associated with all forms of motivation, and both of them with cognition. Human behaviour is imbued with conative, affective and cognitive activities. Conative and affective processes encourage, energize and guide our behaviour, but in a manner that is regulated and lead by our intellect (that is, our perceptions, experiences and thoughts).

Now that we have a better understanding of the processes behind our actions, we can provide a description of the relationships among the four dimensions of the model (see Figure 6.1). As we described above, because the four dimensions are independent they cannot be substituted by each other. Along each dimension, individuals develop through qualitatively different stages, which are built on, and are inclusive of, the core capacities of lower stages, that is, developmental stages as holons (Koestler 1967). The proposed model assumes that the general direction of human development is oriented to more complex and more integrated personality structure. Even if the stage sequence should be invariant, people proceed through the stages at different rates, and some may not reach the highest stages of development. In some rare cases, individuals can even regress to a lower stage of development on some or all dimensions. Although an individual can develop along a single dimension of the model independently of other dimensions, the fact that the conative, cognitive and affective processes are present simultaneously suggests that these may be mutually reinforcing. However, as shown by several examples in practice (for example, Nazi doctors performing inhumane acts) and research (for example, research about emotional intelligence), this mutual dependence is not linear and decreases the more the individual's development is progressing. While we can expect that at the lower stages of development the intellect can be a good indicator of developmental level for the other three dimensions (for example, an individual cannot be expected to give or understand moral judgement without having a proper level of intellectual development), at the post-formal stage of development this is not necessarily the case. Individuals at any given stage have full access to the developmental stages below – or as Hewlett (2003: 17) states: 'each newly emergent holon includes its preceding or lower level holons and adds its own novel or higher level qualities – or in other words, each emergent holon transcends but includes its predecessor'. For example, individuals at the metasystematic level of development will also retain the capacity to function and work efficiently with people at the formal level of development. Nevertheless, individuals do not have access to the stages above their current developmental stage. Even if an individual may in one context show stages of development above their current one, this is only a random event that has nothing to do with the true transformation needed to move from one stage to another.

Two important assumptions underlie our wisdom development model. First, an individual needs to develop along all four domains (that is, cognitive, conative, affective and moral) as any one of them is insufficient for wisdom. Conversely, an individual who displays post-formal development along all four dimensions will not necessarily behave wisely, but their potential for behaving wisely is high. Second, certain relatively independent modes of thought progress through discernible stages of growth (Baldwin 1906/1975; Dawson-Tunik, Commons, Wilson and Fischer 2005). In our model, stages of growth are defined in terms of a developmental logic: that is, there is a process of growth along stages of development characterized in terms of increasing differentiation, integration, complexity and abstraction (Stein and Heikkinen 2008). However, using Kohlberg's (1969) model of moral reasoning, although distinct from reasoning in other domains, presupposes levels of complexity of reasoning.

At the metasystematic stage of development, individuals act to 'integrate systems to construct multisystems or metasystems out of disparate systems; compare systems and perspectives in a systematic way (across multiple domains); reflect on systems ... [and] name properties of systems' (Commons 2008: 312). We now consider each of the four dimensions of the wisdom model at the metasystematic level more closely.

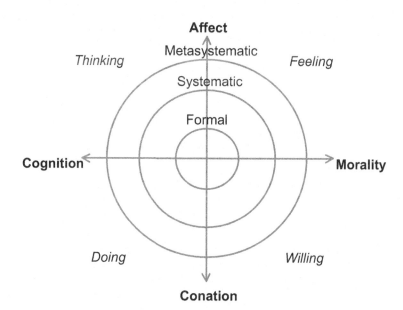

Figure 6.1   Integrated wisdom development model

Cognitive Complexity

Cognitive complexity includes using different aspects when thinking about something, discriminating among the aspects and integrating the information (Warr and Conner 1992). Most researchers agree that cognitive complexity involves the ability to view a given situation from multiple perspectives while screening out irrelevant factors, flexible thinking and possessing a multidimensional view of the world. High cognitive complexity indicates that a decision-maker carefully weighs all the relevant perspectives on an issue and then integrates them into a coherent position. Low complexity, in contrast, indicates that only one viewpoint is considered, which is then maintained with tenacity. This understanding of cognitive complexity includes not just fluid intelligence (the capacity to think abstractly), but also crystallized intelligence (life knowledge) and tolerance of diverse values and uncertainty that are implied in the various schools of wisdom outlined in Table 6.1. Differing levels of cognitive complexity are more pronounced as environmental complexity increases.

The three levels of the individual's cognitive complexity are:

1. *At the formal level of development*, the individual is cognitively capable of shaping and understanding only one aspect of any matter because such people understand every matter merely from their personal uniform viewpoint. Although they are sensible to the context of the matter, their decisions are most of the time subordinate to rules. They are not capable of realizing that different viewpoints can coexist at the same time.
2. *At the systematic level of development*, the individual is aware that different standpoints exist, and perceives knowledge and values as relativistic. Consequently, from among the different standpoints (that is, relations between variables), the individual either works out a compromise or else reactively responds to the negative consequences that result from persisting in one standpoint. The person is searching for a dynamic balance while considering the diverse aspects of the matter.
3. *At the metasystematic level of development*, the individual at the same time integrates the diverse viewpoints on the matter and knows that each of these has its own limitations (that is, the capacity for paradoxical reflection or dialectic thinking). The individual is aware of the fact that the people with whom s/he is in social relationships may hold different viewpoints from their own, and that these viewpoints are as real for other individuals as their own viewpoint is for him/her (that is, the multiple realities of life). This individual is capable of integrating differing viewpoints into the best possible coherent whole in order to come closer to the reality of the task.

Conative Complexity

Moral conation is 'the capacity to generate responsibility and motivation to take moral action in the face of adversity and persevere through challenges' (Hannah, Avolio and May 2011: 664). It could also be considered as an individual's agentive self-control or willpower to fully commit towards achieving a particular goal (Ghoshal and Bruch 2003). Conation is distinguished from motivation in that willpower is linked to activities aimed at achieving a set objective, while motivation merely moves the individual to a state of eagerness, which in an extreme instance may also become quite static. Motivation arises at the moment when the individual, consciously or unconsciously, determines upon a certain goal, while conation enters at the moment when the individual undertakes activities in order to achieve the established aim. As Poulsen (1991) says, motivation is a feeling whereas conation is the style of action that a person uses to respond to that feeling. While a definition for conation is relatively elusive, it is best understood as connecting 'knowledge and affect to behavior ... It is the personal, intentional, planful, deliberate, goal-oriented, or striving component of motivation, the proactive (as opposed to reactive or habitual) aspect of behavior' (Huitt and Cain 2005: 1).

Hannah, Avolio and May (2011) see conation as indirectly related to moral maturation capacities that shape moral sensitivity and moral judgement (moral cognition). Their concept draws from theories of human agency, psychological ownership and engagement as well as self-efficacy, means efficacy and courage. Moral action is seen as the outcome of moral motivation, and these comprise a moral conation process. However, moral conation processes are preceded by moral cognition processes where moral sensitivity leads to moral judgement. It is the gap between moral judgement and moral motivation that is the essence of conation. While moral cognition processes comprise the capacity for moral complexity, meta-cognitive ability and moral identity, moral conation processes depend on the level of moral ownership, moral efficacy and moral courage (Hannah, Avolio and May 2011). Conation, therefore, is the key factor in persisting towards performing moral action.

A positive conative aspect is particularly important when the vision or ambitious goals of the organization are removed in time and which, in their demands, exceed the present capabilities of members of the organization. Conation, therefore, is linked not only to the willpower necessary for fulfilling the set objectives, but also to the perseverance required for achieving the ultimate goal (Corno 1993). Thus, conation, because it involves willpower rather than mere impulse, is linked to virtue because virtue involves choosing for the good regardless. Furthermore, to remain constantly directed towards attaining goals, individuals with strong conation use three reflective techniques (Eccles and Wigfield 2002). They use self-observation to monitor their own activity. They use self-assessment to compare the results of their own activities with the standard norm, or with the results achieved by other individuals in the environment. They also use positive self-reaction: that is, reacting to the results of their activities and, if the results happen to be negative, this provides further stimulus for continuing activities to attain the goal. This reflexive aspect is consistent with the wisdom principles contained in the Berlin School notion of pragmatics, which includes insight into oneself and human existence in general, and in Ardelt's (2003, 2011) reflective dimension.

The three levels of the individual's conative complexity are:

1. *At the formal level of development*, the individual links different motives and situational variables. The individual is aware that different motives and volitional strategies influence final goal achievement, but they can or cannot protect selected intentions from competing action tendencies.
2. *At the systematic level of development*, the individual organizes different motives and volitional strategies into a system. S/he is able to give a conscious personal shape to the image of the goal.

3. *At the metasystematic level of development*, the individual coordinates different systems of motives and volitional strategies and relates them to the type of the set goals. At this level of development, the individual accepts uncertainty as a fact that cannot be disregarded, but which can be mitigated by adopting various behavioural approaches. In no case will the person abandon attaining the goal on account of feeling uncertain.

Affective Complexity

After Wessman and Ricks' (1966) initial work on affective complexity, two aspects have been predominantly emphasized. The first aspect relates to the range or span of different emotions experienced by a person. The second aspect concerns how well a person can distinguish subtle differences among similar emotions. Kang and Shaver' (2004: 689) conceptualized emotional complexity as 'a product of cognitive complexity, personality dispositions, and life experiences [that] leads to empathic understanding of others' feelings and greater interpersonal adaptability'. They hypothesized, and in their study confirm, that individuals with more complex emotional experience are more attentive to their feelings, more open to experience, better able to understand others' feelings and are better adjusted socially.

A person with high affective complexity can benefit from experiencing varied and differentiated emotions in such a way that improves their understanding of others because that often requires that we understand their feelings (Saarni 1997), and to understand their feelings we need to first of all understand our own. Emotional complexity also enhances interpersonal adaptability as empathic understanding of others' feelings increases the likelihood of choosing appropriate responses or reactions (Kang and Shaver 2004). The ability to recognize one's own and other people's emotions as well as the ability to restrain oneself from inappropriate emotional responses represent the focal point of the research on the relationship between wisdom and emotions (Csikszentmihalyi and Nakamura 2005).

The concept of affective complexity shares some similarities with the concept of emotional intelligence developed by Mayer and Salovey (1997) that comprises four types of skills, ranging from the basic psychological processes to the more complex processes of emotional and cognitive integration. The first type of skill represents a group of abilities that enable the individual to recognize, judge and express feelings. These skills include recognizing one's own feelings and those of others, expressing one's own feelings and distinguishing among the emotions expressed by others. The other type of skill includes the use of feelings to alleviate and to order the priority of various ways of thinking. The third group includes skills such as characterizing and distinguishing between emotions, understanding the interlinkages between various feelings and devising the rules relating to them. The fourth type of skill represents the individual's overall ability to control emotions, that is, emotional regulation (Webster 2010). The core of emotional intelligence is the ability to use emotional information and to regulate moods rather than differences in the range of emotional experience. However, the first type of skill – ability to identify one's own emotions – seems to be directly related to affective complexity. The affective domain, incorporating empathy, understanding and control, is strongly represented in the wisdom theory summary provided in Table 6.1. Affective complexity is incorporated as a characteristic of wisdom by all the wisdom researchers considered in our summary analysis above.

Three levels of the individual's affective complexity are:

1. *At the formal level of development*, the individual is capable of linking their own emotional state and those of others to the situation at hand. The individual is aware that feeling states influence immediate perspectives or perception. They are able to imagine themselves in another's position although they cannot relate this emotional disposition to their own.
2. *At the systematic level of development*, the individual organizes feelings into a system that comprehends others' feelings and the context. The individual understands how the context and people involved shape their emotional state, and so is capable of putting their personal emotions into a proper perspective.
3. *At the metasystematic level of development*, the individual is able to take into account that some sets of emotions conflict with other sets (for example, parents' love versus fear of losing a child in adulthood). At this level of development, the individual is fully capable of reflectively regulating, differentiating and expressing their own emotion as well as relating others' feelings to their own.

Moral Complexity

An individual's moral development can be described using Kohlberg's (1969, 1981) three-level model of moral reasoning or ethical criteria (for example, egoism, benevolence and principle). These three criteria correspond to philosophy's three major classes of ethical theory: egoism, utilitarianism and deontology. Cullen, Victor and Stephens (1989) define egoism as being motivated by the wish to maximize one's own interest; utilitarianism as the wish to maximize the interest of oneself and significant others; and deontology as the desire to do what is right, independently of the action's specific outcome. An individual's moral development can even be related to an organization's moral development: as Logsdon and Yuthas (1997: 1216) propose, 'how the organisation views its goals and relationships to various stakeholders is an important indicator of its moral development, just as the moral development of individuals is indicated by whether and how they take others into account'. In a similar way, Piaget (1969) and, after him, Feffer (1970) developed the concept called 'decentring'. Based on their work, moral development can be understood in direct relationship with an individual's ability to maintain a decentred perspective when interacting with others. This means understanding a situation from the other person's viewpoint, not just from one's own, and to behave in a proper way based on it. A commitment to virtuous outcomes is also strongly represented in the empirical researchers' criteria for wisdom, none more so than Sternberg (1998: 356) who asserts that it 'is impossible to speak of wisdom outside the context of a set of values' or the Berlin School who see wisdom as characterized by 'excellence in mind and virtue and ... excellence in the conduct and meaning of life' (Kunzmann and Baltes 2003: 294–5).

The proposed individual's moral complexity is defined as:

> *At the formal level of development* the individual's actions comply with rules (that is, authority) to avoid unpleasant consequences. While an individual's decisions could

serve the interests of others, there is no requirement that they do so. Whatever benefits the individual and some specific people is appropriate if it does not go against prevailing social rules.

At the systematic level of development, an individual understands the structure and functioning of the social order as a whole and their own duties and rights. The focus is on maintaining law and order by following the rules, doing one's duty and respecting authority. This includes accepting responsibilities for specific classes of people.

At the metasystematic level of development, individuals recognize the interconnectedness between them and other natural and social complex systems. Actions are justified on the basis of universal abstract principles. Recognizing that sometimes peer and legal standards are not sufficient to be fully moral, the individual can participate in a dialogue about social values and responsibility to achieve social consensus and tolerance on conflicting issues. The individual is willing to pursue principles of justice and the rights of human beings, even if this is not expected from peers or other people around them. The metasystematic level of the four wisdom dimensions (cognitive, conative, affective and moral) thus provides comprehensive criteria to evaluate whether people are acting wisely.

Methodology

To evaluate whether the Process Wisdom Model measures wisdom potential, we consider the statements provided by two people who are considered outstanding and inspirational humanitarians who have suffered immensely to bring about a better society. Aung San Suu Kyi and Nelson Mandela might reasonably be considered to be two of the most respected, even revered, people living today (2012). They have in common that they have been political prisoners whose persistence and moral authority eventually led to their release and the full or (in Burma's case) partial achievement of humanitarian and democratic political goals. For textual analysis, we have used interviews from Kyi's (1997) and Mandela's (1994) autobiographies. While it could be argued that people's perceptions of themselves could be distorted or unrealistic, in these two instances, the lives of both people have been open to public scrutiny for a very long time. Thus the potential for inaccurate representations is greatly diminished. In any case, it is important to know how they view the world, how they understand themselves and how they explain the extreme courses of action that they took.

Our textual analysis simply involved reading the texts (interview and biography), conscious of the systematic and metasystematic level of the four-dimensional model. This is consistent with Vergne's (2011) methodology of selecting the relevant dimensions of the construct under question and selecting the relevant textual sources for analysis. The third part of that methodology, controlling for spatial bias, is not relevant in this instance as that was taking into account the political biases of the newspapers under study. We employed no coding scheme other than looking for instances of 'embodied' practice of the four wisdom dimensions. Admittedly, this implies a positivist approach to the relationship between text and meaning (Lacity and Janson 1994). That is, we assume that the language corresponds to an objective reality that is understood by those who read the text. The analysis makes no attempt to locate the texts within a discursive framework or the subject positioning of author and reader, which would no doubt yield more useful information. Instead, as readers, we locate ourselves within a Bakhtinian chain of utterances (Lemke 1995) that we claim to share with the writer. Implicit in this is a shared set of beliefs about human rights and human dignity. Although looking specifically for instances of the four wisdom dimensions, we were alert for other possible wisdom indicators.

Findings

COGNITIVE COMPLEXITY

Mandela emphasized the importance of formal education and learning by obtaining an arts degree. Furthermore, to better understand the history of revolution and political economy, he read classic texts such as those by Marx, Mao Tse-Tung and Edgar Snow. To understand warfare, he read von Clausewitz (NM: 239).[1] However, Mandela also showed the importance of diverse experience, not just formal education. When Mandela travelled internationally in 1961 he learnt much from diverse sources, but one of the most important realizations was to recognize his own mindset. As he was boarding a plane in Addis Ababa: 'I saw that the pilot was black. I had never seen a black pilot before, and the instant I did I had to quell my panic. How could a black man fly an airplane? But a moment later I caught myself: I had fallen into the apartheid mind-set' (NM: 254–5).

Kyi considers the notion of truth, asserting that 'The search for truth has to be accompanied by awareness. And awareness and objectivity are very closely linked' (AK: 53). In other words, Kyi sees knowledge as socially constructed and that, jointly, knowledge becomes intersubjective: 'What we need when we come to dialogue is confidence, in ourselves as well as in each other. Truth does not become such a problem if there is confidence in each other' (AK: 39). Such a view of knowledge is consistent with the metasystematic level of cognitive complexity, particularly the tentative and subjective nature of knowledge. As Kyi argues: 'Pure truth – absolute truth – is beyond ordinary beings like us because we cannot see things absolutely and as a whole. ... Truth is something towards which we struggle all the time' (AK: 52). However, truth is not just about intersubjective understanding. There are moments of realization as the metasystematic level brings together differing viewpoints to form the best coherent whole. This does not always mean some sort of middle or compromise position. At one stage, Mandela makes the decision that violence had to replace non-violence (NM: 136–7) as the government simply became even more repressive in response to attempts to negotiate. The ruling National Party's bigoted view of the black people, and their own incapability of sharing national wealth, Mandela realized, left no option.

Metasystematic level cognition, then, is evident insofar that knowledge is understood as constructed in people's minds, that this can be the basis of viewpoints different from our own, and that judgements can be made based on differing viewpoints, even within oneself.

---

1   NM = Nelson Mandela's *Long Walk to Freedom*; AK = Aung San Suu Kyi's *The Voice of Hope*

CONATIVE COMPLEXITY

Conative complexity is an aspect of wisdom that is not very well incorporated in the wisdom models provided by the theorists outlined above. It is especially clear that both leaders have enormous agentive self-control and willpower, not just in committing themselves to the struggle, but also in maintaining it when they were each imprisoned for three decades or more. Kyi says, 'our struggle for democracy is ... not something that you do when you have a bit of free time, or when you feel like it. You have to work at it all the time, because it affects your life all the time' (AK: 108). She claims that 'There's always courage involved in making decisions' (AK: 49). Mandela displayed enormous conative development as he awaited the sentence at his treason trial. Knowing that the death penalty was a likely possibility, Mandela nonetheless vowed not to appeal because 'our message was that no sacrifice was too great in the struggle for freedom' (NM: 326). In this sense, conative complexity to some degree overlaps with moral development, as one has to enact the decision that has been arrived at. Wisdom has to be practical: enacting it can clearly also be dangerous.

Again it is clear that both people combine different motives and volitional strategies to set goals that for them guaranteed suffering and possibly death. They were able to deal with the enormous uncertainty that they faced in dealing with a repressive and violent enemy. They adopted appropriate behavioural approaches to deal with this uncertainty so that they did not abandon the goal. Mandela's and Kyi's conative development is consistent with Hannah, Avolio and May's (2011) model: their moral complexity and moral identity developed a capacity for moral judgement (the moral cognition process) but they also displayed the moral ownership, efficacy and courage to generate the motivation to act.

AFFECTIVE COMPLEXITY

It is clear that Mandela and Kyi have very high levels of affective complexity. An important element is to recognize one's own and other people's emotions. Linked to Kyi's notion of truth is the need for self-truth, which is based on the awareness identified in the cognitive dimension above, for example she acknowledged her weakness of having a short temper (AK: 59). This objective self-awareness also leads to a better understanding of others even when they attempt to intimidate:

> (I)f you are aware of what people are doing you become more objective about them too. For example, awareness means that when you are aware of the fact that somebody is shouting, you don't think to yourself: 'What a horrible man'. That's purely subjective. But if you are aware you know that he's shouting because he's angry or frightened. That's objectivity. Otherwise, without awareness, all kinds of prejudices start multiplying. (AK: 53)

This capacity to deeply understand even one's jailers was evident in Mandela also. He recounts the instance at Robben Island whose warders were the most aggressive and violent Afrikaners who despised the black prisoners. Nonetheless, one of these inhumane warders was ameliorated by Mandela's deft understanding of people's emotions. Mandela asked a colleague to befriend the man as Mandela himself, who was seen as defiant, would arouse suspicion if he appeared courteous and friendly. When the warder asked the other prisoner to lend him his jacket, Mandela nodded agreement. A few days later, the warder threw them a leftover sandwich. Although this act could have been treated with disdain, Mandela considered it best to accept this offer as representing a step forward, however small, in the warder's own humanity. Unbelievably, they later started a political dialogue, with Mandela leading the warder to reappraise his own political beliefs (NM: 365–6).

Kyi had to deal with the affective dimension of her enemy's fear and hate by adopting a serene disposition. She asserts that: 'If you can look upon someone with serenity you are able to cope with the feelings of hatred. But there cannot be serenity if there is fear' (AK: 164). Trust is clearly significant not just in Kyi's cognitive awareness, but also in her affective awareness and disposition. Much discord arises from fear which 'is motivated by lack of trust in oneself', which in turn 'may indicate that you think there are things about yourself which are not desirable' (AK: 40). Her linking of fear and trust is particularly incisive given that there is considerable psychological support for it (Korsgaard, Brodt and Whitener 2002, Lewicki and Bunker 1996). More particularly, wary individuals who lack trust are likely to adopt self-protective behaviour and are likely to have lower expectations about relationships (Cotterell, Eisenberger and Speicher 1992, Kamdar, McAllister and Turban 2006). Hence there is less likelihood of reciprocal relationships.

Both leaders showed a metasystematic level of affective development in their ability to regulate their own emotions and to understand the foundation of the emotions of another person, even one's jailer and torturer. They were able to use this affective complexity to build relationships with others with whom they were implacably opposed.

MORAL COMPLEXITY

Given that Mandela and Kyi are renowned and revered for profoundly suffering for humane political beliefs, it is not surprising that they would display a high level of moral complexity. Kyi refers to it as *purity*, the enemies of which are greed, hatred and ignorance (AK: 53). Mandela founded his political struggle on the desire for human dignity. In summing up his motivation in the treason trial at which he could have been sentenced to death, Mandela stated that he saw the lack of dignity emerging from poverty, the breakdown of family structures, a lack of security and a lack of political and economic equality (NM: 321–2). However, at a more personal level, Mandela faced the moral dilemma of choosing between his family and his political activism. His first marriage ended because his wife, Evelyn, not unreasonably, could no longer endure an almost fatherless family. Although his second wife, Winnie, shared his political convictions, the children from this marriage lost their father for the 30 years that he was imprisoned. Clearly, such moral difficulties are almost impossible to judge given the tension between the greater good of South African black liberation and the personal good of providing a stable family for his children.

Both leaders displayed a metasystematic level of moral development in that they profoundly understood the interconnectedness within complex social systems. Furthermore, they based their political actions on universal abstract principles that, in both instances, required that they act illegally. They were prepared to engage in dialogue with political allies and enemies even when there seemed little chance of reciprocal respect or dialogue.

OTHER FINDINGS

Some important aspects of Mandela's and Kyi's statements also emerged for consideration in a wisdom model. For example, it was clear that Mandela had a deep respect for his elders and for the tradition they carried. He spoke in an earlier trial about listening to his elders in the Transkei village in which he grew up and the importance of tradition in his moral formation (NM: 287). Kyi acknowledges the importance of teachers, but also says that having good friends is important in understanding life (AK: 54). Another important point that Mandela made was that: 'I had no epiphany, no singular revelation, no moment of truth, but a steady accumulation of a thousand slights, a thousand indignities, a thousand unremembered moments' (NM: 83). In other words, wisdom came about by fully experiencing life, engaging in dialogue and being thoughtful about one's experience. A third element that emerged from Mandela's account was discipline, including physical discipline. Mandela maintained his physical fitness even under the most difficult circumstances (NM: 167, 241). The physical and corporeal aspects of wise people should be considered given that wisdom is displayed in enduring patterns of behaviour of those who have it; wise people regularly and predictably act wisely in daily life (Kekes 1983, 1995): 'the whole process of wisdom should entail embodied action' (Yang 2008: 63). Kyi also identified a sense of humour as a device for dealing with vindictiveness (AK: 40). Webster (2007) identifies humour as one of the elements of being wise. In other words, there are possible elements of wisdom that are not effectively covered by the four dimensions of the model. On the other hand, because good theory needs to be parsimonious, it is inappropriate to try to include every possible contributory factor.

Conclusion

Wisdom is a concept that is difficult to define and even more difficult to measure. Basically, we employed a psycho-historical approach – in some ways a psycho-biography (Cara 2007) – to identify components of wisdom displayed by two significant and successful political activists seeking a more humane society. We have tested the four-dimensional model based on our definitions of cognitive, conative, affective and moral development. There was clear evidence that both leaders exhibited metasystematic levels of performance in the four dimensions, providing some face validity to these constructs. As yet, however, there is no empirical research that we know of that collectively operationalizes these concepts for measurement. We believe that in the future the use of 'pattern matching' (Trochim 1985), which is aimed at developing greater construct validity and clearer relationships, will assist in developing wisdom measurements and relationships among constructs. Hence, the questions of reliability and validity of the proposed model should be considered more precisely. More theoretical and empirical dialogue regarding the various wisdom measures, including the four dimensions of this model, can contribute to a better understanding of wisdom as a concept and possible ways in which we can test for wisdom and wise practice.

An important feature of this research is that it moves wisdom research away from personal wisdom (about one's own life), general wisdom (being able to advise others about life issues) and organizational wisdom (creating conditions for organizations to act wisely) to consider wisdom in the political realm. Given the widespread mistrust of politicians, further research into wise political leaders may well contribute to an increased trust in the political process. In the case of these two politicians, we have seen wisdom heroically enacted in pursuit of political ideals that contribute to *eudaimonic* outcomes for society. In applying the findings to an organizational context, there is evidence not just about the cognitive, affective and moral components of wisdom, but also about the conative component and the potential price to be paid by those who display courage in enacting their conative capacity.

We believe that using the narratives and experiences of demonstrably wise people contributes strongly to wisdom research. Although this is already done in research dealing with nominated wise people (Baltes, Staudinger, Maercker and Smith 1995, Orwoll and Perlmutter 1990, Yang 2008), no studies as yet have chosen globally outstanding living nominees. However, such an approach has its own limitation that was well explained by Polanyi (1968) when he said 'people know more than they can say'. The point is that a person may not be able to explain what they tacitly know to another and neither can the person explain it to themselves. We can say that because a psycho-historical approach depends on written statements (that is, explicit knowledge), it understates the value of implicit knowledge that is mostly valued by different wisdom researchers. For example, Sternberg (1998: 351) asserts that knowledge that is not easily communicated is 'at the core of wisdom'. On the other hand, we have provided evidence to support the proposition that wisdom can largely be explained in terms of metasystematic-level performance of the four dimensions. If it is true that most people know wisdom when they see it, listening to what wise people say should help us better understand the factors that define this elusive concept.

Reflective Questions

1. There is a deep cynicism in many democracies about their politicians, and certainly few would be nominated as wise. What factors militate against politicians acting wisely? How might we in the electorate contribute to unwise political outcomes by our own demands and practices?
2. Nelson Mandela and Aung San Suu Kyi displayed great courage, and the description of conation outlined above included moral courage. Can a person who lacks courage be wise?
3. Aristotle proposed that by acting virtuously we contribute to *eudaimonia*, or human flourishing. Is it possible for business organizations to adopt *eudaimonic* outcomes as their foundational principle above all others? If not, what prevents it?
4. How would we assess wisdom in groups, organizations and society? Try to express this in positive terms, rather than the absence of negative elements.
5. Affective complexity involves empathy and emotional regulation. What factors might trigger our emotions sufficiently to reduce our capacity to regulate them, leading to unwise actions? What research method might be useful in investigating this?
6. Is it possible to be wise with relatively low levels of moral complexity? Why?
7. Given that a relatively high level of cognitive complexity underlies each of the four factors, is it possible for a naïve Forrest Gump character to act wisely?

8. The zone of proximal development is a concept developed by Vygotsky and represents the difference between what a learner can do without help and what he or she can do with help. How can this concept be used for wisdom development in political and business leaders?

9. Is a metasystematic level of cognitive, conative, affective and moral development a necessary but not sufficient condition for wisdom? What can prevent wisdom from being expressed by people at this stage of development?

References

Ackoff, R.L. 1996. On learning and systems that facilitate it. *Center for Quality of Management Journal*, 5(2), 27–35.

Ardelt, M. 2003. Empirical assessment of a three-dimensional wisdom scale. *Research on Aging*, 25(3), 275–324.

Ardelt, M. 2004. Wisdom as expert knowledge system: a critical review of a contemporary operationalization of an ancient concept. *Human Development*, 47(5), 257–85.

Ardelt, M. 2011. The measurement of wisdom: a commentary on Taylor, Bates and Webster's comparison of the SAWS and 3D-WS. *Experimental Aging Research*, 37(2), 241–55.

Baldwin, J.M. 1906/1975. *Thought and Things: A Study in the Development of Meaning and Thought or Genetic Logic* (Vols. 1–4). New York: Macmillan.

Baltes, P.B. and Kunzmann, U. 2003. Wisdom. *The Psychologist*, 16(3), 131–3.

Baltes, P.B. and Smith, J. 1990. Toward a psychology of wisdom and its ontogenesis, in *Wisdom: Its Nature, Origins and Development*, edited by R.J. Sternberg. Cambridge: Cambridge University Press, 87–120.

Baltes, P.B. and Staudinger, U.M. 2000. A metaheuristic (pragmatic) to orchestrate mind and virtue toward excellence. *American Psychologist*, 55(1), 122–36.

Baltes, P.B., Smith, J. and Staudinger, U.M. 1992. Wisdom and successful aging, in *Nebraska Symposium on Motivation Volume 39*, edited by T.B. Sonderegger. Lincoln: University of Nebraska Press, 123–67.

Baltes, P.B., Staudinger, U.M., Maercker, A. and Smith, J. 1995. People nominated as wise: a comparative study of wisdom-related knowledge. *Psychology and Aging*, 10(2), 155–66.

Beck, S. 1999. Confucius and Socrates: the teaching of wisdom. [Online] Available at: http://www.san.beck.org [accessed: 1 May 2008].

Biloslavo, R. and McKenna, B. 2011. Wisdom and transformational leadership: a conceptual model. Paper presented at The Seventh International Critical Management Studies (CMS) Conference, Naples, 11–13 July 2011.

Birren, J.E. and Fisher, L.M. 1990. The elements of wisdom: overview and integration, in *Wisdom: Its Nature, Origins, and Development*, edited by R.J. Sternberg. New York: Cambridge University Press, 317–32.

Cara, E. 2007. Psychobiography: a research method in search of a home. *The British Journal of Occupational Therapy*, 70(3), 115–21.

Case, P. and J. Gosling 2007. Wisdom of the moment: premodern perspectives on organizational action. *Social Epistemology*, 21(2), 87–111.

Cattell, R.B. 1971. *Abilities: Their Structure, Growth, and Action*. Boston: Houghton-Mifflin.

Cattell, R.B. 1987. *Intelligence: Its Structure, Growth and Action*. Amsterdam: North Holland.

Commons, M.L. 2008. Introduction to the model of hierarchical complexity and its relationship to postformal action. *World Futures*, 64(5–7), 305–20.

Commons, M.L., Trudeau, E.J., Stein, S.A., Richards, F.A. and Krause, S.R. 1998. The existence of developmental stages as shown by hierarchical complexity of tasks. *Developmental Review*, 8(3), 237–78.

Corno, L. 1993. The best-laid plans: modern conceptions of volition and educational research. *Educational Research*, 22(2), 14–22.

Cotterell, N., Eisenberger, R. and Speicher, H. 1992. Inhibiting effects of reciprocation wariness on interpersonal relationships. *Journal of Personality and Social Psychology*, 62(4), 658–68.

Csikszentmihalyi, M. and Nakamura, J. 2005. The role of emotions in the development of wisdom, in *A Handbook of Wisdom*, edited by R.J. Sternberg and J. Jordan. New York: Cambridge University Press, 220–45.

Cullen, J.B., Victor, B. and Stephens, C. 1989. An ethical weather report: assessing the organization's ethical climate. *Organizational Dynamics*, 18(2), 50–62.

Dawson-Tunik, T.L., Commons, M.L., Wilson, M. and Fischer, K.W. 2005. The shape of development. *European Journal of Developmental Psychology*, 2(2), 163–95.

Eccles, J.S. and Wigfield, A. 2002. Motivational beliefs, values, and goals. *Annual Review of Psychology*, 53, 109–32.

Feffer, M. 1970. Developmental analysis of interpersonal behavior. *Psychological Review*, 77(3), 197–214.

Ghoshal, S. and Bruch, H. 2003. Going beyond motivation to the power of volition. *MIT Sloan Management Review*, 44(3), 51–7.

Greene, J.A. and Brown, S.C. 2009. The Wisdom Development Scale: further validity investigations. *International Journal of Aging and Human Development*, 68(4), 289–320.

Hannah, S.T., Avolio, B.J. and May, D.R. 2011. Moral maturation and moral conation: a capacity approach to explaining moral thought and action. *Academy of Management Review*, 36(4), 663–85.

Hewlett, D.C. 2003. A qualitative study of postautonomous ego development: the bridge between postconventional and transcedent ways of being. PhD thesis, Fielding Graduate Institute [Online]. Available at: http://www.grof-holotropic-breathwork.net/page/doctoral-dissertations [accessed: 4 May 2012].

Horn, J.L. and Cattell, R.B. 1967. Age differences in fluid and crystallized intelligence. *Acta Psychologica*, 26(2), 107–29.

Huitt, W. and Cain, S. 2005. *An overview of the conative domain*. Educational Psychology Interactive. Valdosta State University [Online]. Available at: http://teach.valdosta.edu/whuitt/brilstar/chapters/conative.doc [accessed: 16 December 2008].

Kamdar, D., McAllister, D.J. and Turban, D.B. 2006. All in a day's work: how follower individual differences and justice perceptions predict OCB role definitions and behavior. *Journal of Applied Psychology*, 91(4), 841–55.

Kang, S-M. and Shaver, P.R. 2004. Individual differences in emotional complexity: their psychological implications. *Journal of Personality*, 72(4), 687–726.

Kegan, R. 1982. *The Evolving Self*. Cambridge, MA: Harvard University Press.

Kegan, R. 1994. *In Over Our Heads: The Mental Demands of Modern Life*. Cambridge, MA: Harvard University Press.

Kekes, J. 1983. Wisdom. *American Philosophical Quarterly*, 20(3), 277–86.

Kekes, J. 1995. *Moral Wisdom and Good Lives*. Ithaca: Cornell University Press.

Koestler, A. 1967. *The Ghost in the Machine*. London: Arkana.

Kohlberg, L. 1969. *Stage and Sequence: The Cognitive-Developmental Approach to Socialization.* Chicago: Rand McNally.

Kohlberg, L. 1981. *Essays on Moral Development. Volume 1: The Philosophy of Moral Development.* San Francisco: Harper and Row.

Korsgaard, M.A., Brodt, S.E. and Whitener, E.M. 2002. Trust in the face of conflict: the role of managerial trustworthy behavior and organizational context. *Journal of Applied Psychology,* 87(2), 312–19.

Kramer, D.A. 2000. Wisdom as a classical source of human strength: conceptualization and empirical inquiry. *Journal of Social and Clinical Psychology,* 19(1), 83–101.

Kriger, M.P. and Malan, L.-C. 1993. Shifting paradigms: the valuing of personal knowledge, wisdom, and other invisible processes in organizations. *Journal of Management Inquiry,* 2(4), 391–8.

Kunzmann, U. and Baltes, P.B. 2003. Beyond the traditional scope of intelligence: wisdom in action, in *Models of Intelligence: International Perspectives,* edited by R.J. Sternberg and J. Lautrey. Washington DC: American Psychological Association, 329–43.

Kyi, A.S.S. 1997. *The Voice of Hope: Conversations with Alan Clements.* New York: Seven Stories Press.

Lacity, M.C. and Janson, M.A. 1994. Understanding qualitative data: a framework of text analysis methods. *Journal of Management Information Systems,* 11(2), 137–55.

Lemke, J.L. 1995. *Textual Politics: Discourse and Social Dynamics.* London: Taylor & Francis.

Lewicki, R. and Bunker, B. 1996. Developing and maintaining trust in work relationships, in *Trust in Organizations: Frontiers in Theory and Research,* edited by R. Kramer and T. Tyler. Newbury Park: Sage, 114–39.

Logsdon, J.M. and Yuthas, K. 1997. Corporate social performance, stakeholder orientation, and organizational moral development. *Journal of Business Ethics,* 16(12/13), 1213–26.

Malan, L.C. and Kriger, M.P. 1998. Making sense of managerial wisdom. *Journal of Management Inquiry,* 7(3), 242–51.

Mandela, N. 1994. *Long Walk to Freedom: the Autobiography of Nelson Mandela.* Boston: Little Brown.

Maxwell, N. 1984. *From Knowledge to Wisdom: a Revolution in the Aims and Methods of Science.* Oxford: Basil Blackwell.

Mayer, J.D. and Salovey, P. 1997. What is emotional intelligence?, in *Emotional Development and Emotional Intelligence: Educational Implications,* edited by P. Salovey and D. Slyter. New York: Basic Books, 3–31.

Morrell, A. and O'Connor, M.A. 2002. Introduction, in *Expanding the Boundaries of Transformative Learning,* edited by E. O'Sullivan, A. Morrell and M.A. O'Connor. New York: Palgrave Macmillan, xv–xxi.

Mumford, M.D. 2011. A hale farewell: the state of leadership research. *The Leadership Quarterly,* 22(1), 1–7.

Musek, J. 2003. *Zgodovina Psihologije.* Ljubljana: Filozofska fakulteta Univerze v Ljubljani.

Nussbaum, M. 1994. *The Therapy of Desire: Theory and Practice in Hellenistic Ethics.* Princeton: Princeton University Press.

Orwoll, L. and Perlmutter, M. 1990. The study of wise persons: integrating a personality perspective, in *Wisdom: Its Nature, Origins, and Development,* edited by R.J. Sternberg. Cambridge: Cambridge University Press, 160–77.

Pasupathi, M. and Staudinger, U.M. 2001. Do advanced moral reasoners also show wisdom? Linking moral reasoning and wisdom-related knowledge and judgement. *International Journal of Behavioral Development,* 25(5), 401–15.

Pasupathi, M., Staudinger, U.M. and Baltes, P.B. 2001. Seeds of wisdom: adolescents' knowledge and judgement about difficult life problems. *Developmental Psychology,* 37(3), 351–61.

Piaget, J. 1969. *The Mechanisms of Perception*. London: Routledge and Kegan Paul.

Piaget, J. 1971. *Biology and Knowledge; an Essay on the Relations between Organic Regulations and Cognitive Processes*. Chicago: University of Chicago Press.

Polanyi, M. 1968. Logic and psychology. *American Psychologist*, 23(1), 27–43.

Poulsen, H. 1991. *Conations: On Striving, Willing and Wishing and their Relationship with Cognition, Emotions and Motives*. Aarhus: Aarhus University Press.

Rooney, D., McKenna, B. and Liesch, P. 2010. *Wisdom and Management in the Knowledge Economy*. New York: Routledge.

Saarni, C. 1997. Emotional competence and self-regulation in childhood, in *Emotional Development and Emotional Intelligence: Educational Implications*, edited by P. Salovey and D.J. Sluyter. New York: Basic Books, 35–66.

Schaie, K.W. 2005. *Developmental Influences on Adult Intelligence: the Seattle Longitudinal Study*. New York: Oxford University Press.

Schwaninger, M. 2006. *Intelligent Organizations: Powerful Models for Systemic Management*. Berlin: Springer.

Staudinger, U.M. and Pasupathi, M. 2003. Correlates of wisdom-related performance in adolescence and adulthood: age-graded differences in 'paths' toward desirable development. *Journal of Research on Adolescence*, 13(3), 239–68.

Stein, Z. and Heikkinen, K. 2008. On operationalizing aspects of altitude: an introduction to the LecticalTM assessment system for integral researchers. *Journal of Integral Theory and Practice*, 3(1), 105–38.

Sternberg, R.J. 1990. Understanding wisdom, in *Wisdom: its Nature, Origins and Development*, edited by R.J. Sternberg. Cambridge: Cambridge University Press, 3–9.

Sternberg, R.J. 1998. A balance theory of wisdom. *Review of General Psychology*, 2(4), 347–65.

Sternberg, R.J. 2003. *Wisdom, Intelligence, and Creativity Synthesized*. New York: Cambridge University Press.

Sternberg, R.J. 2004. Positive development: realising the potential of youth. *The Annals of the American Academy of Political and Social Science*, 591(1), 164–74.

Sternberg, R.J. 2005. WICS: a model of positive educational leadership comprising wisdom, intelligence and creativity synthesized. *Educational Psychology Review*, 17(3), 191–262.

Sternberg, R.J., Wagner, R.K., Williams, W.M. and Horvath, J.A. 1995. Testing common sense. *American Psychologist*, 50(11), 912–27.

Sternberg, R.J. et al. 2000. *Practical Intelligence in Everyday Life*. Cambridge: Cambridge University Press.

Trochim, W.M.K. 1985. Pattern matching, validity, and conceptualization in program evaluation. *Evaluation Review*, 9(5), 575–604.

Vaill, P.B. 1998. The unspeakable texture of process wisdom, in *Organizational Wisdom and Executive Courage*, edited by S. Srivastava and D.L. Cooperrider. San Francisco: Jossey-Bass, 25–39.

Vergne, J-P. 2011. Toward a new measure of organizational legitimacy: method, validation, and illustration. *Organizational Research Methods*, 14(3), 484–502.

Warr, P. and Conner, M. 1992. Job competence and cognition, in *Research in Organizational Behavior*, (Volume 6,) edited by L.L. Cummings and B.M. Staw. Greenwich: JAI Press, 91–127.

Webster, J.D. 2007. Measuring the character strength of wisdom. *International Journal of Aging and Human Development*, 65(2), 163–83.

Webster, J.D. 2010. Wisdom and positive psychosocial values in young adulthood. *Journal of Adult Development*, 17(2), 70–80.

Wessman, A. and Ricks, D. 1966. *Mood and Personality*. New York: Holt, Rinehart, and Winston.

Yang, S.-Y. 2008. A process view of wisdom. *Journal of Adult Development*, 15(1), 62–75.

Zimprich, D., Allemand, M. and Dellenbach, M. 2009. Openness to experience, fluid intelligence, and crystallized intelligence in middle-aged and old adults. *Journal of Research in Personality*, 43(3), 444–54.

7

Transformation and Transcendence for Wisdom: The Emergence and Sustainment of Wise Leaders and Organizations

JAY HAYS

Transformation is a possibility in the mind of every social revolutionary and the awakening of consciousness that gives meaning to life for many people. (McWhinney and Markos 2003: 22)

Introduction

This chapter examines the relationships amongst transformational leadership, learning and change (abbreviated as T³ herein), transcendence and wisdom. Building on and integrating three established but disconnected streams of research and practice – T³ – this chapter contributes uniquely to organizational and management scholarship and, particularly, to emerging conceptions and understandings of leadership and wisdom. The primary thesis undertaken in this chapter is that transformation and transcendence play dynamic, synergistic roles in promoting and manifesting wisdom, identifying critical links with leadership and learning. The chapter explores how these factors work in concert in a coevolutionary way for the greater good. It is essentially a model for learning that organizations and communities can employ to change wisely – that is, with an understanding of the implications and consequences of their choices, including the processes they undertake to change. The author emphasizes that we must first transcend and transform ourselves if we intend to change the world. Guidance on achieving such transcendence and transformation is offered.

While the integration of transformational leadership, learning and change (T³) seems reasonable, if not obvious, there has been, to date, no meaningful synthesis – although it may be inferred in some of the richer organizational learning literature (see Altman and Iles 1998). Transcendence is only beginning to surface as a relevant aspiration and topic in leadership and organization studies: Scharmer's *Theory U* work (2001, 2009) and Hays (in press) are notable examples. These sources highlight the inherent potential to transcend the self and the present, or in the vernacular, *to get over ourselves*. This capacity is as crucial as it is fundamental, emphasizing the potential individuals, teams, organizations and societies have to become more than they seem, to realize their fullest potential. Research by Wink and Helson (1997) supports this view. They note the developmental nature of wisdom, distinguish between practical and transcendental wisdom and conclude that, of the two, only transcendental wisdom, which is associated with transcending ego boundaries and capacity for integration, awareness and paradox, correlates with openness to experience, intuition and creativity.

Learning, change and evolution have never been more needed than they are today. The problems confronting organizations, communities and the planet are severe, complex and have proven intractable (Hays 2012). The opportunities for bettering the world are immense, but seemingly elusive. New ways of thinking, operating and being are needed to address these challenges.

We must transform ourselves to transform the world. The wisest amongst us recognize this principle more so than most. But how do we become wise? How do we know what needs to change or how to go about it? This chapter attempts to answer these questions. It emphasizes that wisdom can be developed and fostered. It provides possible ways individuals, organizations and communities can cultivate and make best use of their inherent potential for wisdom and transformation.

A Context for Transformation and the Critical Role of Wisdom

A transformation in the way we lead and develop leaders in keeping with the scope of challenges confronting organizations and nations today is imperative. The consequences of continuing to lead as we have done in the past – with little regard for the greater good and the future of the planet – are dire. We require wise leadership and organizations and societies that act wisely. But how is such transformation achieved? Moreover, once transformed, how can we ensure that leaders and groups continue to do the right thing in an environment that continually poses new threats and opportunities, the seeds many of which we, ourselves, sowed in years past, not knowing or disregarding the risks (Hays 2012).

The answer is deceptively simple. We need to stay in a continuing process of transforming – of becoming – learning, adapting, evolving. Remaining in the process of transforming is crucial to keep pace with change, not to mention anticipating and preparing for threats and opportunities that may arise (see Dey and Steyaert 2007). Remaining in a constant state of becoming requires transcendence – the missing link in understanding and facilitating transformation. If nothing else, transcendence means 'getting over ourselves'. What this entails is the focus of this chapter.

Wisdom is doing the right thing for the greater good, all things considered (Hays 2007). This means going beyond self-interest, having a perspective transcending organizational or national borders, and privileging tomorrow over today. It means redefining the way things are and transforming and evolving ourselves. It means seeing possibilities, drawing on untapped resources and identifying what may be limiting thinking, learning or performance. This may all require openness, flexibility and humility that do not come easily.

Many would agree that these are laudable virtues. Regrettably, some believe they are incompatible with business motives or sit outside corporate responsibility. Such archaic beliefs impede us from forging productive relationships and working in the new and different ways demanded by complex, intractable problems. These and many other subversive beliefs are the more insidious because they usually operate outside our awareness and are, thus, beyond our control.

Mindful awareness is a quality of wisdom (Smith 2007), but where does it come from? How do we become more attentive and perceptive? How do we attain and sustain consciousness of ourselves *and* our dynamic environment as they interact, being both part of and detached from the interaction? Given that extraordinary foresight and insight are possible, how can we see beyond that which we normally see? How can we bring into being that which is yet unconceived (see Hays, in press, and Scharmer 2001, 2009)? As we will see, the transcendence process is the key to opening up new worlds of possibility.

A Dynamic Model of Organizational Wisdom

Figure 7.1 presents a dynamic model of organizational wisdom, highlighting the key contributions of transcendence and transformation. Three transformations – transformational leadership (T^1), transformational learning (T^2) and transformational organizational change (T^3) – are shown within the dotted-line box, labelled collective T^3. Transcendence, or *getting over ourselves*, is the key capacity and the lever that actualizes T^3 and, in particular through them, wisdom.

As indicated by the dotted arrows, each element of the dynamic model interacts individually with another. For example, transcendence and transformational leadership

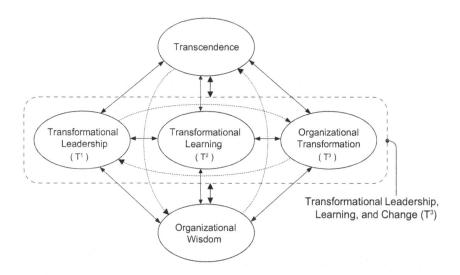

Figure 7.1   Dynamic model of organizational wisdom, showing relationships amongst transcendence, T^3 and wisdom

(T^1) mutually influence one another, implying that they both improve interdependently. Likewise, organizational transformation (T^3) and wisdom interact. As one increases and improves so does the other. More important, however, is the functioning of the three transformations T^1, T^2 and T^3 working in concert (the interactions amongst elements in the box). The most significant relationships are shown in Figure 7.1 as the bold arrows between transcendence and T^3, and T^3 and wisdom. This means, essentially, that the potency of the three transformations is greater in combination – they are synergistic. In practical organizational terms, transformational leadership, transformational learning and transformational organizational change need to be operationalized as a system if leader and organizational wisdom are to be attained.

Transformational leadership, transformational learning and transformational organizational change (T^3) are fairly well understood and represented in a range of scholarly literatures, as covered further on, although they tend to be treated independently. It has long been of interest to the author that 'transformation' has been attached to leadership, learning and change, implying something significant about them individually and hinting that they share certain qualities, but that the three constructs themselves have not been linked. Thorough investigation of each suggests that they have much in common and that this commonality is significant.

The three 'transformations' alone do not guarantee that an organization or its leaders can attain or sustain extraordinary performance that not only meets narrow self-interests but that also contributes to the greater good. In combination with wisdom and transcendence, however, they operate virtuously as a complex adaptive system (Hays 2010a, 2010b, 2012, Lichtenstein et al. 2006, Schneider and Somers 2006) and produce generative learning (McGill, Slocum and Lei 1992, Schein 1999), continuous renewal, innovation and healthy resilience and adaptability to changing environmental conditions.

An organizational system exhibiting these characteristics anticipates and positions itself to contend with problems and opportunities over the horizon (Hays, in press, Scharmer 2001, 2009). It sees beyond its current limitations arising from habit, flawed perceptions and even values that may need revision. Such critical vision is enabled through the process of transcendence, resulting in heightened consciousness and the possibility of redefining the self in relation to the environment (see Sanders III, Hopkins and Geroy 2003, concerning relationships between transcendence and consciousness). This greater state of awareness permits access to untapped resources and novel ways of approaching problems (Smith 2007). When we *get over ourselves* we are freed to see issues differently, explore new possibilities and approach situations in novel ways. It is not that problems are unsolvable; it is merely that we have failed to transform ourselves to more effectively deal with them.

An Emergent Model

There has been no known attempt to integrate or explore relationships amongst T^3, transcendence and wisdom. The dynamic model of organizational wisdom presented here is, thus, new but has solid foundations in the literature, representing a synthesis of several established streams of research. Indicating some progress in this direction previously, Altman and Iles (1998) linked learning, leadership and organizational change, emphasizing leadership and teamwork as transforming processes. Bierly, Kessler and Christensen (2000) made a significant contribution to the literature linking transformational leadership, organizational learning and wisdom. A precedent for the model is found in the determined attempts to map organizational learning and wisdom as dynamic systems (Hays 2007, 2010a, 2010b).

While Hays (2007 2010a, 2010b) did advance the notion of wisdom as a dynamic and collective system, his earlier conceptualizations neglected transcendence, a key concept here. Furthermore, where his complex models contributed significantly to a systems understanding of learning and wisdom, he omitted the role of leaders in transformation, which features prominently in this evolved adaptation. Organizational transformation, itself, plays a more central role in the model proposed here. Continual transformation is the key to organizational survival (Kets de Vries and Balazs 1998) and critical to fulfilment of the corporate social obligation of sustainability.

Since continual change may be stressful, resented or exhausting, the role of a leader in supporting employees through change is paramount. Leaders may need continually to coach, enthuse, inspire, provide hope, instill optimism and so on. This implies that they themselves must undergo renewal (see Preece 2003), tapping into their own sources of inspiration. Not surprisingly, leadership and wisdom are often associated in the literature (Bierl, Kessler and Christensen 2000, Korac-Kakabadse, Korac-Kakabadse and Kouzmin 2001, McKenna, Rooney and Boal 2009, Sternberg 2003), but the link to organizational change is seldom explicitly made.

It is the dynamic interplay of leadership, learning, transcendence and wisdom that enables the organization to survive and innovate in ways that promote the welfare of the greater good. Notions of the greater good are the basis of much of the thinking on wisdom, as acknowledged by Bass and Steidlmeier (1999), Bennet and Bennet (2008), Bierly, Kessler and Christensen (2000), Hays (2007, 2012) and Sternberg (2003). Hinterhuber (1996: 298) went so far as to assert that 'top management [must] take seriously its responsibility for the future of the planet'.

While no sources were identified that linked all factors included in this model or conceived of them in the same way, there have been interesting and constructive usages of and distinctions amongst some of the key terms. Miller (1996) and Miller and Seller (1990) distinguished amongst three teaching orientations: transmission, transaction and transformation. Though these scholars applied the terms differently than they appear in the management literature, it may be reasonable to interpret transformation in both instances as superior to or at least qualitatively more sophisticated than transaction.

Some support for this assertion is found in Gardiner (2006) who places transmission, transaction and transformation on a continuum, and Sanders, Hopkins and Geroy (2003) who arrange them hierarchically. Transformational learning, to illustrate, is held to be deeper, more fundamental and longer-lasting than surface learning (Brown and Posner 2001, Grauerholz 2001, Harris, Lowery-Moore and Farrow 2008, Marsick 1998), the result of learning processes and strategies that are more engaging, integrating and holistic than transmission, which is one-way, or even transaction, which implies a more interactive exchange and involvement (see also Altman and Iles 1998, Yorks and Kasl 2002). Further, Hutchison and Bosacki (2000: 179) expand on the three orientations – transmission, transaction and transformation – by qualifying them as mechanistic, constructivist and organismic respectively, the latter tantamount to transcendence, manifesting '... acts of intuitive insight, moments of wonder and revelation, and peak experiences'.

Wong (2008) has identified qualitative differences in teaching orientations (or relationships with learners) and their effects of relevance here: transaction, transformation and transcendence. Though rare, those teachers operating at a transcendent level were able to achieve extraordinary learning outcomes with their students. The influence they had over learners was in no small part due to the teachers' ability to empathize with, relate to and encourage them, which resembles the character of the influence transformational leaders have over followers (as described in Bass and Avolio 1993, and Sarros and Santora 2001). What was absent amongst the transaction-style teachers and weaker amongst the transformational ones was the ability to stimulate learners to transcend obvious or superficial understandings of material and experience, and to seek deeper insights, explore personally meaningful and relevant connections and forge their own authentic and autonomous points of view.

Transformational Leadership

Transformational leaders approach followers differently than do transactional leaders, appealing to higher values and motives and relating on a more personal level and, thus, inducing greater levels of commitment, performance and innovation from followers (Avolio 2010, Burke and Litwin 1992, Howell and Avolio 1993, and others). Burns (1978) is credited with introducing the concept of transformational leadership to convey the influence that some leaders have to change people and organizations in fundamental ways. It may currently be the most accepted theory of leadership, as suggested by Conger (1999), Judge and Piccolo (2004) and Kim and Hays (2010).

Transformational leaders motivate and enable people to perform exceptionally and to want to continue to learn, develop and change; they instil a sense of pride and possibility (Avolio 2010). They transform people and organizations (Sarros and Santora 2001). Transformational leaders challenge the status quo and encourage others to question, take risks, show initiative and try new things (Avolio 2010). LeBrasseur, Whissell and Ojha (2002: 147, my emphasis) write that: '... the transformational leader *encourages the adoption of new values and beliefs*, endorses the goal of organisational effectiveness, and sustains the effort to [achieve specific changes]'.

Bierly, Kessler and Christensen (2000) stress the role of transformational leadership in promoting organizational wisdom; that is, helping others to become wise. Likewise, Brown and Posner (2001) make the direct linkage between transformational leadership and transformational learning, and less directly to organizational change. They note: 'Today's turbulent economic marketplace requires people who thrive on the challenge of change, who can foster environments of innovation, who encourage trust and collaboration, and who are *prepared to chart a course into uncharted territories*' (Ibid.: 275, my emphasis).

Preece (2003) also directly links transformational learning with transformational leadership, submitting that leaders need to understand the process and pedagogy of transformation if they want to be effective. This suggests that leaders should be learners themselves, and be willing and able to undergo transformation. Kim and Hays (2010) consider 'learnership' a defining feature of leaders in the twenty-first century. Smith, Montagno and Kuzmenko (2004: 85) also make a strong case for the influence of transformational leadership on organizational innovation, noting, for example, that '... transformational behaviors are needed to revitalize organizational processes'.

Finally, Sarros and Santora (2001: 385, my emphasis) commented that '*Transformational leaders raise the consciousness of followers* by appealing to higher ideals and values such as liberty, justice, peace, and equality'. Transcending current practices, policies, perspectives and other limitations is necessary to remain viable in a changing world, as is recognizing that one or one's organization needs to transcend. It is perhaps in recognition of this that some scholars have started to draw attention to transcendent leaders and leadership. Crossan, Vera and Nanjad (2008), Gardiner (2006), and Sanders III, Hopkins and Geroy (2003), for example, emphasize that transcendent leaders continually strive for greater heights of personal performance and effectiveness through raising their own levels of consciousness, and inspire this in those they lead and serve. Crossan, Vera and Nanjad (2008: 578) build a particularly strong case for transcendental leadership and its emergence in their ultimate proposition that 'The transcendental leader, who has high levels of leadership of self, others, and organization, will be associated with the highest level of [sustainable] firm performance', as set apart from transactional and transformational leaders.

These emerging views of transcendent leadership accompany a recognition of the limits of transformational leadership (see Küpers 2011). Transformational leaders may indeed inspire change, but it might not be enlightened change for the greater good, fostering equality, consciousness, emancipation and efficacy, understanding of interdependence or ideals of service and community. Moreover, for our thesis here, transformational leaders may not necessarily transform themselves or even recognize that they may need to. Thus what is needed, at least potentially, is a focus on transcendence. The ideals, process and discipline of transcendence can become integral parts of professional development and relevant higher education curricula such as MBA and executive education programmes.

Transformational Change and Organizational Transformation

Transformational change is qualitatively greater than incremental, gradual, evolutionary change, often seen as improvements to a process (Rafferty and Simons 2006). Transformation is not just improvement, it is invention, maintain Prahalad and Osterveld (1999). Managers and leaders need to be encouraged to envisage the possible, they explain: 'If they cannot imagine the future, they cannot create it' (1999: 7). Transformation is concerned with cultural and structural changes, and learning to think and act differently (Altman and Iles 1998, Chapman 2002).

Citing Bartunek, Bartunek and Louis, Chapman (2002: 16) writes, 'Transformational change within organisations requires a basic shift in attitudes, beliefs and cultural values, [and] reframing'. Reframing or perspective transformation (Brooks 2004, Moore 2005, Preece 2003, Taylor 2008) is a process leading to a change in attitudes, values, beliefs and understandings – the way we define ourselves and our world. Perspective change is essential if there is going to be sustainable change in behaviour and the systems, structures and processes that support it. To change perspectives requires that we are aware of them and how they may be influencing our behaviour, hence the need for transcendence.

Kets de Vries and Balazs (1998) explain the psychodynamics of organizational transformation and change, and provide useful guidance for change agents, including the need to promote and allow positive conflict. Prahalad and Osterveld (1999) stress the relationship between learning and change, and that sometimes positive conflict is needed to promote learning and change. A shake-up may be needed to shift people out of their comfort zones into the 'zone of opportunity' – the unfamiliar.

The stimulus of contradiction, paradox and other tensions is an underlying theme across a range of relevant literatures reviewed for this chapter, including Lichtenstein et al. (2006) and Nicolaides and Yorks (2008). Barge and Little (2002), for instance, speak of 'constructive cacophony', a discordant clashing of perspectives that may provide a springboard to new solutions, better decision-making and innovation and creativity. Hays (2012) makes a strong case for the need to complicate higher education through incorporating complexity, paradox, unpredictability, contention and chaos, in his words, to make it 'wicked', to better equip learners to deal with the realities of the world in which they will find themselves upon graduation.

For Tsoukas and Chia (2002), organizational transformation is a process of continuously becoming. These scholars stress the relevance of intuition, knowledge from within, direct experience, sensing, perception and emergence. They write of the importance of detachment and letting go, and comment on the extraordinary human capacity to reflect on experience and learn from it, to play with ideas, 'draw new distinctions, imagine new things' (Ibid.: 574), suggesting that it is important to think more of the emergence of an organization than change. Drawing on Wittgenstein, they submit that 'managers need to clear their vision to *see* what is going on and, at the same time, help fashion a coherent and desirable *pattern* out of what is going on' (Ibid.: 579, emphasis in the original). Their insights and observations are clearly consistent with other transformational dimensions relevant here, as well as with transcendence and wisdom as conceptualized herein.

Transformational Learning

Learning plays a direct and vital role in wisdom and is an instrumental part of transformation and transcendence. With such a critical part to play, it is essential to understand the nature of learning and, particularly, the distinction between surface and transformational and deep learning.

Surface learning is a shallow or superficial learning, generally insufficient to solving the complex or novel problems people face in organizations. Surface learning does not lead to discovery and development; at best it deals with what is already known (Gow and Kember 1990, Lynch 1999, van Woerkom 2004), but this is insufficient in a world that is unknown, unpredictable and continually changing (Hays 2012). Knapper (2001) asserts that innovative learning is a strategic imperative. Bonnett (2009) states that we should be less preoccupied with the known and attend more to the unknown, less with mastery (that is with knowing) and more with cultivation of receptivity to knowledge, less with inquiry and more with listening and responding responsibly.

Mezirow (1991, 1997, 2000) is the 'father' of transformational learning, and the foremost proponent of transformational learning theory. Transformative or transformational learning is learning that fundamentally changes a person in some way. It is not merely an accretion of skills or knowledge, but a quantum leap in ability or understanding. Once transformed, you cannot really be the person you were (Hays 2008). Grauerholz (2001) described deep learning as profound, meaningful and lasting shifts in cognitions, attitudes, emotions and values. Citing Miller, he defined deep learning as: 'transformational, in which the point is not simply intellectual development but also physical, emotional, aesthetic, moral, and spiritual growth' (Ibid.: 44). Likewise, Warburton (2003) stressed the importance of deep learning and its relationship to transformation. Deep learning, he maintains, '... promotes and is characterised by holistic insight, the ability to see complex relationships and to organize and structure disparate types of information into a coherent whole' (Ibid.: 45). Linking adult and transformational learning theories, Illeris (2003) described transcendent learning as transformational, expansive, significant and critical.

Harris, Lowery-Moore and Farrow (2008) posit that under the right conditions a fundamental shift in the learner's view of self or the world allows him or her to operate differently and more efficaciously. Learners come to understand themselves and how they interact with the world better, achieved, they maintain, through continually reflecting on behaviour and the assumptions and beliefs that underpin it.

Transformational learning not only influences what a person thinks, but *how* he or she thinks (Bushe and Kassam 2005, Moore 2005), perceives, feels and experiences him- or herself in relation to the world (Bennet and Bennet 2008, Taylor 2008, Torosyan 2001). At least some measure of transformational learning has to do with the development of the learner's awareness, both of internal thought processes and of his or her surroundings (Illeris 2003, McWhinney and Markos 2003). Elias (1997: 12, my emphasis) has observed: 'Transformative learning is the *expansion of consciousness* through the transformation of basic worldview and specific capacities of the self', a point endorsed by Preece (2003) who added that it represents movement toward self-actualization and self-transcendence.

Attending to one's learning and thought processes and deliberately and reflectively working on and with them is liberating and empowering. People are neither oblivious to their reactions and interactions nor hapless victims to them, but accept responsibility and assert authority over how they perceive, interpret and act in response. Individuation is an important aspect of transformational learning (Cranton and Roy 2003). Taylor (2008: 7) explains: 'individuation [is] a lifelong journey of coming to understand oneself [involving] discovery of new talents, a sense of empowerment and confidence, a deeper understanding of one's inner self, and a greater sense of self-responsibility'.

Transformational learning is sometimes described in both individual and social terms (McWhinney and Markos 2003, Nicolaides and Yorks 2008, Quay 2003). Transformational learning strives to help individuals create better lives for themselves and make their organizations and communities better places to work and live in (Brooks 2004, Preece 2003, Taylor 2008). This is consistent with the greater good aspect of wisdom emphasized herein (Bennet and Bennet 2008, and Sternberg 2003, as examples). While theory and approaches to transformational learning have been criticized for an emphasis on rational discourse and critical reflection, as alluded to by Taylor (2008), Taylor emphasizes the holistic nature of transformational learning, recognizing 'the role of feelings, other ways of knowing (intuition, somatic), and the role of relationships with others' (Ibid.: 11) and 'personal contextual influences' (Ibid.: 7). Transformational learning concerns the whole person and, by extension, the whole community or organization, suggesting the need to consider and address the richness and complexity of individuals and their environments, including diverse ways of learning and knowing.

Fundamental to transformational learning theory and practice is the critical role of reflection, with many sources on transformational and deep learning accentuating its importance (Boström and Lassen 2006, Grauerholz 2001, Hays 2008, Taylor 2008, van Woerkom 2004). Schwandt (2005), for instance, writes of emancipatory knowledge derived from self-reflection and questioning of assumptions – those beliefs and practices that perpetuate the status quo. Citing Mezirow, he explains, 'Critical reflection on prior interpretation of the meaning of one's experience in order to guide future actions becomes a 'transformational' learning process that leads to individual perspective change' (Ibid.: 180).

Exemplifying a holistic approach to transformational learning as suggested above, Jordi (2011: 182) recommends reflective practices that foster body–mind integration, dialogues between the mind (conceptual aspects of consciousness) and body (implicit embodied experience): 'Embodied reflective practices can encourage an integration of varied and often disconnected aspects of our human experience and consciousness'.

Emancipation is a central theme running throughout the literature on transformational learning, with Percy (2005), Quay (2003) and Taylor (2008) as examples. In *Pedagogy of the Oppressed*, Freire (2000) describes emancipatory education as involving the learner as an active participant in designing learning. The learner asks, 'What do I want to learn? Why am I learning this? How can my learning liberate and empower me?' Thus one of the key objectives and natural outcomes of transformational learning is liberation, in terms of both mind and circumstance (see also Cacioppe and Edwards 2005, and McWhinney and Markos 2003). Emancipation may be understood as a freeing of the beliefs, values, assumptions and biases that we have adopted that limit perception, understanding and effective action (see Cranton and Roy 2003). Unencumbered by these restrictions, we can make more informed decisions, solve problems more effectively and act in the world more potently; thus, we are *emancipated*. Emancipation is critical to transcendence.

With deep, transformational learning the learner develops breadth and depth of understanding regarding problems and solutions. The learner is able to contextualize and generalize. Having learned something deeply, a learner should be able to apply it in diverse or unfamiliar situations (Havard, Du and Olinzock 2005, Hays 2012, Marsick 1998). Moreover, learning how to learn and solve problems independently and collaboratively is at least as important as learning knowledge *of* or *about* any particular knowledge domain (Boström and Lassen 2006, Hays 2012, Knapper 2001, Marsick 1998).

Getting people to think and behave differently has major implications for the way we teach and the way we conduct business (Hays 2012). Amongst other things, we tend to teach (and learn) backwards, when we need to be looking forward – attempting to make sense of what lies beyond our limited field of attention. We tend to teach (and learn) what is proper and tangible, ruling out more than we rule in. What we need to be doing is exploring the improbable and drawing out possibilities and extending the range of alternatives. This means going where no one else has gone or drawing new lessons and insights from the previously traversed.

The task for leaders and educators is to create conditions for transformative learning that stimulate creativity, autonomy and critical thought (Altman and Iles 1998, Marsick 1998), to build capability for sustainable learning and change rather than competence (Fraser and Greenhalgh 2001) – that is, teaching for the unknowable (Hays 2012). Learning and preparing for the unknowable and uncertain futures is a continuing theme through a range of literatures (see, as examples, Karp 2004, and Stacey 1992), and plays a critical role in transcendence.

Knowing in the face of mystery (Gherardi, referenced in Dey and Steyaert 2007) requires humility and courage or permits, if not necessitates, 'not knowing'. Admission of not knowing has been linked to learning and wisdom (Hays 2007). Relatedly, scholars are increasingly speaking of unlearning behavioural and cognitive habits that undermine performance and innovation (Becker 2005, Kim and Hays 2010, Sinkula 2002) and making room for what might come (Dey and Staeyert 2007, Rafferty and Simons 2006, Smith 2007).

Transcendence

Transcendence is a process and state of mind that allows us to see deeper within and further without (Hays, in press, Scharmer 2001, 2009). It is a mechanism that contributes to continuous, purposeful and conscious learning and change – transformation and the cultivation of wisdom (Bennet and Bennet 2008). While transcendence may be thought the province of an elite or fringe minority, it is available to most of us. Moreover, it is requisite if we are to undo the damage of the past and create a sustainable world for ourselves. If we want to transform the world, we must first transform ourselves (Smith 2007). Transcendence informs us what needs to transform, why and how, and helps us *get over ourselves* so that we can more accurately and objectively see things as they truly are, become more receptive to possibility and overcome habits that impede our capacity to effectively act in and on the world (Shefy and Sadler-Smith 2006, Sanders III, Hopkins and Geroy 2003).

Bennet and Bennet (2008) explore the relationship between wisdom and transcendence and the process of transcending. For them, wisdom is an expression directed toward the greater good, enabled by extraordinary consciousness and moderated through systemic understanding and values concerning unity and interdependence. Extraordinary consciousness permits the surfacing and application of tacit, unconscious knowledge and attentiveness to external stimuli. Richer intuition and observed accuracy enable one to more effectively act in and on the world.

Boström and Lassen (2006) describe meta-learning – consciousness of how one thinks and learns – and its importance. This 'meta' perspective and capacity is transcendent. We must get outside and rise above ourselves to objectively assess who we are and who we are not, what we know and can do and what we need to know and be able to do. Meta-learning, Boström and Lassen (2006) assert, permits learning expansion. This comes about through reflection. One's perception and learning horizons can be extended; that is, we can transcend our limits through reflection (see Shefy and Sadler-Smith 2006) and, to some measure, through mindfulness training (see Carroll and Edmondson 2002, or Jordan, Messner and Becker 2009). Adopting Laurer's concept of the transcendent episteme, Torosyan (2001) notes that transcendence is a function of 'self-reflexiveness', a consciousness of one's own active engagement with pursuits that matter. Transcendence involves developing a voice of one's own, seeking linkages, holism, integration and developing empathy (Cacioppe and Edwards 2005, Shefy and Sadler-Smith 2006). This means finding *and* getting over ourselves: joining with the universe while not losing ourselves.

Brown and Posner (2001: 274, my emphasis) make the link between transformational learning and transcendence, arguing that transformational learning involves a *'dramatic and fundamental change in the way we see ourselves and the world in which we live'*. They note that Kegan suggested transformational learning represents an 'expansion of consciousness', *transcending a simple accretion of knowledge.* Citing Clark, who has observed that transformational learning 'shapes' learners, they conclude that having undergone a transformational learning experience, people are substantially different in some regard in ways that both they and others can recognize.

Berger (2004) submits that the most powerful transformative learning occurs when learners are pushed to the edges of their understanding. The tension between not knowing and desire for understanding seeks resolution. 'It is in this liminal space', she writes, 'that we can come to terms with the limitations of our knowing and thus begin to stretch those limits' (Ibid.: 338). She alludes to the importance of conceiving of the edge as 'the threshold of meaning making [rather than as the limits] of their store of knowledge' (Ibid.: 342). These ideas appear to be particularly relevant to the notion of transcendence. As leaders and learners we need to be able to reach the edge of knowing and unknowing and be able to remain in that state as we make sense of our perceptions and experiences, evolving as clarity emerges and obscures.

Cacioppe and Edwards (2005) conclude that *the pinnacle of learning is heightened consciousness*, which they characterize as having the following attributes: pluralistic, collectivistic, socially aware and responsible, holistic/integrated, global, visionary, spontaneous, ecological, service-oriented and liberated – all terms that fit with notions of transcendence and wisdom. Compton (2006: 3) discusses holism and explains that it is comprised of agency, communion, self-adaptation, self-dissolution and self-transcendence: self-transcendence being '... the creative force of evolution itself, manifested in the emergence of something new', indeterminate and not-yet-manifested potential.

This suggests that transcendence is possible, natural and not entirely volitional. It is an appreciative process seeking possibility, and the self evolves as does learning. Writing on metamorphosis, Sullivan (1998) likewise claims that self-transcendence is a natural, creative act, part of life and the evolutionary process (see also Norton and Smith 2011). Chaos (purposeful disorder) can create the conditions for metamorphosis to a new order. This is in keeping with the notions of positive conflict mentioned earlier. Such tensions can fuel change and sustain effort.

Miller and Seller (1990: 167) highlight the aims of transformation as 'self-actualization, self-transcendence, and social involvement'. The evolutionary trajectory is toward greater fulfilment, potential and integration (see Norton and Smith 2011). To become 'one with' involves giving up something of the self – ideas to which we are attached, beliefs that prevent us from moving forward – so that we are free to embrace greater perspective and possibility. This is part of the emancipatory nature of transformation and transcendence discussed earlier.

Berger (2004: 338) writes that '... to begin the transformative journey is to give up an old perspective, to actually lose a sense of the former world before the new world is fully articulated'. Norton and Smith (2011) have suggested that self-transcendence requires the relaxation of belief systems. It permits evolutionary vision, which is creative, generative and unbounded. These scholars make the case that transcendence can lead to transformation. This important point lends credence to the thrust of this chapter that transcendence may lead to extraordinary performance, innovation and sustainability, a point supported by Wink and Helson (1997), who link transcendent wisdom and creativity, both depending on openness and intuition.

Linking oriental wisdom and Western leadership, Hinterhuber (1996: 295) stresses the need to build capacity to 'prepare for a variety of situations which cannot be anticipated ... in order to take advantage of unforeseen opportunities and/or to limit the losses due to a badly calculated risk'. He uses the Sufi concept 'self-remembering' to describe what is essentially a transcendent process, explaining that there are two levels of observation. The first is of 'facts, trends, and critical issues', while the second is observing the observer, that is, 'observing the behavior of oneself and one's unit in the context of the whole … and surrounding environment. [Such a view can free the individual or organization] from old habits and lead to the discovery of new opportunities or threats' (Hinterhuber 1996: 297).

Clearly what Hinterhuber (1996) and the other scholars covered in this section on transcendence suggest is that leaders and organizations increasingly need to develop the capacity to see beyond the present and the expected. Bound by belief, assumption and bias, reinforced by experience and tradition, we cannot objectively and sufficiently perceive our environment, assess ourselves with respect to it or respond in the most constructive way possible. Self-transcendence is essentially a matter of 'getting over ourselves' – expanding consciousness, as described by Norton and Smith (2011), Sullivan (1998) and others. We need to be conscious of and ready to transcend ourselves in order to learn and change productively. This applies equally to collectives, and, while posing additional challenges, may be even more important. Hays (in press) is one scholar who has applied the notions of transcendence and transformation to organizations, in this instance to teams, arguing that the learning they enable is essential to improved performance and productivity.

Conclusions and Contributions

Having ranged widely in our explication of transformation and transcendence but now bringing our journey to a close, a number of significant and related conclusions can be drawn. Each of the points below provides topics for further dialogue and inquiry.

GROUNDBREAKING PROGRESS

This chapter cuts across and ties together a range of seemingly disparate literatures, all contributing to a richer understanding and conceptualization of organizational learning, transformation, sustainability and wisdom. The parallels and complementarity amongst philosophy, management and education that this study has revealed have generally been overlooked to date. This lack of integrated thinking may have impeded the potential of these individual elements to produce desired results. Conceiving transformation and transcendence as a dynamic system with potential virtuous properties presents opportunities for researchers to examine related organizational phenomena and especially wisdom more completely. Practitioners, too, may benefit, as organizational systems and processes can be designed or enhanced to accommodate and integrate all of the elements and, thus, optimize their potential for enacting and realizing wisdom.

TRANSCENDENCE – AN INDIVIDUAL AND ORGANIZATIONAL PROCESS

Transcendence is not merely an individual process, although even individual transcendence has organizational and societal implications, particularly as a catalyst for change. When we *get over ourselves*, we are able to more objectively see the bigger picture and freer to engage in thinking and behaviour that transcend self-interest, ego influence and perceptual blinders (Shefy and Sadler-Smith 2006) and are, thus, more likely to effectively and wisely act in and on the world. For Sanders, Hopkins and Geroy (2003: 22), transcendence implies 'above experience or beyond ego'. Similarly, an organization, under the aegis of enlightened transformational leaders, can continually transcend its limits, seeking renewal, redefinition and expansion of conscience and consciousness toward wiser forms of practice (Cacioppe and Edwards 2005, McWhinney and Markos 2003, Preece 2003).

A WORK-IN-PROGRESS

Transcendence is an ongoing process of pushing the boundaries of knowing, performance and effectiveness and promoting transformation to ever-greater being and lived wisdom (Preece 2003, Wink and Helson 1997). It is not a quality anyone attains once and for all, rather of *ever-becoming* (see McWhinney and Markos 2003, and Tsoukas and Chia 2002). People continue to learn and develop; organizations adapt and innovate as opportunities arise and challenges present themselves and, by this, potentially cultivate wisdom.

WE MUST TRANSFORM OURSELVES TO TRANSFORM THE WORLD

Wisdom is itself and comprises a range of virtues, including ideals of justice, equality, service and empowerment, continuous seeking to know and understand more, and having awareness and courage to do the right thing in the face of opposition. Konorti and Eng (2008) are amongst those scholars who link courage – along with wisdom and vision – to the potency of transformational leadership. Striving to develop these qualities in ougerselves and in others can make a great difference in our communities and organizations. As described before, we must *'get over ourselves'* or transcend, if we are to transform (Smith 2007). Conscious and purposeful undergoing of personal transformation for the better gives us then the guidance as to how others may be encouraged and supported through transformation towards a wiser way of living.

PUT REFLECTION TO WORK!

Readers interested in cultivating their own wisdom and transcendent capacities, as well as supporting their development amongst colleagues and clients, might benefit from adopting practices and seeking disciplines that virtually everyone can do. Since consciousness, awareness and mindfulness are essential aspects of learning leading to transformation (Nicolaides and Yorks 2008), reflection is essential. It leads to wholeness and authenticity, serving to connect and engage us in very real and immediate ways with people and possibilities, as McWhinney and Markos (2003), Shefy and Sadler-Smith (2006), Taylor (2008) and others scholars cited herein have suggested.

LEARNING IS TRANSCENDING AND CHANGE

People and organizations cannot or will not change more than superficially if they do not deeply learn. To achieve unprecedented levels of performance, they need to learn not only new competencies and knowledge, but must also unlearn the habits of body and mind that limit them (Sinkula 2002). Cranton and Roy (2003) provide a helpful discussion on the impeding nature of habits of mind and how transformative learning represents supplanting them with more accurate and realistic frames of reference. Transcending themselves facilitates individuals and organizations in seeing beyond who they thought they were to embrace a new way of being, thinking and acting.

IT'S OBVIOUS ... OR IS IT?

The aspect of transcendence that is of most relevance here is the capacity to perceive and make sense of what may not be obvious to others. This includes the ability to see patterns – to connect the dots in ways others might not think of, to see possibilities where others see nothing, to see opportunities when many see problems, to distinguish what might be important from all that might be insignificant. Of particular value is the ability to discern what is new and novel from that with which we are more familiar. Our minds work quickly to identify, organize and classify, and we tend to arrange what we perceive in accordance with prior experiences and understandings (Sinkula 2002). As this happens virtually automatic and beyond our awareness, we are likely to fail to see the unique and to distinguish the new from the old. This is why it is of the utmost importance to consciously monitor the thought process and keep our blinders in check – to see things as they are, not as we are or want them to be. Knowing that there will be novelty in every situation and striving to see it allows for the emergence of new possibilities (Barge and Little 2002).

WITHIN REACH

Few might believe that transcendence is available to them, something that they could achieve. On the contrary, one of the main purposes of this chapter is to bring transcendence within reach of managers, teachers and organizational or team members, to help readers understand it and to realize that with discipline and effort many people can develop the capacity for ongoing transcendence. The ten exercises provided at the end of the main text of this chapter are designed to develop reflective and transcendent capacities, enabling personal and collective transformation and development of wisdom.

PROSPECTIVE LEARNING

Where transformational leadership concerns inspiring and enabling change, transcendent leadership is about identifying what is most worth changing. It is also about sensing what is yet to come and grasping its implications (Hays, in press, Scharmer 2001, 2009), and allowing it to come into being (Dey and Steyaert 2007; Tsoukas and Chia 2002). Most importantly, it concerns the ongoing self-transcendence and personal transformation to greater levels of functioning needed to lead and support organizations and communities into the future. This feeds back into transformational leadership as the vision of the future, the mission to fulfil and the learning and capability-building needed to prepare oneself and others to contend with emerging challenges and realize opportunities as they crystallize. More forward-looking and conscious than intuitive, incidental or retrospective learning, the prospective stance involves planning to learn before experience takes place (Mumford 1995). Imagine how constructive it could possibly be to ask what knowledge and skills you or your organization will need in five years, or ten, and how you might go about building them?

TAKE A STAND!

One thing individuals, units and organizations can do to create a climate in which transcendence, transformation and wisdom may flourish is to take a stand: a public declaration for the greater good. Commitment to an important purpose can focus and galvanize attention and effort, providing meaning to what people do. Wisdom is not merely possessing knowledge and skills or knowing what the right thing to do is. It is about taking action – doing the right thing for the greater good, all things considered (Hays 2007). The positive stands that we take individually and collectively are visible signs of our lived wisdom, as well as evincing commitment to the continued betterment of ourselves and our world.

Parting Thoughts

This chapter introduces a new model for organizational wisdom by highlighting the critical role that transformation and transcendence play in organizational learning, change and important organizational performance areas such as innovation and sustainability. Transformation and transcendence are complex concepts and may at first seem lofty and abstract. The author has attempted to make them more accessible and practical. First, this was done by relating transformation to three key forms which are firmly established in the literature – learning, leadership and change – and explaining their contribution to wisdom. Second, it was done by clarifying how transcendence is essentially a matter of 'getting over ourselves'. Self-transcendence is shown to be an essential capacity if we want to transform ourselves or our world. We need to know how our minds and behaviours restrict possibilities and become able to stretch beyond these limits. This is the only way that we will be able to solve persistent and complex problems or develop new technologies that will improve the quality of our lives without doing damage to our precious and delicate planet.

The ten exercises following this conclusion are also designed to bring transformation and transcendence down to earth. Each takes a main idea covered in this chapter and provides a practical application of it. The guiding questions can be used by individual organizational members or leaders to assess themselves and develop personal action plans, or they may be used with teams and groups. Ideally, working through these exercises will lead to a deeper understanding of real problems and identification or clarification of impediments as well as ways for solving them – including how our thinking and behaviour may be limiting possibilities. Thus, what we learn through the exercises may lead to wiser decisions and their more effective implementation.

Developing wisdom is an ongoing, lifelong project, as transcendence is a continual process of renewal and pushing the boundaries (Norton and Smith 2011). The laudatory pursuit of wisdom should be encouraged and reinforced not only in workplaces, but also in families, schools and communities. Yet how do we do that? There is no simple, guaranteed path to wisdom, but there are productive actions we can take. We must first remember that wisdom arises from a dynamic interaction amongst a number of factors.

This chapter has identified several, notably: transformational learning, leadership and change and transcendence. There are, no doubt, others but we know that these factors, if present, can operate synergetically and virtuously to expand consciousness and enhance performance – the very capacities and capabilities we need to make a positive difference. Moreover, the wiser we become, the more likely we are to attend to T^3 and transcendence, as well as appreciating the vital roles they play.

Finally, organizations and their members and leaders can and should become wise. Their wisdom can become evident in their continual learning, refocusing and renewing. Wise, they seek to understand their environment, themselves and their place in the world. Importantly, they look beyond what is obvious, certain and easily 'knowable', trying to anticipate and prepare for possibility – to learn forward. They do this by transcending themselves and, thus, enabling their own transformation and evolution. For this, they constantly surface, explore and challenge their competencies and confidence, as well as the beliefs, biases and assumptions underpinning them. Demonstrating wisdom, these individuals and organizations strive to do the right thing to the best of their ability. In so doing, they set the example for others to emulate, and they inspire and support those they serve to transform themselves, their organizations and their communities.

Reflective Exercises

1. The dynamic model of organizational wisdom emphasizes the importance of five factors working in concert (transformational learning, leadership and change (T^3), transcendence and wisdom). Assess any professional development programme of which you are aware for the incorporation and integration of these factors. Explain how it might be improved by incorporating and integrating these factors!
2. Transcendence and transformation operate at both individual and collective levels. Describe how transcendence and transformation might be approached or fostered in your team or organization. What would individuals do? How could they leverage their individual efforts and talents to achieve more collectively?
3. Transcendence and transformation represent a work in progress, an ongoing process of pushing the boundaries and renewal. Explain where you are in the process right now, and what you might need to do differently to accelerate the process or make it more meaningful.
4. We must first transform ourselves if we wish to make the world a better place. To transform ourselves, must we first transcend i.e. getting over ourselves. Consider what you might benefit from changing or learning to become more effective at leading change and transformation. What is standing in the way of you becoming a better, wiser person?
5. Reflection is central to the process of transcendence, learning and change. Shared reflections may be the key to transforming teams and communities. How might you promote the rich sharing of reflections necessary to lead to positive learning and change in a group with which you are involved? What themes or questions would be useful? How could you best encourage participation in joint reflecting?
6. Learning is tantamount to change. Much learning is superficial and does not lead to transformation. Often we are not aware about how we learn, what learning would be most benefical for us or what we need to unlearn. Assess your own learning habits

and their sufficiency. Identify any beliefs, assumptions, biases or values that may be impeding your effectiveness and needs of unlearning or supplanting.

7. Important capacities of wisdom include discerning patterns in seeming chaos, separating important phenomena from noise, appreciating the big picture and being able to see what is new and unique about situations and problems that seem otherwise familiar. Take any problem or issue you are working on and identify all the particulars about it that may be new, unique and different. Identify any trends or patterns that might be operating beyond the obvious symptoms. Taking a new look, separate what must be central aspects from those that are merely distractions and extraneous (red herrings).

8. Wisdom is within reach of most of us. Enumerate your beliefs about wisdom and your own or the capacity of others to attain it. What would wisdom look like for you? Given what you know about transcendence and transformation, what can you or suggest to others that they begin doing to cultivate wisdom in your respectively their life, organization or community?

9. Wisdom is less what one knows or is able to do than it is about learning and preparing for an uncertain future. Make a list of skills, knowledge or practices that you might need or want to do in five years from now, and define some of the ways you might go about learning forward. You might alternatively do this for a team or organization, in which case you might enlist the aid of one or more free thinkers to help envisage possible futures and their requirements.

10. Wisdom is manifest in action, and often involves commitment to a worthy cause and courage to pursue a course of action that may be difficult, unpopular and offer no guarantee of success. Identify one 'stand' that you are personally willing and able to take or to champion in your organization or community – a commitment to a greater purpose and 'beyond business as usual'. Explain why this is so important, what the benefits will be and what the consequences of inaction are.

References

Altman, Y. and Iles, P. 1998. Learning, leadership, teams: corporate learning and organizational change. *Journal of Management Development*, 17(1), 44–55.

Avolio, B. 2010. *Full Range Leadership Development: Building the Vital Forces in Organizations*. Thousand Oaks: Sage.

Barge, J. and Little, M. 2002. Dialogical wisdom, communicative practice, and organizational life. *Communication Theory*, 12(4), 375–97.

Bass, B. and Avolio, B. 1993. Transformational leadership and organizational culture. *Public Administration Quarterly*, 17(1), 112–21.

Bass, B. and Steidlmeier, P. 1999. Ethics, character, and authentic transformational leadership behaviour. *Leadership Quarterly*, 10(2), 181–217.

Becker, K. 2005. Individual and organisational unlearning: directions for future research. *International Journal of Organisational Behaviour*, 9(7), 659–70.

Bennet, A. and Bennet, D. 2008. Moving from knowledge to wisdom, from ordinary consciousness to extraordinary consciousness. *VINE: The Journal of Information and Knowledge Management*, 38(1), 7–15.

Berger, J. 2004. Dancing on the threshold of meaning: recognizing and understanding the growing edge. *Journal of Transformative Education*, 2(4), 336–51.

Bierly, P., Kessler, E. and Christensen, E. 2000. Organizational learning, knowledge and wisdom. *Journal of Organizational Change Management*, 13(6), 595–618.

Bonnett, M. 2009. Systemic wisdom, the 'selving' of nature, and knowledge transformation: education for the greater whole. *Studies in Philosophy and Education*, 28(1), 39–49.

Boström, L. and Lassen, L. 2006. Unraveling learning, learning styles, learning strategies and meta-cognition. *Education & Training*, 48(2–3), 178–89.

Brooks, A. 2004. Transformational learning theory and implications for human resource development. *Advances in Developing Human Resources*, 6(2), 211–25.

Brown, L. and Posner, B. 2001. Exploring the relationship between learning and leadership. *Leadership and Organization Development Journal*, 22(6), 274–80.

Burke, W. and Litwin, G. 1992. A causal model of organizational performance and change. *Journal of Management*, 18(3), 523–45.

Burns, J. 1978. *Leadership*. New York: Harper and Row.

Bushe, G. and Kassam, A. 2005. When is appreciative inquiry transformational? A meta-case analysis. *Journal of Applied Behavioral Science*, 41(2), 161–81.

Cacioppe, R. and Edwards, M. 2005. Seeking the holy grail of organisational development: a synthesis of integral theory, spiral dynamics, corporate transformation and action inquiry. *Leadership & Organization Development Journal*, 26(2), 86–105.

Carroll, J. and Edmondson, A. 2002. Leading organizational learning in health care. *Quality and Safety in Health Care*, 11(1), 51–6.

Chapman, J. 2002. A framework for transformational change in organisations. *Leadership & Organization Development Journal*, 23(1–2), 16–25.

Compton, V. 2006. Perched on the outside of the box, clinging to the threads of familiarity: incubating imagination through meditation practice in teacher education. Paper presented at the 4th Annual International Conference of the Imaginative Education Research Group, *Opening Doors to Imaginative Education*, Vancouver, BC, 11–15 July.

Conger, J. 1999. Charismatic and transformational leadership in organizations: an insider's perspective on these developing streams of research. *Leadership Quarterly*, 10(2), 145–79.

Cranton, P. and Roy, M. 2003. When the bottom falls out of the bucket: toward a holistic perspective of transformative learning. *Journal of Transformative Education*, 1(2), 86–98.

Crossan, M., Vera, D. and Nanjad, L. 2008. Transcendent leadership: strategic leadership in dynamic environments. *Leadership Quarterly*, 19(5), 569–81.

Dey, P. and Steyaert, C. 2007. The troubadours of knowledge: passion and invention in management education. *Organization*, 14(3), 437–61.

Elias, D. 1997. It's time to change our minds. *ReVision*, 26(1), 3–12.

Fraser, S. and Greenhalgh, T. 2001. Coping with complexity: educating for capability. *BMJ*, 323(6 October), 799–803.

Freire, P. 2000. *Pedagogy of the Oppressed*. 30th Anniversary Edition. London: Continuum International.

Gardiner, J. 2006. Transactional, transformational, and transcendent leadership: metaphors mapping the evolution of the theory and practice of governance. *Leadership Review*, 6, 62–76.

Gow, L. and Kember, D. 1990. Does higher education promote independent learning? *Higher Education*, 19(3), 302–22.

Grauerholz, L. 2001. Teaching holistically to achieve deep learning. *College Teaching*, 49(2), 44–50.

Harris, S., Lowery-Moore, H. and Farrow, V. 2008. Extending transfer of learning theory to transformative learning theory: a model for promoting teacher leadership. *Theory into Practice*, 47(4), 318–26.

Havard, B., Du, J. and Olinzock, A. 2005. Deep learning: the knowledge, methods, and cognition process in instructor-led online discussion. *Quarterly Review of Distance Education*, 6(2), 125–35.

Hays, J. 2007. Dynamics of organisational wisdom. *The Business Renaissance Quarterly*, 2(4), 77–122.

Hays, J. 2008. Threshold and transformation. *European Journal of Management*, 8(3), 24–46.

Hays, J. 2010a. The ecology of wisdom. *Management & Marketing Journal*, 5(1), 71–92.

Hays, J. 2010b. Mapping the wisdom ecosystem. *Management & Marketing Journal*, 5(2), 19–66.

Hays, J. 2012. Wicked problem: educating for complexity and wisdom. Paper presented at the Wise Management in Organisational Complexity Conference, 23–24 May 2012, Shanghai, China. Revised version, same title (in press), in *Wise Management in Organisational Complexity*, edited by M. Thompson and D. Bevans. Basingstoke: Palgrave Macmillan.

Hays, J. (in press) Theory U and team performance: presence, participation, and productivity, in *Perspectives on Theory U: Insights from the Field*, edited by O. Gunnlaugson, C. Baron and M. Cayer. Publication details pending.

Hinterhuber, H. 1996. Oriental wisdom and Western leadership. *The International Executive*, 38(3), 287–302.

Howell, J. and Avolio, B. 1993. Transformational leadership, transactional leadership, locus of control, and support for innovation: key predictors of business-unit performance. *Journal of Applied Psychology*, 78(6), 891–902.

Hutchison, D. and Bosacki, S. 2000. Over the edge: can holistic education contribute to experiential education? *The Journal of Experiential Education*, 23(3), 177–82.

Illeris, K. 2003. Workplace learning and learning theory. *Journal of Workplace Learning*, 15(4), 167–78.

Jordan, S., Messner, M. and Becker, A. 2009. Reflection and mindfulness in organizations: rationales and possibilities for integration. *Management Learning*, 40(4), 465–73.

Jordi, R. 2011. Reframing the concept of reflection: consciousness, experiential learning, and reflective learning practices. *Adult Education Quarterly*, 61(2), 181–97.

Judge, T. and Piccolo, R. 2004. Transformational and transactional leadership: a meta-analytic test of their relative validity. *Journal of Applied Psychology*, 89(5), 755–68.

Karp, T. 2004. Learning the steps of the dance of change: improving change capabilities by integrating future studies with positive organisational scholarship. *Foresight*, 6(6), 349–55.

Kets de Vries, M. and Balazs, K. 1998. Beyond the quick fix: the psychodynamics of organizational transformation and change. *European Management Journal*, 16(5), 611–22.

Kim, C. and Hays, J. 2010. Renaissance leaders: global trends and emerging forms of leadership. *I-manager's Journal on Management*, 4(3), 1–27.

Knapper, B. 2001. Lifelong learning in the workplace, in *Systems, Settings, People: Workforce Development Challenges for the Alcohol and Other Drugs Field*, edited by A. Roche and J. McDonald. Adelaide: NCETA.

Konorti, E. and Eng, P. 2008. The 3D transformational leadership model. *Journal of the American Academy of Business*, 14(1), 10–20.

Korac-Kakabadse, N., Korac-Kakabadse, A. and Kouzmin, A. 2004. Leadership renewal: towards the philosophy of wisdom. *International Review of Administrative Sciences*, 67(2), 207–27.

Küpers, W. 2011. 'Trans- + - form' leader- and followership as an embodied, emotional and aesthetic practice for creative transformation in organisations. *Leadership & Organization Development Journal*, 32(1), 20–40.

LeBrasseur, R., Whissell, R. and Ojha, A. 2002. Organisational learning, transformational leadership and implementation of continuous quality improvement in Canadian hospitals. *Australian Journal of Management*, 27(2), 141–62.

Lichtenstein, B., Uhl-Bien, M., Marion, R., Seers, A., Orton, J. and Schneider, C. 2006. Complexity leadership theory: an interactive perspective on leading in complex adaptive systems. *Emergence: Complexity and Organization*, 8(4), 2–12.

Lynch, R. 1999. Seeking practical wisdom. *Business and Economic History*, 28(2), 123–35.

Marsick, V. 1998. Transformative learning from experience in the knowledge era. *Daedalus*, 127(4), 119–36.

McGill, M., Slocum, J. and Lei, D. 1992. Management practices in learning organizations. *Organizational Dynamics*, 21(1), 5–17.

McKenna, B. and Rooney, D. and Boal, K. 2009. Wisdom principles as a meta-theoretical basis for evaluating leadership. *Leadership Quarterly*, 20(2), 177–90.

McWhinney, W. and Markos, L. 2003. Transformative education: across the threshold. *Journal of Transformative Education*, 1(1), 16–37.

Mezirow, J. 1991. *Transformative Dimensions of Adult Learning*. San Francisco: Jossey-Bass.

Mezirow, J. 1997. Transformative learning: theory to practice. *New Directions for Adult and Continuing Education*, (74), 5–12.

Mezirow, J. 2000. Learning to think like an adult: core concepts of transformation theory, in *Learning as Transformation: Critical Perspectives on a Theory in Progress*, edited by J. Mezirow. San Francisco: Jossey-Bass.

Miller, J. 1996. *The Holistic Curriculum*. Toronto: OISE.

Miller, J. and Seller, W. 1990. *Curriculum: Perspectives and Practice*. Toronto: Copp Clark Pitman.

Moore, M. 2005. The transtheoretical model of the stages of change and the phases of transformative learning: comparing two theories of transformational change. *Journal of Transformative Education*, 3(4), 394–415.

Mumford, A. 1995. Four approaches to learning from experience. *Industrial and Commercial Training*, 27(8), 12–19.

Nicolaides, A. and Yorks, L. 2008. An epistemology of learning through life. *Emergence: Complexity and Organization*, 10(1), 50–61.

Norton, F. and Smith, C. 2011. Embodying evolutionary vision: an action-based experiment in non-dual perception. *World Futures*, 67(3), 201–12.

Percy, R. 2005. The contribution of transformative learning theory to the practice of participatory action research and extension: theoretical reflections. *Agriculture and Human Values*, 22(2), 127–36.

Prahalad, C. and Osterveld, J. 1999. Transforming internal governance: the challenge for multinationals. *Sloan Management Review*, 40(3), 31–9.

Preece, J. 2003. Education for transformative leadership in Africa. *Journal of Transformative Education*, 1(3), 245–63.

Quay, J. 2003. Experience and participation: relating theories of learning. *The Journal of Experiential Education*, 26(2), 105–16.

Rafferty, A. and Simons, R. 2006. An examination of the antecedents of readiness for fine-tuning and corporate transformation changes. *Journal of Business and Psychology*, 20(3), 325–50.

Sanders III, J., Hopkins, W. and Geroy, G. 2003. From transactional to transcendental: toward an integrated theory of leadership. *Journal of Leadership and Organizational Studies*, 9(4), 21–31.

Sarros, J. and Santora, J. 2001. The transformational-transactional leadership model in practice. *Leadership and Organization Development Journal*, 22(8), 383–93.

Scharmer, C. 2001. Self-transcending knowledge: sensing and organizing around emerging opportunities. *Journal of Knowledge Management*, 5(2), 137–50.

Scharmer, C. 2009. *Theory U: Leading from the Future as it Emerges*. San Francisco: Berrett-Koehler.

Schein, E. 1999. Empowerment, coercive persuasion and organizational learning: do they connect? *The Learning Organization*, 6(4), 163–72.

Schneider, M. and Somers, M. 2006. Organizations as complex adaptive systems: implications of complexity theory for leadership research. *Leadership Quarterly*, 17(4), 351–65.

Schwandt, D. 2005. When managers become philosophers: integrating learning with sensemaking. *Academy of Management Learning & Education*, 4(2), 176–92.

Shefy, E. and Sadler-Smith, E. 2006. Applying holistic principles in management development. *Journal of Management Development*, 25(4), 368–85.

Sinkula, J. 2002. Market-based success, organizational routines, and unlearning. *Journal of Business & Industrial Marketing*, 17(4), 253–69.

Smith, B., Montagno, R. and Kuzmenko, T. 2004. Transformational and servant leadership: content and contextual comparisons. *Journal of Leadership and Organizational Studies*, 10(4), 80–91.

Smith, C. 2007. Working from the inside out: management and leadership through the lens of the perennial wisdom tradition. *Journal of Management Development*, 26(5), 475–83.

Stacey, R. 1992. *Managing for the Unknowable: Strategic Borders between Order and Chaos in Organizations*. San Francisco: Jossey-Bass.

Sternberg, R. 2003. WICS: a model of leadership in organizations. *Academy of Management Learning and Education*, 2(4), 386–401.

Sullivan, T. 1998. Leading people in a chaotic world. *Journal of Educational Administration*, 37(5), 408–23.

Taylor, E. 2008. Transformative learning theory. *New Directions for Adult and Continuing Education*, (119), 5–15.

Torosyan, R. 2001. Motivating students: evoking transformative learning and growth. *Et Cetera*, 58(3), 311–28.

Tsoukas, H. and Chia, R. 2002. On organizational becoming: rethinking organizational change. *Organization Science*, 13(5), 567–582.

van Woerkom, M. 2004. The concept of critical reflection and its importance for human resource development. *Advances in Developing Human Resources*, 6(2), 178–92.

Warburton, K. 2003. Deep learning and education for sustainability. *International Journal of Sustainability in Higher Education*, 4(1), 44–56.

Wink, P. and Helson, R. 1997. Practical and transcendent wisdom: their nature and some longitudinal findings. *Journal of Adult Development*, 4(1), 1–15.

Wong, P. 2008. Transactions, transformation, and transcendence: multicultural service-learning experience of preservice teachers. *Multicultural Education*, 16(2), 31–5.

Yorks, L. and Kasl, E. 2002. Toward a theory and practice for whole-person learning: reconceptualizing experience and the role of affect. *Adult Education Quarterly*, 52(3), 176–92.

8 Students of Wisdom: An Integral Meta-competencies Theory of Practical Wisdom

ALI INTEZARI AND DAVID J. PAULEEN

Introduction

One of the critical questions with regard to wisdom is, can wisdom be taught and learnt or is it a God-given gift? Is it a set of intrinsic personal/behavioural characteristics or a set of meta-competencies that can be learnt and developed? As we argue in this chapter, some meta-competencies and capacities (henceforth called wisdom meta-competencies) can be learnt and developed. However, there are some other competencies for which teaching strategies or learning practices have not yet been adequately developed. We see this as an opportunity for educators, especially in business education.

The world we live in is characterized as being volatile and unpredictable: in a word, complex. The events of the future will not necessarily reflect those of the past. Merely relying on lessons learnt from the past, ingrained habits and beliefs rooted in individual and communal values, social assumptions and theories extensively contextualized and restricted in their time–space frameworks might be insufficient for managing future complexity, where emergent phenomena may require seeking new ways of handling unpredictable situations.

Despite two decades of theoretical and practical development of Knowledge Management (KM), the results of KM programmes in real world organizations are mixed at best. One of the critical reasons for such mediocre results is the basic (mis)understanding of knowledge that underlines KM. Instead of focusing on the management of knowledge, we argue that organizations and managers require complementary meta-competencies: a set of critical competencies and skills that enable them to more completely understand situations and to consider the effects of decisions not only on organizational interests but those of the larger community as well. In sum, we ask, is it possible for business education to develop and foster wisdom to enable students and practitioners to be better prepared to live and work in a world fraught with uncertainty and unpredictability?

In this chapter we first discuss the limitations of knowledge as it is generally understood in the KM field when applied in complex, emergent situations. Then we argue how practical wisdom, in the form of meta-competencies, can lead to wise actions that may circumvent these limitations. We present a four-level theory of wisdom, 'the meta-competencies theory', which integrally links the meta-competencies and which can form the basis of a systematic pedagogy for management education.

Knowledgeable from the Past, Unknowledgeable for the Future

Complex systems include innumerable possible states, agents' unstructured interactions and unpredictable behaviour of individual elements as well as the system as a whole (Battram 1998). This is an apt description of the world we live in – considered by Snowden and Boone (2007) to be an unordered entity, in which there is no simple relationship between cause and effect. This is the world into which business students graduate. Our individual lives are intricately connected to the complex, emergent social system we live in. To survive and even thrive, we, as individuals, must also in a sense be emergent. This is why knowledge, which is largely based on such past-oriented entities as data, information and experience, by itself may be insufficient in ensuring appropriate decisions and effective actions in emergent situations in a complex world.

While we assume tomorrow will be much like today, as today was to yesterday, the 'unpredictable' future can be characterized as the shadow side of a future that will not correspond to circumstances experienced in the past. While we can be reasonably certain that spring will follow winter, we are much less certain about whether it will be a dry or wet, or warm or cool spring. This chapter is not arguing that knowledge will be of no value in complex situations. Rather, we argue when teaching the skills of creating, sharing and applying knowledge that the lesson of unintended consequences is also covered. We further argue, however, that there will always be situations, for example the BP oil spill in 2010 or the Japanese tsunami in 2011, in which making decisions and taking action based only on experience and information-derived knowledge will not necessarily be adequate. Rather, in complex situations such as these we must be taught to understand the inherent limitations of knowledge and be educated and ready to implement another skill set and abilities – that of practical wisdom in the form of *wisdom meta-competencies*.

As is the case with organizational KM, practical wisdom has not been given much attention in knowledge-based educational systems. Knowledge systems are mainly aimed at transferring accumulated knowledge and enabling business students[1] to effectively apply knowledge in practice and to develop and create knowledge. To this, practical wisdom would add the consideration of ethics, stakeholders' values and interests, emotion, as well as sound judgement, insight and the awareness of the fallibility of knowledge in uncertain circumstances (Begley 2006, Bierly, Kessler and Christensen 2000, Nonaka and Takeuchi 2011, Sternberg 2004, Tredget 2010).

More than just a set of applied skills, however, wisdom includes the desire and ability to see what is of value in life (Maxwell 1984). Practical wisdom as an intellectual virtue is not something apart from moral virtue when applying right reason to action (O'Toole 1938). This means, when teaching practical wisdom, the norms of ethical behaviour must necessarily be a part of business education. As some scholars such as Steutel and Spiecker

---

1   Here we note that 'business students' means not just university students and those who academically study business, but also practitioners who take short or long business courses. Similarly, in this chapter where we talk about 'education' it refers to all academic systems, education programmes and practical courses.

(1997) argue, wisdom and morality are therefore closely linked, and the promotion of intellectual virtues needs to be an important goal of education.

Complexity and Unpredictability

The most significant characteristic of today's world is unpredictability. Innumerable nonlinearly related subsystems, the behaviours of which are not easy to predict, make the behaviour of the world as a whole unpredictable (Bennet and Bennet 2004, Lazanski and Kljaji 2006). To tackle complexity issues, scholars in management and organization studies have looked to complexity science (for example, Nonaka 1988, Stacey 1992, 1993, 1995), and to consider organizations as complex systems consisting of nonlinearly interacting agents (Schneider and Somers 2006, Stacey 2007). By adopting complexity theories, organizational theorists and practitioners have tried to gain a better understanding of organizations. Nonetheless, according to this theory, the future still remains inherently unpredictable and unstable (Kelly 1998, Tetenbaum 1998). So, despite the contribution of complexity theories to the study of organizations and social systems, unpredictability is still a challenge that is fostered by the complexity of human social interactions at the organizational level on the one hand, and the turbulence of the business and wider world on the other.

The characteristic of unpredictability can also be seen in the theory of quantum. According to this theory, which derived from the study of subatomic particles (Shelton and Darling 2001), uncertainty is not a momentary limitation, but a rule (Lunca 2006). Perhaps, accordingly, the only thing we can be sure of is that the future is unpredictable and unknowable (Uhl-Bien and Marion 2008).

So, 'simple common mechanistic or linear ways' may not be able to help us understand the complex 'intricately related' world (Battram 1998: v). As argued in the following section, the unpredictability of the complex world on the one hand, and the nature of knowledge as a past-oriented entity on the other lead us to believe that teaching knowledge alone is not sufficient for preparing business students to cope with real world complexity.

The Limits of Knowledge

In management literature knowledge has been described as the combined form of information, experience and one's interpretation in a significant context (Nonaka 1994). Knowledge is processed and validated information (Firestone 2003), it develops over time through experience (Davenport and Prusak 1998) and involves one's interpretation of the world, as it is a 'meaning' made by one's mind (Marakas 1999). In the industrial era knowledge was based upon technical rationality and order, but today it is believed that interpretations and discourse between different people are the base of knowledge (Bhatt 2000).

Whether as technical rationality or human discourse, knowledge does not go beyond humans' predictive capacity. It is accumulated, evolves, is reformed and tailored over time for either current, or what is believed to be future, needs. If we accept that providing a precise picture of the future, even by using cutting-edge technologies and scientific studies of past and current trends, is impossible in practice, we should admit that the future will always encompass emergent phenomena and surprising situations. This shadow side and unpredictable portion of the future is where our knowledge is most likely to fall short.

The constituent elements of knowledge such as data, as discussed later in this chapter, may be universal in meaning but this in no way means, as argued above, that they are necessarily universally applicable in the future. Information that, for example, has been gathered by a particular business in the last couple of years, while still possessing the same meaning as before, may or may not be useful in future situations.

Accordingly, business courses and programmes that concentrate on the accumulation and dissemination of knowledge, information and data may not necessarily be preparing students for situations where there is no sign of similarity to the past. We argue instead that this inherent limitation may be overcome by a set of competencies we call *wisdom meta-competencies* that are related to wisdom and complement and enhance knowledge activities. Maxwell (1984: 65) declares that 'the philosophy of wisdom is designed to overcome the fundamental and profoundly damaging defects of rationality inherent in the philosophy of knowledge'. In consonance with Maxwell, David Rooney (Chapter 4) suggests that epistemology must be replaced with a wisdom-based methodology, *phrónêsiology*. So it is, arguably, crucial that practical wisdom meta-competencies be taught to students so that they can apply them to evaluate complex real world business situations (Small 2004).

Wisdom Meta-competencies: An Integral Meta-competencies Theory of Practical Wisdom

In this section, we introduce four levels of wisdom and the meta-competencies each level encompasses. The four levels include: collection (creating, acquiring and/or developing knowledge), cognition (understanding of complex situations), connection (decision-making) and conduct (acting/doing rightly). While all four levels are directed towards achieving the right ends, the level of conduct is specifically about achieving that right end in a right manner. Each level is in fact a category of interconnected, wisdom-related meta-competencies that have been distilled from the literature and which we believe are useful for taking proper action in and coping with a complex world. These are: reflection, insight and intuition, awareness of knowledge fallibility, making sound judgements, consideration of individual and communal interests, emotions, ethical considerations and taking actions i.e. doing things right.

These meta-competencies function in an integrated manner, as wisdom, according to Blatner (2005: 30), 'requires the integration or judicious balancing of two or perhaps several ... skills and principles'. A proper action will be the result of a balanced interaction between different wisdom meta-competencies and levels. At the *Collection* level, one begins acquiring or developing the knowledge required for gaining an accurate understanding of the situation or phenomena on which a decision is to be made. *Cognition*, as proposed by the theory, refers to one's capacities and competencies to gain a correct understanding of emergent circumstances and phenomena. *Connection* refers to the nexus between cognition and conduct, and brings individual and communal interests together through the process of decision-making. *Conduct* is simply where cognition through connection manifests in practice in forms of doing things in a right manner. These four levels of wisdom competencies are explained below.

LEVEL OF COLLECTION: MANAGING KNOWLEDGE

This level refers to the activities and abilities one needs for acquiring and developing the required information and knowledge. Knowledge is considered one of the main components of wisdom (Garrett and College 1996, Lehrer and Smith 1996). Wise decisions and action, however, are not based merely on knowledge. A wise person not only possesses knowledge (Maxwell 1984), but also has the ability to use that knowledge (Birren and Fisher 1990).

This level indeed includes much from the field of knowledge management, where the main objective is to identify, exploit and share knowledge, whether for organizational (see Hislop 2009) or personal purposes (see Pauleen and Gorman 2011). At the organizational level, knowledge is systematically acquired, organized and communicated to enable organizational members to use it for further productivity and efficiency (Alavi and Leidner 2001). At the personal level the goal is to enhance individual effectiveness in personal, organizational and social environments (Pauleen 2009), allowing individuals 'to choose what information to collect, how to structure it, and who to share it with' (Jefferson 2006: 36).

The level of collection plays a complementary role to the cognitive meta-competencies (level of cognition). At this level one's initial understanding of situations and phenomena is developed, assessing, analyzing and exploring different aspects of the situation based on existing and available knowledge and experience. Whether or not existing knowledge and experience is appropriate is a question addressed by one's cognitive meta-competencies and capacities at the level of cognition.

Experience is critical in developing knowledge and a main source of knowledge (Roberts and Armitage 2008). It is also closely linked to, and necessary, although not sufficient, for wisdom (Baggini and Fosl 2007). Experience, and more importantly the lessons learnt from it, expand and develop one's knowledge capacity. In teaching and learning wisdom it is very important to know that while knowledge abilities can be taught and learnt (that is, *tékhnê*), experience has a subjective nature that is gained through personal exposure to and involvement in 'real' events. Although case study simulations may give business students a taste of the real world, true experience requires the *touch* of the real world which is difficult to simulate. However, essential to becoming wise is not just gaining, accumulating and having (knowledge and) experience, but also becoming experienced by learning from and reflecting on experiences, which calls for a higher level of understanding and internalization: the level of cognition.

LEVEL OF COGNITION: UNDERSTANDING AND ASSESSING COMPLEX SITUATIONS

Within this level we explore the meta-competencies required to gain accurate understanding of complex situations upon which wise actions are based. These cognitive competencies include: *reflection, insight and intuition* and *awareness of knowledge fallibility*.

Wisdom, as Csikszentmihalyi and Rathunde (1990) explain, is reliant on holistic cognitive processes providing a universal awareness of interrelated systems that moves beyond all known conventional relationships. A lack of cognitive competencies – reflection, insight and intuition and awareness of knowledge fallibility – will most likely lead one to make wrong decisions and take inappropriate actions.

Understanding is the capacity to sum up circumstances, and according to Aristotle is a requisite for practical wisdom (2009: 1143a 1–20). Understanding the truth of (or behind) complex events and phenomena entails critical reflection on our knowledge and experience, insight into the events and awareness that our existing knowledge and experiences may fall short in dealing with the events and phenomena. In complex situations, where emergence is a significant feature (Tredinnick 2009), knowledge needs to be continuously checked against current reality, as in changing situations 'there will always be new relations which ultimately threaten our current cognitive constructions' (Andrade 2004: 125). Cognition and accurate understanding of complex situations support the meta-competencies at the higher level of connection – making sound judgements, consideration of individual and communal interests and consideration of ethics – that are required for making sound decisions.

Reflection

As a connection between the world of experience and the world of ideas, John Dewey (1933: 118) defines reflection as 'active, persistent, and careful consideration of any belief or supposed form of knowledge in the light of the grounds that support it and further conclusions to which it tends'.

In complex situations, this ability is needed for *understanding and assessing complex circumstances* in order to get closer to the truth by taking account of emotion and cognition, as well as being aware of the fact that knowledge is intrinsically fallible and there are always unknowns inevitably surrounding us in a complex world. As Felten, Gilchrist and Darby (2006: 42) describe, effective reflection in service-learning is a process which involves 'the interplay of emotion and cognition in which people (students, teachers, and community partners) intentionally connect service experiences with academic learning objectives'. So in the pedagogy of reflection, it is important to ensure that reflections concentrate on both thinking and emotion that leads to learning (Correia and Bleicher 2008).

Insight and intuition

Insight and intuition are critical for developing one's cognition. They construct the rational and irrational dimensions of cognition. Incorporating these two is crucial for the level of cognition, as truth arises from both reason and emotion. While insight is a reason-based inference, intuition is associated with and mainly based on emotion. As Heath (2003: 1) defines the concepts, while 'insight is an inference that is validated by reason, [i]ntuition is an inference that is validated by the thinker's belief systems'.

Insight in psychology refers to the understanding one obtains of the functional relationships between component parts of a specific situation in a particular way (Marková 2005). Adopted from psychology, we define insight, being closely linked to reflection and awareness of the limits of knowledge (at the level of cognition) and judgement (at the level of connection), as the awareness and deep understanding concerning one's own condition(s) in a particular situation at a given time, as well as the capacity to explore possible meaningful relationships between apparently unrelated events and phenomena pertinent to that situation. Put simply, insight enables one to comprehend the obscure aspects of situations and events, recognize their interrelationships and gain a true, deeper and wider understanding of the bigger picture and of the dynamics taking place.

Insight is one of the key components of wisdom (Pasupathi and Staudinger 2001, Rooney, McKenna and Liesch 2010), as wise practice in a complex world requires an accurate assessment of a complex situation, which means an understanding of the nature of nonlinear interactions of events and phenomena. A practical wise person is able to grasp and comprehend what is blurred and obscure at first sight (Tredget 2010). So a true understanding of complex situations in a particular time will not be gained through a superficial evaluation of events, but through deep insight.

Awareness of the limits of knowledge

Another component required for understanding complex and unpredictable situations is an *awareness of the limits of knowledge*. Students must be aware that what they learn now is likely to be time-proscribed, given a constantly changing future. Even if we can ascribe some degree of stability to changing situations 'we [still] cannot plausibly claim to have a definite picture of a reality which undergoes change' (Andrade 2004: 125). Complexity theory holds that the reality of the world is what we perceive of the world (Keene 2000), and, accordingly, it may not match what we are taught. Clearly, a business graduate of the 1980s will not succeed in the current virtual trading environment if reliant only on what was learned at school.

LEVEL OF CONNECTION: DECISION-MAKING

The level of connection is the link between one's cognition and conduct. At this level one's judgement abilities, consideration of ethics and consideration of individual and communal interests engage. Practices and actions taken in a particular time when facing a complex situation are to a great degree based upon one's understanding of the situation and its interacting component parts. After understanding and reflecting on a situation, one can apply judgement in order to make an appropriate decision. The level of connection is based on one's judgement ability, which is directed by considering codes of ethics and by concerns, considered central to ethics, for other individuals, organizations and society.

At this level the wise person enters the decision-making process, through which various options are evaluated according to a set of criteria to resolve a problem. We believe making the right decision that will most likely lead to wise actions when confronting complex situations greatly depends on four meta-competencies embodied by wisdom, discussed in the following sections. These are the ability to make sound *judgements*, consideration of *ethics*, balancing *emotion* and the consideration of *individual and communal interests*.

Judgement

'Virtue is a state of character concerned with choice' (Aristotle 2009: 1106b 35). This conveys that doing the right thing requires right judgement (Shenbai 2009). To realize what is right and correct as opposed to wrong and incorrect and to discriminate between right and wrong, judgement is a crucial ability, one clearly required for right decision-making. Bennis and O'Toole (cited in Gibson 2008) point out that most difficulties managers face challenge their ability to judge rather than merely accumulate facts. Wise people thus are more likely to succeed in such situations.

As Bierly, Kessler and Christensen (2000) argue, one of the distinctive characteristics of wise people compared to merely knowledgeable ones is the ability to form sound judgements regarding the conduct of life. A wise person possesses the skills or abilities required for making 'all of the variety of judgments only an expert can make' (Ibid.: 4). They go on to say that knowledge does not necessarily 'give this sort of ability or skill' (Ibid.). The significant kind of judgements that wise experts are able to form are the judgements that involve evaluation (Smith and Lehrer 1996), and this involves knowledge and *emotions* (Saaty 1994).

Emotion

Practical wisdom is not a pure cognitive entity: it also involves emotional characteristics (Baltes and Kunzmann 2003, Tredget 2010). Aristotle (2009) said that virtue is concerned with emotions and actions. With respect to practical wisdom, 'emotion' is a matter of one's ability to strike a balance between being overly affected by emotions or remaining ignorant of them when making decisions and taking actions. Birren and Fisher (1990: 321) refer to this as 'emotional mastery', explaining that a 'wise person is thought to show emotional mastery such that his or her decisions are not likely to be dominated by such passions as anger or fear'. Virtuous decisions and acts are not made and affected by extremes.

Passion, according to Garrison (1997: 80) 'is a part of practical reasoning; [and] nothing is called into existence without it'. So bringing awareness to the reality of emotions and passions is vital. Aristotle argued that habituation could be used to educate and refine emotions and lead to appropriate behaviour (1999: 1103b 15–21).

As with ethics, emotion plays an integral role among the four levels. Emotion is reflected through judgement (Saaty 1994) at the level of connection, and engaged with cognition through reflection (Correia and Bleicher 2008, Felten, Gilchrist and Darby 2006) at the level of cognition.

Consideration of ethics

Although ethics has been depicted as a part of the level of connection in Figure 8.1, it is in no way separable from the other wisdom meta-competencies. Ethics indeed unifies all the other wisdom meta-competencies, and plays the role of a filtering mediator to integrate the other wisdom competencies with practice. Ethics is directly linked to reflection and to practice.

Ethics is broadly defined as 'having to do with what is right, good, and/or virtuous' (Tjeltveit 2000: 243). This requires the consideration of individual and communal interests and values. As related to practical wisdom, ethics is, according to Melé (2010: 638), 'an intrinsic dimension of any decision, and practical wisdom is essential in perceiving such a dimension and in making sound moral judgments in the making of decisions'. Hence, practical wisdom intimately embraces ethics (Steutel and Spiecker 1997) as it helps people find out what is of value and how it can be realized (Maxwell 1984).

Ethics sanctions knowledge activities as sometimes unwise even when applied successfully and efficiently. Ethics and morality are key in this theory as they distinguish the teaching of knowledge from the teaching of wisdom. As Pantzar (2000: 231), in emphasizing the deep lack of wisdom in the current world, put it, '[m]ere information or raw knowledge [...] will not be enough to reduce poverty, unemployment, solitude, anxiety, crime, feelings of insecurity or war'. Gathering, transferring and applying information and knowledge can be done to achieve either good or bad ends. However, in wise actions, morality and practice are not separated. According to Baggini and Fosl (2007: 153) prudence (practical wisdom) is the effective deliberation and sound reasoning that leads to 'morally right practice'. In the realm of wisdom, as Aristotle (2009) believed, *being good* and *achieving good ends* are two qualities not only inseparable but also one thing in essence.

The emergence of new fields such as 'sustainability management' in organizations shows the responsibility organizations and managers have to take for their decisions and actions (Küpers 2011). The mutual effects of business and society on one another, the interwoven natures of economic and social growth and development and the increasing importance of bio-environmental issues all require business people to ultimately shift their decisions from being made based solely on the trade-off between ethics and benefits, and rather on the extensive interdependence of financial success and social credibility which is mainly acquired from socio-environmental acceptance and development. This requires organizations and business people to look beyond the realm of individuality to the group and organizational interests, and beyond the organizational level to society by integrating individual, group, organizational and social interests and values.

Balancing individual and communal interests

At the level of connection, considering both 'individual and communal interests' is the integrating point of knowledge abilities with ethics and moralities. With respect to the business world, this allows such terms as success, rightness, goodness and appropriateness in the business world to gain meanings far beyond mere financial success. Through this meta-competence, wisdom connects individuality with communality. As argued by Sternberg's (1998) balance theory of wisdom, wisdom is involved when a balance is struck between one's self-interests and others' interests. This meta-competency underlines the ultra-personal nature of wisdom, referring to one's capacity for looking beyond individual interests and points of view to an integration of individual and communal multiple and sometimes opposing interests.

At the individual level wisdom improves cognition and helps one gain true understanding of situations. In complex situations, prudently wise people consider and act on matters in a way that goes beyond the realm of individuality to that of society by taking into account what is of value for both oneself and others (Maxwell 1984). In this sense, students should learn that as human beings (Baggini and Fosl 2007) they should consider what is good not only for themselves, but also for others. Organizations gain their credibility from society. This leads students to take the morality of social interactions into account, as well as the larger area of global sustainability.

LEVEL OF CONDUCT: TAKING ACTIONS PROPERLY AND DOING THINGS RIGHT

While the level of connection centred a great deal on choosing the right things to do, the level of conduct deals with doing things 'rightly'. That is, to be a practically wise person requires that knowledge, judgement and decisions result not only in actions, but in *proper* actions (Beck 1999, Garrett and College 1996). Wisdom encompasses one's thoughts, feelings and actions (Nozick 1989) and displays itself in action (Aristotle 2009).

The mean[2] of moral virtue will differ according to the person (O'Toole 1938); the appropriateness of actions is evaluated according to the extent to which one's perception of the situation represents the reality. This concern takes on more importance in complex situations, where the intricate interaction of phenomena is difficult to understand. Edwards (Chapter 10), in considering environmental complexity, proposes a wisdom typology, which includes transformative, transitive, innovative, conformative and adaptive wisdom. He argues that when facing different levels of environmental turbulence, organizational responses may vary based on these five types of wisdom.

As discussed in the previous section, ethics is one of the critical indicators of the properness of actions. A 'proper action' is, therefore, assessed according to the integration of three factors:

- *Effectiveness*: the extent to which a decision achieves desired goals;
- *Interpretation*: the decision-maker's understanding of the situation in which an action is taken;
- *Ethics*: the degree to which both individual and social values and interests have been considered in decision-making.

The four levels of collection, cognition, connection and conduct, their interrelationships, and the interactions of wisdom meta-competencies will be discussed in the next section.

A Model for Teaching Wisdom

Practical wisdom is the 'intelligence inspired by a moral intuition of what is or is not virtue' (Roca 2007: 198) and, as the basis of action (Robinson 1990), it enhances learners' cognitive capacity to go beyond the formulation of logic and reason, and rather promotes their judgement skill and deliberative ability to 'act appropriately in specific instances, including situations where there is no established formula' (Roca 2007: 197). So the acquisition of practical wisdom and moral virtues is vitally important and, as Begley (2006) asserts, it must be facilitated in order to enable people to make sound ethical judgements in practice.

Figure 8.1 illustrates our theory which illuminates the concepts of wisdom and being wise, and provides an integrated approach for illuminating the concept of wisdom and for teaching wisdom meta-competencies in business pedagogies. According to this theory, managing complex situations entails not only being knowledgeable and capable

---

2   'Doing what is right is always a sort of mean between two extremes, each of which is wrong' (Shenbai 2009: 618). This, indeed, refers to what Aristotle believed as the 'intermediate between excess and deficiency' (2009: 1106a 30).

of creating and sharing knowledge in a given context, but also being practically wise. A wise person, as Bierly, Kessler and Christensen (2000: 602) argue, not only possesses knowledge, 'but uses his or her intellectual grasp and insight to practically apply it'. As a vital nexus between existing knowledge (at the level of collection) and practice (at the level of conduct), sound decisions are made based on an accurate understanding of circumstances. Although this understanding is basically created from knowledge, a true and comprehensive understanding is obtained by reconciling insight and intuition, and refining one's knowledge regularly through reflection. This is based upon the proposition that wise people are aware of the limitations and the fallibility of knowledge (Baltes and Kunzmann 2004, Holliday and Chandler 1986, Sternberg 1990). A wise person therefore shows a balance of certitude and doubt which enables them to benefit from past mistakes through evaluative and reflective skills (Sternberg 1985). In order to know the limitations of their knowledge, wise people need to be capable of self-examination, or reflection. They know that their perception of the world, and their knowledge, may be different from others. Reflection also has a mutually constructive correlation with the other three levels of collection, connection and conduct. In order to make a wise decision and take a right action, we argue that one needs to reflect on other competencies and the consequences of actions. In the model, reflection plays the critical role of providing feedback.

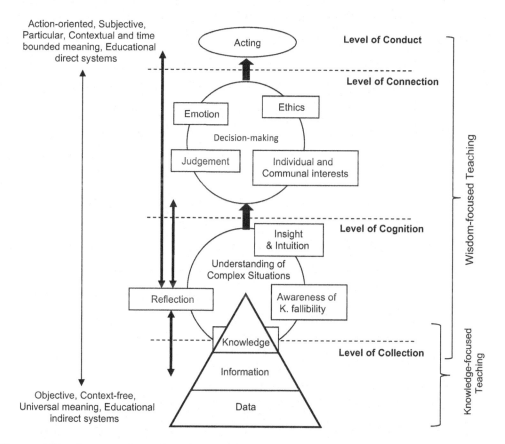

Figure 8.1 Integration of an integral meta-competencies theory of practical wisdom into business education programmes

After coming to an understanding of a complex situation (that is, levels of collection and cognition), one should be able to articulate and define problems, assess alternatives and choose the best possible solution (that is, level of connection) based on the criteria that the decision will lead not only to effective actions and consequences but also to *right actions* by *right means* (that is, level of conduct); 'right' not only for the decision-maker but for all those likely to be affected by the decision. To achieve such right results and actions, judgement is a crucial ability. So, judgement is critical when making right decisions (Saaty 1994) and is vital as one of the wisdom competencies for dealing with complex situations.

The hierarchical data–information–knowledge approach, as a 'taken-for-granted' model in the literature of information and knowledge (Rowley 2007), as illustrated, is still useful. In this approach knowledge is believed to derive from information and data (Alavi and Leidner 1999, Davenport and Prusak 1998). Information is the analysed form of data, and it becomes knowledge once it has been combined with an individual's experience (Alwis and Hartmann 2008, Nonaka 1994).

As mentioned, one of the main differences between wisdom and knowledge is the ethical aspect of wisdom, which differentiates a wise person from a merely knowledgeable one. As Roca (2007) emphasizes, being practically wise is essentially impossible without being good. Nobody will be called a prudently wise person without taking ethics into account in the creation, sharing and application of knowledge. Accordingly, as depicted in Figure 8.1, knowledge abilities (for example, knowledge creation, knowledge sharing and knowledge implementation[3]) are considered a part of wisdom when done in a *good manner* and for *good ends*. That is, knowledge-related activities done through levels of cognition and connection, which are based on an ethical framework applied for achieving good ends, are important aspects of practical wisdom.

An important point is that the goodness and rightness of an action does not depend on what we want or on the actual results of an action, but rather on the circumstances and factors that will be affected beyond the primary action (Field 1966). Moral virtues may not be the same for all people and may differ according to the individual or society: that is, the mean of moral virtue 'is not universal and unchangeable' (O'Toole 1938: 84). This implies that the *rightness* of an action is not necessarily a universal concept in practice. This links the concept of *ethics* to *reflection*, as reflection 'acknowledges that there are multiple perspectives to any phenomenon, each with their own vocabularies, theories, interpretations and frames' (Rooney and McKenna 2005: 314). The ability to acknowledge and consider differences (for example, individual, cultural and so on) is an important part of the wise person's repertoire.

The integral involvement of ethics and morality in taking a course of action in complex circumstances means wise decisions and actions are highly context-oriented. While data can be processed and applied to various situations and evaluated as a context-free quality, a wise decision is extensively grounded in the context in which the action is taken. This, we believe, requires a reconfiguration from theory-based business programmes to practice-based educational systems.

This theory does not suggest that wisdom meta-competencies are restricted to these seven competencies. Clearly others, for example the ability to assess the consequences

---

3   Knowledge abilities may also include such activities as knowledge acquiring, knowledge evaluation, knowledge internalization and so forth. The discussion of these issues is outside the scope of this chapter.

of an action, although depicted in Figure 8.1 as a part of reflection, could explicitly be illustrated as separate though related to reflection. Nor do we suggest that one of the two teaching approaches (teaching knowledge and teaching wisdom) is better than the other. We do, however, try to make the case that practical wisdom is developed based on a set of competencies, capacities, skills and abilities that are beyond those usually taught in management training programmes. These meta-competencies, we argue, can be integrated into an educational approach that would better enable students to manage complex situations more successfully with due consideration of what is ethically of value at both the individual and social level.

Moreover, the levels of wisdom (and in turn wisdom competencies) interact in a recursive manner rather than a strictly linear way. A causal relationship does not necessarily exist among the abilities at each level and/or between levels. Rather, the meta-competencies interact in a non-causal yet multidirectional manner. Some levels may require more attention than others, depending on such elements as the social context in which a decision is made, the decision-maker's information needs and the level of ambiguity that is surrounding the decision-making circumstances. The importance of the levels of connection and conduct may increase in circumstances where, for instance, cultural variety is high, whilst the levels of cognition and collection may play a more critical role in dealing with ambiguity. Ethics is actively engaged in all meta-competencies. Existing information and knowledge may be required at any stage in which the wise person realizes their need. Judgement ability is not restricted to the level of connection as gathering information, reflection and evaluating the applicability of existing knowledge all require a high level of judgement ability. The development of the meta-competencies therefore requires an integrating approach that in bringing these competencies together leads to the development of practical wisdom in practice. Introducing a four-dimensional model, Biloslavo and McKenna (Chapter 6) argue that such an integrating approach is required. They suggest that the personal development of wisdom entails achieving a proper level of development in several domains, including cognitive, conative, affective and moral domains, rather than just one.

Developing Practical Wisdom in the Classroom[4]

According to Aristotle, practical wisdom can be taught (Telfer 1990). In book VI of *The Nicomachean Ethics* Aristotle (2009) argues that the exercise of practical wisdom involves one's knowledge and awareness of right values and of what is good for human beings, as well as one's ability to apply that knowledge in particular situations. Aristotle (2009) further argues that virtues are acquired and developed through exercising them and habituation: a kind of practice makes perfect. As held by this theory, success in coping with complexity and in living well requires teaching that concentrates on knowledge, wisdom meta-competencies, ethics and practice, rather than just knowledge.

In the realm of business education, however, teaching such meta-competencies, even just virtue, have not been given much focus. While there have been ways and techniques of teaching proposed for some of the meta-competencies such as reflection, others, such

---

4   Due to space limitations, this section has been greatly abridged. Table 8.1 serves as an outline of possible teaching strategies. The authors hope to include the material originally in this section in an upcoming publication.

as insight, have not been given much attention. Teaching these meta-competencies (for example, insight and intuition) need to be studied further. In Table 8.1, we have listed the meta-competencies and the teaching strategies and techniques that are available.

The teaching strategies for developing wisdom outlined in Table 8.1 are not discrete: rather they must be considered and applied in an integrated manner, as according to Küpers (2007: 176), 'any single perspective is likely to be partial, limited and maybe distorted'. In order to avoid reductionist fallacies, understanding wisdom in management and organizations requires an integrated, multilevel and comprehensive framework

Table 8.1 Teaching strategies of wisdom meta-competencies

Wisdom Meta-competencies	Teaching Strategies and Techniques
Reflection	Learning the art of questioning Reflective group sessions.
Insight and intuition	Although believed by Buddhists to be developed by meditation, no academic, practical, significant technique has been proposed in the business literature (see Peter Case, Chapter 3).
Awareness of knowledge fallibility	Case studies that represent business failures arising from exclusively relying on current knowledge and experience Encouraging innovation and innovative thought as well as innovative problem solving.
Judgement	Setting up and involving business students in judgement situations Encouraging them to seek out all related features in that given situation, in order to ensure all relevant aspects are considered '(C)onfronting the person with a wide variety of other cases which resemble in one way or another the case they are looking at' (Hare 1971: 248).
Emotion	It would be senseless to claim that business decisions and practices must be made and taken totally independent of any emotional effects. However, through practice and habituation, one will be able to make appropriate decisions by striking a balance between emotional tendencies.
Ethical consideration	Awareness of the right values Being aware of society and stakeholders' values and beliefs Society culture is as important as organizational culture and personal values so they must be fully respected. So cultural studies need to be one of the initial and necessary steps to take in any business. Taking a cross-cultural approach to events Habituation.
Consideration of individual and communal interests	Developing students' competencies to see phenomena through a multilevelled approach Jay Hays (Chapter 7) has proposed a set of exercises that are helpful for developing this ability.
Acting rightly	Closely linked to *Ethics* Informing students that various ways may lead to the same end A group of students can be asked to list as many ways to achieve a predefined certain goal as possible. Then they can be asked to evaluate and comment on each other's solution based on ethics and consideration of individual and communal interest.

(Küpers 2005, 2007). Moreover, the way wisdom competencies can be taught, and the extent to which one may be able to develop one's competencies and skills to properly and wisely handle complex situations may vary.

This theory does not assume that teaching wisdom in the classroom is similar to teaching or transferring knowledge. However, the fundamental assumption of the model is that some meta-competencies can be developed through teaching (for example, reflection and awareness of knowledge fallibilities) which in combination with some other criteria and competencies (for example, code of ethics, and the integration of both individuals and communal interests) will guide decisions and actions that over time will more likely be considered wise.

Conclusion

The rapid growth of knowledge management thought and practice over the last two decades has turned the attention of a number of academics and practitioners in business and management toward the utility of knowledge. Much has been written regarding knowledge, and the knowledge activities business students, practitioners and even organizations need to learn and apply in the real world of business. The complexity of the business world however, in light of the extensive contribution of complexity theories to the study of organizations, requires business pedagogical programmes to develop students' knowledge management abilities by providing them with additional complementary skills towards making right decisions and taking right actions.

In this chapter, we argue that although the dynamics of knowledge and its vital role in business courses is undeniable, the past orientation of the formative components of knowledge entails a re-orientation to a new understanding of what constitutes a relevant learning focus in business programmes. The meta-competencies of reflection, understanding and assessing complex situations, applying insight and intuition, making sound judgement, balancing emotions, considering individual and communal interests, making right decisions considering moral codes and of taking proper actions through appropriate means when unpredictability is significant are the meta-competencies we suggest business students also need to learn.

The aim of this chapter is to offer a fresh perspective for business teaching programmes. This approach explores new features we think are necessary for success in a complex business world. This chapter attempts to shed light on the educational dimensions of business courses that appear to be crucial in aligning conventional knowledge-concentrated abilities with practical wisdom meta-competencies.

Future research should more clearly focus on further exploring, developing and evaluating additional methods and content for teaching wisdom in business programmes. The effects of various qualities of moral and intellectual virtues on knowledge management initiatives need to be examined and clarified with respect to the different aspects of work and life at individual, group and organizational levels. In addition, educational theory and pedagogy that can align practical wisdom, knowledge management and decision-making in a complex world need to be further developed.

Reflection and Critical Thinking

This section asks some simple, yet important, questions to help the reader reflect on their own perceptions of wisdom.

Reflect on your way of living life, whether organizational or personal daily life. Regularly ask yourself the following questions. Keep a record of your answers and compare them over time.

- What personal, behavioural and emotional characteristics do you think wise people have?
- To what extent do you think you are a wise person? Have you ever thought how you could become a wise/r person?
- What thinking and practices do you think you should follow to make wise decisions that have 'good' results?
- Have you ever thought how could you bring your children up, treat family members, help friends, teach pupils, cooperate with colleagues and develop your subordinates' capacities, skills and abilities to make them more capable of making wise decisions and taking wise actions?

As a practitioner ...

- How would you look beyond your personal interests when making decisions and taking actions?
- How can you integrate personal, organizational and society's interests?
- Have you ever asked yourself, your colleagues or your employees the same questions?
- How would a wise business person act in the business world?

As an educator ...

- How can you act in the classroom to model wisdom and so serve as a role model for your students?
- To what extent do you think the current education system allows the development of wisdom in students?
- How would you change or improve it if you were asked to do so?
- Do you think teaching wisdom necessarily requires a wise teacher?

As a student ...

- What exercises and practices do you think you need to do to become wise rather than just being knowledgeable?
- What would be the role of the education system, teachers and your classmates in such activities?
- What course materials do you think you would require for developing wisdom competencies in yourself?
- Do you think you are on the right track now toward becoming a wise person? Why?

References

Alavi, M. and Leidner, D. 1999. Knowledge management systems: issues, challenges and benefits. *Communications of the Association for Information Systems*, 1(7), 2–36.

Alavi, M. and Leidner, D.E. 2001. Knowledge management and knowledge management systems: conceptual foundations and research issues. *MIS Quarterly*, 25(1), 107–36.

Alwis, R.S. and Hartmann, E. 2008. The use of tacit knowledge within innovation companies: knowledge management in innovative enterprises. *Journal of Knowledge Management*, 12(1), 133–47.

Andrade, R.P. 2004. On fallible knowledge. *Nove Economia, Belo Horizonte*, 14(1), 123–49.

Aristotle 2009. *The Nicomachean Ethics*, translated by D. Ross. Oxford: Oxford University Press.

Baggini, J. and Fosl, P.S. 2007. *The Ethics Toolkit: A Compendium of Ethical Concepts and Methods*. Malden: Blackwell Publishing.

Baltes, P.B. and Kunzmann, U. 2003. Wisdom: the peak of human excellence in the orchestration of mind and virtue. *The Psychologist*, 16(3), 131–3.

Baltes, P.B. and Kunzmann, U. 2004. The two faces of wisdom: wisdom as a general theory of knowledge and judgment about excellence in mind and virtue vs. wisdom as everyday realization in people and products. *Human Development*, 47(5), 290–299.

Battram, A. 1998. *Navigating Complexity*. London: Robert Hyde House.

Beck, S. 1999. Confucius and Socrates: the teaching of wisdom. [Online]. Available at: http://www.san.beck.org [accessed: 10 January 2012].

Begley, A.M. 2006. Facilitating the development of moral insight in practice: teaching ethics and teaching virtue. *Nursing Philosophy: An International Journal for Healthcare Professionals*, 7(4), 257–65.

Bennet, A. and Bennet, D. 2004. *Organizational Survival in the New World: The Intelligent Complex Adaptive System*. Burlington: Elsevier.

Bhatt, G.D. 2000. Organizing knowledge in the knowledge development cycle. *Journal of Knowledge Management*, 4(1), 15–26.

Bierly, P.E., Kessler, E.H. and Christensen, E.W. 2000. Organizational learning, knowledge and wisdom. *Journal of Organizational Change Management*, 13(6), 595–618.

Birren, J.E. and Fisher, L.M. 1990. The elements of wisdom: overview and integration, in *Wisdom: Its Nature, Origins, and Development*, edited by R.J. Sternberg. New York: Cambridge University Press, 317–32.

Blatner, A. 2005. Perspectives on wisdom-ing. *ReVision*, 28(1), 29–33.

Correia, M.G. and Bleicher, R.E. 2008. Making connections to teach reflection. *Michigan Journal of Community Service Learning*, 14(2), 41–9.

Csikszentmihalyi, M. and Rathunde, K. 1990. The psychology of wisdom: an evolutionary interpretation, in *Wisdom: Its Nature, Origins, and Development*, edited by R.J. Sternberg. New York: Cambridge University Press, 25–51.

Davenport, T. and Prusak, L. 1998. *Working Knowledge*. Boston: Harvard Business School Press.

Dewey, J. 1933. *How We Think: A Restatement of the Relation of Reflective Thinking to the Educative Process*. Boston: Heath.

Felten, P., Gilchrist, L.Z. and Darby, A. 2006. Emotion and learning: feeling our way toward a new theory of reflection in service-learning. *Michigan Journal of Community Service Learning*, 12(2), 38–46.

Field, G.C. 1966. *Moral Theory: An Introduction to Ethics*. London: Methuen.

Firestone, J.M. 2003. *Enterprise Information Portals and Knowledge Management*. Amsterdam: KMCI/ Butterworth-Heinemann.

Garrett, R. and College, B. 1996. Three definitions of wisdom, in *Knowledge, Teaching, and Wisdom*, edited by K. Lehrer, B.J. Lum, B.A. Slichta and N.D. Smith. Dordrecht: Kluwer Academic Publishers, 221–32.

Garrison, J. 1997. *Dewey and Eros: Wisdom and Desire in the Art of Teaching*. New York: Teachers College Press.

Gibson, P.S. 2008. Developing practical management wisdom. *Journal of Management Development*, 27(5), 528–36.

Hare, W. 1971. The teaching of judgment. *British Journal of Educational Studies*, 19(3), 243–9.

Heath, I. 2003. The pursuit of truth: reason and intuition. [Online]. Available at: http://www. modern-thinker.co.uk/1a%20-%20Reason%20and%20Intuition.htm [accessed: 21 May 2012].

Hislop, D. 2009. *Knowledge Management in Organizations: A Critical Introduction*. 2nd Edition. Oxford: Oxford University Press.

Holliday, S.G. and Chandler, M.J. 1986. *Wisdom: Explorations in Adult Competence*. Basel: Karger.

Jefferson, T.L. 2006. Taking it personally: personal knowledge management. *The Journal of Information and Knowledge Management Systems*, 36(1), 35–7.

Keene, A. 2000. Complexity theory: the changing role of leadership. *Industrial and Commercial Training*, 32(1), 15–18.

Kelly, K. 1998. *New Rules for the New Economy*. New York: Viking.

Küpers, W.M. 2005. Phenomenology and integral pheno-practice of embodied well-be(com)ing in organizations. *Culture and Organization*, 11(3), 221–32.

Küpers, W.M. 2007. Phenomenology and integral pheno-practice of wisdom in leadership and organization. *Social Epistemology: A Journal of Knowledge, Culture, and Policy*, 21(2), 169–93.

Küpers, W.M. 2011. Integral responsibility for a sustainable practice in organisations and management. *Corporate Social Responsibility and Environmental Management Journal*, 18(3), 137–50.

Lazanski, T.J. and Kljaji, M. 2006. Systems approach to complex systems modelling with special regards to tourism. *Kybernetes*, 35(7–8), 1048–58.

Lehrer, K. and Smith, N.D. 1996. Introduction, in *Knowledge, Teaching, and Wisdom*, edited by K. Lehrer, B.J. Lum, B.A. Slichta and N.D. Smith. Dordrecht: Kluwer Academic Publishers, 3–17.

Lunca, M. 2006. The quantum turn in cybernetics. *Kybernetes*, 35(7–8), 1241–55.

Marakas, G.M. 1999. *Decision Support Systems in the Twenty-first Century*. Englewood: Prentice Hall.

Marková, I.S. 2005. *Insight in Psychiatry*. Cambridge: Cambridge University Press.

Maxwell, N. 1984. *From Knowledge to Wisdom: a Revolution in the Aims and Methods of Science*. Oxford: Basil Blackwell.

Melé, D. 2010. Practical wisdom in managerial decision making. *Journal of Management Development*, 29(7–8), 637–45.

Nonaka, I. 1988. Creating organizational order out of chaos: self renewal in Japanese firms. *California Management Review*, 30(3), 57–73.

Nonaka, I. 1994. A dynamic theory of organizational knowledge creation. *Organization Science*, 5(1), 17–37.

Nonaka, I. and Takeuchi, H. 2011. The big idea: the wise leader. *Harvard Business Review*, 89(5), 58–67.

Nozick, R. 1989. What is wisdom and why do philosophers love it so? in *The Examined Life*, edited by R. Nozick. New York: Touchstone, 267–78.

O'Toole, C.J. 1938. The teaching of intellectual and moral virtues. *Ethics*, 49(1), 81–4.

Pantzar, E. 2000. Knowledge and wisdom in the information society. *The Journal of Future Studies, Strategic Thinking and Policy*, 2(2), 230–236.

Pasupathi, M. and Staudinger, U.M. 2001. Do advanced moral reasoners also show wisdom? Linking moral reasoning and wisdom-related knowledge and judgement. *International Journal of Behavioral Development*, 25(5), 401–15.

Pauleen, D.J. 2009. Personal knowledge management: putting the 'person' back into the knowledge equation. *Online Information Review*, 33(2), 221–4.

Pauleen, D.J. and Gorman, G.E. (eds) 2011. *Personal Knowledge Management: Individual, Organizational and Social Perspectives*. Farnham: Gower.

Roberts, J. and Armitage, J. 2008. The ignorance economy. *Prometheus*, 26(4), 335–54.

Robinson, D.N. 1990. Wisdom through the ages, in *Wisdom: Its Nature, Origins, and Development*, edited by R.J. Sternberg. New York: Cambridge University Press, 13–24.

Roca, E. 2007. Intuitive practical wisdom in organizational life. *Social Epistemology*, 21(2), 195–207.

Rooney, D. and McKenna, B. 2005. Should the knowledge-based economy be a savant or a sage? Wisdom and socially intelligent innovation. *Prometheus*, 23(3), 307–23.

Rooney, D., McKenna, B. and Liesch, P. 2010. *Wisdom and Management in the Knowledge Economy*. New York: Routledge.

Rowley, J. 2007. The wisdom hierarchy: representations of the DIKW hierarchy. *Journal of Information Science*, 33(2), 163–80.

Saaty, T.L. 1994. How to make a decision: the analytic hierarchy process. *Informs*, 24(6), 19–43.

Schneider, M. and Somers, M. 2006. Organizations as complex adaptive systems: implications of complexity theory for leadership research. *The Leadership Quarterly*, 17(4), 351–65.

Shelton, C.K. and Darling, J.R. 2001. The quantum skills model in management: a new paradigm to enhance effective leadership. *Leadership & Organization Development Journal*, 22(6), 264–73.

Shenbai, L. 2009. Responsibility for 'doing what is right': Aristotle's approach and difficulties. *Journal of Chinese Philosophy*, 36(4), 618–28.

Small, M.W. 2004. Wisdom and now managerial wisdom: do they have a place in management development programs? *Journal of Management Development*, 23(8), 751–64.

Smith, N.D. and Lehrer, K. 1996. Introductory essay: knowledge, teaching and wisdom, in *Knowledge, teaching and wisdom*, edited by K. Lehrer, B.J. Lum, B.A. Slichta and N.D. Smith. Dordrecht: Kluwer Academic Publishers, 3–16.

Snowden, D. and Boone, E. 2007. A leader's framework for decision making. *Harvard Business Review*, 85(11), 69–76.

Stacey, R.D. 1992. *Managing the Unknowable: the Strategic Boundaries between Order and Chaos*. San Francisco: Jossey-Bass.

Stacey, R.D. 1993. *Strategic Management and Organisational Dynamics*. London: Pitman.

Stacey, R.D. 1995. The science of complexity: an alternative perspective for strategic change processes. *Strategic Management Journal*, 16(6), 477–95.

Stacey, R.D. 2007. *Strategic Management and Organizational Dynamics: The Challenge of Complexity*. 5th Edition. Harlow: FT/Prentice Hall.

Sternberg, R.J. 1985. Implicit theory of intelligence, creativity, and wisdom. *Journal of Personality and Social Psychology*, 49(3), 607–27.

Sternberg, R.J. 1998. A balance theory of wisdom. *Review of General Psychology*, 2(4), 347–65.

Sternberg, R.J. 2004. What is wisdom and how can we develop it? *Annals of the American Academy of Political and Social Science*, 591, 164–74.

Sternberg, R.J. (ed.) 1990. *Wisdom: Its Nature, Origins, and Development*. New York: Cambridge.

Steutel, J. and Spiecker, B. 1997. Rational passions and intellectual virtues: a conceptual analysis. *Studies in Philosophy and Education*, 16(1–2), 59–71.

Telfer, E. 1990. The unity of the moral virtues in Aristotle's Nicomachean Ethics. *Proceeding of the Aristotelian Society*, 90, 35–48.

Tetenbaum, T.J. 1998. Shifting paradigms: from Newton to chaos. *Organizational Dynamics*, 26(4), 21–32.

Tjeltveit, A. 2000. There is more to ethics than codes of professional ethics, and managed care. *The Counseling Psychologist*, 28(2), 242–52.

Tredget, D.A. 2010. Practical wisdom and the rule of benedict. *Journal of Management Development*, 29(7–8), 716–23.

Tredinnick, L. 2009. Complexity theory and the web. *Journal of Documentation*, 65(5), 797–813.

Uhl-Bien, M. and Marion, R. (eds) 2008. *Complexity Leadership. Part I: Conceptual Foundation.* Charlotte: IAP.

9

University Presidents as Wise Leaders? Aristotle's Phrónêsis and Academic Leadership in Germany

BERND KLEIMANN

Introduction

The task of combining the concept of practical wisdom with the concept of university leadership is threefold. Firstly and generally, the chapter tries to mobilize conceptual evidence for the claim that it is a valuable endeavour for organizational research to describe university leadership in terms of the ancient concept of (practical) wisdom. Hence, it will investigate possible conceptual insights through applying the notion of wisdom to the current roles and tasks of university presidents in Germany.

Secondly and more concretely, it shall fill a tiny, but interesting research gap of leadership studies. While wisdom of leadership in general has already been the focus of different research strands (for example, Rooney, McKenna and Liesch 2010, Grint 2007), it has not been applied to university leadership in the German context. Therefore, the chapter will use Aristotle's concept of the right mean in order to develop an alternative description of university leadership practices that are usually described as 'dilemma management' (Schneidewind and Dettleff 2007) or as 'balancing contradictory expectations' (Pellert 1999: 175).

Thirdly, our considerations in this chapter will lead to some concluding remarks on further research questions and practical challenges pertaining to the investigation and encouragement of practical wisdom.

This attempt to theorize German university leadership in terms of Aristotelian ethics has two origins. The first one is the presumption that a description of university leadership can probably benefit from the enduring philosophical study of practical wisdom due to an intriguing correspondence between Aristotelian ethics and management theory. This correspondence refers to the link between practical reasoning and virtuous action in the Aristotelian sense. Virtuous action aims at doing things as well as possible; that is, at perfecting one's course of action in accordance with the specific situational circumstances. This aim is a common idea in the theory and practice of management and leadership, too ('doing things the right way'; cf. Drucker 2001).

Another origin is the fact that Aristotle has unfolded a highly differentiated account of practical reasoning, prudence or wisdom, distinguishing different virtues that reflect different aspects of deliberation and decision-making processes. Thus, he provides an interesting starting point for analysing contemporary decision-making processes of university presidents in a different way.

In order to prepare the application of Aristotle's concept of practical wisdom to university leadership, two preceding steps have to be taken. First of all, an overview of Aristotle's account of intellectual virtues shows what practical wisdom originally was and what it can mean for a study of academic leadership. Then we have to approach some of the key structures of the German university as well as some key features of the president's role.

Aristotle's Ethics and the Virtue of *Phrónêsis*

Even if the combination of wisdom and leadership at first sight may seem to be an arbitrary, if not completely questionable coupling (given contemporary and recent experiences from the political and business sector like the worldwide financial crisis), the intertwining of both goes far back into the cultural history of Western political and philosophical thought. It was Plato who introduced in book VII of his work *The Republic* (Politeia, Plato 1991) the figure of a philosopher-king as the best ruler of the state. According to his utopian, although repressive or totalitarian (Popper 1945) conception of state-order, philosopher-kings are distinguished through their wisdom since they have access to the eternal ideas of truth, beauty and goodness. Hence, it is their philosophical knowledge that enables them to foresee the right course of the 'ship' of state. This well-known, highly disputed and provocative approach of a philosophically informed leadership is based on Plato's idealism and metaphysics. Hence, it is nearly impossible to adapt it for today's leadership challenges. This is the reason why we should not go back to the Platonian virtue of wisdom incorporated into philosopher-kings, but turn to some of the ethical concepts of Aristotle, especially to the notion of *phrónêsis* and to other dianoetic or intellectual virtues. Before we can have a closer look at what *phrónêsis* is, we have to bring up some basic features of Aristotelian ethics.

In perfect accordance with ancient thought, Aristotle claims that the highest good in human life is happiness or *eudaimonia* (cf. Eikeland 2008; other translations are flourishing or doing well, cf. Pakaluk 2005). 'Happiness in particular is believed to be complete without qualification, since we always choose it for itself and never for the sake of anything else' (Aristotle 2009: 1097a–b). Since each being is striving to carry out its own kind of action as perfectly as possible, happiness is the consummate execution of this characteristic kind of action. Moreover, since the essence of human beings is encapsulated in their rational capabilities, their happiness lies in perfectly developing and exercising the rational abilities and virtues of men. 'For a human being, therefore, the life in accordance with intellect is best and pleasantest, since this, more than anything else, constitutes humanity. So this life will also be the happiest' (Aristotle 2009: 1178a). Hence, the characteristic activity of a human being is 'the exercise of reason: that is what, Aristotle thinks, makes human beings what they are. The good of a human being, then, will be exercising that capacity well' (Crisp 2009: xiii). This argument of Aristotle has been subject to criticism along with the objectivism of his ethics, which consists of his proposition that practical wisdom means grasping practical truth – a truth independent of our empirical notions. On the other hand, Aristotle admits that human action is always embedded in concrete situations, and so practical wisdom requires experience and sensitivity to situational circumstances.

Unlike modern ethics, Aristotle's theory is not about moral rules and their foundation, but about virtues. The concept of virtue is crucial to his ethics since – as already demonstrated – 'the human good turns out to be activity of the soul in accordance with virtue' (Aristotle 2009: 1098a). Since ancient ethics has mainly to do with the question of what one should do to live a happy life, virtues are of major importance to ethical reasoning and moral practice. In the ancient sense, virtues are 'dispositions engendered in us through practice or habituation' (Crisp 2009: xv). They are dispositions or habits (*hexis*; cf. Hinman 2012) of human beings who are striving to perform their own characteristic activities as well as they can. Virtue is 'what makes something work at its best' (Eikeland 2008: 53); it 'is a matter of getting it right within particular spheres of human life' (Crisp 2009, xxiv). In the *Nicomachean Ethics*, Aristotle discusses a lot of virtues in a detailed way while applying his famous 'doctrine of the mean' that has experienced both great impact and strong criticism (Williams 1985: 36, Hursthouse 1999). The mean Aristotle bears in mind is not moderation of our desires, but the appropriate middle between two vices or two undue states of mind. 'Virtue, then, is a state involving rational choice, consisting in a mean relative to us and determined by reason ... It is a mean also in that some vices fall short of what is right in feelings and actions, and others exceed it, while virtue both attains and chooses the mean' (Aristotle 2009: 1107a). This applies, for example, to the virtues of character as Aristotle (2009: 1106b) points out:

> *For example, fear, confidence, appetite, anger, pity, and in general pleasure and pain can be experienced too much or too little, and in both ways not well. But to have them at the right time, about the right things, towards the right people, for the right end, and in the right way, is the mean and best; and this is the business of virtue.*

Hence, the mean Aristotle has in mind is not the arithmetic mean on a scale between two extremes, but the ability to determine one's own actions in perfect accordance with the particular circumstances of a particular situation.

Another aspect of Aristotelian ethics is its normative character. Ancient ethics is not a neutral analysis of moral rules or beliefs, but a value-laden approach to the question of how human beings should live their lives. So even if Aristotle does not provide rules that tell us how to live a good life and how to realize the highest good, his account of what is virtuous and good is inevitably normative. Bearing these aspects of Aristotelian ethics in mind, we can now proceed to the so-called intellectual virtue of practical wisdom that Aristotle calls *phrónêsis*.

In his ethical writings, especially in the *Nicomachean Ethics* (Aristotle 2009), Aristotle distinguishes different kinds of virtues on different levels. Basically, he differentiates between two kinds of virtues, viz. *ethical* or *character-related moral virtues* like courage, temperance, generosity, truthfulness, magnanimity and so on on the one hand and *dianoetic* or *intellectual virtues* on the other (Pakaluk 2005, Eikeland 2008). Aristotle divides these intellectual virtues into practical, productive and theoretical virtues, which are separated, but partly overlapping dispositions.

The theoretical virtues are scientific knowledge (*epistêmê*) which is concerned with eternal and necessary things like mathematics, intellect (*nous*) as a capacity of intuitive understanding of first principles that cannot be demonstrated and contemplative,

Table 9.1 **Virtues in Aristotle's *Nicomachean Ethics***

Virtues (*aretai*)			
Character-related Moral Virtues (selection)		**Intellectual Virtues**	
Andreia	Courage	*Epistêmê*	Theoretical, 'scientific' knowledge
Sôphrosunê	Temperance	*Nous*	Intellect or intuitive understanding
Eleutheriotês	Generosity	*Sophía*	Contemplative, transcendental wisdom
Megalopsuchia	Magnanimity	*Phrónêsis*	Practical wisdom
Alêtheia	Truthfulness	*Tékhnê*	Instrumental knowledge, 'knowing how'

transcendental wisdom (*sophía*) as the knowledge of the eternal forms or ideas, the ends-in-themselves. However, wisdom is not really a virtue on its own, but a combination of scientific knowledge and intellect being concerned with most honourable subjects like philosophy (Crisp 2009) or quasi-theological truths (Lear 2004).

The virtue concerned with instrumental knowledge is skill (*tékhnê*). It tells us how things that are not necessarily predetermined and that 'do not have an inner purpose' (Grint 2007: 234) are to be done (art, skill, craftsmanship). 'Every skill is to do with coming into being, and the exercise of the skill lies in considering how something that is capable of either being or not being, and the first principle of which is in the producer and not the product, may come into being' (Aristotle 2009: 1140a). Therefore, skill (*tékhnê*) is crucial to instrumental activities in all spheres of human life.

The virtue especially relevant to this paper is *phrónêsis* which is usually translated as *practical wisdom* or prudence. According to Aristotle it is the most important intellectual virtue. He characterizes *phrónêsis*/practical wisdom through describing a person that is practically wise (cf. Flyvbjerg 2001). 'It seems to be characteristic of the practically wise person to be able to deliberate nobly about what is good and beneficial for himself, not in particular respects, such as what conduces to health or strength, but about what conduces to living well as a whole' (Aristotle 2009: 1140a). Hence, practical wisdom comprehends deliberation about what is good for the individual conduct of life in general, for the household and for the political community (Hutchinson 1995). In other words, practical wisdom is 'a true and practical state involving reason, concerned with what is good and bad for a human being' (Aristotle 2009: 1140b). 'Practical wisdom ... is concerned with human affairs, namely, with what we can deliberate about. For deliberating well, we say, is the characteristic activity of the practically wise person above all' (Aristotle 2009: 1141b). Furthermore, practical wisdom is based on experience, and so it is found more often in older people 'since experience takes a long time to produce' (Ibid.: 1142a). Then, even if practical wisdom is oriented towards the practical truth in human life and tries to grasp it, it basically consists of deliberation, which is dealing with particulars, that is, things that can be otherwise. According to Aristotle, *phrónêsis* deals with particulars since it concerns our course of action, 'and action is concerned with particulars' (Ibid.: 2009: 1141b). We are all always acting under specific circumstances and in concrete situations, and practical wisdom is the capability to adequately determine what to do in these situations while taking into account what is truly good. This is why, eventually, practical wisdom as a 'type of mediation of the universal and the particular' (Bernstein 1986: 110) commands human actions regarding both proper means for certain ends and the ends we strive for, with happiness (*eudaimonia*) respectively acting well (*eu praxía*) and living well (*éu zén*), being the highest end.

Based on this brief elaboration on *phrónêsis* and regarding the purpose of this chapter (that is, the combination of practical wisdom and university leadership), it is useful to explore Aristotle's four subjacent intellectual virtues, too. They complete the list of capabilities that are possibly relevant to leadership.

The first of these virtues is good deliberation (*euboulia*) – the faculty of deliberating properly about what has to be done to achieve the right ends (Aristotle 2009). However, *euboulia* is not only deliberation with regard to the results, but also to the means of deliberation. Aristotle claims that it is 'possible to achieve something good through false inference, that is, to achieve the right result, but not by the right steps, the middle term being false' (Ibid.: 1142b). This means that deliberation achieving the right results, but not by the rights steps, 'is not yet good deliberation either' (Aristotle 2009: 1142b).

The second intellectual virtue is understanding, good judgement or astuteness (*sunesis*) as 'the capacity to discern the proper thing to do within a given context by attending not only to the peculiarities of the situation but also to the perspective, advice, and counsel of others' (Long 2004: 148). According to this interpretation, astuteness (*sunesis*) exceeds the perspective of the individual actor and takes into account what other actors may think. Hence, it can be seen as a kind of empathetic judgement that is closely connected to dialogue (Eikeland 2008).

The third virtue is cleverness (*deinotes*) as the capability to 'do the actions that tend towards the aim we have set before ourselves, and to achieve it' (Aristotle 2009: 1144a). The value of cleverness depends on the end it deals with (Dahl 1984): 'If the aim is noble, then the cleverness is praiseworthy; if it is bad, then it is villainy' (Aristotle 2009: 1144a).

The fourth virtue is discernment (*gnomê*) as the 'correct judgement of what is equitable' (Aristotle 2009: 1143a). It has to do with the fairness of practical deliberation and judgement with regard to the community of human beings (Fink 1970).

Embracing these different, but closely interrelated virtues, we can summarize that Aristotle characterizes the intellectual virtues of practical wisdom, good deliberation, good judgement, cleverness and discernment as capabilities or dispositions to:

- determine the course of action properly with regard to good and bad;
- act, combining particular circumstances and universal aspects;[1]
- act in a way that integrates the perspective and advice of others;
- act so that the proposed aims can be achieved in the right way; and to
- act on the basis of a proper discrimination of what is fair or equitable.

This interpretation of practical wisdom obviously does not confine itself to the virtue of *phrónêsis* alone, but comprises the four subjacent intellectual capabilities, too. These virtues are different from practical wisdom, but they might be of importance for the description of academic leadership. Hence, when the term *phrónêsis* is used in the following parts of this chapter, these virtues are also included.

---

1   Kant has worked out his concept of the faculty of judgement in a similar way: the *determining judgement* identifies and characterizes particulars in the light of universal rules, whereas the *reflecting judgement* tries to find general rules starting from the particular (cf. Kant 1974).

Practical Wisdom and University Leadership

Based on this brief account of *phrónêsis* and its related virtues, we can now turn to investigating whether Aristotle's practical wisdom encompasses capabilities and qualities that are relevant to leadership in universities. Our premise here is that even if discourse on wisdom in organizations may partly seem to be a new scientific fad adorning social science with reputable notions from the past (due to the demand for a new momentum in the never-ending scientific innovation cycle), there is more to the discussion of practical wisdom in organizations than this cursory and biased glance reveals. Not only has the new interest in the concept of *phrónêsis* exerted a remarkable influence on the methodology and self-understanding of the social sciences (Flyvbjerg 2001, Flyvbjerg, Landman and Schram 2012), it has also elicited new approaches to organizational theory (Tsoukas and Cummings 1997, Statler 2005, Statler, Roos and Victor 2006, Statler and Roos 2007) and inspired the development of a metatheoretical framework of practically wise leadership in organizations (Küpers and Statler 2008) that seeks to overcome individualistic and rationalistic restrictions of existing accounts of practical wisdom in leadership theory. Compared to these ambitious and wide-ranging approaches, our task here is rather modest due to its strictly limited conceptual aspiration and its specific subject. The aim is neither to propose a new model of practically wise leadership, nor to cover all aspects of the Aristotelian notion, but to focus on some aspects of *phrónêsis* in order to explore their interpretative capacity with regard to the leadership practice of university presidents in Germany.

Based on the outline of Aristotle's concept of *phrónêsis*, we can now try to examine to what extent the structures of practical wisdom might be constitutive of leadership practices of university presidents today. The hypothesis I want to put forward is expressed in the claim that there are different structural correspondences between practical wisdom on the one hand and the current requirements of academic leadership on the other, as shown in Table 9.2.

Table 9.2   Structural correspondences between practical wisdom and presidential leadership

Structural Correspondences between	
Practical Wisdom	**Presidential Leadership in Academe**
Goal: individual good in the long term	Goal: organizational good of the university in the long term
Reflecting on both ends and means regarding the individual good	Reflecting on both ends and means of the organizational good (university strategy and steering instruments)
Determination of will	Making binding decisions for the organization
Deliberation without rules that could definitely guide practical orientations	Decisions without rules guaranteeing organizational success
Continuous search for the right mean	Constantly balancing conflicting interests and expectations

1. Aristotle asks what is good for individual human beings in the long term and what can be considered to be the common good. Accordingly, university presidents have the duty to ask what is good for their organizations in the long term. Hence, the ancients as well as university leaders must embark on deliberation processes that take into account those ends that represent the sound and reliable interests of individuals on the one hand and of the organization on the other. Furthermore, since public universities depend on material (budget, buildings and so on) and immaterial (legitimacy) societal resources, their reasonable ends must correspond to political and societal expectations.

2. Someone who exercises practical wisdom (*phrónêsis*) must not only deliberate adequately, they must also ask how the good can be achieved. They have to take into account both ends and means since Aristotelian *phrónêsis* deals with particulars, too. In a similar way, leadership decisions include both ends and means; university presidents have to deliberate about what the university shall become in the future (strategic perspective) and how it can get there – even if the means are only reflected on a rather abstract level.

3. Practical wisdom in the Aristotelian sense not only includes deliberation, but also the determination of will, the ability to command one's course of action (cf. Reeve 1992). 'Unlike judgment, practical wisdom involves the virtuous person's commanding himself to perform what is called for in the circumstances' (Crisp 2009: xxv). Those who are not capable of steering their behaviour according to their deliberation cannot be considered practically wise people. This thought may be interpreted along the lines of system theory as follows: if we agree with Aristotle on the fact that practical wisdom includes the ability to command one's will, we can conclude that a decision of a leader is no decision at all if it is not put into practice – and that means, if it is not at least communicated. As Niklas Luhmann (2006) has argued, a decision in an organization is basically a communicative event that is (correctly or incorrectly) attributed to a person. Hence, it may be valuable for the purposes of organization theory to consider practical wisdom not only as a personal feature or capability (as I have done so far), but as a quality of organizational decisions. These decisions consist of communicative events that exercise formal power and that might be attributed to individual leaders, collective actors or to structural circumstances.

4. Another interesting aspect of Aristotle's account of practical wisdom is that there is no rule to guide practical deliberation. Practical wisdom is inevitably situational, and it refers to the individual character and talents of a virtuous person. Similarly, there is no rule that could determine the decisions of academic leaders who are concerned with extremely complex situations, too. Moreover, organization theory is well aware that an organization whose members strictly follow rules must inevitably fail (cf. Ortmann 2004). Thus, the absence of rules that could guide someone who is exercising practical wisdom corresponds to the absence of rules in the case of university presidents who are trying to steer a complex and often inert organization.

5. Finally, Aristotle describes the endeavour to live a virtuous life and to act practically wise as the continuous search for the right mean. Correspondingly, university presidents have to permanently balance (cf. Rooney, McKenna and Liesch 2010) conflicting or even contradictory interests, interpretations and expectations in an ongoing process of 'muddling through' (Lindblom 1959).

These structural correspondences between the features of practical wisdom *sensu* Aristotle and some of the professional requirements of university presidents provide a reference point for my claim that the description of academic leadership might profit from the application of the ancient concept of *phrónêsis*.

Limitations

However, in opposition to the potential benefits of an adaptation of *phrónêsis*, there are also certain limits that restrict the chances of transferring this notion into the context of current leadership theory. These limits arise from the following characteristics of the Aristotelian concept of practical wisdom that do not really match the requirements of an up-to-date account of university leadership:

1. Aristotle's ethics do not primarily adopt the deontological viewpoint of moral duty, but reflect on what is good for an individual, for me, you, him or her:

   There is nothing in Aristotelian ethics inconsistent with the idea that all your reasons for action, or for living a certain kind of life or for being a certain kind of person, ultimately rest on the advancement of your own good. Nowhere in Aristotle is there a recommendation of any kind of genuine self-sacrifice. (Crisp 2009: xf.)

   Even if astuteness (*sunesis*) takes into account the perspectives of others, practical deliberation in Aristotle is primarily aiming at individual well-being (which, however, is conceived of as a common good for everybody). In contrast to that, university presidents as professionals are supposed to reflect on what is good for their organization and not to deliberate and act for their own sake.

2. Furthermore, the Aristotelian objectivism of what is worth striving for (cf. Bolton 1991) is to be rejected. According to Aristotle (2009: 1139b) what is really good for human beings can be determined objectively since *phrónêsis* as practical wisdom is one of 'five ways in which the soul arrives at truth by affirmation and denial'. This means that *phrónêsis* is to do with an objective goal of human endeavour, a state that can be discerned like theoretical phenomena can be recognized through rational understanding. Happiness in the Aristotelian sense is not something that is up to us, but something that is determined by our function or essence (cf. Reeve 2006). Obviously, this is not the case for academic leadership today: the goals of universities are far from being clearly defined, instead they are subject to massive conflicts of interests and ongoing debates. Hence, Aristotle's concept of what is good has to be 'socialized' and pluralized if we want to transfer it to organization theory.

3. Moreover, we have to remove the notion of *phrónêsis* from its original ethical context in order to shake off its metaphysical and objectivist implications and to turn it into a kind of analytic instrument. Admittedly, this is a radical operation since the virtue of *phrónêsis* is at the heart of Aristotle's ethics, but the attempt might be valuable nonetheless. Consequently, if we take practical wisdom in a non-ethical, rather utilitarian way, we have to do without the concept of virtue, too, since virtue is too

closely tied to the normative concept of what it means to live a happy life through perfect exercise of one's essential activity.

These are only some examples of a broader range of conceivable reasons that might speak against the idea of applying the concept of practical wisdom to university leadership. However, regarding the aforementioned overlaps, there are also good reasons to proceed in the attempt to combine both concepts and to explore the possible results of this operation.

Leadership

This requires, beforehand, a working definition of the notoriously ambiguous and intensely discussed term 'leadership' (cf. Wunderer 2007, Bolden, Petrov and Gosling 2008, Northouse 2010, Yukl 2010). According to Yukl (2010: 26), 'leadership is the process of influencing others to understand and agree about what needs to be done and how to do it, and the process of facilitating individual and collective efforts to accomplish shared objectives'. It is worthwhile to extract the main features from this definition and to reconsider them in order to emphasize what leadership is about and how it can be linked to the concept of practical wisdom:

- First of all, leadership is a process, not a single event. It can be regarded as a special type of a continuous interpersonal relationship.
- Then, leadership is exerting an influence on people. However, this influence does not consist of physical force, but usually aims at understanding and agreement on the part of those who are led.
- Leadership is concerned with action and with its ends and its means. It is about the question of which things are to be done and how.
- Leadership does not consist only of mere pressure, but comprises facilitating the efforts of individual or collective actors (Scharpf 1997, Schimank 2010), for example enlarging their opportunities to act and to achieve certain goals.
- Eventually, leadership is relative to objectives that are shared by those who lead and those who are led. However, I think that this claim of Yukl is too strong since it ties leadership to a consensus about the ends. In contrast, I think it is enough that there is a sufficient intersection of interests or at least a combination of different, but complementary goals of the leaders and the members of the organization (Luhmann 1964, Kühl 2011).

Furthermore, I claim five aspects should be added to Yukl's definition in order to adapt it to our purposes:

1. First, leadership is a bi- or multidirectional relationship (Wunderer 2007). Its effectiveness as well as its efficiency depends on the behaviour of both leaders and organization members as well as their interrelationships (Küpers 2007, Küpers and Weibler 2008).
2. However, leadership is an asymmetrical relationship: the leader is usually more powerful and has greater resources to impose his will than the people he leads.

3. Then, leadership – as I see it here – is personal: in contrast to governance or steering which are based on impersonal rules and regulations that have been set up to steer human behaviour, leadership is carried out by individuals (cf. Wunderer 2007).
4. Leadership occurs in formal and informal contexts, which means that its influence is either based on formal authority (hierarchy) or on informal influence potentials (Schimank 2010).
5. Leadership is predominantly concerned with personal decision-making and communication since – according to empirical studies – managers have to spend the biggest amount of time on communicating with internal and external stakeholders (Walgenbach and Tempel 2002).

It is particularly this last aspect that provides an interesting link to the Aristotelian virtue of practical wisdom portrayed above. Leaders, for example individuals trying to influence others through decisions and communication, have to rely on capabilities and personal qualities that correspond to Aristotle's concept of *phrónêsis*. This especially applies to university leaders in Germany, who are compelled to act practically wisely in the light of many conflicting expectations and incompatible structures moulding the university as well as the presidential position.

Structures of the German University and the President's Position

Before we look at the role that intellectual virtues may play in presidential leadership, it is necessary to briefly outline the organizational peculiarities of the German university which have a strong influence on the professional role of the academic leader. German universities today form a specific type of organization defined by structural tensions affecting the university's tasks, knowledge basis and internal organization.

First of all, German universities as public institutions consist of two *often conflicting social orders*: the academic corporation or profession (for example, academic staff) on the one hand and the (state) administration on the other. The traditional gaps between these orders are becoming deeper today since the external pressure on universities with regard to improving their operational and administrative processes is still increasing. Due to this pressure, members of the academic profession are very afraid of an accelerating 'de-professionalization' (Enders and Schimank 2001, Koschorke 2004, Schimank 2005).

Since their medieval beginning in Paris and Bologna (Weik 2011), universities have been *loosely coupled systems* (Weick 1976, Orton and Weick 1990, Nickel 2007) consisting of widely independent faculties with heterogeneous organizational cultures. Hence, universities are often presumed to be virtually uncontrollable by a centralized leadership. This is one of the reasons why legislators in Germany have strengthened the role of university presidents over the last ten years.

Furthermore, German universities are rooted in *two societal subsystems*: education and science/research. Therefore, they have to follow two completely different kinds of logic, which turns them – at least according to system theory – into 'anomalous' (cf. Luhmann 1992) or 'inter-systemic' organizations (cf. Guggenheim 2007).

Another aspect of the university is its traditional *multidisciplinarity*. Irrespective of specialist organizations (for example, polytechnics or business schools) and in spite of the prevailing demand for clear-cut university profiles, German universities still tend to be a sort of 'department store' (Schimank 2001) comprising different scientific disciplines with widely varying cultures and working processes.

Traditionally, professors regard teaching and research as *unclear technologies* (Cohen, March and Olsen 1972, Musselin 2007) that cannot be controlled like, for example, industrial production. Nowadays, the audit society (Powers 1999) strikes back and tries to control these technologies through imposing a broad range of quality management measures on universities and academic staff. This increases the pressure on teachers, scholars and university leaders and forces the latter to balance collegial and managerial expectations.

Regarding the *autonomy* of higher education, some federal states have conferred selected responsibilities and competencies on the universities over the last decades. But since higher education institutions are often not prepared for making this autonomy productive, the state in turn restores governmental control and state hegemony on a different level or with different means.

The last structural problem that is relevant here is the *intricate mode of decision-making* in universities. Universities are 'organized anarchies' (Cohen, March and Olsen 1972) since decisions are made without the decision-makers running the risk of being held responsible for them. This has been another reason for legislators to strengthen the role of university leaders in order to facilitate faster and better decisions.

These are some of the structural tensions and contradictions characteristic of the German university as well as of other educational organizations (Laske, Meister-Scheytt and Küpers 2006). Their relevance for this chapter lies in the fact that these tensions affect the role of the university president in a way that forces incumbents to *balance* conflicting expectations, interests and values. German university presidents have to act as mediators between different areas, political fields and internal and external stakeholder groups. As a consequence, the equilibristic nature of their daily practice corresponds to the core meaning of practical wisdom as the constant search for the right mean.

In order to reveal this equilibristic nature of the university presidency, it is reasonable to concentrate on its tasks, its knowledge base and the structural conditions of the presidential position.

As far as *tasks* are concerned, presidents must alternate not only between different organizational tasks like research, teaching, economic effectiveness, legal accountability, ecological sustainability, social responsibility, technological innovation and so on, but also between the fundamental extremes of *change* and *continuity*. They are expected to make decisions that trigger reforms and organizational innovations as well as decisions that stabilize the existing order and uphold traditional processes and beliefs.

As principal agent theory has convincingly shown (Ebers and Gotsch 2006), managers generally lack the *knowledge* that is necessary to effectively control the work of subordinate staff. This applies in an even greater extent to university presidents who are confronted with a multitude of scientific disciplines, with a huge variety of statutes, regulations and laws in the administrative area and with a vast network of interpersonal relations and enmities all of which they have to keep in view. Hence, presidents have to find the appropriate balance between their need for reliable information as a means for appropriate decisions and the impartiality and neutrality of their decisions.

Furthermore, in the wake of new legislation, the *structural conditions* of the role of the university's top management have changed. Traditionally, the position of the German rector was rather symbolic and equipped with only a few responsibilities. Rectors were seen as *'primi inter pares'*, that is, academic colleagues, and their main task was to represent the university in official contexts, but not to lead or steer it. Nowadays, the traditional model of rectorship has been overlaid by a managerial model. In spite of inconsistent legislation (cf. Hüther 2009, 2010), the tendency to strengthen the top management is obvious. The aim behind this new legislation is to improve the efficiency of decision-making processes through the transfer of competencies from academic self-governance to hierarchical self-governance.

Correspondingly, the president's position has been turned into a full-time job with an extended term of office and with the opportunity of re-election. Some laws even allow the universities an additional full-time vice-president. Moreover, all German federal state laws enable the recruitment of external people who are not professors. This shows that the traditional model of rectorship has been abolished and that the legislators provide for the recruitment of professionals from other societal sectors. However, as far as universities are concerned, presidents are usually still professors since there is strong resistance to managerial governance in the universities – and since the presidential position may not be very attractive to external managers.

Furthermore, the election mode of presidents has been changed: in more than half of all federal states the presidents are elected with the participation of the university council, and the council also often plays a role when presidents are to be voted out of office. This indicates a tendency to make university presidents more independent from internal powers.

Regarding the recruitment of professors, the presidents' abilities to intervene have been strengthened. Today, in ten federal states it is possible or mandatory that professors are appointed by the presidents and not by the minister. Thus, the potential influence presidents can exert on the strategic development of their organization has been expanded considerably. Additionally, in most federal states the presidents have the right to propose candidates for the vice-president positions. This gives them the opportunity to work with colleagues they trust. In five federal states presidents have the right to propose deans, and in six states deans can only be appointed with the president's consent. Ultimately, in some federal states presidents are allowed to control and distribute financial and personnel resources, veto important decisions, make agreements on objectives with the ministry, establish or disband organizational units and to define guidelines for vice-presidents and deans.

Along with the strengthening of the formal position of presidents, expectations and requirements regarding presidential leadership have changed and increased significantly. The number of voices demanding that assertive, entrepreneurial managers equipped with experience in leading scientific organizations should be chosen as university presidents has increased (Weibler 2007). Other clues for growing expectations and the attribution of increased significance are an emerging job market for university presidents, increasing attention of the media, awards for university leaders ('rector' or 'university manager of the year'; cf. Krüger and Rudinger 2010, Schmidt 2011) and finally the fact that university leadership in Germany is nowadays considered to be an interesting research topic (Schimank 2008, Krücken 2009).

However, the legal strengthening, the growing expectations and the attribution of increased significance are only one side of current university leadership. Reconsidering the aforementioned features of the German university, it is apparent that the new managerial role of the top management is contrary to the older rector model that is deeply rooted in the institutionalized self-image of the academic profession.

The overlay of these two models of university leadership results in a mixed structure that I call the *integrative-paradoxical structure* of university leadership. It is *integrative* insofar as the president is supposed to combine the role of a collegial rector with the role of a superior manager who is able to make binding decisions.[2] At the same time the mixed structure is *paradoxical* because the rector and the manager model are contradictory in many respects and cannot be combined harmoniously.

Thus, university presidents have to mediate between contradictory elements, actors, value systems, interests and tasks. I will briefly outline a few of these contradictions here:

1. University presidents have to balance their managerial role (giving them more responsibilities and increasing their hierarchical power) on the one hand and the traditional habits, expectations and routines that define their intra-organizational position as a colleague or *primus inter pares* on the other hand (*integrative-paradoxical structure*).
2. They must mediate between the different parts of the university, that is, the sector of the academic profession and the administrative sector with its strong ties to the state bureaucracy.
3. They have to mediate between value orders, belief systems and interests of different external actors like ministries, corporations, political bodies (these requirements often being highly contradictory in themselves) and those of internal actors like deans, departments, administration staff, professors and so on. What is often required here is 'double talk' (Schimank 2008) that serves to break up persistent oppositions between actor groups.
4. University presidents have to mediate between the requirements of research and teaching. This concerns many issues like allocation of resources, defining institutional goals, rewarding intramural achievements and so on.
5. They have to take into account the heterogeneity of scientific disciplines and the particular interests of departments while at the same time trying to establish a visible scientific profile of the university as a whole. This task is one of the most demanding challenges for university leadership these days.
6. They have to navigate between the claim of autonomy and the persisting financial dependency on the state, which is difficult to do especially in times of budget cuts.
7. Finally, they are supposed to make binding decisions in a loosely coupled system and to ensure that these decisions are put into practice. At the same time, they have to respect academic self-governance with its fragmented and often slow decision-making processes, and they must be aware of opposition to their decisions from different parties at different times.

Hence, university presidents have a highly contradictory job. Research into higher education has ascertained that university leadership is ambiguous (Cohen and March 1986), substantially paradoxical (Laske and Meister-Scheytt 2003) and can be described

---

2   Even if the notion of a partly integrative structure of academic leadership uses a similar term as accounts that theorize organizational governance under the label of 'integral leadership' from a holistic perspective (Deeg, Küpers and Weibler 2010), it is not related to these approaches. In this chapter, the attribute 'integrative' is only meant to denote the integration of collegial and managerial traits in the current role of German university presidents.

as a kind of contradiction or dilemma management (Pellert 1999, Schneidewind and Dettleff 2007). In my terms, the current structure of university management in Germany can be specified as integrative-paradoxical since it oscillates incessantly between extremes and has to find a way to face uncertain, contradictory and highly complex situations.

Taking this diagnosis as a starting point, we can now ask in which way Aristotle's concept of practical wisdom can help us to better understand the practice of German university presidents. To what extent does the notion of practical wisdom provide a new or at least modified perspective on university management?

University Presidents as Wise Leaders

What can be gained from applying the concept of *phrónêsis* to university leadership is a subtler sense of the oscillating nature of presidential decision-making and communicating, an attentiveness to its integral-paradoxical character, a deepened understanding of the fact that leading a university equals dealing with uncertain and contradictory situations in which there is an ongoing search for the right mean without a rule that unmistakeably shows where to find it.

Specifically, we can see that Aristotle's practical wisdom enables us to formulate a revised description of leadership practice that raises our awareness of its illogical, paradoxical and antithetic moments. What university presidents do is deliberate, negotiate, make decisions and communicate these decisions, and these activities can – at least partly – be described in terms of Aristotle's *phrónêsis*. The reason for this consists in structural analogies between the way university presidents are supposed to make decisions and to communicate and the way a practically wise person deliberates and acts. Some of these analogies will be outlined at the end of this chapter.

Aristotle claims that a practically wise person must be able to determine their course of action properly with regard to what is really good for their life. *Phrónêsis* means that the practical truth is grasped – which is not easy to do and requires experience, long deliberation, cleverness and a strong will. Correspondingly, university presidents must be able to determine measurements and activities so that aims can be achieved that are really good for the university as an organization. This task is also very difficult to fulfil since usually there are highly contradictory opinions about what is good for a university. Yet even if the criteria of what is good and what is bad for the organization are diverse and differ between stakeholder groups and individuals, the claim to act on behalf of the university's true aims is crucial to the president's role.

Happiness in the Aristotelian sense consists of exercising one's own characteristic activity perfectly and is taken as the highest good for human beings. In analogy to this, the highest good of a university can be defined as the fact that the university perfectly exercises its characteristic activities: research and teaching. In order to enable the university to live up to this 'idea of the university' (Jaspers 1946), presidents have to provide the appropriate conditions and resources from material resources to legitimacy. This means that the president's highest good would be the exercise of successfully providing the conditions under which a university can prosper and improve its own performance.

However, we have to keep in mind that the Aristotelian essentialism of the highest good cannot be transferred unmodified to a modern organizational context. Even if research and teaching are undeniably the core academic activities, universities – as shown – are characterized by a multiplicity of tasks and societal requests. There is no metaphysical, transhistorical idea of the university, but a field of various, ever-changing, often conflicting and struggling expectations and demands which institutions of higher education have to meet or to cope with.

According to Aristotle, practically wise people are able to deal with particular situations in the light of their universal aim (*eudaimonia* as the highest good). Accordingly, university presidents only arrive at good decisions if particular circumstances of the university and general developments, trends or rules are appropriately taken into account. University presidents must be able to specify general circumstances (for example, changing political, economic or judicial frameworks) properly to determine particular actions and specific measurements, and they must know how to interpret and evaluate particular situations in the light of general facts. In short, they must dispose of superior judgement, which is generally a major characteristic of authority (Sennett 1980) and is often based on 'ontological acuity' (McKenna and Rooney 2008) as the capacity to understand epistemic foundations of belief systems. It is this judgement that can be called a 'sense' or 'intuition' for existing opportunities and restrictions, that is, 'an "eye" … or a "nose" for what is salient in concrete situations' (Dunne 1993: 368).

In our interpretation of astuteness (*sunesis*), Aristotle explains that wise practical reasoning has to take into account the perspective and counsel of other people. This is a counterweight to his concentration on what is good for the individual actor. Accordingly, information about and support of others are crucial to the success of decisions of university presidents who spend a lot of their time gathering information and opinions through personal conversation, endless series of meetings and reading reports and official documents. In order to anticipate and overcome resistance, to rally support and to do successful networking, they are dependent on excellent knowledge of what other university members and external stakeholders think and favour. Hence, sensitivity to other opinions and openness to the advice of people who the presidents can trust and who are intimately acquainted with the needs, procedures and organizational logic of a contemporary university are definitely key success factors for university leadership.

As we have seen, according to Aristotle, practical wisdom does not consist only of clever deliberation and decisions, but encompasses the ability and determination to implement the decisions that have been made. University presidents certainly must be equipped with both abilities. Given a certain decision, they need to know how to communicate it, how to use available governance means that promote the implementation of the decision, how to distribute material and immaterial resources in order to motivate people, how to persuade or impress university members as well as important external players, how to set up new regulations that stabilize innovations and so on – and they must be able to put this knowledge into practice. However, unlike the practically wise person in Aristotelian ethics, university leaders do not have to command only their own actions in order to act virtuously, but are supposed to elicit, control or hinder actions of other organizational actors, since that is what leadership is all about.

Eventually, discretion or fair judgement (*gnomê*) is a necessary prerequisite for the success of presidential action, especially with regard to presidential communication and with respect to the deeply rooted do's and don'ts of the academic world. Therefore, a reason for failure can be an inappropriate kind of communication with university members or the inability to properly judge the capacity of the university to adapt to further innovations. So even if being tough and resolute, innovative and bold (where necessary) may be an important ingredient of the managerial side of the presidential role, the respect for the equitable in different contexts is another one.

These are some analogies between practical wisdom and the requirements of university leadership. However, even if it is interesting to consider university presidents as 'wise leaders' in the Aristotelian sense, this approach neither provides rules for successfully leading a university nor is it intended (or appropriate) to promote a heroic picture of leadership.[3] There are no rules that could exactly guide action as Aristotle clearly shows in his ethical reflections, nor is everybody who has the disposition to deliberate and act in accordance with situational circumstances and one's own true ends practically wise in the Aristotelian sense.

On the contrary, the Aristotelian approach to university leadership is instead suited to outlining how delicate and challenging the pursuit of individual happiness as well as the exercise of university leadership is – notwithstanding their undeniable differences. Both require a kind of practical wisdom that is far from being easily cultivated (Kemmis 2012).

Conclusion and Open Questions

With the last remark emphasizing the difficulties of developing and teaching practical wisdom, we have already proceeded to some concluding thoughts about possible consequences for further research that can be drawn from this chapter. There is a plethora of intriguing research paths that could be followed in the future – paths that are linked to different aspects of Aristotle's work, to different scientific disciplines and to different research questions within these disciplines. However, I will only very briefly hint at some open questions and challenges for prospective research on theoretical and practical aspects:

1. Aristotle has derived theoretical differentiations from his observation of the contemporary discourse on ethical phenomena. Thus, he is well aware that concepts like *phrónêsis* or *gnomê* are attributed (Aristotle 2009) to particular people on account of particular circumstances – which means that he, even if unknowingly, acknowledges the social constructivist nature of ethical predicates. This leads to the empirical question of which criteria are to be applied when a course of action or a person is called practically wise. For example, under which circumstances are people willing to call leaders wise – instead of using other attributes? The challenge here is especially the set-up of an adequate methodology for empirical research – be it quantitative or qualitative, observing or even experimental. In spite of the evident difficulties of wisdom research (Rooney, McKenna and Liesch 2010), we should try to find methodologies that are based on a full-fledged theoretical account of wisdom, that provide new insights into empirical phenomena related to practical wisdom and that refer to a broad body of knowledge about organizational issues. Developing, applying, testing and discussing such methodologies could help to further unravel, for example, the 'enigma' of wise leadership behaviour.

---

3   It does not promote a post-heroic account of leadership as these accounts get caught up in the paradox of promoting a heroic servant-leader (Western 2008).

2. A second desideratum involves the inter- and transdisciplinarity of research on *phrónêsis* and its related concepts. At present, psychology, organization theory, organization sociology, management and leadership studies and philosophy tend to primarily or exclusively pursue their own research agendas. However, there are many opportunities to address cross-disciplinary research questions – for example regarding the use of present-day vocabulary synonymous with 'practical wisdom' in different social and organizational contexts or the relation of wisdom to other personal capacities and social norms.

3. A third dimension that has only been touched upon in this chapter concerns the following question: what distinguishes practically wise leadership from acting practically wise in general? Moreover, what distinguishes practically wise leadership in business contexts from – say – academic leadership, from leadership in public administration (Rooney and McKenna 2008), in non-profit or high-risk organizations (Rooney, McKenna and Liesch 2010)? To put it in a more general way: do the features of practical wisdom and practically wise leadership depend on the social context in which they are situated – and, if yes, to which extent and in which ways? Comparative studies on these issues could further our understanding of a possible context-relatedness of wisdom and wise leadership.

4. The discussion of practical wisdom, respectively of wise leadership and of wise academic leadership, could benefit from placing the concept in the context of a corresponding social theory like neo-institutionalism (Lawrence, Suddaby and Leca 2009), structuration theory (Giddens 1984) or even systems theory (Luhmann 2006, Baecker 2003). There are likely to be advantages for both sides. If models of practically wise behaviour were permanently isolated from social theory, their impact would necessarily remain strictly limited. Vice versa, notably actor- and decision-oriented social theories could beneficially make use of an elaborated concept of practical wisdom in order to refine their account of human agency.

5. Finally, with regard to leadership practice, the question of teachability of practical wisdom will remain relevant to all institutions dealing with leadership training and qualifications. As far as university leadership is concerned, it will be interesting to see whether and how the prevailing reservations about formal education for (prospective) leaders today will be overcome or which alternative ways of conveying the necessary leadership knowledge at the top management level – for example, through one's own and others' practical experiences as Kemmis (2012) contends – will be developed in the future. Moreover, especially in times of a strong drift of higher education towards highly regulated occupational and professional education, universities should not only be seen to be led wisely, but should also systematically provide the necessary environments for exercising and reflecting practical wisdom across different scientific disciplines.

Answers to these questions will not only advance research with regard to the multifaceted meaningfulness of Aristotelian thought in contemporary social theorizing, but might at the same time extend our understanding of how universities and other educational organizations that are girded by increasingly turbulent and uncertain environments can be led wisely through *phrónêtic* deliberation and decisions.

References

Aristotle 2009. *Nicomachean Ethics*, translated and edited by R. Crisp. 2nd Edition. Cambridge: Cambridge University Press.

Baecker, D. 2003. *Organisation und Management*. Frankfurt am Main: Suhrkamp.

Bernstein, R.J. 1986. *Philosophical Profiles. Essays in a Pragmatic Mode*. Philadelphia: University of Pennsylvania Press.

Bolden, R., Petrov, G. and Gosling, J. 2008. Tensions in higher education leadership: towards a multi-level model of leadership practice. *Higher Education Quarterly*, 62(4), 358–76.

Bolton, R. 1991. Aristotle on the objectivity of ethics, in *Aristotle's Ethics*, edited by J.P. Anton and A. Preus. Albany: State University of New York Press, 8–28.

Cohen, M.D. and March, J.G. 1986. *Leadership and Ambiguity: the American College President*. 2nd Edition. Boston: Harvard Business School Press.

Cohen, M.D., March, J.G. and Olsen, J. 1972. A garbage can model of organizational choice. *Administrative Science Quarterly*, 17(1), 1–25.

Crisp, R. 2009. Introduction, in *Nicomachean Ethics*, edited by R. Crisp. 2nd Edition. Cambridge: Cambridge University Press, vii–xxxv.

Dahl, N.O. 1984. *Practical Reason, Aristotle, and Weakness of the Will*. Minneapolis: University of Minnesota Press.

Deeg, J., Küpers, W. and Weibler, J. 2010. *Integrale Steuerung von Organisationen*. München: Oldenbourg.

Drucker, P. 2001. *The Essential Drucker*. New York: HarperCollins Publishers.

Dunne, J. 1993. *Back to the Rough Ground. 'Phrónêsis' and 'Téchnê' in Modern Philosophy and in Aristotle*. Notre Dame: University of Notre Dame Press.

Ebers, M. and Gotsch, W. 2006. Institutionenökonomische Theorien der Organisation, in *Organisationstheorien*, 6, edited by A. Kieser and M. Ebers. Auflage. Stuttgart: Kohlhammer, 247–308.

Eikeland, O. 2008. *The Ways of Aristotle. Aristotelian Phrónêsis, Aristotelian Philosophy of Dialogue, and Action Research*. Bern: Peter Lang.

Enders, J. and Schimank, U. 2001. Faule Professoren und vergreiste Nachwuchswissenschaftler? Einschätzungen und Wirklichkeit, in *Die Krise der Universitäten. Leviathan Sonderheft 20*, edited by E. Stölting and U. Schimank. Wiesbaden: Westdeutscher Verlag, 159–78.

Fink, E. 1970. *Metaphysik der Erziehung im Weltverständnis von Plato und Aristoteles*. Frankfurt am Main: Vittorio Klostermann.

Flyvbjerg, B. 2001. *Making Social Science Matter: Why Social Inquiry Fails and How It Can Succeed Again*. Cambridge: Cambridge University Press.

Flyvbjerg, B., Landman, T. and Schram, S. (eds) 2012. *Real Social Science: Applied Phrónêsis*. Cambridge: Cambridge University Press.

Giddens, A. 1984. *The Constitution of Society: Outline of the Theory of Structuration*. Cambridge: Polity Press.

Grint, K. 2007. Learning to lead: can Aristotle help us find the road to wisdom? *Leadership*, 3(2), 231–46.

Guggenheim, M. 2007. Beobachtungen zwischen Funktionssystemen. Umweltdienstleistungsfirmen als intersystemische Organisationen. *Soziale Welt*, 58(4), 419–38.

Hinman, L.M. 2012. *Ethics: A Pluralistic Approach to Moral Theory*. 5th Edition. Belmont: Wadsworth.

Hursthouse, R. 1999. A false doctrine of the mean, in *Aristotle's Ethics. Critical Essays*, edited by N. Sherman. Lanham: Rowman & Littlefield, 105–19.

Hutchinson, D.S. 1995. Ethics, in *The Cambridge Companion to Aristotle*, edited by J. Barnes. Cambridge: Cambridge University Press, 195–232.

Hüther, O. 2009. Hochschulräte als Steuerungsakteure? *Beiträge zur Hochschulforschung*, 31(2), 50–73.

Hüther, O. 2010. *Von der Kollegialität zur Hierarchie? Eine Analyse des New Managerialism in den Landeshochschulgesetzen*. Wiesbaden: VS Verlag für Sozialwissenschaften.

Jaspers, K. 1946. *Die Idee der Universität*. Berlin: Springer.

Kant, I. 1974. *Kritik der Urteilskraft*. Frankfurt am Main: Suhrkamp.

Kemmis, S. 2012. Phron sis, experience and the primacy of praxis, in *Phron sis as Professional Knowledge: Practical Wisdom in the Professions*, edited by A. Pitman and E.A. Kinsella. Rotterdam: Sense Publishing, 147–62.

Koschorke, A. 2004. Wissenschaftsbetrieb als Wissenschaftsvernichtung. Einführung in die Paradoxologie des deutschen Hochschulwesens, in *Universität ohne Zukunft?* edited by D. Kimmich and A. Thumfart. Frankfurt am Main: Suhrkamp, 142–57.

Krücken, G. 2009. Kommunikation im Wissenschaftssystem – was wissen wir, was können wir tun? *Hochschulmanagement*, 4(2), 50–6.

Krüger, T. and Rudinger, G. 2010. Rektor und Wissenschaftsminister des Jahres 2010. *Forschung & Lehre*, (3), 178–81.

Kühl, S. 2011. *Organisationen. Eine sehr kurze Einführung*. Wiesbaden: VS Verlag für Sozialwissenschaften.

Küpers, W. 2007. Perspectives on integrating leadership and followership. *International Journal of Leadership Studies*, 2(3), 194–221.

Küpers, W. and Statler, M. 2008. Practically wise leadership: toward an integral understanding. *Culture and Organization*, 14(4), 379–400.

Küpers, W. and Weibler, J. 2008. Inter-leadership: why and how should we think of leadership and followership integrally? *Leadership*, 4(4), 443–75.

Laske, S. and Meister-Scheytt, C. 2003. Wer glaubt, dass Universitätsmanager Universitäten managen, glaubt auch, dass Zitronenfalter Zitronen falten… in *Universitätsentwicklung – Strategien. Erfahrungen. Reflexionen*, edited by J. Lüthje and S. Nickel. Frankfurt am Main: Peter Lang Verlag, 163–87.

Laske, S., Meister-Scheytt, C. and Küpers, W. 2006. *Organisation und Führung*. Studienreihe Bildungs- und Wissenschaftsmanagement Series, edited by A. Hanft. Volume 3. Münster: Waxmann.

Lawrence, T.B., Suddaby, R. and Leca, B. (eds) 2009. *Institutional Work. Actors and Agency in Institutional Studies of Organizations*. New York: Cambridge University Press.

Lear, G.R. 2004. *Happy Lives and the Highest Good: An Essay on Aristotle's Nicomachean Ethics*. Princeton: Princeton University Press.

Lindblom, C.E. 1959. The science of muddling-through. *Public Administration Review*, 19, 79–88.

Long, C.P. 2004. *The Ethics of Ontology. Rethinking an Aristotelian Legacy*. Albany: State University of New York Press.

Luhmann, N. 1964. *Funktionen und Folgen formaler Organisation*. Berlin: Duncker und Humblot.

Luhmann, N. 1992. *Die Wissenschaft der Gesellschaft*. Frankfurt am Main: Suhrkamp.

Luhmann, N. 2006. *Organisation und Entscheidung*. 2nd Edition. Wiesbaden: Verlag für Sozialwissenschaften.

McKenna, B. and Rooney, D. 2008. Wise leadership and the capacity for ontological acuity. *Management Communication Quarterly*, 21(4), 537–46.

Musselin, C. 2007. Are universities specific organisations?, in *Towards a Multiversity? Universities between Global Trends and National Traditions*, edited by G. Krücken, A. Kosmützky and M. Torka. Bielefeld: Transcript Verlag, 63–86.

Nickel, S. 2007. *Partizipatives Management von Universitäten. Zielvereinbarungen – Leitungsstrukturen – Staatliche Steuerung*. München: Rainer Hampp Verlag.

Northouse, P.G. 2010. *Leadership. Theory and Practice*. 5th Edition. Los Angeles: Sage.

Ortmann, G. 2004. Schmuddelkinder der Logik. Paradoxien des Organisierens. *Berliner Debatte Initial*, 15(1), 18–27.

Orton, J.D. and Weick, K.E. 1990. Loosely coupled systems: a reconceptualization. *Academy of Management Review*, 15(2), 203–23.

Pakaluk, M. 2005. *Aristotle's Nicomachean Ethics: An Introduction*. New York: Camridge University Press.

Pellert, A. 1999. *Die Universität als Organisation. Die Kunst, Experten zu managen*. Wien: Böhlau.

Plato 1991. *The Republic: the Complete and Unabridged Jowett Translation*. New York: Vintage Books.

Popper, K.R. 1945. *The Open Society and its Enemies*. London: Routledge.

Powers, M. 1999. *The Audit Society. Rituals of Verification*. Oxford: Oxford University Press.

Reeve, C.D.C. 1992. *Practices of Reason – Aristotle's Nicomachean Ethics*. Oxford: Clarendon Press.

Reeve, C.D.C. 2006. Aristotle on the virtues of thought, in *Aristotle's Nicomachean Ethics*, edited by R. Kraut. Oxford: Blackwell, 198–217.

Rooney, D. and McKenna, B. 2008. Wisdom in public administration: looking for a sociology of wise practice. *Public Administration Review*, 68(4), 709–21.

Rooney, D., McKenna, B. and Liesch, P. 2010. *Wisdom and Management in the Knowledge Economy*. New York: Routledge.

Scharpf, F.W. 1997. *Games Real Actors Play. Actor-Centered Institutionalism in Policy Research*. Boulder: Westview Press.

Schimank, U. 2001. Festgefahrene Gemischtwarenläden – Die deutschen Hochschulen als erfolgreich scheiternde Organisationen, in *Die Krise der Universitäten. Leviathan Sonderheft 20*, edited by E. Stölting and U. Schimank. Wiesbaden: Westdeutscher Verlag, 223–42.

Schimank, U. 2005. Die akademische Profession und die Universitäten: 'New Public Management' und eine drohende Entprofessionalisierung, in *Organisation und Profession*, edited by T. Klatetzki and V. Tacke. Wiesbaden: VS Verlag für Sozialwissenschaften), 143–64.

Schimank, U. 2008. Double Talk von Hochschulleitungen, in *Universität und Lebenswelt – Festschrift für Heinz Abels*, edited by W. Jäger and R. Schützeichel. Wiesbaden: Verlag für Sozialwissenschaften, 154–72.

Schimank, U. 2010. *Handeln und Strukturen. Einführung in die akteurtheoretische Soziologie. 4., völlig überarbeitete Auflage*. Weinheim: Juventa.

Schmidt, M. 2011. Die besten Alphatiere an den Unis. *Financial Times Deutschland*, 21 October. [Online]. Available at: http://www.ftd.de/karriere-management/management/:hochschulmanager-des-jahres-2011-die-besten-alphatiere-an-den-unis/60118827.html [accessed: 5 September 2012].

Schneidewind, U. and Dettleff, H. 2007. Hochschulsteuerung als Dilemmata-Management – Ist reflexives Hochschulmanagement ein Garant für bessere Führung? *Hochschulmanagement*, 2(3), 63–7.

Sennett, R. 1980. *Authority*. New York: Knopf.

Statler, M. 2005. Practical wisdom and serious play: reflections on management understanding, in *Sophisticated Survival Techniques: Strategies in Art and Economy*, edited by M. Brellochs and H. Schrat. Berlin: Kulturverlag Kadmos, 399–412.

Statler, M. and Roos, J. 2007. *Everyday Strategic Preparedness: The Role of Practical Wisdom in Organizations*. Basingstoke: Palgrave MacMillan.

Statler, M., Roos, J. and Victor, B. 2006. Illustrating the need for practical wisdom. *International Journal of Management Concepts and Philosophy*, 2(1), 1–30.

Tsoukas, H. and Cummings, S. 1997. Marginalization and recovery: the emergence of Aristotelian themes in organization studies. *Organization Studies*, 18(4), 655–83.

Walgenbach, P. and Tempel, A. 2002. Management als soziale Praxis – konzeptionelle und methodische Ansatzpunkte für die interkulturell vergleichende Managementforschung, in *Managementsoziologie*, edited by R. Schmidt, H.-J. Gergs and M. Pohlmann. München: Hampp, 168–83.

Weibler, J. 2007. Führung von Universitäten? Anmerkungen zu einem verordneten Wandel. *Forschung & Lehre*, 14(1), 13–15.

Weick, K.E. 1976. Educational organizations as loosely coupled systems. *Administrative Science Quarterly*, 21(1 March), 1–19.

Weik, E. 2011. The emergence of the university: a case study of the founding of the University of Paris from a neo-institutionalist perspective. *Management & Organizational History*, 6(3), 287–310.

Western, S. 2008. *Leadership: A Critical Text*. London: Sage.

Williams, B. 1985. *Ethics and the Limits of Philosophy*. Cambridge, MA: Harvard University Press.

Wunderer, R. 2007. *Führung und Zusammenarbeit. Eine unternehmerische Führungslehre, 7., überarbeitete Auflage*. Köln: Luchterhand.

Yukl, G. 2010. *Leadership in Organizations*. 7th Edition. Upper Saddle River: Pearson.

10 *Wisdom and Integrity: Metatheoretical Perspectives on Integrative Change in an Age of Turbulence*

MARK G. EDWARDS

Introduction

In times of turbulence, is the wisest course of action to boldly step out, introduce large-scale change and risk everything or is it to do nothing or, at least, very little and safeguard those recently hard-won gains? If there is much to lose and if the welfare of many others is at stake, might not the wiser option be to remain conservative, just do a modest bit of innovation and to let others take the first big step? On the other hand, being conservative might also have unintended negative consequences. In basing their estimations of future levels of economic growth on criteria that emphasize stability, regularity and predictability, organizations might be locking themselves and their stakeholders into calamitous and widespread failure. Organizations, managers and leaders today face the paradox of needing to respond to the imperative for radical transformation while also safeguarding the current welfare and the financial, psychological and professional investments of their members and key stakeholders. When do we make the call to accept the challenge of transformation and risk much and when do we decide to withdraw into our shells, reflect on what we have and conserve what we can?

The quality of wisdom is deeply concerned with this kind of discernment. This chapter will discuss, from a metatheoretical perspective, the relationship between wisdom and organizational change in times of economic and social turbulence. To explore these issues a typology will be presented which describes different kinds of wisdom and their relationships to types of environmental change. Wisdom is a complex notion that incorporates many different capacities and advanced skills. Holding these qualities within an overarching and balanced integrity is vital for enabling wise decisions and actions to be exhibited in different ways across different contexts. To adequately investigate these integrated qualities, our conceptualizations and theories of wisdom need to have the requisite level of sophistication. Hence, we take a metatheoretical approach to building an understanding of wisdom as it applies in times of rapid change. This chapter is structured as follows: after discussing some definitional issues around the core topics of wisdom, metatheory and integration, a detailed overview of wisdom and transformative change is presented. Following this, a metatheoretical framework is developed which describes a typology of various kinds of wisdom and their relationships to different levels of turbulence in organizational environments. This leads to a section that discusses what happens to wisdom and high-level capacities when integration is not present. While the scientific literature on wisdom has often emphasized the importance of integration, there has been little discussion of what happens to very advanced capacities of leaders in organizations when integrative aspects are missing. It is proposed here that, when otherwise high-performance organizations and their leaders lack integrity and integrative capacities, seriously negative impacts on societies and environments ensue, and this is particularly so in times of turbulence and rapid change. Next, the metatheoretical model is applied to the challenging topic of climate change and the responses that organizations make in the face of the transformational imperatives that flow from this kind of global crisis. The chapter concludes with a brief discussion of some of the implications of the metatheoretical framework for studies of organizational wisdom.

Metatheoretical Research

The distinguishing feature of metatheoretical research is that it takes other theories as its 'data'. Consequently, wherever there are diverse and contested theories for a certain topic of study, metatheorizing can be a valuable research tool. Just as conventional theories are built and tested from the analysis of empirical data and phenomenal events, metatheories are built and tested from the analysis of theoretical models and conceptual data. As such one of the uses of metatheories is to map the extant range of theories and, in so doing, to identify gaps and possibilities for new directions. Abrams and Hogg (2004: 98) say that:

> A metatheory is like a good travel guide – it tells you where to go and where not to go, what is worthwhile and what is not, the best way to get to a destination, and where it is best to rest a while. Metatheoretical conviction provides structure and direction, it informs the sorts of questions one asks and does not ask, and it furnishes a passion that makes the quest exciting and buffers one from disappointments along the way.

One way in which metatheorizing provides this 'structure and direction' is through its integrative capacity. By adopting a 'metaperspective' (Gioia and Pitre 1990) on the range of theories within a particular domain, a researcher can develop an overarching framework that integrates the different primary models into a more encompassing overview or secondary model. Anchin (2008: 804) describes this integrative function as follows: 'Among vital purposes served by metatheory is its function as scaffolding for integrating more specific theories that conceptually and empirically map different aspects of the phenomena under study'.

Metatheoretical analysis examines theories to 'determine the *link* between the theoretical perspective that frames each primary study and the methods, findings, and conclusions of the research' (Bondas and Hall 2007: 115, emphasis added). This linking and integrative function is only one of the aims of metatheoretical research. Identifying metatheorizing as a specific form of research helps enable researchers to treat 'the multiplicity of theorizations as an opportunity for multiple operations of analysis and synthesis' (Weinstein and Weinstein 1991: 140). This activity of analysis and synthesis allows for several aims (Colomy 1991, Ritzer 2007) including: 1) the review of existing theories (MR), 2) the preparation of new middle-range theory (MP), 3) the building and testing of new overarching metatheory (MO) and 4) the assessment of other theories and metatheories (MA).

In the following pages MR research will be undertaken in order to build an MO, more specifically, a review of models of organizational change during times of turbulence will be performed to build an overarching model of organizational wisdom. The resulting model will be applied to the topic of climate change to explain the variety of responses that organizations can make to this critical feature of the contemporary organizational environment.

The Meanings of Wisdom

Wisdom is a 'polysemantic concept' (Rowley and Slack 2009: 110) that evokes many different images and meanings and definitive qualities.[1] Wisdom can mean to be street-wise, to be clever at surviving in the often harsh conditions of urban life or it can refer to the profound states of insight and spiritual knowledge that great sages possess and exhibit. Wisdom can refer to a collective quality that is seen in, for example, the 'wisdom of crowds' (Surowiecki 2004) and the ability of groups to produce deeply practical and healthy solutions to complex problems as much as to the knowledge and capacities of individuals. It is also used to describe the characteristics of extraordinary individuals who possess highly developed skills, insights and capacities to make prudent judgements. English dictionary definitions often privilege the notion of judgement in relation to behaviour and decisions when defining wisdom. In contrast however, the notion of wisdom in the East is more associated with subjective states of insight and of existential being rather than with decision-making and doing. The contexts in which we set the notion of wisdom can range from the quiet cloisters of monastic settings to the hurly burly of political and organizational life. Wisdom can be seen in the actions and words of local community representatives and in the decisions and speeches of world leaders. Wisdom can be associated with powerful capacities for reasoning as well as non-rational visionary abilities. So where do we draw the definitional boundaries around such a global and many-sided term?

Scholars have taken several different tacks in trying to capture the core meaning of wisdom. Applying a metatheoretical perspective, McKenna and Rooney (McKenna, Rooney and Boal 2009, Rooney and McKenna 2007) distilled wisdom into five core principles. They found that wisdom is: 1) based on reason and careful observation, 2) includes non-rational and subjective elements when making decisions, 3) directed towards humane and virtuous outcomes, 4) concerned with the practical and the everyday, including work and 5) articulate, aesthetic and intrinsically rewarding and incorporates emotion. There are many researchers who have offered other such lists of characteristics. From their extensive research on wisdom, Baltes and Staudinger (2000) concluded that there are five criteria for assessing wise behaviour: 1) the possession of rich factual knowledge and 2) rich procedural knowledge, 3) the ability to contextualize events within the overarching

---

1   Hence, metatheoretical approaches can be very usefully applied to the topic (see, for example, Baltes and Staudinger 2000 and McKenna, Rooney and Boal 2009).

frame of lifespan development, 4) an appreciation for the relativism of values and life priorities and 5) the recognition and management of uncertainty. A more recent study sees wisdom as the confluence of a number of quite diverse capacities: knowledge, the translation of that knowledge into action, the capacity to experience forms of optimal enjoyment and, finally, the capacity for feelings of deep contentment and happiness (Rowley and Slack 2009). These capacities can be applied across very wide-ranging situations and include being able to persuade and lead others, see the big picture, the context, the long-term implications, being flexible as circumstances change, able to see things from many perspectives, able to cope with uncertainty and being prepared for multiple contingencies.

The variety of proposed sets of definitive characteristics of wisdom points to another aspect of research on this complex notion. For wisdom to be present and for wise decisions to be made, it is not sufficient to possess or display one, two or even several of these qualities, nor is it enough that individuals and organizations occasionally tap into one or other of these diverse skills. Authentic wisdom requires that most if not all of these qualities be present and that there be an integration of these abilities; a capacity for and display of integrity that brings coherence and wholeness to what might otherwise be simply an assemblage of expert skills and high-performance abilities.

Wisdom and Integration

Given that several studies have identified wisdom as consisting of these diverse sets of characteristics, it is not surprising that some researchers have also proposed that a key aspect of wisdom is the ability to integrate a range of capacities into a coherent and immediate response to a problem or situation (Rowley and Slack 2009). Baltes and Staudinger (2000: 132) suggest that this integrative aspect of wisdom is an overarching metaheuristic: 'that organizes, at a high level of aggregation, the pool (ensemble) of bodies of knowledge and commensurate, more specific heuristics that are available to individuals in planning, managing and evaluating issues surrounding the fundamental pragmatics of life'.

Birren and Fisher (1990: 324) describe wisdom itself as 'an integrative aspect of human life' where wisdom integrates such capacities as subjective experience, cognitive abilities and affect at both the individual and the societal level. Similarly, in her critique of wisdom as expert knowledge, Ardelt (2004: 257) sums up her view of wisdom as 'an integration of cognitive, reflective, and affective personality characteristics'. In perhaps the most thorough-going attempt to develop an integrative understanding of wisdom, Küpers and Statler (2008: 380) propose an 'integral understanding' that aims to develop 'an integral model of wisdom that accommodates multiple dimensions and multiple levels of human experience, and thereby serves as a metatheoretical framework for contemporary theories of practical wisdom'.

The authors see wisdom as 'covering various levels and spheres of wisdom in organizations' including the intrapersonal, interpersonal, organizational and social (Küpers and Statler 2008: 380). Drawing on the metatheories of Wilber (1999, 2000), Baltes and Staudinger (2000) and Edwards (2005), Küpers and Statler (2008: 384) conclude that:

... the interior and exterior dimension as well as individual and collective spheres of wisdom and its specific interconnected processes of intentional, behavioural, cultural and social domains are considered. With this, the inner spheres of wisdom and the external, behavioural aspects as well the collective embedment within an organizational community and culture and the external structural–functional realms of wisdom can be assessed together.

Küpers and Statler highlight the multiple dimensions of wisdom and that they are 'interconnected' and are to be 'assessed together'. That interconnectedness and integration may itself be the most definitive feature of wisdom, a fundamental 'metaheuristic', as Baltes and Staudinger call it, that coordinates and balances whatever other qualities and characteristics may constitute wisdom.

So what happens to wisdom when the integrative capacity is weak or largely absent? What does wisdom become when expert knowledge, personal charisma, forthright leadership and the ability to deal with uncertainty are no longer balanced by an integrative metaheuristic? How do organizations, which are constituted by knowledgeable, highly skilled and educated and, potentially at least, wise individuals respond to turbulent environments when their resources for taking action, developing strategies, making crucial judgements and balancing the needs of their stakeholders are not integrated by an overarching scaffold? In short, what does wisdom look like when it is not held together by an integrative ethic?

The integrative dimension of wisdom facilitates the construction of a meaningful whole out of disparate, ambiguous and often contradictory sources of information and knowledge. One of the most important of these sources is the situational context in which decisions are made and actions taken. But when the situational context is one of mixed signals and extreme instability, what then? For organizations immersed in turbulent economic, social, political and environmental change it becomes even more important to be clear about the organizational core purpose and mission when setting strategic directions in such conditions. I will explore these questions later, but before that, I will look more closely at the relationship between wisdom and turbulent organizational environments.

Wisdom and Transformation in the Age of Turbulence

The immensely complex challenges that global environments throw up for organizations today surely demand the wisdom of Solomon if they are to be addressed with some semblance of adequacy. Given this complexity and the role of psychological and socio-cultural factors in how we respond to these challenges, it is not likely that a purely scientific or technological approach will be sufficient for dealing with the economic, environmental and social crises that beset us. A large dose of practical wisdom on a global scale, involving leaders and organizations of all kinds, will be needed if human communities and their natural surrounds are to emerge from the present problems with vitality and a capacity for long-term sustainability.

Environmental turbulence refers to the amount of change and complexity in an organization's environment. That environment consists not only of other businesses and commercial players but the whole range of physical, ecological, technological, economic, social and cultural dynamics that constitute the planetary system. Environmental turbulence increases with an increase in the number of these factors to be considered and the greater the level of change that exists within each of them. Environmental volatility and instability have been increasing for the past 100 years. In times of great social and global turbulence the level of change required to adaptively meet the challenges posed by hyper-change or 'raplexity', as Harrison Owen calls it, becomes a question of qualitative transformation rather than translation or incremental adaptation. Here is what Owen (1987: 3) says about the world of raplexity and his comments, now more than two decades old, are as relevant today as ever:

> *The world of raplexity is a different world indeed. We can't continue with business as usual. Indeed, our business and the organisations which do that business are being transformed whether we like it or not. Like the dinosaurs, we are discovering that when the environment radically alters, such that the old way of being is no longer appropriate, the choice is fairly clear. Evolve, or go extinct. The dinosaurs apparently didn't get the picture, and some of our organizations appear to suffer from a similar lack of perception. But for the rest, we may hope that the search for a better way to be, now initiated, will be carried to some reasonable and successful conclusion. There are, of course, no guarantees. The odds, however, may be improved to the extent that we possess some accurate understanding of what is transpiring, coupled with the ability to facilitate the process.*

Owen speaks here of the process of transformational and discontinuous change that is required if organizations are to respond adaptively to the world of raplexity. Transformational change can be contrasted with translational change which is concerned with maintaining the status quo and the stability that is required for any organization to retain its current mode of operating, cultural and functional identity and so on. Bringing together these two ways of conceptualizing change creates a powerful metatheoretical lens (Edwards 2010b) that can be used to unlock new insights into how organizations respond to challenging environments.

Transformation refers to radical change that includes the whole system of the organization and its organizing capacities across its people and their behaviours and its cultural identity and operational systems. This whole-of-system shift is a radically developmental one that requires the qualitative rearrangement of the core archetype of the organization. Change of this nature is discontinuous in that one stage is qualitatively different from, but inclusive of, preceding stages. Many theorists have offered stage-based developmental models that capture this kind of transformational insight (Bleicher 1994, Golembiewski 1989, Lester, Parnell and Carraher 2003, Torbert 2004). Although various models have been presented that articulate this kind of radical reordering of organizational capacities and identities, they all describe a movement that starts from a relatively simple, short-term and reactive mode of organizing to a more conventional and conformist mode and, finally, to a more integrative and complex mode of organizing.

Other terms that are commonly used synonymously with transformation are radical, discontinuous, deep, revolutionary, qualitative, gamma, second-order change and paradigmatic change (Fletcher 1990). While there are nuances between these varying terms, the common element is the idea of a qualitative shift, leap or dramatic emergence into a new stage of organizing. These terms and their antonyms are frequently used to describe the contrast between transformation and other, non-transformative, types of change such as incremental or translational change. Where transformation is about radical shifts, translation is about the ongoing transactions that maintain an organization's stable functioning and coherent identity. This distinction has been applied to organization theory by Ford and Backoff (1988). They describe transformation as occurring between 'vertical dimensions' of organizing while '[m]ovements within hierarchical levels are horizontal movements and are termed *translations*' (1988: 105). Figure 10.1 shows this distinction between transformation and translation. The figure gives a stylized representation of these movements and uses Dexter Dunphy's (2003) Corporate Sustainability model as an example. Transformation is never a simple, progressive movement from one level to another, but always involves complex transitional tracks that are idiosyncratic to each organization (Greenwood and Hinings 1988). This does not mean that qualitative and discontinuous stages of transformation are not possible, only that the transitional process and the means for displaying those stages are unique to each organization.

Ford and Backoff see translational or 'horizontal' change as alterations that occur within the structures and systems that pertain to a particular stage of organizing. Translational growth is focused on the integration, stabilization and balancing processes and structures within one level of organizational identity and operation. 'Translations, therefore, are concerned with morphostasis' (Ford and Backoff 1988: 106). It is important to recognize that, because translational change is ongoing and supports the stability and coherence of organizational forms, it plays an important role in the transformational

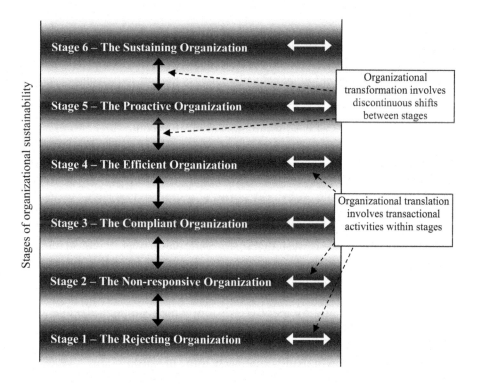

Figure 10.1 Transformational and translational change using Dunphy's Corporate Sustainability model as an example

process. Consequently, any integrative approach to transformation will need to accommodate some account of translational change. To put it mildly, balancing the multidirectional demands of transformational and translational change in turbulent environments is a difficult business and requires knowledge and wisdom management skills and capacities. In the following section this transformation–translation lens will be used to develop a typology of kinds of wisdom that come to the fore when dramatic change is in the air.

A Wisdom Typology for Turbulent Times

If organizations are to respond with any level of wisdom to the contemporary global conditions, they will need to develop not only an astute process of knowledge management but also of wisdom management. Thierauf and Hoctor (2006) refer to the knowledge management and wisdom management (KM/WM) nexus as a form of organizational intelligence that can respond to problems and also generate new potentials. They point out that (2006: x–xi):

> [W]isdom is the umbrella that brings together not only knowledge in the form of business intelligence and optimization, but also provides the means to assist decision-makers in reaching optimal and wise decisions over time. From this view, a new type of systems, that is, optimal KM/WM systems, can be defined. Such systems are forward-looking by utilizing creativity and problem finding to the highest degree possible. They utilize the latest new business models that are integrated with e-commerce and the Internet. Overall, optimal KM/WM systems draw upon the basic concepts found in knowledge management, business intelligence, and optimization. As noted earlier, these new of type systems provide a company's decision-makers with the ability to connect 'points of wisdom' so that optimal decisions regarding forthcoming opportunities and upcoming problems can be reached today and into the future.

What might be the varieties of wisdom management that could direct an organization's response to complex conditions of rapid change? We can consider organizational responses to hyper-turbulence to be associated with: 1) the level of environmental imperatives for change, and 2) the capacity to respond either with transformational or translational adaptations. This model results in five categories of responses (see Figure 10.2).

The model suggests that organizations can offer wise responses to environmental conditions in both turbulent and relatively stable conditions through: 1) transformative wisdom which supports whole-of-system transformational change for radical transitioning, 2) transitive wisdom which supports translational change for stable transitioning, 3) innovative wisdom which supports localized transformative innovation in times of stability, 4) conformative wisdom which supports translational change that conforms to environmental conditions and 5) adaptive wisdom which supports flexible adaptation to the range of environmental conditions. Each of these five response types can be associated with rationales for pursuing particular strategies for dealing with turbulent environments. In the following I describe each form of wisdom and give examples of these strategies.

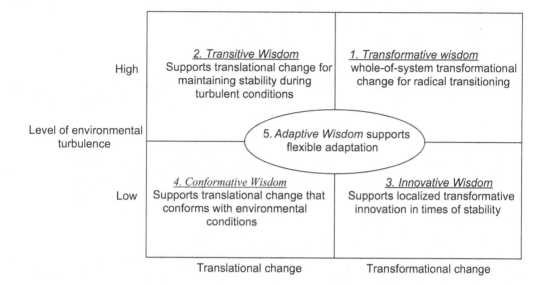

Figure 10.2 A wisdom typology for turbulent organizational environments

1. *Transformative Wisdom* is concerned with innovative, radical change and the factors that trigger and generate that change. The current global state of turbulence in world markets, collapsing natural environments, dramatically changing social and political conditions mean that transformational wisdom is a much needed quality for meeting contemporary organizational challenges. For example, transformational wisdom in organizational responses to the environmental crisis calls for a dramatic reordering of priorities from traditional cycles of consumption and production to radically new visions of how we view natural resources (Hargroves and Smith 2005). In response to the question 'Is that wise?', the transforming organization says that radical change in environmental conditions demands radical organizational change. Completely new qualities are required to meet the environmental imperatives. Wisdom from this perspective consists not only of marshalling existing organizational capacities but also of finding emergent innovations that can develop the requisite capacities for responding to and strategically adapting to turbulent environments. Transformative wisdom, both in terms of individual leadership skills and collective capacities, requires a profound understanding of developmental capacities such as core values and ethical virtues, intelligence and analytical skills and a familiarity with leading-edge practices. An organization that possesses transformative wisdom does not only rely on a senior executive group or a CEO to lead it through the process of radical change (Avolio 2007). Transformative wisdom requires top-down, bottom-up and reciprocating capacities in such areas as organizational governance, leadership and decision-making to be embedded across organizational structures and management processes (Edwards 2010a, Küpers 2007).
2. *Transitive Wisdom* supports a strategy of stability that also recognizes the need for change. It comes out of an awareness that change is needed but that the best way of meeting this challenge is to incrementally improve upon the organization's current mode of operations. From this perspective the strategy of dealing with turbulent

environments is one of translation rather than transformation. This more conservative path is seen as the wisest course of action because, even though there is awareness of radically changing environmental forces, there is recognition of the need for stability, for maintaining a solid identity and for integrating the capacities that are currently possessed by the organization even as new organizing capacities are developed.

3. *Innovative Wisdom* supports localized transformative innovation in times of stability and low turbulence. This is the sort of wisdom that prepares for dramatic change by nurturing and providing space for creative work, the outcomes and products of which can be crucial when challenging external conditions, are actually encountered. In contemporary times, when there is almost a permanent state of transformational imperative in organizations, this kind of innovative wisdom should be a prominent feature of organizational planning and long-range environmental scanning. Innovative wisdom at this level often takes the form of small teams of research and development personnel who are permitted time and space to develop imaginative solutions to old problems, new technologies, new products and services and creative potentials for building on organizational resources and strengths. Innovative wisdom is not just about technological innovation or product transformation but incorporates a far broader range of activities including organizational purposes and culture, core goals, workplace relations and relationships with extended communities of stakeholders.

4. Where transformative wisdom is all about the dramatic rearrangement of an organization's core identity and functional form, *Conformative Wisdom* focuses on alignments with environmental contingencies to ensure that there are strong connections between organizational activities and those of the extended family of stakeholders. The *trans-form-ative* is about the radical change of organizational form whereas the *con-form-ative* is about the astute alignment of organizational forms with environmental contingencies. Conformative wisdom is not simply about conforming to conventional values or systems of behaviour. There are powerful commercial reasons for aligning organizational economic policies and goals with those of the market. Conformative wisdom is more than this. Conformative wisdom takes into account and conforms to prevailing economic goals but also displays integrity across different social, environmental and cultural boundaries. Conformative wisdom would tell us, for example, that, where a very significant proportion of customers hold the view that food and beverage companies should ensure their products are labelled with adequate dietary information, organizational activities should conform to those customer expectations. Traditional qualities such as integrity in maintaining existing values, the maintenance of important stakeholder relationships and honouring established agreements are all aspects of conformative wisdom.

5. *Adaptive Wisdom* Organizational environments can, of course, be a mixture of many different factors and categories of turbulence. The patchwork nature of these environments can mean that many different kinds of organizational responses are called for. Consequently, while there may be relatively pure forms of wisdom management capacities required for particular situations, overall a more adaptive and flexible form of wisdom is often needed. For example, skills in managing translational change are always in demand because an organization must always retain its identity and core purpose irrespective of the level of radical change it needs to undertake. So, transformational wisdom will always need to balance the demands of translational wisdom in navigating a course through the difficult territories of

radical organizational change. Similarly, a conformative wisdom that conserves and nurtures existing relationships will be needed to complement and support innovative aspects of wisdom that seek out new possibilities. Adaptive wisdom draws on each of these forms of wisdom as required. Once again we see that the integration and timely balancing of wisdom capacities is a meta-level characteristic of wise judgement and behaviour. Adaptive wisdom draws on the qualities of flexibility, timeliness, sophisticated environmental scanning, tolerance for uncertainty and a kind of receptive insight that does not pre-empt judgement even where there might be considerable pressure to do so.

And Where Integration is Lacking?

The preceding discussion describes a typology of wisdom management capacities. However, it is during times when transformational demands are at their greatest and environmental turbulence at its peak that wisdom can be in shortest supply. During times of low turbulence, when current strategies work reasonably well and the imperative for change is low, conventional modes of organizing and managing dominate. As conditions become more unpredictable and the need for wisdom capacities rises, it becomes more crucial but also more difficult for the wisdom resources within an organization to be usefully deployed.

Figure 10.3 maps out the hypothetical relationship between the level of environmental turbulence and organizational capacities for developing and utilizing wisdom management competencies. At low levels of turbulence, for some organizations, the need for change management capacities of any kind is not acknowledged ('There are no problems') and so there are no provisions made for considering those anomalies that signal potential change. In contrast to the notion of organizational wisdom, we might characterize the predominant ethic of these organizations as being one of deliberate complacency towards potential challenges that lie on the horizon. Organizations with a more established culture of wisdom management resources will move towards experimentation and

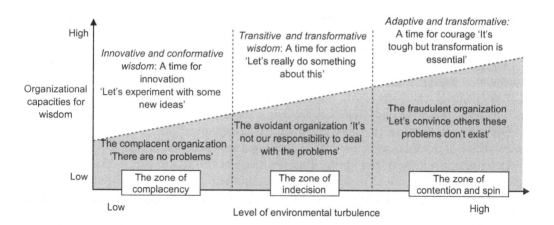

Figure 10.3 Organizational responses to turbulence as a function of wisdom capacities

nurturing innovative new ideas (*innovative wisdom*) while also retaining a strong focus on environmental scanning and the conventional contingencies that shape strategic plans and goals (*conformative wisdom*). The trap with highly stable environments is that organizations grow complacent and do not pursue innovation or develop corresponding knowledge or wisdom management capacities.

As turbulence grows, the tendency is for more organizations to be drawn into avoiding the growing challenges that accrue ('It's not our responsibility to deal with the problems') and to shrink from concrete measures that deal with the crisis. While many organizations are aware of the crises that emerge from turbulence, few of them take decisive action ('Let's really do something about this') or call on their capacities for *transitive or transformative wisdom*. In contrast, a growing number of organizations respond to uncertain environmental conditions by simply avoiding the imperative to change. Many examples of this kind of avoidance can be cited. For example, oil companies are currently not addressing the need for an industry-wide response to the challenges thrown up by BP's Deepwater Horizon disaster in the Gulf of Mexico (Houck 2010). The plastics manufacturing industry is avoiding such issues as plastic pollution in the oceanic gyres (Moore and Phillips 2011). Governments appear incapable of agreeing to a global response to climate change (Neuhoff 2010). Facing up to market turbulence, many organizations are unsure how to deal with these complex and pressing issues and get caught in a zone of avoidance, indecision and hesitancy and they often abrogate their responsibility to act and wait for others to do so.

As levels of turbulence reach a critical point, some organizations will call on their *adaptive and transformative wisdom* capabilities ('It's tough but we have to change') to develop and utilize their capacities for qualitative change and so shift to new values and systems at a systemic level. In these challenging environments, there will be even more organizations whose activities will aim not only to avoid the reality of transformational imperatives, but to convince as many other players as possible, for example customers, other industry members and political groups, that the conditions for change are in dispute ('Let's convince others these problems don't exist'). At this point, the reality of change is denied, the need for transformation is rejected, the proponents of change are demonized and organizational and industry resources are directed to the purpose of projecting a counter-reality where the status quo is reaffirmed as the only possible path to take. For these organizations the manufacturing of doubt about the need for change is a primary objective (Oreskes and Conway 2010).

The movement from passive complacency to active avoidance and finally to targeted fraudulence is one that some large corporations and privately funded organizations have increasingly taken towards the crises that contemporary organizations are faced with at both the local and global levels. The concept of 'organizational isomorphism' is relevant here because the growing inability of organizations to display even basic forms of wisdom, such as *conformative* and *innovative wisdom*, seems to be related to the intense uniformity in the kinds of leadership, structures and cultures that currently define organizational identity and behaviour. In their paper on the need to develop organizational wisdom at the international level, McKenna, Rooney and Liesch (2006: 285) state that: 'Organisational isomorphism occurs because populations of organisations develop historically in a shared environment, facing similar challenges. Unsurprisingly, because many within a population of organisations make similar decisions about how to deal with the constraints and opportunities facing them, the result is a homogeneity across their structures, cultures and output'.

Organizational isomorphism operates at both the structural level as well as the cultural level and this homogeneity is one of the reasons why the expression of wisdom is so difficult in times of radical turbulence. Consequently, we find that, in times of crisis, instead of human and organizational resources being dedicated to actions that might be categorized under our wisdom typology, we see energy and knowledge being subverted to shadow forms of activity.

The Shadow Side of Wisdom and the Example of Climate Change

Bowles (1991) and others have written of the concept of organizational shadow. All organizations can be regarded as having a shadow side that can be a source of motivation that often goes unacknowledged within an organization. Lichtenstein (1997: 394) writes that the shadow:

> ... involves the unacknowledged or hidden issues that show up as a loss of meaning, dispirited morale, sabotage, cynicism and gaps between what is espoused in the organization's mission statement and what is actually enacted. By facing the organizational shadow, the creative and vital resources at work can be unleashed for a greater purpose.

On the other hand, if the shadow is not integrated or acknowledged in some way with the ongoing activities of the organization then collective pathologies can develop and these often take the form of directed antagonisms towards internal and external groups that are demonized in some way. As Bowles (1991: 392) points out: 'The Organization Shadow will normally be directed towards particular groups who challenge the managerial direction or its supremacy. At a more extreme level, the projection of the Shadow can lead to an organizational pathology'.

Figure 10.3 suggests that there can be a shadow side to each of the forms of wisdom management that are appropriate for various levels of environmental volatility and that, as that volatility grows, these shadowy currents will tend to come to the fore in organizational activities. The shadow side of wisdom is not its absence as in straightforward ignorance; it is not just lack of knowledge or poor decision-making. Rather, it is the use of expertise, high-performance skills and high-functioning abilities and expert knowledge to deny, undermine and emasculate an organization's or a community's capacity to respond to challenges or initiate actions with integrity, responsibility and vision.

The global crisis of climate change provides a good example for describing this shadow aspect of wisdom and how it relates to turbulent environments. The reality of climate change presents a case where all the various types of wisdom outlined in our typology, and particularly *transformative wisdom* and *adaptive wisdom*, are required in large doses. And yet, the presence of organizational capacities to deal with these emergencies seems to be less prevalent now than ever before. Not only is there denial and avoidance but organizations are strategically channelling enormous resources into what I call in Figure 10.2, the zone of spin. This is the zone where public relations, image advertising and corporate branding are all designed to remove any sense that transformational imperatives actually exist. As is the case with all social entities, organizations have strong motivations to retain the status quo and to reject the need to go through the laborious and often unsuccessful process of transformation. There are not only financial and economic reasons for denying the need for change but also political and social power issues related to the maintenance of established power structures and forms of decision-making. In these cases considerable intellectual resources of organizations and industry groups are poured into the spin zone of creating front groups, blog sites, lobby groups, funded 'research' and political and media opportunities that distort the science with the aim of injecting doubt and confusion into the public mind. The recent actions of such organizations as 'The Heartland Institute in America', who associate the views of convicted murderers with those of climate scientists (Nuwer 2012), and the Murdoch media, which, through their newspapers, for example the *Australian* (Lewandowski 2011), and their cable news networks, for example *Fox News* (Armoudian 2012, Hill 2011), are examples of this kind of pathology. These are powerful and sophisticated organizations consisting of highly educated and skilled professionals whose actions are not merely to be explained by ignorance or self-interest. The notion of a pathological form of wisdom/ knowledge management can contribute significantly to understanding the behaviour of these kinds of organizations.

While some organizations, particularly those with much to lose in a world undergoing climate change, take the path of spin and manipulating public opinion, the vast majority of organizations seem to fall within the zone of avoidance which is the shadow side to the zone of realization and action. Avoidance is about denial, minimizing the risks and pretending that minor adjustments in technology or some other convenient process will be all that is needed. Organizations that fall into the zone of avoidance do not take strategic actions to manipulate attitudes, promote inaccuracies or inhibit the expression of scientific knowledge but they do actively avoid and deny realities that demand transformational change. The existence of this shadow suggests that we need to be more sophisticated in recognizing pathological or shadow forms of knowledge and wisdom management. The shadow use of the notion of 'wisdom' becomes one of reframing so that to be 'wise' means anything but responding to challenging times with integrative insight and judicious action. There are shadow forms of each of the wisdom types that we have been discussing.

The *conformative shadow* is the use of organizational resources to maintain the current status quo at any cost. With regard to climate change this essentially means to be inactive while pretending inaction to be a wise and deliberate strategy of 'wait and see'. The end result of the *conformative shadow* is that everyone waits for everyone else which risks the crossing of various tipping point thresholds that dramatically escalate the urgency and size of requisite responses. Australia has taken a *conformative shadow* approach in its government's climate change policy by deliberately arguing that we should not take the first step in mitigation strategies. The reasons offered for this are that we will be disadvantaged by going first and that we need to see how other countries respond before committing ourselves to action. These arguments are made despite Australia being the highest per capita emitter of carbon pollution in the world.

The *transformative shadow* occurs when the instinct for transformative growth is channelled into regressive change or into aggressively rearranging corporate ownership structures that provide very little improvement in efficiency and extensive downsides for many stakeholders. In Fletcher's (1990: 105) review of meanings of organizational transformation, she quotes Jean Bartunek as saying that:

> *Some [transformations] are partly the result of mergers and acquisitions ... These types of changes end up being by definition transformations, changing organizations' understanding of themselves. ... I think the political, economic, and social situation in the country right now is extremely conducive to that kind of situation and absolutely not at all to my ideal of a desirable transformation ... I'm talking about a mass negative transformation happening in most organizations, with a few people getting rich from it and lots of people losing.*

This negative transformation is a regressive state of change rather than a progressive one. It seeks to introduce change that takes organizations back to more primitive forms of organizing so that more elementary goals of competitive and economic gain can be achieved with little recognition of broader social goals (Kilburg, Stokes and Kuruvilla 1998). The *transformative shadow* can often be framed as the call for a 'return to basics', 'return to traditional values' and 'the need for reform'. We see this in the climate change area where nuclear power is touted as the best way to create non-carbon-based economies. There have been concerted efforts to revitalize the nuclear power industry and to repackage it as a transformative option that could address the climate change issue. While the benefits and potentials of nuclear power are a matter of ongoing debate, there is strong evidence that nuclear power will significantly add to, rather than mitigate, carbon emissions (Kleiner 2008).

The *adaptive shadow* is the world of covering all bases and not making a decisive judgement about the direction for change. This is the world of indecision, flip-flopping and vacillation between alternative strategies for dealing with turbulent environments. Many theories of wisdom point to its judicative characteristics, that is, to the capacities that wise individuals and wise collectives show in making clear decisive decisions. The adaptive shadow shows up when organizations hedge their responses between introducing superficial programmes for saving energy, publicly criticizing governments and community groups calling for major change, providing money for politicians campaigning on climate sceptic policies and running greenwash advertising campaigns that present a clean and green image to consumers. The *adaptive shadow* flows from a distorted form of postmodern and relativist position that does not recognize the priority of some ethical horizons over others. It takes root in organizations that do not possess a diverse values base, that do not see the fundamental connection between ethics and business and whose management systems might be described as amoral in that they do not include moral vision in the setting of organizational goals and policies.

The *innovative shadow* is that dark aspect of knowledge and technical ingenuity which reduces all problems to one of technological innovation or to innovations that do not require substantive changes in values, mindsets and forms of collective culture. The focus is on engineering magic bullet solutions that derive from technical expertise. Innovation gets reduced to hyper-technologies and in the climate change arena we see solutions being offered requiring geo-engineering and space sunshields and several other high-tech alternatives that require no cultural change, no change in consumption and production patterns.

These shadows are all distortions of wisdom potentials that almost all people and all organizations possess in some fashion. To finish the discussion of the shadow side of various forms of change wisdom I want to turn to *transitive wisdom*. The *transitive shadow* seeks to reframe transformation as translation and argues that we can meet the challenge of transformational imperatives with merely improved ways of doing what we already do now. It assumes that deep change can be achieved through quantitative increase and higher rates of efficiency while still utilizing the dominant forms of organizing, planning and managing: 'We don't need to change what we do, just do it better'. The *transitive shadow* casts a powerfully disabling influence on our capacities to really engage in forms of change that are actually required in the present times. What it does is supplant transformative growth with increased translational growth and so the need to move to a completely new stage of organizational behaviour and culture is used as a rationale for increased translational and economic growth. The *transformative wisdom* is sublimated into a one-sided concern for quantitative increase rather than qualitative development. Organizations and their leaders see the importance of radical change, but avoid authentic transformational growth and focus instead on 'the malfunctioning source code' of pure financial increase and the profit motive (Henderson 2006). The result is a global concern for economic growth and a deliberate blindness to the global degradation of nature.

In pursuing largely translational change strategies to address problems that require authentic transformation, the *transitive shadow* locks organizations and their communities into ways of thinking and acting that exacerbate the problem. They look to growth and the creation of even more economic 'wealth' as a solution to the sustainability dilemma. Luke (2006) calls this approach 'sustainable degradation'. He argues that the 'strategies of sustainable degradation' offer justifications for ongoing translational growth so that the deep cultural and structural changes that environmental sustainability actually calls for can be evaded. There is an appearance of ecological issues being represented in managerial, commercial and judicial decision-making, but, as Luke contests (2006: 112), 'in reality, the system of sustainable degradation enables capital to extract even more value by maintaining the appearances of creating ecological sustainability while exploiting the realities of environmental degradation'.

And so we have the vicious circle of increased economic activity being seen as the solution to problems caused by increasing levels of production and consumption (Sonntag 2000). In other words, organizations are ramping up their translational growth goals and activities to address problems largely caused by excessive translational growth. The demands and benefits of true interior and exterior transformation are being eschewed in favour of translational cycles of change that do not question the basic issues of excessive production and consumption (Kimerling 2001). This is essentially a conservative approach to change; one that is suspicious of transformative change and is reluctant to admit to the need for radically new ways of dealing with pressing environmental and social problems.

Conclusion

In this paper I have taken a metatheoretical perspective on some aspects of organizational wisdom. The approach has been metatheoretical in that the large-scale conceptual lens of transformation–translation has provided a basis for considering aspects of wisdom in turbulent environments. Adopting a metatheorizing discourse to reconsider the place of wisdom in organizations is timely now for several reasons. First, the territories covered by various understandings of the term 'wisdom' are vast and often in contention. If wisdom-based ideas are to be applied to the pragmatic world of organizational life then researchers will need approaches that find points of connection between, for example, organizational behaviour and challenging environments. The metatheorizing pursued here has demonstrated that the notion of wisdom can be usefully applied to explore these types of connections. Second, there are important implications of the many understandings of wisdom for the field of organizational change and transformation. Leadership is obviously one domain where such considerations are relevant and there are many others. Healthy and pathological organizational responses to change, the critical analysis of organizational moves to avoid change and the usurping of the long-term visioning by short-term expediency are all examples of domains where wisdom can be insightfully applied. Third, in moving ideas across philosophical and scientific demarcations, theorists need to enlist methods that can cope with the demands that such large-scale visioning necessarily involves. By providing means for building connection as well as critical analysis, metatheoretical research is not simply a holistic totalizing of the many into a unified lump. Metatheorizing acknowledges diversity and so accommodates rather than assimilates, it integrates rather than subsumes and it acknowledges difference rather than trying to explain difference away. In effect, metatheorizing shows some of the qualities of wisdom management capacities that have been explored in this chapter. Just as we might expect organizational practices to change in ways that can face global climate change and other crises, we might also expect that our scientific work develops meta-level capabilities that display a similar level of responsiveness and integrity.

Exploring and integrating diverse understandings of wisdom has much to offer the study of organizational behaviour. Two avenues have been explored in detail in this chapter: 1) a typology of forms of wisdom has been described and linked with different kinds of organizational environments, and 2) this typology has been explored in terms of shadow or pathological sides of wisdom. There are implications of this typology for both the development of theories of organizational change and for management practices. With regard to the latter, the principles emerging from this analysis are proposed as useful resources for reflecting on the responses that managers and leaders at all levels make towards transformational imperatives in their environments. When facing contending imperatives during times of crisis it is useful to have frameworks that provide a broad overview. If only for creating a space to breathe and to open up to the big picture, these principles offer a worthwhile addition to the growing literature on organizational wisdom and transformational change. The paper also has implications for the development of theory. Being able to grasp the connections between crisis and opportunity, between change and purpose, between high performance and wise behaviour are all important for developing theories that have relevance and utility in the challenging environments in which contemporary organizations aim to prosper.

In conclusion, a number of questions arising from these foregoing considerations can be posed. Given that wise action on the part of organizations is so sorely needed to meet current challenges, how are organizations best able to introduce and support capacities that enable adaptive and transformative forms of wisdom? Conversely, given the power of organizations to influence the political and social perception of challenges like climate change, how can the pathological side of organizational wisdom be countered? In other words, how can high-level organizational capacities and expertise that are detached and compartmentalized from ethical considerations be reconnected with the well-being of communities and environments both local and global? How can the self-interest of organizations be aligned with the general welfare of natural and human systems? Developing responses to these and similar questions will be among the most important tasks for twenty-first century organizational science.

References

Abrams, D. and Hogg, M.A. 2004. Metatheory: lessons from social identity research. *Personality & Social Psychology Review*, 8(2), 98–106.

Anchin, J. 2008. The critical role of the dialectic in viable metatheory: a commentary on Henriques' tree of knowledge system for integrating human knowledge. *Theory & Psychology*, 18(6), 801.

Ardelt, M. 2004. Wisdom as expert knowledge system: a critical review of a contemporary operationalization of an ancient concept. *Human Development*, 47(5), 257–85.

Armoudian, M. 2012. Murdoch finds it's not easy being green. *Columbia Journalism Review*, 50(6), 1–15.

Avolio, B.J. 2007. Promoting more integrative strategies for leadership theory-building. *American Psychologist*, 62(1), 25–33.

Baltes, P.B. and Staudinger, U.M. 2000. Wisdom: a metaheuristic (pragmatic) to orchestrate mind and virtue toward excellence. *American Psychologist*, 55(1), 122–36.

Birren, J.E. and Fisher, L.M. 1990. The elements of wisdom: overview and integration, in *Wisdom: Its Nature, Origins, and Development*, edited by R.J. Sternberg. New York: Cambridge University Press, 317–32.

Bleicher, K. 1994. Integrative management in a time of transformation. *Long Range Planning*, 27(5), 136–44.

Bondas, T. and Hall, E.O.C. 2007. Challenges in approaching metasynthesis research. *Qualitative Health Research*, 17(1), 113.

Bowles, M.L. 1991. The organization shadow. *Organization Studies*, 12(3), 387–404.

Colomy, P. 1991. Metatheorizing in a postpositivist frame. *Sociological Perspectives*, 34(3), 269–86.

Dunphy, D. 2003. Corporate sustainability: challenge to managerial orthodoxies. *Journal of the Australian and New Zealand Academy of Management*, 9(1), 2–11.

Edwards, M.G. 2005. The integral holon: a holonomic approach to organisational change and transformation. *Journal of Organizational Change Management*, 18(3), 269–88.

Edwards, M.G. 2010a. Metatheorising transformational management: a relational approach, in *Cybernetics and Systems Theory in Management: Tools, Views and Advancements*, edited by S.E. Wallis. Hershey: IGI Global, 127–50.

Edwards, M.G. 2010b. *Organizational Transformation for Sustainability: An Integral Metatheory*. New York: Routledge.

Fletcher, B.R. 1990. *Organization Transformation Theorists and Practitioners*. New York: Praeger.

Ford, J.D. and Backoff, R.H. 1988. Organisational change in and out of dualities and paradox, in *Paradox in Transformation: Toward a Theory of Change in Organisation and Management*, edited by R.E. Quinn and K.S. Cameron. Cambridge, MA: Ballinger Publishing, 81–122.

Gioia, D.A. and Pitre, E. 1990. Multiparadigm perspectives on theory building. *The Academy of Management Review*, 15(4), 584–602.

Golembiewski, R.T. 1989. *Ironies in Organizational Development*. London: Transaction.

Greenwood, R. and Hinings, C.R. 1988. Organizational design types, tracks and the dynamics of strategic change. *Organization Studies*, 9(3), 293.

Hargroves, K. and Smith, M.H. 2005. *The Natural Advantage of Nations*. London: Earthscan.

Henderson, H. 2006. Twenty-first century strategies for sustainability. *Foresight: the Journal of Futures Studies, Strategic Thinking and Policy*, 8(1), 21.

Hill, J. 2011. Media, politics and the portrayal of 'Climate-gate' by CNN and Fox News, MA thesis, University of Denver.

Houck, O.A. 2010. Worst case and the deepwater horizon blowout: there ought to be a law. *Tulane Environmental Law Journal*, 24(1), 1–18.

Kilburg, R.R., Stokes, E.J. and Kuruvilla, C. 1998. Toward a conceptual model of organizational regression. *Consulting Psychology Journal: Practice & Research*, 50(2), 101–19.

Kimerling, J. 2001. 'The human face of petroleum': sustainable development in Amazonia? *RECIEL*, 10, 65–81.

Kleiner, K. 2008. Nuclear energy: assessing the emissions. *Nature Reports*, 2, 130–31.

Küpers, W. 2007. Perspectives on integrating leadership and followership. *International Journal of Leadership Studies*, 2(3), 194–221.

Küpers, W. and Statler, M. 2008. Practically wise leadership: toward an integral understanding. *Culture & Organization*, 14(4), 379–400.

Lester, D.L., Parnell, J.A. and Carraher, S. 2003. Organizational life cycle: a five-stage empirical scale. *International Journal of Organizational Analysis*, 11(4), 339–54.

Lewandowski, S. 2011. Selling climate uncertainty: misinformation and the media. *The Conversation*, 29 August, [Online]. Available at: http://theconversation.edu.au [accessed: 5 May 2012].

Lichtenstein, B.B. 1997. Grace, magic and miracles: a 'chaotic logic' of organizational transformation. *Journal of Organizational Change Management*, 10(5), 393.

Luke, T.W. 2006. The system of sustainable degradation. *Capitalism, Nature, Socialism*, 17(1), 99.

McKenna, B., Rooney, D. and Boal, K.B. 2009. Wisdom principles as a meta-theoretical basis for evaluating leadership. *The Leadership Quarterly*, 20(2), 177–90.

McKenna, B., Rooney, D. and Liesch, P. 2006. Beyond knowledge to wisdom in international business strategy. *Prometheus*, 24(3), 283–300.

Moore, C. and Phillips, C. 2011. *Plastic Ocean*. New York: Avery.

Neuhoff, K. 2010. *Climate Policy after Copenhagen: The Role of Carbon Pricing*. Cambridge: Cambridge University Press.

Nuwer, R. 2012. Heartland pulls billboard on global warming. *New York Times*, 5 May [Online]. Available at: http://green.blogs.nytimes.com/2012/05/04/a-new-tactic-for-climate-skeptics/ [accessed: 5 May 2012].

Oreskes, N. and Conway, E.M. 2010. *Merchants of Doubt: How a Handful of Scientists Obscured the Truth on Issues from Tobacco Smoke to Global Warming*. New York: Bloomsbury Press.

Owen, H. 1987. *Spirit: Transformation and Development in Organizations*. Potomac: Abbott Publishing.

Ritzer, G. 2007. Metatheory, in *Blackwell Encyclopedia of Sociology*, edited by G. Ritzer. London: Blackwell Publishing.

Rooney, D. and McKenna, B. 2007. Wisdom in organizations: whence and whither. *Social Epistemology*, 21(2), 113–38.

Rowley, J. and Slack, F. 2009. Conceptions of wisdom. *Journal of Information Science*, 35(1), 110–19.

Sonntag, V. 2000. Sustainability – in light of competitiveness. *Ecological Economics*, 34(1), 101–13.

Surowiecki, J. 2004. *The Wisdom of Crowds: Why the Many are Smarter than the Few*. London: Abacus.

Thierauf, R.J. and Hoctor, J.J. 2006. *Optimal Knowledge Management: Wisdom Management Systems Concepts and Applications*. Hershey: Idea Group Publishing.

Torbert, W.R. 2004. *Action Inquiry: The Secret of Timely and Transforming Leadership*. San Francisco: Berrett-Koehler.

Weinstein, D. and Weinstein, M.A. 1991. The postmodern discourse of metatheory, in *Metatheorizing*, edited by G. Ritzer. Newbury Park: Sage, 135–50.

Wilber, K. 1999. *Collected Works, Volumes I–IV*. Boston: Shambhala.

Wilber, K. 2000. *Collected Works, Volumes V–VIII*. Boston: Shambhala.

Index

Note: page numbers in *italic* type refer to
Figures; those in **bold** type refer to Tables.
Page numbers followed by 'n' and another
number refer to Footnotes.